THE JOURNAL OF INDUSTRIAL ECONOMICS

Volume XVIII NOVEMBER 1969 No. 1

LOUIS PHLIPS
Business Pricing Policies and Inflation—Some Evidence from E.E.C. Countries.

A. MERCER
Operational Marketing Research.

EARL R. BRUBAKER
Some Effects of Policy on Productivity in Soviet and American Crude Petroleum Extraction.

J. L. FORD and J. J. WARFORD
Cost Functions for the Water Industry.

DOUGLAS WOOD
The Water Supply System up to A.D. 2001.

Symposium on Advertising and Concentration:

ROBERT B. EKELUND, Jr. and CHARLES MAURICE
An Empirical Investigation of Advertising and Concentration: Comment.

H. M. MANN, J. A. HENNING and J. W. MEEHAN, Jr.
Testing Hypotheses in Industrial Economics: a Reply.

L. G. TELSER
Another Look at Advertising and Concentration.

H. M. MANN, J. A. HENNING and J. W. MEEHAN, Jr.
Statistical Testing in Industrial Economics: a Reply on Measurement Error and Sampling Procedure.

BASIL BLACKWELL OXFORD ENGLAND

Price — 15s. net or $2.10. Annual subscription: 30s. or $4.20

CONTRIBUTORS TO THIS NUMBER

LOUIS PHLIPS: Professor of Economics at the Université Catholique de Louvain; Visiting Professor at the Université de Montréal, Winter Semester 1968.

A. MERCER: Professor in Operational Research, University of Lancaster.

EARL R. BRUBAKER: Assistant Professor of Economics, University of Wisconsin (Madison).

J. L. FORD: Senior Lecturer, Department of Economics, the New University of Ulster, Coleraine, Northern Ireland; formerly Lecturer at University of Manchester.

J. J. WARFORD: Lecturer in Economics, University of Manchester.

DOUGLAS WOOD: Lecturer in Economics, Manchester Business School, University of Manchester.

ROBERT B. EKELUND, Jr.: Assistant Professor of Economics, Texas A&M University.

CHARLES MAURICE: Assistant Professor of Economics, Texas A&M University.

H. M. MANN: Associate Professor of Economics, Boston College; on leave 1968-69 as Special Assistant to the Assistant Attorney General, Antitrust Division.

J. A. HENNING: Associate Professor of Economics, Syracuse University.

J. W. MEEHAN, Jr.: Assistant Professor of Economics, Northeastern University.

L. G. TELSER: Professor of Economics, University of Chicago.

THE JOURNAL OF INDUSTRIAL ECONOMICS

Volume XVIII APRIL 1970 No. 2

R. ROBSON

Project Evaluation of Multinational Plants in Africa.

DONALD STEVENSON WATSON and MARY A. HOLMAN

The Concentration of Patent Ownership in Corporations.

RONALD S. KOOT and DAVID A. WALKER

Short-Run Cost Functions of a Multi-Product Firm.

C. J. HAWKINS

On the Sales Revenue Maximization Hypothesis.

J. F. PICKERING

Effective Competition in the Television Rentals Industry: a Note.

IRA HOROWITZ

A Note on Advertising and Uncertainty.

J. M. ALLEN

A Survey into the R & D Evaluation and Control Procedures Currently Used in Industry.

BASIL BLACKWELL OXFORD ENGLAND

Price — 15s. net or $2.10. Annual subscription: 30s. or $4.20

CONTRIBUTORS TO THIS NUMBER

R. Robson: Regional Adviser on Industry attached to the United Nations Economic Commission for Africa, and has been for the last five years engaged in promoting industrial development on the African continent. Prior to that he was Economist to the Cotton Board in Britain and then to the Iron and Steel Board.

Donald Stevenson Watson: Professor of Economics at The George Washington University.

Mary A. Holman: Associate Professor of Economics at The George Washington University.

Ronald S. Koot: Assistant Professor of Quantitative Business Analysis, The Pennsylvania State University.

David A. Walker: Assistant Professor of Quantitative Business Analysis, The Pennsylvania State University.

C. J. Hawkins: Lecturer in Economics and Economic Theory, the University of Southampton.

J. F. Pickering: Lecturer in Economics at the University of Sussex.

Ira Horowitz: Professor of Business Administration at Indiana University.

J. M. Allen: Member of a group at the Post Office working on the appraisal and programming of telecommunications research projects. Previously a Research Associate with the R & D Research Unit at Manchester Business School, where the work described in this article was carried out.

THE JOURNAL OF INDUSTRIAL ECONOMICS

Volume XVIII JULY 1970 No. 3

DENNIS LEES and JOHN MORLEY
Competition in the Sausage Market.

R. C. SKINNER
The Determination of Selling Prices.

BELA GOLD, WILLIAM S. PEIRCE and GERHARD ROSEGGER
Diffusion of Major Technological Innovations in U.S. Iron and Steel Manufacturing.

A. DALE TUSSING
Meaningful Bank Failure: a Proposal.

L. S. ZUDAK
Productivity, Labor Demand and Cost in a Continuous Production Facility.

E. A. LOWE and R. W. SHAW
The Accuracy of Short-Term Business Forecasting: an Analysis of a Firm's Sales Budgeting.

C. M. CANNON
The Board of Trade Capital-Investment-Forecasts: the Prediction of Gross-Fixed-Capital-Formation in U.K. Manufacturing Industry and Business Expectations.

BASIL BLACKWELL OXFORD ENGLAND

Price — 15s. net or $2.10. Annual subscription: 30s. or $4.20

CONTRIBUTORS TO THIS NUMBER

DENNIS LEES: Professor of Industrial Economics, Nottingham University.

JOHN MORLEY: Economic Adviser at the Department of Employment and Productivity; formerly lecturer in the Department of Industrial Economics, Nottingham University.

R. C. SKINNER: Senior Lecturer in Accountancy, University of Otago, New Zealand; formerly Lecturer in Accountancy, University of Liverpool.

BELA GOLD: Timken Professor of Industrial Economics and Director of the Research Program in Industrial Economics, Case Western Reserve University.

WILLIAM S. PEIRCE: Assistant Professor of Economics, and Research Associate in the Research Program in Industrial Economics, Case Western Reserve University.

GERHARD ROSEGGER: Associate Professor of Economics, and Research Associate in the Research Program of Industrial Economics, Case Western Reserve University.

A. DALE TUSSING: Associate Professor of Economics, Syracuse University.

L. S. ZUDAK: Associate Professor of Economics at the University of Miami in Coral Gables, Florida; formerly Assistant Professor of Economics in the University of Western Ontario.

E. A. LOWE: Senior Lecturer in Management Accounting, Manchester Business School, University of Manchester.

R. W. SHAW: Lecturer in Economics at the University of Stirling; formerly of the School of Economic Studies, Leeds University.

C. M. CANNON: Lecturer in Economics, University of Leeds.

BUSINESS PRICING POLICIES AND INFLATION—SOME EVIDENCE FROM E.E.C. COUNTRIES*

by Louis Phlips

1. INTRODUCTION

This paper presents some empirical evidence, for Belgium, the Netherlands and France, on the so-called 'administrative inflation' hypothesis. The hypothesis might be defined as saying that price increases are higher in more concentrated industries, given positive changes in demand and costs. Empirically speaking, it implies that, for a cross-section of industries, wholesale-price changes are a positive function of concentration ratios, for given increases in demand and unit costs. Although any relevant evidence would be an interesting contribution to the present discussion about the Common Market's antitrust policy, the hypothesis has never been confronted—to my knowledge—with data from E.E.C. countries.

It was Gardner Means who formulated the idea that prices are characterized by upward flexibility in concentrated industries, in a presentation before the Kefauver Committee.[1] Since then, the idea seems to have gained some acceptance. But the case is rather weak.

It would indeed be difficult to defend the hypothesis on theoretical grounds. As G. J. Stigler puts it: 'The traditional economic theory argues that oligopoly and monopoly prices have no special relevance to inflation. A monopolist (to take the simpler case) sets a profit-maximizing price for given demand-and-cost conditions. If inflation leads to a rise in either demand or costs, a new and usually higher price will be set. The price will usually be above the competitive level at any given time, but its pattern over time will not be other than passively responsive to monetary conditions.'[2]

On the empirical level, there is room for discussion. For obvious reasons, the profession could not accept as valuable evidence the now famous charts presented by G. Means before the Kefauver Committee. The first serious statistical analysis is due to DePodwin and Selden.[3] These authors concluded that their simple correlation

* I am grateful to Mrs. Vuylsteke, M. Biart and J. Garcia dos Santos for research and programming assistance and to A. Jacquemin, R. Leroy, J. Miller, E. Van Broekhoven and L. Weiss for comments on earlier drafts. This paper is part of a report written for and at the request of the Commission of the European Communities. The Commission is not, of course, responsible for the analysis and opinions contained in it.

[1] *Hearings before the Subcommittee on Antitrust and Monopoly of the Committee on the Judiciary*, United States Senate, 1957, pp. 124–5; 1959; *a*, pp. 4746–58; 1959; *b*, pp. 4897–910.

[2] 'Administered Prices and Oligopolistic Inflation', *Journal of Business*, XXXV, No. 1, January 1962, p. 8.

[3] 'Business Pricing Policies and Inflation', *Journal of Political Economy*, April 1963.

analysis of 1953–59 price changes and concentration ratios of some U.S. industries were adequate evidence to 'put the administrative inflation hypothesis to rest'.

In a more recent article,[4] Leonard W. Weiss emphasized the necessity of introducing demand and cost changes in the analysis, to separate their influence. Utilizing the same sample, he found a small positive effect of concentration on price changes for the period 1953–59; for 1959–63, the relationship became negative and not significantly different from zero, however.

The evidence presented in this paper is limited to the 1958–65 period, because of the difficulty in collecting comparable data for earlier years. As we were more familiar with Belgian data, Belgium was selected as a test case to determine the most appropriate empirical specification of the hypothesis. A few changes in Weiss's approach proved to be beneficial and are discussed in section II together with the data and results obtained for Belgium. In section III, results for the Netherlands are compared with the Belgian evidence on the basis of an analysis of covariance. Section IV introduces France while the last section draws some conclusions as to the validity of the hypothesis in a European framework.

II. BELGIUM

(*a*) *Data*

Data collection represented a problem—as is invariably the case in Europe. No concentration ratios are available for Belgium[5] (nor for any other E.E.C. country). We had therefore to calculate[6] them from the 1961 Industrial Census,[7] utilizing frequency distributions of firms by number of employees.[8] Except for the very few cases where one or several classes happened to include exactly the four largest firms, we had to interpolate following the method utilized by J. S. Bain.[9] The industries, as defined in the Belgian Census, are 'three-digit': some correspond to the American 'four-digit' industries, others are somewhat larger but always smaller than two-digit.

Official wholesale price indexes are available for only a very limited number of corresponding industries. Fortunately, we had

[4] 'Business Pricing Policies and Inflation Reconsidered', *Journal of Political Economy*, April 1966.

[5] Except for two-digit industries, where they seem meaningless when unweighted.

[6] I wish to express my thanks to Michel Biart who calculated these concentration ratios with great care and patience.

[7] *Recensement de l'industrie et du commerce*, 31 décembre 1961, Tome 4 (Institut National de Statistique, Brussels, 1967).

[8] Frequency distributions by shipments are not available.

[9] *International Differences in Industrial Structure*, Studies in Comparative Economics, No. 6 (Yale University Press, New Haven, 1966), pp. 27–8.

access to the files of the *Centre de Recherches Economiques* (University of Louvain) which constructs its own indexes for a much larger number of industries. These indexes were used here.

Data on shipments, production worker payroll, salaries and materials cost were taken from the annual surveys of manufactures which the *Institut National de Statistique* started in the 1950s—but only for a limited number of industries.[10] Each year, a number of industries were added to the list.

Given this set of constraints, it was possible to construct comparable series for a maximum number of 17 manufacturing industries only, for the period 1958–64. In one case, data were lacking on production worker payroll, in another on materials cost. As a result, some regressions are based on only 16 or 15 observations.[11]

(*b*) *Using Weiss's approach*

To facilitate comparisons of methods of analysis, the same concepts were used as in the *J.P.E.* articles mentioned above. It might be useful to recall briefly the significance of the following symbols:

S_t = Value of industry shipments in year t;
P_t = Industry price level in year t (always part of a price index expressed as P_t/P_0);
Q_t = Industry output in year t, measured by deflating S_t;
C = Four firms concentration ratio for the given industry;
W_t = Total production worker payroll for the industry in year t;
SW_t = Total salaries and wages for the industry in year t.

We will also introduce

MC_t = Total cost of purchased fuel and materials less the net increase in inventories in year t.

A simple regression of the 17 price indexes on the 17 concentration ratios gave the following (standard errors are between brackets):

$$\frac{P64}{P58} = \underset{(6.81)}{125.51} - \underset{(.132)}{.310}\, C$$

with $r = .52$. Of course, this does not allow the conclusion that concentrated industries increased prices less than unconcentrated.

[10] See the annual issues of *Annuaire Statistique de la Belgique*.

[11] The 17 manufacturing industries included in the sample are: sugar, tobacco, shoes, pulp and paper mills, paper and paperboard products, leather tanning, rubber, cleaning and toilet goods, clay products, glass, iron and steel, nonferrous metals, pottery, yarn mills, weaving mills, fats and oils, cokeries.

We have to correct for influences of demand and costs. When the output variable, defined as

$$\frac{Q64}{Q58} = \frac{S64}{S58} \Big/ \frac{P64}{P58}$$

is introduced, output has a negative effect (as in Weiss's paper):

$$\frac{P64}{P58} = \underset{(21.73)}{169.96} - \underset{(.124)}{.386}\,C - \underset{(.142)}{.303}\,\frac{Q64}{Q58} \qquad \begin{array}{l} \bar{R}^2 = .37 \\ (D.F. = 2, 14) \\ (F\text{-ratio} = 5.7) \end{array}$$

where D.F. designates the degrees of freedom. Industries with greater increases in production increased prices less, which indicates that changing costs (per unit of production) are likely to have played an important role. It is necessary then to introduce changes in such key cost factors[12] as labor and materials costs per unit of production

$$\left(\text{defined as } \frac{W64}{W58} \Big/ \frac{Q64}{Q58} \text{ or } \frac{SW64}{SW58} \Big/ \frac{Q64}{Q58} \text{ and } \frac{MC64}{MC58} \Big/ \frac{Q64}{Q58}\right).$$

Table I gives the results from a set of regressions with different combinations of the cost variables. A striking result is that the coefficients of the labor-cost variables (W or SW) are not significantly different from zero,[13] whereas the coefficients of the materials cost variable (MC) are always significant (although with variable sign). This is, to say the least, surprising. As for concentration, it appears with coefficients which are either negative or not significantly different from zero, as in equation 1.3 which stands out as the 'best' in terms of explained variance.

One explanation of these strange results is that our sample is too small and/or our data too bad. But another (possibly concomitant) explanation is that the specification of the model has to be improved.

(c) *Alternative specifications*

The foregoing approach gives equal weight to increases in unit labor or materials cost, irrespective of the importance of these elements in total average cost. It is clear, however, that capital-intensive industries should worry less about a given percentage change in unit labor cost than labour-intensive industries, and that producers of margarine should pay more attention to a given percentage change in unit materials cost than producers of bricks. A

[12] Changes in the cost of capital, per industry, are neglected because of the difficulty of measuring them.

[13] We adopt the convention that a regression coefficient is not significantly different from zero when less than twice its standard error.

TABLE I

BELGIUM (Unweighted cost variables)

	Constant	C	$\frac{Q64}{Q58}$	$\frac{W64}{W58} / \frac{Q64}{Q58}$	$\frac{SW64}{SW58} / \frac{Q64}{Q58}$	$\frac{MC64}{MC58} / \frac{Q64}{Q58}$	$\bar{R}^2$	D.F.	F-Ratio
I.1	229.5 (30.7)	−.500 (.094)	−.608 (.143)	−.145 (.099)			·73	3,12	13.92**
I.2	89.8 (92.1)	−.307 (.153)	−.157 (.217)		.500 (.559)		·36	3,13	4.01*
I.3	87.2 (72.3)	−.247 (.137)	−.209 (.215)	.197 (.339)		.371 (.185)	·79	4,10	13.89**
I.4	164.1 (91.7)	−.492 (.159)	−.513 (.261)		.640 (.502)	−.342 (.123)	·56	4,11	5.72**

* significant at the 95 per cent level.
** significant at the 99 per cent level.

natural procedure is then to multiply the cost variables by percentages of wage and materials expenses in the value of shipments.[14] The results are presented in Table II.

Improvements are substantial. Equation II.2 clearly stands out with a remarkable $\bar{R}^2$ of .89. It corresponds to the fully specified model with production worker payroll (deflated by production) as the labor-cost variable. Firms appear to adjust prices positively to wage increases, especially when production is labor-intensive. But the administrative inflation hypothesis does not derive any support from the results.

There remains an uneasy feeling, however.

First, the regression coefficients of most variables are unstable. Second, standard errors are generally very high, especially for the output variable and the concentration ratio. Third, the regression coefficients of the output variable are difficult to interpret. In Weiss's interpretation, Q64/Q58 should measure the impact of demand, once the cost variables enter the regression. But why should an increase in demand lead to smaller price increases or be without impact?[15] Finally, the variables are defined in such a way that Q64/Q58 enters in the denominator of the cost variables. As Q64/Q58 is itself highly correlated with the concentration ratio, a huge amount of multicollinearity may be suspected.

The analysis of multicollinearity has been facilitated by the recent contribution of D. E. Farrar and R. R. Glauber.[16] Their paper introduces three tests of multicollinearity:

(a) an approximate chi-square transformation of the determinant of the matrix of correlation coefficients, to judge the presence and severity of multicollinearity between the independent variables;

(b) F-tests to indicate the dependence of a particular variable on other variables;

(c) *t*-tests to determine which variables are collinear with each other.

Applying these three tests to equation 1.3 (Table I), we find χ^2 (6) = 30.8 where the critical value at the 95 per cent level is only 12.6. The F-tests indicate that all four independent variables

[14] The percentages were calculated for the year 1964.

[15] Weiss offers the explanation that a non-significant coefficient for Q64/Q58 might indicate that firms have been working in the range of constant marginal costs. In the standard textbook case, a movement to the right of the demand curve does not affect price if costs are *decreasing*, however.

[16] 'Multicollinearity in Regression Analysis: the Problem Revisited', *The Review of Economics and Statistics*, February 1967.

TABLE II

BELGIUM (Weighted cost variables)

		C	$\frac{Q64}{Q58}$	$\frac{W64}{W58} \cdot \frac{W64}{S64} / \frac{Q64}{Q58}$	$\frac{SW64}{SW58} \cdot \frac{SW64}{S64} / \frac{Q64}{Q58}$	$\frac{MC64}{MC58} \cdot \frac{MC64}{S64} / \frac{Q64}{Q58}$	$\bar{R}^2$	D.F.	F-Ratio
II.1	157.3	−.268	−.321	.518			.77	3,12	18.51**
	(18.6)	(.095)	(.101)	(.215)					
II.2	104.2	−.175	−.171	1.118		.303	.89	4,10	29.36**
	(32.2)	(.090)	(.137)	(.286)		(.127)			
II.3	183.4	−.298	−.403		.336	−.193	.50	4,11	4.75*
	(65.1)	(.182)	(.278)		(.518)	(.236)			

are affected by multicollinearity: the $F(3, 11)$ values are 12.0 for the concentration ratio, 16.3 for output, 8.8 for wages and 8.3 for materials costs. Furthermore, each variable is linked to each of the remaining variables, with the exception of wages and materials costs for which the *t*-ratio is .32.

Our weighting procedure makes things worse, as exemplified by equation 11.2 which is gratified with a $\chi^2\ (6) = 26.6$, F values of 9.4, 12.2, 18.8 and 12.6 and *t*-ratios indicating that all variables are dependent upon *all* the others.

These results are not surprising and confirm the objections raised earlier. Furthermore, as the percentage of wages in the value of shipments is negatively correlated with the percentage of material costs, the weighting procedure had to destroy the independence between the two cost variables.

Multicollinearity, however, is a fact of life. In principle, nothing can be done about it.[17] In practice, one has to try to rearrange the problem at hand. In this context, it seemed reasonable to leave the production variable (Q64/Q58) out, given its dubious economic significance and its high correlation with the concentration ratio. We also wondered whether an *ad hoc* specification, in which one cost variable only would be weighted, would not give a better fit.

Rearrangements along these lines were rewarding (see Table III). When Q64/Q58 is deleted, the coefficients of the cost variables have the correct (positive) signs (compare regressions III.1 and III.2 with I.3 and I.4). This might indicate that a correct specification of the model does not include the production variable. After all, the influence of demand might already be reflected in the variation of the cost variables. On the other hand, weighting wage cost only leads to a gain in explained variance ($\bar{R}^2$ is higher in III.3 than in II.2, although one independent variable was deleted). Notice that the χ^2's are not only reduced—as is inevitable—but also turn out to be above the 95 per cent significance level of 7.815 in Table III.A and below in Table III.B.

Table III leads to the following conclusions:

(a) Belgian firms tended to increase prices when unit wage and/or materials cost went up;
(b) price changes in response to changes in unit wage cost were a positive function of labor intensity (equation III.3 and III.5);
(c) price reacted directly to changes in unit materials costs, in the sense that these changes were given equal weight;

[17] See H. Theil, *Economic Forecasts and Policy* (North-Holland, Amsterdam, 1965), p. 216.

TABLE III
BELGIUM (Final Results)

A. *Unweighted cost variables*

		C	$\frac{W64}{W58} / \frac{Q64}{Q58}$	$\frac{MC64}{MC58} / \frac{Q64}{Q58}$	$\frac{SW64}{SW58} / \frac{Q64}{Q58}$	$\bar{R}^2$	D.F.	F-Ratio	χ^2 (3)
III.1	20.83 (23.43)	−.134 (.072)	.400 (.265)	.472 (253)		.78	3, 11	18.3**	11.05
III.2	27.91 (28.84)	−.147 (.077)		.510 (.181)	.304 (.351)	.76	3, 11	15.8**	13.20

B. *One cost variable weighted*

		C	$\frac{W64}{W58} \cdot \frac{W64}{S64} / \frac{Q64}{Q58}$	$\frac{MC64}{MC58} / \frac{Q64}{Q58}$	$\frac{W64}{W58} / \frac{Q64}{Q58}$	$\frac{MC64}{MC58} \cdot \frac{MC64}{MC58} / \frac{Q64}{Q58}$	$\frac{SW64}{SW58} \cdot \frac{SW64}{S64} / \frac{Q64}{Q58}$	$\frac{SW64}{SW58} / \frac{Q64}{Q58}$	$\bar{R}^2$	D.F.	F-Ratio	χ^2 (3)
III.3	46.66 (7.32)	−.030 (.043)	.633 (.107)	.516 (.063)					.94	3, 11	72.1**	7.28
III.4	6.63 (31.33)	−.159 (.102)			1.028 (.275)	.086 (.125)			.62	3, 11	8.6**	3.95
III.5	45.58 (9.45)	−.050 (.054)		.530 (.081)			.505 (.124)		.90	3, 11	42.1**	6.82
III.6	8.45 (35.09)	−.178 (.099)				.127 (.129)		1.182 (.314)	.62	3, 11	8.7**	4.13

(d) the calculations do not allow any conclusion to be drawn as to the role demand could have played;
(e) there is no support whatsoever for the administrative inflation hypothesis, all the regression coefficients for C being negative in all cases. Of course, this negative sign does not imply that concentrated industries had a stabilizing influence on prices,[18] since the coefficients of C are not significantly different from zero in the 'best' regressions (III.3 and III.5).

III. BENELUX

For the Netherlands, a sample of 43 three- or four-digit industries could be collected, the four-digit products belonging to the textile industry. Wholesale price indexes for 1964 (1958 = 100) were furnished by the *Centraal Bureau voor de Statistiek*. Concentration ratios were calculated by interpolation from the (unpublished) Industrial Census of October 15th, 1963, using frequency distributions of firms by number of employees. The other data are taken from the *Produktiestatistieken* which are published each year for a number of particular industries.

There are no data on wages and salaries separately for a sufficient number of industries.

The regressions give results which confirm those obtained for Belgium. Equation III.2 (from Table III) may be compared with the following result for the Netherlands:

$$\frac{P64}{P58} = \underset{(10.85)}{36.99} - \underset{(.060)}{.090}\,C + \underset{(.080)}{.467}\,\frac{MC64}{MC58}\Big/\frac{Q64}{Q58} + \underset{(.079)}{.211}\,\frac{SW64}{SW58}\Big/\frac{Q64}{Q58} \qquad \text{(IV.I)}$$

$$\bar{R}^2 = .57 \text{ (D.F.} = 3.\ 39)$$
$$\text{F-ratio} = 19.91^{**}$$
$$\chi^2\ (3) = 9.11$$

with F-statistics of 3.98, 2.83 and 4.03 for each independent variable respectively.

A natural question is to ask whether Belgium and the Netherlands are homogeneous insofar as their slope coefficients are concerned and to set up a 'within' analysis of covariance using a 'combined'

[18] In the regressions with unweighted cost variables, the negative effect of concentration on prices is probably due to the negative relation between concentration and labor intensity.

regression.[19] Combining equations III.2 (for Belgium) with equation IV.1 (for the Netherlands), we obtain the following weighted coefficients[20] =

$$-.113\,C + .484\,\frac{MC64}{MC58}\Big/\frac{Q64}{Q58} + .228\,\frac{SW64}{SW58}\Big/\frac{Q64}{Q58}$$
$$(.047)\qquad(.069)\qquad\qquad(.074)$$

The 'within' analysis of covariance leads to

Source	*SS*	*D.F.*	*M.S.*	*F-ratio*
Combined regression	6012.91	3	2004.30	33.48
Difference of regressions	52.69	3	17.56	.29
Residual	2993.40	50	59.87	
Total within	9059.00	56	161.77	

Belgium and the Netherlands are clearly homogeneous, as is indicated by the F-ratio of .29 which lies in the acceptance region of the null hypothesis that the differences between the 'national' regression coefficients are zero. Notice that for both countries combined, the regression coefficient for C appears as significantly different from zero. But it still remains to verify how this coefficient behaves when SW is weighted by its percentage in the value of shipments.

For the Netherlands alone, we get:

$$\frac{P64}{P58} = \underset{(9.04)}{39.56} + \underset{(.053)}{.020}\,C + \underset{(.071)}{.504}\,\frac{MC64}{MC58}\Big/\frac{Q64}{Q58} + \underset{(.153)}{.592}\,\frac{SW64}{SW58}\,\frac{SW64}{S64}\Big/\frac{Q64}{Q58} \qquad \text{(IV.2)}$$

$$\bar{R}^2 = .63$$
$$\text{F-ratio} = 25.54^{**}$$
$$\chi^2\,(3) = 5.28$$

and F-statistics of 2.36, 1.06 and 1.84.

A combination of regressions III.5 (for Belgium) and IV.2 (for the Netherlands) gives the slope coefficients

$$\underset{(.042)}{.001}\,C + \underset{(.058)}{.511}\,\frac{MC64}{MC58}\Big/\frac{Q64}{Q58} + \underset{(.110)}{.574}\,\frac{SW64}{SW58}\cdot\frac{SW64}{S64}\Big/\frac{Q64}{Q58}$$

and an F-ratio of .21, which is again non-significant. Indeed, we can set up the table

[19] For similar applications of analysis of covariance, see e.g., H. Houthakker, 'New Evidence on Demand Elasticities', *Econometrica,* XXXIII (April 1965) or E. Kuh, *Capital Stock Growth: A Micro-Econometric Approach* (Amsterdam, 1963), chap. 5.

[20] Using a moment matrix which is the sum of the two national moment matrices.

Source	*SS*	*D.F.*	*M.S.*	*F-ratio*
Combined regression	6701.56	3	2233.85	47.99
Difference of Regressions	29.86	3	9.95	.21
Residual	2327.58	50	46.55	
Total within	9059.60	56	161.77	

We conclude that the administrative inflation hypothesis definitely does not derive any support from Benelux data.

At this point, we have to pause a moment and face an important objection. Are the results reported thus far relevant to the hypothesis to be tested? An implicit assumption is that concentration ratios measure monopoly power. Is it reasonable to admit that national concentration ratios bear any relation to market power in economies as open as those of Belgium and the Netherlands? In such countries, they certainly do not measure market shares: Belgium, for example, exports 40 per cent (if not more) of its production while imports represent a substantial part of consumption.

I do not think the objection is very damaging. Case studies show that in concentrated industries prices are determined in a national framework, in the sense that national producers fix prices in their national market, while importers adjust as price-followers, taking over the same price for comparable products. International agreements on sales conditions (such as basing-point systems, exclusive dealing, etc.) give these *ententes* an operational character, separating the markets while allowing for substantial imports—even in Benelux.[21] Although many more case studies would be needed, I do believe that national concentration ratios are good proxies for the control national producers have over prices in their domestic market. In this sense, they may be used to test the administrative inflation hypothesis.

This is only a statement of belief, however. It is important, therefore, to provide evidence for economies as 'closed' as the American. Fortunately enough, the analysis could be carried out for France, which can be considered as sufficiently 'closed' to allow comparisons with the U.S.: if American concentration ratios measure any such thing as monopoly power, then French concentration ratios also do.[22]

IV. FRANCE

Forty wholesale price indexes for 1965 (1959 = 100), for indus-

[21] Three cases were analysed in some detail in my dissertation *De l'intégration des marchés* (Nauwelaerts, Louvain), 1962. Of course, the enforcement of articles 85 and 86 of the Roman Treaty may change all this.

[22] Given the absence of frequency distributions, even for the number of employees, no concentration ratios could be calculated for Germany. As for Italy, it was impossible to obtain wholesale price indexes for industries defined according to the classification used in the Italian Industrial census and the annual surveys on value added.

tries corresponding to the N.A.E. classification (Nomenclature des Activités économiques), were provided by I.N.S.E.E. This classification is also used in the 1962 Industrial Census[23] and in the B.I.C. statistics (Bénéfices industriels et commerciaux). We could thus proceed, utilizing these three sources.

The findings are very similar indeed to the results reported above. The following regression

$$\frac{P65}{P59} = \underset{(11.50)}{37.28} + \underset{(.067)}{.069}\,C + \underset{(.072)}{.465}\,\frac{MC65}{MC59}\Big/\frac{Q65}{Q59} + \underset{(.082)}{.203}\,\frac{SW65}{SW59}\Big/\frac{Q65}{Q59} \qquad (V.1)$$

$$\bar{R}^2 = .60 \quad D.F. = 3, 36$$
$$F\text{-ratio} = 69.89^{**}$$
$$\chi^2\,(3) = 9.81$$

can be combined with regressions III.2 (for Belgium) and IV.1 (for the Netherlands) to give

$$\underset{(.039)}{-.045}\,C + \underset{(.049)}{.460}\,\frac{MC65}{MC59}\Big/\frac{Q65}{Q59} + \underset{(.054)}{.210}\,\frac{SW65}{SW59}\Big/\frac{Q65}{Q59}$$

This combined regression is gratified with a significant F-ratio of 51.70. Belgium, the Netherlands and France appear as homogeneous, as far as the national regression coefficients are concerned, for we obtain an F-ratio of 1.22, with 6 and 86 degrees of freedom, indicating that differences between these coefficients are not significantly different from zero. When we weight salaries and wages, the fit is somewhat inferior, however, and the coefficient of SW is not significant[24] =

$$\frac{P65}{P59} = \underset{(10.37)}{50.12} + \underset{(.070)}{.084}\,C + \underset{(.075)}{.516}\,\frac{MC65}{MC59}\Big/\frac{Q65}{Q59} + \underset{(.215)}{.259}\,\frac{SW65}{SW59}\cdot\frac{SW65}{S65}\Big/\frac{Q65}{Q59} \qquad (V.2)$$

$$\bar{R}^2 = .56 \quad D.F. = 3, 36$$
$$F\text{-ratio} = 17.07^{**}$$
$$\chi^2\,(3) = 8.27$$

But the combination of V.2 with III.5 (Belgium) and IV.2 (the Netherlands) gives

[23] *Recensement de l'industrie en France en 1962*, Vol. III, Paris, 1968.

[24] My guess is that this result might be due to political interference within the framework of the *Plan*.

$$\underset{(.037)}{.024}\,C+\underset{(.045)}{.512}\,\frac{MC65}{MC59}\Big/\frac{Q65}{Q59}+\underset{(.100)}{.508}\,\frac{SW65}{SW59}\cdot\frac{SW65}{SW65}\Big/\frac{Q65}{Q59}$$

with an F-ratio of 58.58. As for the differences between the national regression coefficients, an F-ratio of .66 with 6 and 86 degrees of freedom indicates that they can be considered as negligible.

V. CONCLUSIONS

The absence of comparable and systematic production statistics (such as annual surveys of manufactures, concentration ratios, etc.) for the six E.E.C. countries places a heavy burden on empirical work in the field of business policies and industrial organization. One of the aims of the present paper is to show that quantitative analysis is nevertheless possible.

Analysis of covariance appeared as a useful tool to compensate for the losses in information due to the non-comparability of national statistics. It also allowed interesting comparisons.

For our problem, the comparison of France with Benelux countries played a crucial role. If the results for France had been different, it would have been difficult indeed to interpret our findings for economies as open as those of Belgium and the Netherlands, because of the dubious significance of national concentration ratios in these countries. The striking homogeneity of all three countries analysed suggests that our calculations are relevant to the administrative inflation hypothesis and leads to the conclusion that this hypothesis does not derive any support from the European evidence collected.

Concentrated industries appear to behave in the same way as unconcentrated industries, as far as upward price flexibility is concerned. Prices tend to follow increases in unit costs, while market structure does not appear to have any particular influence.

Of course, the reader should not infer from this that concentrated industries adopt competitive prices: the *level* of prices might still be 'too high', leading to 'excessive' profits. But that is another matter.

CATHOLIC UNIVERSITY OF LOUVAIN
and UNIVERSITY OF MONTREAL

OPERATIONAL MARKETING RESEARCH*

by A. Mercer

General Introduction

Operational Research was born of necessity. The need of this country to defend itself against a potential enemy. When peace was finally restored after the Second World War, the first organization in which Operational Research became established was the National Coal Board. In those days of austerity and shortages, coal could not be produced fast enough and the emphasis was quite rightly on production and transportation. As a consequence, operational research established a reputation in those areas and a chain reaction, which led to more research on such problems to the exclusion of others, was started. Apart from this historical accident the retarded growth of operational research in the marketing field can be attributed to the difficulties of producing mathematical models, which are essentially cause and effect relationships, of the behaviour of frequently irrational customers in markets where the efforts of an organization are affected by its competitors' actions.

Whilst the mathematical models of marketing might be very different from those used for production processes, they are the unifying feature of operational research. It is their construction and manipulation, rather than the subsequent results, which characterizes the subject. Consequently I propose to illustrate the underlying methodology of operational marketing research by describing applications with which I have been closely associated in the areas of consumer marketing, industrial marketing and retailing. These applications will not provide universal marketing laws which can be used for other products but they will indicate the direction of future research.

Introduction to Consumer Marketing

In its report on the supply of household detergents, the Monopolies Commission concluded that Unilever and Proctor & Gamble should make substantial percentage reductions in their wholesale selling prices for household detergents. It recommended that the Board of Trade should decide the appropriate reductions in consultation with the two companies, which would be encouraged to agree that a 40 per cent reduction of the selling expenses should accompany the price reduction. The Commission then suggested that the price consultations with the companies might well begin on the basis of an

* An inaugural lecture delivered in the University of Lancaster on March 5th, 1969.

average 20 per cent reduction. When subsequently explaining his decision not to implement the contents of the Commission's report, the then President of the Board of Trade told the House of Commons that too little is known about the economic effects of advertising in

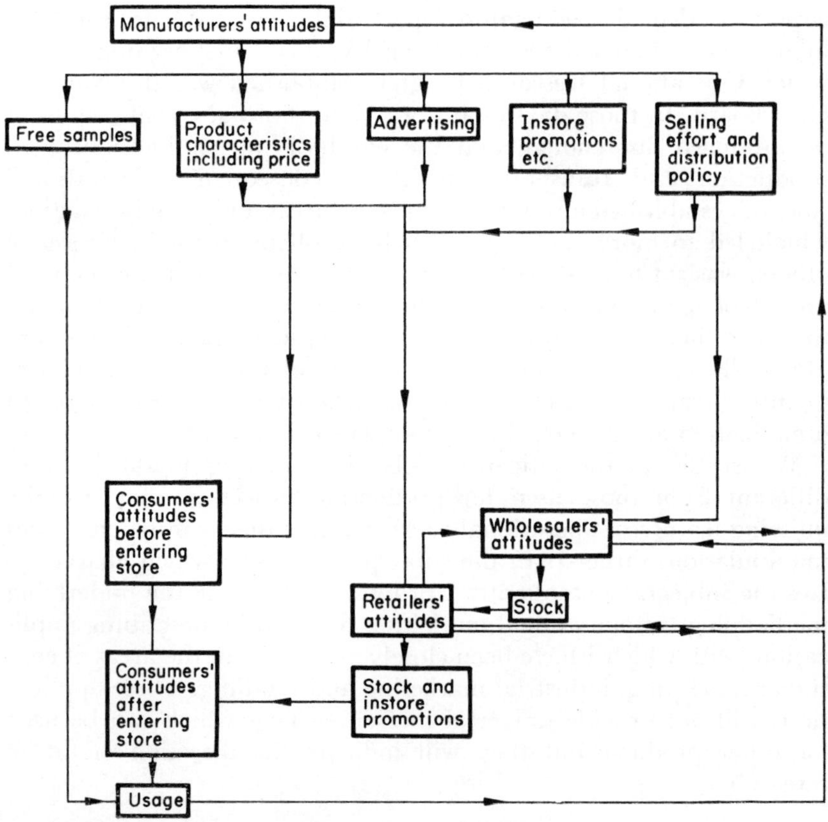

Fig. 1 Market interactions

general and its relation to competition. Therefore it was surprising that less than eighteen months later, the National Board for Prices and Incomes should make recommendations in its report on the costs and prices of the chocolate and sugar confectionery industry, which implied that these effects were capable of being understood in the near future. Although the Board admitted that there are considerable technical difficulties in intensive evaluation, it suggested that when the Ministry of Agriculture, Fisheries and Food considers proposals for price increases, it should require evidence of the extent to which a company has given attention to ensuring the cost-effectiveness of its selling efforts. Traditionally there has been a preoccupation with the effect of price on sales but as both the Monopolies Commission and the Prices and Incomes Board have acknowledged, advertising must also be considered in any marketing study. Price and advertising are themselves only two of the main factors which influence a consumer purchase. The marketing process is illustrated diagrammatically in Fig. 1.

The Consumer Marketing Problem

In the confectionery market a potential consumer will see advertisements on television, in the press, at the cinema and on poster sites. The manufacturer hopes that these advertisements will create a favourable disposition towards his products so that the consumer will either seek them actively or select them when making an impulse purchase. If he makes a purchase on impulse, then he will buy products immediately available. Because two-thirds of confectionery sales fall in this category, manufacturers seek wide distribution for their products. To obtain this distribution salesmen call on the retailers and apart from using their powers of persuasion, offer such financial incentives as increased profit margins or extended credit facilities. The manufacturer seeks to convince the retail outlet that not only should it stock its products but also display them prominently. Often the manufacturer provides special display cabinets and in-store advertising material in an attempt to influence a purchaser at the point of sale. Obviously both price and packaging will affect the consumers' choice of the outlet. They might also be significant in determining their predisposition towards the products. When a consumer buys and eats the product, the experience he acquires will affect his attitudes in a similar manner to advertising, except that product quality, taste and perceived value for money will be important. Not only will the purchaser influence the consumer but the retailer will be more prepared to give good display to a product which appears to be selling well. Equally a retailer will be more likely to stock a product which is widely advertised in the belief that the sales will be higher for a heavily promoted product. Thus the marketing and selling process is a complex, non-linear feedback system in which the manufacturer, retailer and consumer all influence each other. The mathematical components of this system are the two models, representing the effect of the manufacturers and retailers on the consumers and the effect of the manufacturers and consumers on the retailers.

Relationships and Aggregate Data

The simplest and oldest method of deriving such relationships is to take sales data aggregated over customers or time and try to relate these to the comparable advertising expenditures, price and other factors thought to be relevant. For example, the sales might be the total for a product in different months or years, or they might be those in different geographical areas for the same month or year. The report of the Prices and Incomes Board attempts to use such methods.

TABLE I

SALES AND ADVERTISING AND PROMOTIONAL COSTS OF PRINCIPAL CHOCOLATE AND SUGAR CONFECTIONERY LINES

Size of lines	*Total tonnage (thousands)*	*Advertising and promotion cost*	
		(thousand pounds)	*(pounds per ton)*
Over 7000 tons	117	3861	33
5001–7000 tons	83	3237	39
2001–5000 tons	60	2640	44
2000 tons and below	19	152	8

The data given in the second column of Table I are the total tonnages for lines of different sizes and the corresponding advertising and promotion costs are given in the third column. One can conclude that the higher the total expenditure on advertising and other promotional activities, the greater the volume of annual sales, though advertising expenditure per ton tends to decline as the volume of sales increases. Unfortunately such statements are of no operational significance because they do not distinguish cause from effect. Whilst sales might increase because of the advertising and promotional activities, it might well be that manufacturers feel that they can afford to spend more money on those lines which are selling well and generating good profits. In other words, fitting simple statistical relations to such data is meaningless and only non-linear mathematical models of plausible market mechanisms, which reflect the behaviour of customers, should be considered.

In markets such as that for confectionery, aggregate statistics invariably ignore important effects. For example, the total expenditure on press and television advertising conceals the trend of some companies to move from press to television. One company delivers almost 50 per cent directly to the retailers whereas another only services 10 per cent directly. Any manufacturer which operates the latter distribution system risks having less influence over the retailers. Consequently it is often necessary either to give large margins or to advertise more heavily in order to persuade the consumer and effectively bypass the retailer. Thus advertising and distribution costs are partly substitutable as well as being complementary. Although the use of adaptive aggregate-type models may be adequate in some markets, the rapidly changing complex interactions in markets for heavily advertised, low cost products has resulted in the need for methods of analysis using detailed data.

Consumer Data and Simulation

The data which are obviously needed are the purchases of individual consumers and the sales of individual retail outlets. Consumer data are usually obtained from direct records of a sample of users, who will note every purchase together with information about promotions taking place in the outlet at the time. Retail outlet data are obtained by periodically auditing a sample of shops to determine what has been sold, what is in stock and the promotions taking place. The market research organizations which currently collect such data devote an enormous effort to analysing it. Unfortunately the output simply consists of aggregate statistics which are only related qualitatively to the marketing pressures. Thus these statistics do not identify cause and effect and are in no sense representative of the behaviour of customers. Their only virtue is that they are simple to use and enable the marketing man to know more about what is happening than would otherwise be the case.

The process which characterizes the purchases of consumers in rapidly changing markets is so enormously complex that the only feasible mathematical technique to use appears to be that of simulation. This creates within a computer a representation of a large number of retail outlets and consumers who are exposed to the marketing and selling efforts of the manufacturers. The research with which I have been concerned has been influenced greatly by the work of behavioural scientists. A mathematical model, based on stochastic learning theory, has been constructed for the behaviour of consumers when exposed to marketing pressures. After the fundamental characteristics of purchasers have been determined from their reactions in a known environment, it is possible to simulate how they would behave if a manufacturer were to change his strategy. As well as being technically difficult, such studies are expensive because of the large quantities of data which must be collected and the subsequent long computing times. However, the first results are very encouraging for the extreme predictions made by the simulation calculations have been confirmed by actual marketing changes. In the market, which differs from that considered by the Prices and

Incomes Board, small decreases in the advertising cost for the brand leader would have little effect on sales and a 30 per cent decrease in advertising costs would result in a 7 per cent decrease in sales. In contrast, if the brand leader were able to reduce the proportion of shops that were out of stock during price promotions, then its sales would increase by 25 per cent. The computations also showed that there would be a 10 per cent increase in the sales of a competitor if the product carried the same weight of advertising as the brand leader.

Of course there have been other behavioural models, particularly in the advertising area, but these are essentially non-mathematical. For example, as early as 1925 there was the Starch model which stated that for an advertisement to be successful, it must be seen, be read, be believed, be remembered and be acted upon. This and later models suffer from the defect that they are ambiguous and operationally unmeasurable, as well as not being supported by empirical evidence. Thus multiple brand purchases of competing products are inconsistent with a conversion process.

Data Difficulties and Experiments

Consumer panel data are most easily collected when housewives make fairly regular purchases to take home and virtually impossible to obtain with any degree of accuracy for markets in which impulse purchases are made. For example, the confectionery market is complicated because nearly 20 per cent of sales are made to children and almost 40 per cent to men. Shop audit data are inaccurate because one large chain of retail outlets, with an estimated 8 per cent of sales, cannot be audited. An alternative of observing the purchases of a sample of shoppers as they leave outlets is only useful for products whose annual sales exceed a million pounds. Thus the data required for detailed analysis cannot be collected in the confectionery market and even if they were available, the technical problems would be the most difficult imaginable. When the variations in flavour etc. are considered, there are hundreds of competing products, all of which differ in taste. Another serious complication in the confectionery market is the effect of coinage so that the sales of products priced at say 7d. will be affected by children having only 6d. to spend. If the price were changed to 6d. by reducing the weight then the perceived value for money might change radically even when the actual value remained unchanged.

When it is not possible to collect the detailed data, then it is necessary to resort to carrying out experiments, as has happened in the confectionery market. Essentially a company deliberately varies some of the factors in the marketing mix and notes the effect on its sales. It is necessary to plan the experiment so that the factors outside the experiment do not cause the answers to have ambiguous interpretations. Because competitors' actions cannot be controlled, there is a need for large experiments if useful predictions are to be made. However, these are difficult to perform and are expensive, with advertising research in the confectionery market typically costing ten thousand pounds per television area per annum. In many cases large experiments cannot be carried out because of the limitations on the number of subjects available. For example, the size of a television experiment is restricted by the small number of commercial television areas. In the confectionery market, experiments involving wholesalers are difficult to plan because one hundred wholesalers can account for as much as half of a company's sales. Consequently experiments must take place consecutively rather than concurrently. This obviously increases the time scale for research. It also creates new problems in the statistical design of experiments because marketing pressures often have an extended effect and it is necessary to ensure that an experiment is not ruined by carry-over effects from previous ones. However, where experiments can be conducted successfully, the results, whilst being useful in their own right, are only used to maximum advantage when they form the input to a total model of consumer behaviour.

The Bidding Problem and the Wrong Approach

The problems of data collection in industrial markets are much greater than for consumer products in that continuous market research is virtually non-existent. Consequently, experiments must be used frequently. However, when sales are obtained by bidding for contracts, it may be possible to obtain the identities of the winning bidders or the winning prices or both. The prices of a sequence of all winning bids for the sales of a product whose value is simply assessed by its weight, are plotted in Figs. 2, 3 and 4 for between two and three years. There are eleven selling companies competing and it will be seen the price is gradually declining as time progresses. The problem facing a company is to decide what price to quote whenever a contract comes up for tender. One approach might be to collect recent winning bids for all contracts of a similar size and to use these to obtain a probability distribution of winning prices. It would then be possible to determine a price, such that in the recent past, 95 per cent of winning prices have been higher. Thus if a tender were put in at that price, then hopefully there would be a 95 per cent chance of winning the contract. Unfortunately competitors would immediately react and start putting in similar bids. Soon what had been a lower tail of the probability distribution of winning bids would quickly become a central value, so that the chance of winning a contract at the previous price would be dramatically reduced. However, the process could be continued and a new probability distribution determined. Again a bid which had a 95 per cent chance of winning the contract could be determined but competitors would take similar action to reduce the chance of the bid being successful. The process could be repeated and each time competitors would react and the price would rapidly be reduced. Thus the analysis has only succeeded in taking all the profit out of the business. Inevitably and deservedly the analyst will lose his job! Of course, the same situation could have arisen simply by uninformed management taking similar decisions without the help of the analyst. In one such market the profit margin has fallen during the last eight years from 10 per cent to $1\frac{1}{2}$ per cent. Capital is turned over three times a year, so that the return on the investment has been reduced from 30 per cent per annum to $4\frac{1}{2}$ per cent per annum.

Company Bidding Policies

What has gone wrong with the previous analyses is that the use of probabilities in particular and statistics in general is, in many situations, an admission of failure. The use of probabilities enables one to rationalize the apparently irrational. They aggregate over those factors which are imperfectly understood. In the bidding problem, this is equivalent to ignoring the detailed reasons for organizations making particular bids and for customers accepting them. It is as though a selling organization were just as likely to put in a high price as a low price. Now from Fig. 2, the winning bid of company one is sometimes high, sometimes low and sometimes it lies in the middle. It might therefore be concluded that company one has an irrational bidding policy, but this is far from the case. The way of analysing bidding markets is to understand how manufacturers and consumers behave when tenders are put out and bids are accepted. In the particular market considered the purchasers invariably take the lowest price since quality is the same for all suppliers. The behaviour of the marketing organizations is determined by their own company policies. Thus what is needed is a mathematical model of the company policies of those organizations selling in the market.

It might be thought that with only the winning bids given in Figs. 2, 3 and 4 available, it would not be possible to estimate the company policies of the eleven competitors in the market. However, this can be accomplished with the aid of a powerful computer and the estimated policy of company one is given in Table II. Company one started off the period under consideration by being far less aggressive than the majority of the competitors in the market but as time went by, it became progressively more and more aggressive. It was for this reason that company number one won some contracts with high bids. However, this company has always believed in giving large discounts for large quantity orders and therefore it won some contracts with very low prices. Because it has a large and extensive distribution system, it can afford to charge distribution costs only

TABLE II

STRATEGY OF COMPANY I

1. *Basic Price*

Day	*Price Differential compared with Average*
200	15
400	9
600	6½

2. *Quantity Discounts*

Quantity	*Discounts Differential*	*Average Differential*
100	11	10
10,000	25	23
1,000,000	36	32

3. *Distribution Policy*

An allowance for the distribution cost, which is included in the price, is based on the distance from the warehouse rather than the factory. It discriminates against long journeys so that only 4 per cent of contracts more than twenty-five miles from the warehouse are won.

from its local warehouses and it pursued a policy of attempting to get business near to these. Other business was not won because it deliberately charged high prices to cover the high cost of haulage. To summarize the policy of company number one, it was being very aggressive for large contracts near its warehouses and being very unaggressive for other contracts. This behaviour explains the results shown in Fig. 2. Estimates of the policies of the other bidders enabled the resulting operational system to predict the winners of contracts better than management could.

In creating mathematical behavioural models of companies in this industrial market, missed sales and realized sales have both been used in the analysis. Similarly in the simulation of the consumer expendable market, the purchases by customers of the products of all competitors were considered. To the operational research worker, it is always surprising that organizations only analyse their own sales

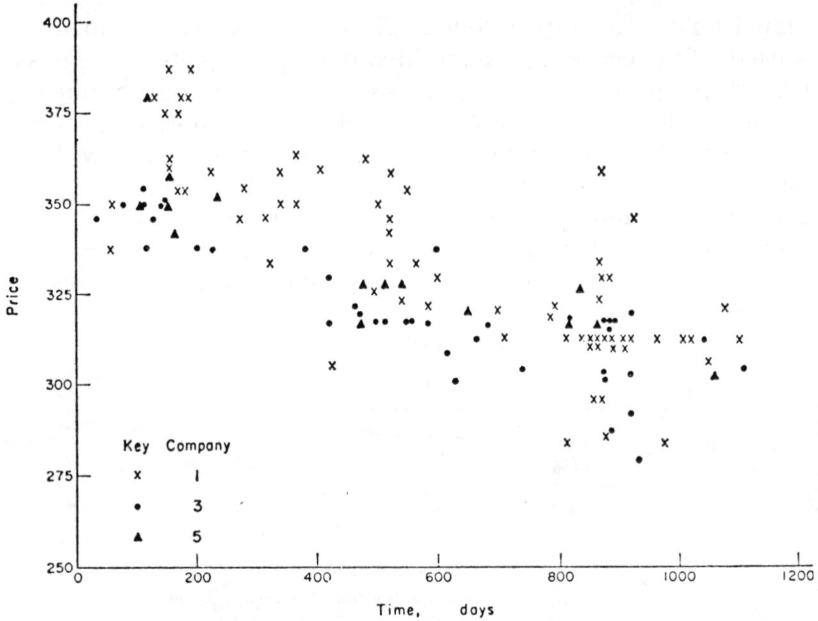

Fig. 2 Winning bids for companies one, three and five.[1]

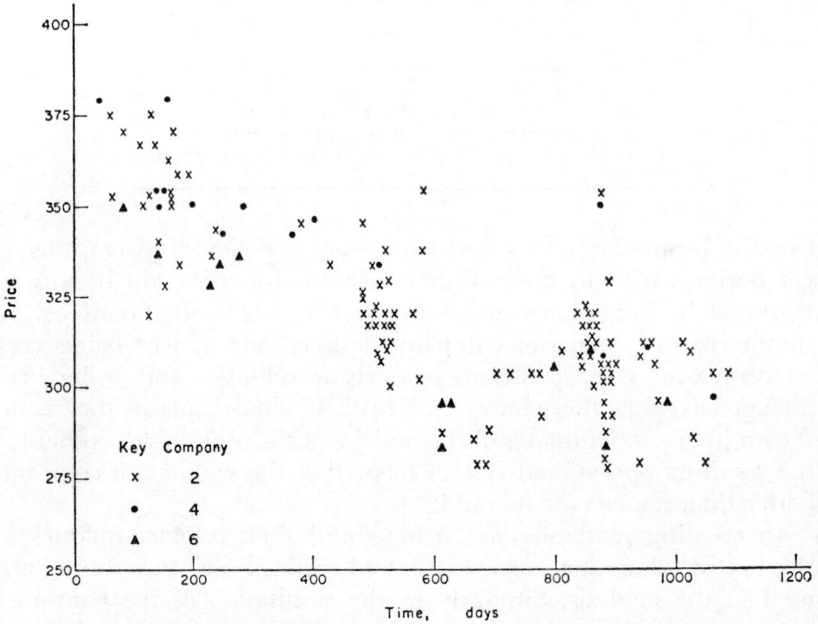

Fig. 3 Winning bids for companies two, four and six[1]

[1] Reproduced by courtesy of the Editor, *Operational Research Quarterly*, from 'Recurrent Competitive Bidding' by A. Mercer and J. I. T. Russell, Vol. 20, No. 2, 1969.

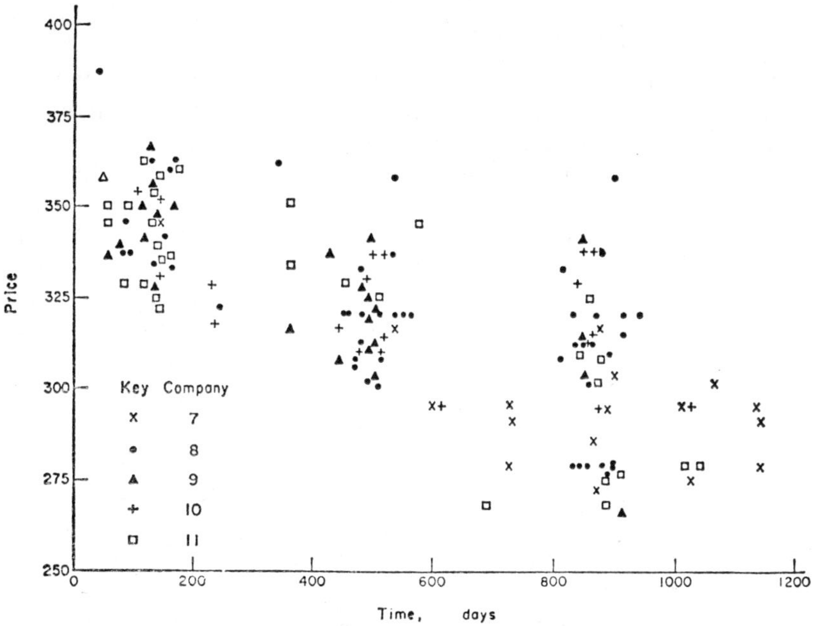

Fig. 4 Winning bids for companies seven, eight, nine, ten and eleven.[1]

when they wish to achieve an increase in sales by winning business from their competitors. The reasons are that the data are not readily available and the computations are difficult. This is particularly true for the more complex bidding processes. For example, each contract may be for a different specification, as in some markets for industrial machinery. A bidder may wish to gain experience in a different field. After-sales service may be important so that the lowest bid does not necessarily win the contract and purchaser behaviour must then be considered.

When the actions of customers and competitors can be anticipated, an organization can tender a winning bid at a price only slightly less than that of the nearest comparable competitor's bid. However, any attempt to secure an untypically large share of the market, even in the short term, might be disastrous because it would invite aggressive action by the competitors. A strategy which has been used successfully is for an organization to obtain the market share which it traditionally held but to win those contracts which are most profitable to itself. This does not necessarily mean that the competitors' profits will be reduced. For example, if the competitors have different strengths, then all could benefit by a company not winning unsuitable contracts.

The Retailing Centralization Problem

The operational problems in retailing may be described as those of getting a customer into a shop and then of making a sale, irrespective of the brand. Consequently, the retailer's objective differs from that of the manufacturer, who is only concerned to sell his own brands, irrespective of the outlet. However, the operational research analyst is presented with the same difficulties of collecting data to construct mathematical models of consumer behaviour, although this might not be immediately obvious. For example, a retailing organization selling consumer durables wanted to know whether to centralize or decentralize its warehousing and distribution system. Over a hundred retail outlets sell a wide range of electrical appliances such as washing machines, radiograms, refrigerators, electric fires, etc. Customers enter the retail outlets and make the purchase of their choice. Unless this is small, it will be delivered to the customer's home. However, the customer will not receive the model which he saw in a retail outlet, but rather one of the same type which has come directly from a store.

The question interesting the organization was whether there should be one large central store or whether there should be a large number of stores scattered in different parts of the country. Now there are considerable economies in having a centralized system. First, a large warehouse can be operated much more cheaply than a small warehouse. For example, it is possible to use fork-lift trucks which can lift appliances to considerable heights so that they may be stacked on modern racking equipment one on top of another. There is clearly a great saving in space with this sort of system. The appliances can be moved around much more quickly than would be the case if one or two men were using a barrow. Secondly, if manufacturers are only going to deliver to one store, then they ought to achieve considerable economies in their own distribution systems. A large retailer will naturally expect that some of these economies of scale should be passed on to him by the manufacturer. These will be passed on in the form of higher discounts. A third economy for the retailer is that he will need to keep less stock to prevent running out if only one warehouse is used than if a large number of warehouses are used. This is simply because the peaks and troughs of demand in different places will be smoothed out overall as opposed to having to be satisfied individually for a decentralized system. Of course, someone has to pay for the distribution costs to the consumers so that if a centralized system is used, then the retailer will have to transport appliances over greater distances and consequently his distribution costs will be increased. Thus the decision as to whether to centralize or decentralize is a question of whether the saving in warehousing costs, the saving in inventory costs and increased discounts are greater or less than the retailer's increased cost of distribution.

Inventory and Consumer Choice

Now in determining how much stock should be kept at each warehouse there are some very difficult problems of forecasting the sales of consumer appliances. This is because each year one or more manufacturers will change a model. Since all choice is comparative those manufacturers who had a good model and therefore did not change it, may find that in a succeeding year the preference for their model had been replaced by that for a newer model of a competitor. Consequently it is true to say that the models on the market change from year to year even if this is not physically the case for all models. Since the sales of many appliances are seasonal, it is necessary to analyse more than one year's data in forecasting what the sales might be. For example, in the winter the sales of refrigerators go down and the sales of electric fires go up.

Once the forecasts have been made, then it is necessary to determine how much stock should be held. This is done by defining the service level, which is essentially the proportion of a product for which demand can be met immediately from stock. Thus one describes a product as being stocked with a 90 per cent service level if 90 per cent of demand can be met from stock. In determining the inventory in a warehouse of the retailer, it is necessary to consider the stock of each brand of each appliance. Now it would be reasonable to assume that if ten different brands of an appliance were stocked but if one happened to be out of stock during the visit to the outlet of a potential purchaser, then there is a chance that that purchaser will switch to another brand of the same appliance. Thus if ten appliances were normally stocked with the nominal 90 per cent service level, one would expect to give a better than 90 per cent service. In other words, the chance of losing a sale would be expected to be less than 10 per cent. It is therefore necessary to determine precisely what the chance would be of losing a sale. This probability can only be obtained by examining the behaviour of customers in the retail outlets. Therefore for a period of two weeks the shop assistants in all the retail outlets filled in questionnaires whenever a sale was made and whenever a sale was missed. Fortunately the organization had a decentralized system and the range of stock varied from warehouse to warehouse. The probabilities were determined in two different ways,[2] and they were obtained both from the questionnaires filled in when sales were made and from the questionnaires filled in whenever sales were missed. It has been argued that since salesmen are always optimistic after making a sale, they will be likely to say that they could have made a sale irrespective of the product range and therefore underestimate the probability of missing a sale because of the range. When they have missed a sale, they will be likely to say that no-one could have made it and therefore they would overestimate the effect of the range. For the study in question, the upper and lower bounds were so close as to define the relationship almost precisely. This is yet another example of the benefits to be obtained from analysing missed sales. Obviously the results varied numerically from product to product. For one range of appliances, the chance of losing a sale because of the stock position was 15 per cent if eight brands were available. This rose to 37 per cent if the choice was restricted to four brands and to 84 per cent if only one brand was stocked. The market share of the brand leader was 16 per cent and it is interesting to note that for all appliances considered, the probability of making a sale when only one brand was stocked was equal to the brand share of the market leader. This suggests the retailers would have no difficulty in determining the brand if they are only going to stock one. For the stocking policy to be decided, the effect of the available consumer choice must be combined with the possible service levels. The probability of losing a sale is given in Fig. 5 for different stock ranges of the previous appliance at the 60 per cent and 90 per cent service levels. At the 90 per cent level, the chance of losing a sale as denoted by the lower curve is greater than the chance of being out of stock of a given brand, denoted by the lower line, unless twelve brands are stocked. The upper curve and line show that seven brands are needed if the whole range is not to do worse than expected for a particular brand when the service level is reduced to the untypically low level of 60 per cent. Quite clearly the potential purchaser is discriminating against buying in those outlets where the product range is low. The results suggest that the organization would be wrong to reduce the range of products sold unless the change was accompanied by a price reduction or some other incentive to purchase.

Profits and Costs

All the factors influencing the decision were put together to produce the annual net-profits before selling expenses of the retail

[2] 'Estimating the Effect of Variety on Sales' by M. C. J. Elton and A. Mercer, *Operational Research Quarterly*, Vol. 20, No. 3, 1969.

outlets and the once only warehousing capital investment for the various possible systems. The results are given in Tables III, IV and V for pessimistic, expected and optimistic estimates of future dis-

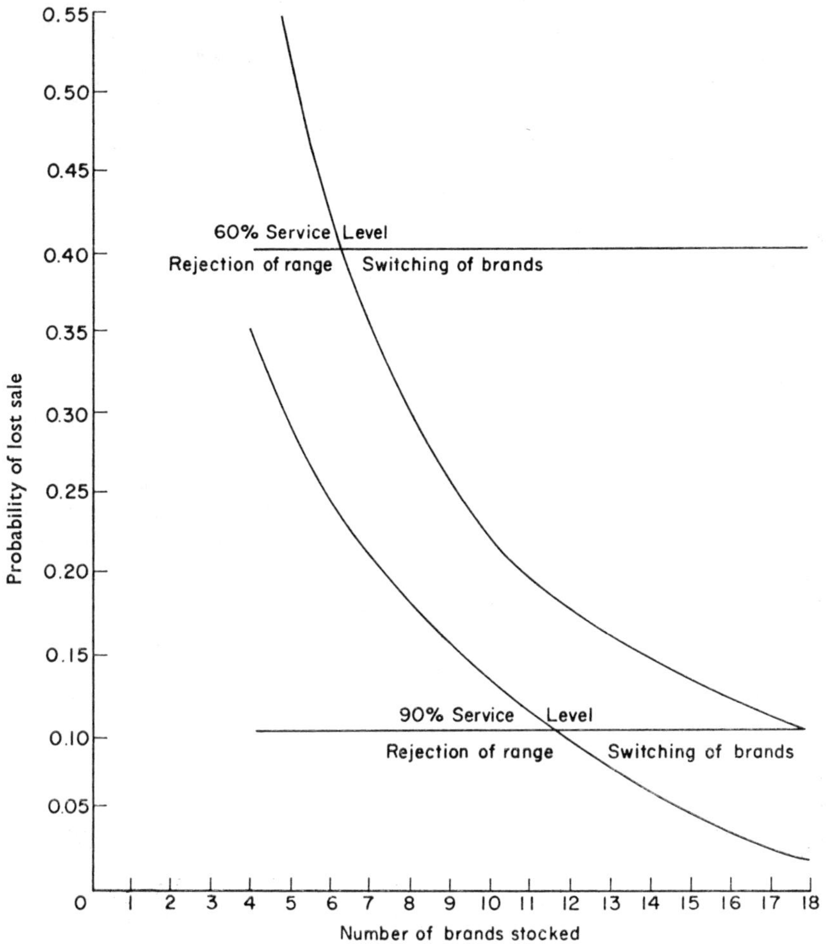

Fig. 5 The probability that a sale is lost because of the stock position

counts respectively, which were obtained by interviewing senior purchasing and marketing executives. Alternative service levels are also included and the calculations have been done for the current demand with the normal and with a reduced product range. The normal product range is essentially that being carried at the time of the study and the reduced product range represents that which would be available if a reduction were to be made.

TABLE III

NET PROFITS AND WAREHOUSE CAPITAL COSTS FOR THE PESSIMISTIC DISCOUNTS AND CURRENT DEMAND

		Normal range		Reduced range	
Service level (percentage)	*Configuration*	*Net profits (£'000)*	*Warehouse capital cost (£'000)*	*Net profits (£'000)*	*Warehouse capital cost (£'000)*
80	Decentralized	1316	215	1222	216
	Centralized	1299	74	1206	79
90	Decentralized	1304	226	1224	226
	Centralized	1303	104	1223	97
95	Decentralized	1293	235	1216	235
	Centralized	1302	125	1224	125
97·5	Decentralized	1284	242	1207	242
	Centralized	1297	144	1217	130

The profit is not particularly sensitive to the service level but the warehousing cost increases as the service level increases. In this case it is therefore not desirable always to give the highest possible service level. Obviously the profits increase considerably as the discounts become more generous but this does not necessitate a large increase in the investment in warehousing. In all cases it pays handsomely to stock the normal range rather than a reduced range, thus confirming the tentative conclusion arrived at from examining the graphs in Fig. 5. The net profits and warehousing capital costs were calculated with increased demand and various other possible changes in the market. In all the most likely cases, it was found that a centralized

TABLE IV

NET PROFITS AND WAREHOUSE CAPITAL COSTS FOR THE EXPECTED DISCOUNTS AND CURRENT DEMAND

		Normal range		Reduced range	
Service level (percentage)	*Configuration*	*Net profits (£'000)*	*Warehouse capital cost (£'000)*	*Net profits (£'000)*	*Warehouse capital cost (£'000)*
80	Decentralized	1359	222	1276	215
	Centralized	1381	67	1285	67
90	Decentralized	1342	233	1273	227
	Centralized	1381	90	1295	89
95	Decentralized	1322	245	1251	237
	Centralized	1376	118	1293	117
97·5	Decentralized	1300	262	1225	247
	Centralized	1366	148	1286	135

TABLE V

NET PROFITS AND WAREHOUSE CAPITAL COSTS FOR THE OPTIMISTIC DISCOUNTS AND CURRENT DEMAND

		Normal range		*Reduced range*	
Service level (percentage)	*Configuration*	*Net profits (£'000)*	*Warehouse capital cost (£'000)*	*Net profits (£'000)*	*Warehouse capital cost (£'000)*
80	Decentralized	1404	230	1338	217
	Centralized	1485	73	1381	66
90	Decentralized	1384	238	1325	227
	Centralized	1484	93	1399	89
95	Decentralized	1366	248	1310	237
	Centralized	1478	122	1397	115
97·5	Decentralized	1344	267	1282	247
	Centralized	1472	147	1394	136

system was much better than one involving two or more warehouses. This study illustrates how marketing interacts in a complex way with the stocking and distribution of the retailing chain and how the operational research analyst could not have solved the organization's problem without creating a mathematical model of the behaviour of customers in retail outlets.

The Location of Retail Outlets

The previous study only considered the in-store behaviour but it is equally important for the retailer to understand the decision process which causes a customer to visit one shopping centre rather than another and to enter a particular outlet.

In studies to determine how shoppers discriminate between outlets, it is necessary to make counts of pedestrian traffic passing each competing store and the numbers of entries. These require either a large number of observers or a complex, statistically designed counting timetable which will allow adjustments to be made for the variations occurring naturally from hour to hour during the day. Departmental stores, which are basically large collections of different outlets, cause problems because it is not possible to count the entries to a particular department. Attractiveness must be defined operationally in a number of alternative ways and models built to determine which is the most satisfactory. As retailers have discovered, the rateable value is invariably the best single predictor of the number of customers who will enter an outlet. This is not surprising since it is a composite measure based on size and location but better models of the behaviour of shoppers can be obtained. Retailers also attempt to persuade customers to visit their stores by advertising in the local press. These effects can be evaluated by carrying out experiments which must be designed to eliminate the interactions between the different advertisements. The results of such experiments frequently result in savings for the outlets. For example, large advertisements for consumer durables may be no more effective than small ones because potential buyers are looking for them. The effect of advertisements for ladies dresses often simply produces sales earlier in the season rather than more sales.

Evaluating why a customer visits a particular shopping centre is one of a whole hierarchy of planning problems. At one extreme, there is the problem of warehouse location which has been successfully solved using operational research techniques because customers will visit the nearest warehouse. At the other, there is the complete planning of a large urban area which includes many interacting facilities. It can be argued that the behaviour of the potential customers for the services being built should be taken into account more, so that the problem has all the features of a marketing study. Between the two extremes, the location of shopping centres involves the same considerations and operational research methods as the siting of churches. In the work done for the Church of England in Preston,[3] it was found that individual churches have a self-perpetuating attractiveness for particular classes of people so that many worshippers do not attend the nearest church although few travel more than 20 per cent further than the distance to the nearest church. The techniques which can be used for locating shopping centres will be used to site churches in the new town to be based on Chorley, Leyland and Preston. Like all the other operational marketing research studies, it uses mathematical behavioural models with data which have been difficult to obtain and what started as research will finally become operational.

[3] See 'The Churching of Urban England', by A. Mercer, J. S. O'Neil and A. J. Shepherd, paper read at IFORS Conference, to be published in Proceedings, 1970.

SOME EFFECTS OF POLICY ON PRODUCTIVITY IN SOVIET AND AMERICAN CRUDE PETROLEUM EXTRACTION*

by Earl R. Brubaker

I. INTRODUCTION

A primary purpose of positive economic investigation is generation of confidence in predictions about the response of society to alterations in public policy, the rules of the game. The rules are of particular interest because they often are thought to be subject to relatively costless manipulation with beneficial effects on performance. The American crude petroleum extracting industry[1] is a clear example of the latter propositions. In recent years most serious writers discussing the rules under which the industry has operated, though often outsiders, i.e., academicians and some journalists, have surprised industry members by suggesting that efficiency could be improved by policy changes *reducing* the degree of regulation by various government agencies. According to an estimate by Professor M. A. Adelman [1] the possible savings are quite impressive, amounting to something on the order of $2.5 billion per year at the levels of crude petroleum production existing in the United States in the 1960s. The gains would come largely through the elimination of excess capacity which, accepting Adelman's estimate, is of the same order of magnitude as the well-known excess capacity in American agriculture [32, p. 322].

The alleged inefficiency notwithstanding, the United States has been the world's largest producer of petroleum. Well behind but secure in second place has been the Soviet Union with a substantial crude oil output of its own. In contrast to the voluminous literature on the American industry little has been published in the West about the activity in the U.S.S.R. Under what rules of the game has the Soviet industry achieved second place? Does it suffer from inefficiencies similar to those of the American industry? Is it beset by

* Thanks are due to Charles Butler, David Granick, Al Pope, Judith Thornton, Dean A. Worcester, Jr., and an anonymous referee all of whom have made helpful suggestions. Remaining defects in the paper are of course the responsibility of the author.

[1] Production, extraction, or lifting of petroleum all refer to the process of transporting inventories of crude oil and natural gas from underground reservoirs to the surface of the earth. It includes maintenance and operation of wells, separators, emulsion breakers, desilting equipment, and all other activities incident to making oil and gas marketable up to the point of shipment from the producing property. This activity is narrower than that defined by the Standard Industrial Classification, Crude Petroleum and Natural Gas Fields (Industry code 131.2), which in addition to the above, includes exploration for crude oil and natural gas, and also drilling, completing, and equipping wells.

inefficiencies of its own? If so, to what extent are they related to the rules of the game under which the Soviet producers operate? Can differences between Soviet and American rules be related to differences in observed performance? Can the answers to these questions help to evaluate the predictions of writers who have argued that efficiency would rise if the government reduced its interference with the activities of crude oil operators? This paper attempts to advance understanding of the answers to these questions through a relatively thorough quantitative investigation of comparative factor productivities in Soviet and American crude petroleum production.

The investigation proceeds as follows. First, in order to establish a frame of reference, we present in summary fundamental features of the competitive compulsory unitization model. This model is regarded by some as an ideal and by many as clearly superior to American policies [1; 7, p. 252; 8, pp. 100, 107; 21, p. 110; 22; 23, p. 119]. Then we trace essential features of Soviet and American economic organization and petroleum production policies focusing on how they conform to or deviate from the normative model. Finally we use data on output per unit input as indicators of performance with each country regarded as a standard for the other.[2] A theoretically more satisfying procedure would be to obtain a measure of the optimum rates of production per well and per man in each economy and to determine the extent to which the actual productivities fall short of the optimum in each case. Measures of optimum productivities at any level of aggregation are, unfortunately, very difficult to obtain, and none has been computed here. Thus the expedient frequently followed under the circumstances, use of observed output per unit factor input at a certain time and place as a standard for other times and places, has been employed again.

II. COMPULSORY UNITIZATION AND COMPETITION

A. *Compulsory Unitization*

Technical considerations dictate highly coordinated development, preferably under unit management, of any single geologically defined petroleum pool. This proposition seems to be almost universally accepted, the consensus being at least sufficiently broad to encompass the views of Soviet as well as American analysts. Because each pool is an isolated hydrodynamic system, events in any part of which may affect significantly the remainder, technically optimum

[2] Performance of an economic system or sector may be measured in terms of a number of criteria. Output per unit input and its growth are two of the major ones most frequently used.

development requires a single management. It appears that most geologists believe crude oil migrates under pressure through porous rock or sand until it is trapped by a layer of impervious material. There it remains, at pressures varying with depth but commonly on the order of 150 atmospheres, until a channel is cut permitting the fluid to flow to the surface. Although no two reservoirs are exactly alike, depending on the particular case, one, or a combination of three general sources of pressure may provide the energy for lifting the oil. These sources are: (1) dissolved gas, (2) free gas collected in a cap above the crude oil, or (3) water. Especially where the latter two types of drive are involved, carefully coordinated development of the reservoir under a complex and delicate model often is required to achieve a technical optimum. Less suitable procedures may result in premature escape of gas from the cap or in the by-passing of oil by the encroaching water which may flow through the oil toward points of low pressure, i.e., the wells. In both cases large quantities of petroleum which could have been obtained at low cost under the technical optimum become available only with steeply rising outlays for productive services. Because of the need for careful coordination, technically optimum development of most pools is best accomplished by a single management with unlimited access to the entire surface area covering the reservoir.

B. *The Competitive Firm and Industry*

The notable normative status of the competitive model in economics has prompted a number of investigators to suggest that competition among sellers of petroleum from unitized pools may constitute an optimum organization, or at a minimum, a decided improvement over the one that has developed historically in the U.S. Thus it is desirable to summarize the basic mode of operation of a competitive firm developing an isolated petroleum reservoir with natural drive.[3] Assume the firm has opportunities for leasing any from a large number of such deposits. Given a perfect market and perfect foresight the firm can obtain the right to develop a deposit for the net revenue (excluding entrepreneurial services) obtainable from its exploitation. Once the lease has been secured the objective of the management is to choose a time distribution of production that will maximize the present net worth of the firm. On the revenue side the firm estimates a pattern for future prices and interest rates to determine the present values of gross revenue associated with the

[3] The model of the petroleum lifting firm follows closely the one developed more fully in [21, pp. 101–10].

alternative schemes for distributing output. On the cost side the firm similarly estimates the present values of outlays for productive services. The management then chooses the scheme that maximizes the positive difference between the present values of the revenue flows and the outlay flows.

So far the description applies to any firm engaged in the sale of a stock resource, but there is a highly important characteristic peculiar to petroleum. Namely the nature of many reservoirs is such that, given a fixed number of wells, over a significant range of output the share of petroleum *in situ* which is commercially recoverable varies inversely with the rate at which it is produced. In other words from a normal reservoir with a fixed complement of wells there is a rate of production, the TMER,[4] beyond which the ultimate economically feasible recovery declines rapidly. Within wide limits, however, the rate of production can be increased without reducing ultimate recovery provided that there are also increases in the number of wells draining the pool.[5] Thus in maximizing present net worth one of the manager's basic decisions involves balancing advantages of present income against the cost of constructing more wells and/or against the cost of producing at a rate above the TMER. If he chooses the latter, he foregoes not only the opportunity for future sales of inventories put on the market in the present but also the opportunity for selling the additional portion of the crude oil *in situ* that, as a practical matter, is irrevocably lost.

It is held that under competitive compulsory unit operation market forces would guide the firms and industry to optimum employment of productive services in the activity. No more labor and capital would be allocated than would be required to obtain the desired time distribution of extraction, which also would be determined by market forces. Calculations of producers analyzing market data would provide a criterion for the desirable degree of intensive and extensive development of crude oil deposits, thereby giving guidance for distributing productive services through time to exploration for new reserves.

C. *The Production Function*

Output of crude petroleum may be regarded as a function of

[4] Petroleum reservoir engineers label this rate the MER or maximum efficient rate. A technical concept (TMER) and an economic concept (EMER) may be distinguished. TMER refers to the maximum rate of production from a given number of wells consistent with maximum ultimate recovery of oil *in situ*. EMER refers to the rate of production that maximizes present net worth of the firm exploiting the reservoir.

[5] Often, however, for a given percentage increase in output an even greater percentage increase in the number of wells is necessary if a decline in ultimate recovery is to be avoided [21, p. 106].

inputs of productive services. It will be useful to describe the nature of the relationship between output and the major inputs.

It seems clear that inventories and wells constitute two of the important capital inputs into the activity. The inventories and wells provide necessary services for which there is little possibility for substitution. Without the channel for flow to the surface that wells provide, no production can take place, and clearly there can be no extraction of oil where there is none to extract. In lifting petroleum the substitutability of any other productive service, including labor in particular, for wells or for inventories is highly inelastic.

In proportion to the number of wells a capacity (C) is needed for operating and maintaining them.[6] Such capacity can be provided by varying proportions of labor and capital, and historically innovation of more sophisticated equipment has increased the range of combinations available to the manager.

Thus it is convenient to think of a petroleum production function in which output depends upon labor and upon two types of capital—one for which labor can be substituted hardly at all and a second for which labor is rather easily substitutable. In mathematical notation we may write $O = f(W, C)$ where O is output of petroleum and W is the number of wells. We also write $C = g(L, K)$ where L and K represent, respectively, services of labor and of capital other than wells. The aggregate petroleum production function for a set of deposits is assumed to have the same form.

As usual we hardly expect the 'independent' variables to explain completely intertemporal and interspatial differences in output, and we shall think of the function as subject to shifts under the influence of other factors. The latter might include any or all of the prominent candidates such as technical progress, public policy, or qualities of inputs, that have been put forward in attempts to explain shifts in production functions relating GNP to aggregate inputs of labor and of capital in a given economy. In addition factor endowments and the historical stage of development might be capable of significantly influencing the relation between output of petroleum on the one hand, and inputs of labor and of capital on the other.

[6] Requirements for capital services necessary to accomplish elementary collection, storage, and refining processes that are dependent more on the volume of extraction than on the number of wells are neglected. Since the capacity to operate and maintain wells varies with their number and not with the level of production, output per well and output per unit of well-servicing capacity tend to be highly correlated. For this reason where the level of surface mechanization is similar, both Soviet and American studies [18, p. 46; 30, p. 190] indicate a strong positive correlation between output per man and output per well. Data from [6] tend to substantiate these results. Thus, after initiation of the Korean conflict in 1950, output per well increased by 13.6 percent in 1951 while output per man-year rose by 13.4 percent, and hours worked per week by production workers in SIC 131.2 (crude petroleum and natural gas fields) increased less than 1 percent.

III. COMPARATIVE RULES AND ENVIRONMENT

A. *United States*

In the U.S. varying degrees of monopoly power in product and/or factor markets, aggregate instability, featherbedding, trade secrets, and other such features of the economic milieu, traceable to some extent to public policy and common in varying degree to almost all industry, may have affected considerably output per man, O/L, and output per well, O/W, in lifting crude petroleum. It is, however, in the area of petroleum policy *per se* that the effects of government intervention are most clearly visible. In the first place, the domestic industry appears to have been subsidized through favored tax treatment in the form of the depletion allowance, through fast write-off of intangible[7] outlays for exploration and development, through the ability to apply capital gains tax rates to sales of inventories of crude oil discovered by wildcatting, and through restriction of imports. Subsidies generally permit continuation of less efficient operations and possibly lower O/L and O/W. No attempt is made here to relate quantitatively the effects of such subsidies on the productive process. Instead attention is focused on policies directly regulating production.

In the U.S. the direct regulatory role of the state governments has dominated in setting the rules for the industry. Thus the statutes of 37 states, as they have evolved over approximately a century, along with their interpretation by the judiciary and their administration by various and sundry state conservation commissions, contribute to the hodgepodge of rules under which crude oil has been extracted.[8] The nature and effects of these policies already have been discussed at length in the literature cited above, so that here a brief summary, though of necessity an extreme simplification, will suffice.

Cutting through the details it seems clear that in contrast to the competitive compulsory unit norm, three fundamental policies have been pursued in the U.S.—unregulated rule of capture, regulated rule of capture, and regulated unit operation. According to the rule of capture lifting petroleum to the earth's surface within the boundaries of an individual's property establishes his ownership. Where a reservoir can be drained from several properties, rule of capture provides a powerful incentive—in the form of a negative user's cost—for each landowner to drill offset[9] wells and to produce from

[7] Items having no salvage value.

[8] See [17] for a detailed survey covering all 37 states. See also [19] for a sophisticated summary of policies affecting efficiency.

[9] Offset wells are drilled on the boundary of a property to drain oil from the portion of a reservoir under neighboring land.

them at a very high rate. Under these circumstances the number of wells tends to depend more on surface property lines than on technical principles of reservoir economics and engineering.

The principal consequences of unregulated rule of capture are the following. Output per well from any given reservoir surges to a peak but soon subsides, and national average *O/W* fluctuates as large new fields are developed quickly and then decline. Under the unregulated rule of capture reservoir energies are rapidly dissipated; total recoveries are reduced; an uneconomically large number of wells are drilled; and the distribution of production over time alternately encourages profligate use and rations severely.

A second major American policy has been regulated rule of capture. Under such regulation owners of land overlying petroleum reservoirs are permitted to produce according to a quota set by a state commission. Although in recent years the formula for setting quotas has been much improved by paying more attention to spacing, the fundamental requirement for 'allowable' production during most of the era of regulation has been the well. Thus the operators have had an incentive to drill more than might otherwise be required. Then too, often any holder of surface rights, no matter how small, has been permitted to withdraw oil from the pool. Where property is finely subdivided, the result is many more wells than normally would be deemed appropriate under economic and technical criteria applied to the reservoir as a unit. In the period under consideration here the unneeded wells and curtailment of production to 'market demand' as estimated by the commissions, i.e., at rates often far below reservoir TMER's, have tended to lower national average *O/W*. A third policy calls for the development of reservoirs as a unit under single management. Land owners share in the profits or losses according to a mutually agreeable formula. Compared with both varieties of rule of capture this policy reduces the incentive for unnecessary drilling, but output from existing wells again may be restricted by the regulatory agencies to the 'market demand' associated with the established price.

During the years for which Soviet–American comparisons have been made, regulated rule of capture constituted the basic policy under which most American crude oil producers operated. Totally unregulated rule of capture was important only in Illinois where the share in national output was less than 5 percent for most years. Regulated unit operation also was comparatively unimportant. United States Government legislation and policy have been relatively favorable to unitization of reservoirs on federal lands, and a number of states have, at various times since 1945, compelled cooperation of recalcitrant property owners for unitization where certain special conditions obtain. But since the later 1920s the overwhelming majority of domestic petroleum production has come from states such as Texas, Oklahoma, and Louisiana where regulated rule of capture has dominated.

B. *U.S.S.R.*

Although government ownership and management have assured unit operation of all petroleum reservoirs in the U.S.S.R.,[10] some features of economic policy deviating considerably from the competitive unit ideal almost certainly detracted from the attained level of performance. Both autarky and conservatism in allocating productive services to risky petroleum exploration may have contributed toward lower O/L and O/W than might have been achieved under a closer approximation to ideal policy.[11] Of primary concern here, however, are the general dysfunctional effects stemming from ascendancy of command over market features of industrial organization [12; 14]. That is, Soviet economic policy has been characterized by: (1) centralized planning and centralized physical allocation of a wide range of intermediate products, (2) use of physical output as the primary managerial success criterion, (3) target planning, i.e., setting plans for output very high so as to stimulate utilization of all capabilities of the enterprise as well as its superior agencies, (4) an informal priority system to achieve a modicum of decentralization providing thereby some flexibility needed for the functioning of the system, (5) extreme pressure for demonstrated evidence of managerial capability with an important result a high rate of managerial turnover, and (6) no formal interest charge, though possibly a rather high *implicit* discounting of future output by the manager because of his short expected tenure.

The implicit interest rate is of special importance in crude petroleum production because of the latter's inventory aspect and because of its high capital intensity. Net interest was eliminated as a category of Soviet enterprise cost in 1931 and was reintroduced at an apparently nominal level only in 1965. The consequences of a zero charge for capital in an economy where it was anything but free have been described carefully and perceptively by Professor Gregory Grossman [15]. As Professor David Granick has pointed out, however, the zero nominal charge did not necessarily imply a corre-

[10] On the strength of universal unit operation within the U.S.S.R., Soviet economists confidently assert the overall superiority of their system [9, p. 82; 20, p. 84].

[11] If the Soviet government had been willing to allocate more resources to exploration, the prolific deposits of the Urals–Volga region may have been discovered and exploited sooner.

spondingly low implicit discount rate in the calculations underlying enterprise decisions [12, pp. 121–2]. Given the very rapid rate of managerial turnover there existed a tendency to discount future output rather heavily, as would be appropriate considering the general scarcity of capital in the economy.

While these features have had aspects functional from the viewpoint of the directors of the system, they have contributed to certain dysfunctional side effects as well. There have been, for example, a whole series of undesirable responses by managers to the situation in which they find themselves. These include: (1) the 'free goods' treatment for materials allocated in excess of needs, (2) disregard for aspects of operations involving the longer term interests of the enterprise, for example, low priority for research and development, for maintenance of plant and equipment, and for developing a labor–management team, (3) a 'search for slack', i.e., attempts to reduce plans by hiding resources, covert reduction in quality of product, hoarding of scarce materials, and integration vertically. In conjunction with all this a self-reinforcing tendency for uneven plan fulfillment with consequent shortages of material inputs and costly work stoppages has pervaded the system.

Although it seems quite likely that the efficiency of the crude petroleum industry in particular was affected to some extent by all these aspects of the Soviet system, it has not proven possible to appraise quantitatively all their impacts. However, certain of these factors, namely the regime's stress on short-run results, gross physical output as the manager's success indicator, and policies causing high rates of managerial turnover, have a distinct appeal as explanations of certain deficiencies in extraction of petroleum in particular. Specifically there seem to be clear examples of the tendency to neglect considerations involving the long-term interests of the enterprise. This is apparent in: (1) production above capacity[12] with probable detrimental effects on ultimate recovery, and (2) failure to keep pace with technical developments in the West. Some of the evidence for these effects and some indications of their quantitative significance are discussed in more detail below.

IV. COMPARATIVE PERFORMANCE

A. *Some Basic Measurements*

For purposes of this paper crude oil and natural gas are regarded as homogeneous products measurable in physical units, but in fact crude oils vary widely in their chemical and physical properties

[12] The term capacity as used here is synonymous with TMER.

and hence in their usefulness as a raw material. Since rational production could involve higher marginal costs to obtain the higher quality crude oils, measuring output in physical terms involves some error. In the U.S.S.R. where quality has been of lesser concern, this element of rationality is missing [5, p. 50]. In the U.S. differences in productivity as measured physically may be due partially to variations in the quality of crudes.

Major specific inputs, labor and capital, also are assumed to be homogeneous and, corresponding to the production function elaborated above, are measured in physical units, production workers and wells. Homogeneity of labor inputs is a traditional assumption in studies of this type. The assumption of the homogeneity of oil wells is less common but may do little more violence to reality, and the use of the mere number of wells has some advantages. First, a physical indicator excludes effects of progress outside the specific activity being analyzed. Secondly, using simply the number of wells tends to eliminate the effects of the greater capital expenditures needed to develop deeper deposits, which are more indicative of inferior natural resources than of inefficiency. Third, although there are other important physically measurable inputs, wells probably account for the major part of total money outlays for capital items.

Major features of intercountry and intertemporal differences in relations between observed specific inputs and output are summarized in Table I. As is frequently the case in such comparisons, O/L is higher in the U.S., but output per unit of the capital item is lower. National average O/W in the U.S., $(O/W)_U$, rose with minor fluctuations, from 330 tons per well in 1925 to 590 tons per well in 1961. On the other hand O/W in the U.S.S.R., $(O/W)_R$, fluctuated violently, rising from 3000 tons per well in 1925 to 4900 tons per well in 1931, then dropping to 2400 tons per well in 1940, and even further to 1700 tons per well in 1945. After a period of stability at a low level during 1945–52, $(O/W)_R$ rose rapidly and by 1960 reached 4600 tons per well, still short of the prewar peak attained in 1931. Intercountry comparisons show that $(O/W)_R$ ranged from approximately 3 to 14 times $(O/W)_U$.

In contrast national average output per production worker in the U.S.S.R., $(O/L)_R$, ranged from 20 percent to 60 percent of $(O/L)_U$. In the U.S. O/L grew with only minor fluctuations from 2400 tons per man in 1939 to 7100 tons per man in 1960. In the U.S.S.R., on the other hand, O/L nearly tripled between 1928 and 1930, but fell precipitously by 1940 and further by 1950 after which it began to rise again. The prewar peak was regained, however, only by 1957.

Of course the statistics provide a picture of apparently fine resolution, which might, nevertheless, be deceptive. For example, the category in Soviet employment statistics most nearly comparable with production workers in the U.S. is wage workers (*rabochie*). Thus where comparisons refer to production workers the Soviet category, *rabochie*, was used. In order to achieve closer comparability with data on production workers as defined by the U.S. Bureau of the Census employment of minor service personnel, guards, apprentices, working foremen, and certain non-industrial personnel should be

TABLE I

U.S. AND U.S.S.R.: GROSS OUTPUT OF CRUDE OIL PER WELL AND OF CRUDE OIL AND NATURAL GAS PER PRODUCTION WORKER, SELECTED YEARS, 1925–61[a]

Year	*Output of Crude Oil Per Well* (*Metric tons per well*)		*U.S.S.R. ÷ U.S.*	*Output of Crude Oil and Natural Gas*[b] *Per Production Worker* (*Metric tons per production worker*)[c]		*U.S.S.R. ÷ U.S.*
	U.S.	*U.S.S.R.*		*U.S.*	*U.S.S.R.*	
1925	330	3000	9.1	N.A.	N.A.	N.A.
1928	370	3230	8.7	N.A.	477	N.A.
1929	430	3500	8.1	N.A.	559	N.A.
1931	350	4910	14.0	N.A.	780	N.A.
1932	340	4390	12.9	N.A.	1020	N.A.
1938[d]	430	3750	8.7	2400	1410[e]	0.59
1940	460	2410	5.2	N.A.	821	0.34
1945	550	1720	3.1	N.A.	N.A.	N.A.
1950	580	2040	3.5	3900	674	0.17
1955	640	2560	4.0	5000	1080	0.22
1960	590	4560	7.8	7100	2040	0.29

[a] [6, pp. 135–41].
[b] Natural gas was converted to oil equivalents at the rate of 0.0000248 metric ton per cubic foot. This is the conversion factor implied in [24, pp. 203, 209, 211] corrected for measurement at 60° F.
[c] Unless otherwise noted data on output do not include associated or non-associated natural gas. Data on labor input do not include employment in extracting non-associated gas.
[d] Datum for the U.S. refers to 1939.
[e] Includes associated gas.

added to the data on Soviet wage workers. According to Professor Walter Galenson's estimates, employment in the excluded categories in 1938 amounted to about 10 percent of the total [11, p. 100]. Data on the Russian Republic (R.S.F.S.R.) in [26, p. 36] suggest that in 1960 this percentage may have fallen to only 2. Errors introduced by these omissions in our basic computations may be offset to a significant degree, however, by relatively large employment of salaried managerial, technical, and staff employees in the U.S. [6, pp. 59–60]. Relative productivity in the Russian industry is understated further because the Soviet data exclude: (1) production of associated gas which amounted to about 4 percent of crude oil output (calorific equivalents) in the 1950s [25, pp. 174, 177] and (2) the activity of extracting non-associated gas, where it appears that productivity was greater than in joint production of crude oil and associated gas. Inclusion of the non-associated gas extraction for the U.S.S.R. would increase productivity relative to the U.S. from 0.22 to 0.24 in 1955 and from 0.29 to 0.35 in 1960. Exclusion of the non-associated gas productive activity from the U.S. data probably would have a somewhat greater effect because of its greater share in American output and employment.[13] Further differences in statistical definitions and in collection procedures may introduce incomparabilities and unavoidable errors of unknown size. It is, however, doubtful that they are so great as to affect significantly either the orders of magnitude shown in Table I or our general conclusions.[14]

B. *Policy and Productivity*

1. *Excess capacity in the U.S.*

Perhaps the most visible impact of government policy on the American industry has been the creation of excess capacity, but what is its extent?[15] Estimates of capacity for producing crude oil in the U.S. have been prepared each year since 1954 by the Independent Petroleum Association of America. According to these estimates unused capability for output grew from about 25 percent in the mid-1950s to almost 40 percent in 1963 [16]. It was even greater at the more prolific pools since stripper wells operated essentially unlimited. Thus excess capacity at non-stripper well fields apparently amounted to about 30 percent in the mid-1950s and reached about 50 percent in the late 1950s and early 1960s.

Given such attribution of all surplus capacity to the superior resources, a hypothetical capacity flow per non-stripper well may be calculated. Such calculations indicate that in 1955, for example, operation of the more prolific U.S. fields at full capacity may have eliminated the need for large numbers of stripper wells and may have reduced $(O/W)_R$ from 4.0 times $(O/W)_U$ to as little as 1.2 times $(O/W)_U$.[16]

[13] This larger share may stem from greater American efficiency in the broader, allocative sense, which is not, however, within the scope of this paper.

[14] For a detailed discussion of these and other possible measurement errors see [6, pp. 16–34].

[15] See [2] and [19, pp. 97–102, 268–71] for excellent analyses of capacity and difficulties in its measurement in the American crude petroleum industry.

[16] Basic data for the computation are from [3, pp. 31, 38–9, 41; 16]. See also [6, p. 146].

2. *Productivity and the unit rule on federal lands*

In general, information about unitized pools in the United States is scarce. There are, however, some data pertaining to U.S. Government lands, where the unit rule enjoyed somewhat greater prominence. Here again the evidence, while not as ample as might be desired, points in the direction of greater *O/W* where the degree of unitization is greater.

Data for 1957 show that at least 40 percent of production from U.S. Government lands was from unitized fields [29]. Of course 40 percent, though probably quite high relative to the share of production from unit operations in the nation as a whole, may be regarded as rather low when compared with the 100 percent that would be required under the ideal.

Suppose, nevertheless, that we were to compare output per unit input on Government lands with the national averages. Other things equal, output per unit input should be higher on Government lands because of the presumably greater (though still small) degree of unitization. Actually a more satisfactory comparison can be made. From readily available evidence it is possible to show that during 1948–57 *O/W* on Government lands was on the order of 30 to 75 percent higher than that in the remaining regions of states containing such lands [29; 3, pp. 30–1, 40–1, 67–8, 72].[17] In this way 'other things' such as differences in geological conditions and state regulations are less likely to reduce the reliability of the test.

The reasons for the indicated numerical outcome are not completely clear. It may reflect the fact that the regulations of some states have allowed higher quotas where more rational development involving wider well spacing has occurred. To the extent that this is so, our data provide yet another indication of the gains that might accrue from requiring unitization. Although possibly the net effect of many factors, the comparatively high output per well on Government land is, nevertheless, consistent with the prediction of greater efficiency where the degree of unitization is higher.[18]

[17] For a complete description of procedures used see [6, pp. 77–80].

[18] A question may arise as to whether or not unit rule might be consistent with excess capacity because of a continuing high cartel price with free entry. Furthermore might not this excess capacity also result in low *O/W* and *O/L* relative to that attainable given both unit rule and elimination of the cartel? Certainly cartelization and the unit rule are not mutually exclusive policies. It would seem, however, that if both a cartel and the unit requirement were instituted, excess capacity would take the form largely of inventories in terms of discovered oil reservoirs and of capabilities for exploration. Quotas presumably would be set essentially in proportion to reserves in the various pools, since there would be concern only about the quantity of oil that each enterprise marketed. Under these circumstances there would be an incentive to obtain a quota by giving evidence of holding proved reserves. There would be no incentive, however, to develop capacity to lift any petroleum beyond that permitted by the quota. The only wells to be drilled would be operated to their individual capacity, and no more wells would be drilled than would be required

3. *Soviet production exceeding TMER*

In contrast to the unused capacity in the U.S. stands production over and above capacity in the U.S.S.R. leading to somewhat higher performance (as measured by O/L and O/W)[19] in the 1950s at the expense of the future.[20] In the years preceding World War II petroleum pools apparently were developed rapidly with little regard for TMER [28, p. 41]. Since World War II, however, application of more advanced reservoir engineering techniques progressed rapidly, and it seemed that excesses were being meticulously avoided. However, there have been indications of production above the maximum efficient rate at the giant *Romashkino* field, where, since 1950, a significant percentage of Soviet crude oil has been produced. Despite doctrine calling for pressure maintenance by water injection from the very beginning of exploitation, reservoir pressures have consistently fallen in the various sectors of the field from 1950 to 1962 [10, p. 10; 30, pp. 82–3]. As a result, hundreds of formerly flowing wells stopped producing, and a reporter for *Ekonomicheskaia gazeta* has charged that 'oilfield operators, striving to make up for declines in output regardless of the cost, produce at excessive rates from the remaining active wells, thereby grossly violating the principles of petroleum reservoir development' [10, p. 10].

The result of these violations has become apparent also in data on output by type of lift. In 1961 production by the flowing method had attained an unprecedented 74 percent of the total. The prewar peak was less than 48 percent in 1930, when flush production from new fields may have been important. By 1940 it had declined to little more than 23 percent. After steady advance in the postwar period to the peak in 1961 the share of flowing production began to descend, falling from 73.2 percent in 1962 to 64.4 percent in 1965 [6, pp. 104–5; 25, p. 176].

to fill the quota. Similarly there would be no incentive for excess surface capacity to operate wells. Under these circumstances it could very well turn out that O/W and O/L would be just as great as in the absence of the cartel. But perhaps more important, unit operation would eliminate the major current reason for cartelization, the negative users' cost implicit in operating with many holders of rights of access to the pool. Cartelization resulted through 'conservation' as the outgrowth of a rational attempt to reduce the obvious waste of unregulated rule of capture. But with such waste eliminated by the unit rule the rationale for 'conservation' and the associated cartelization would disappear.

[19] This illustrates the hazards of focusing on one or a few narrowly defined indicators of performance. The Soviet system would appear to deserve credit for obtaining high O/W by limiting wells to the minimum necessary for draining any given reservoir, but a more comprehensive indicator would account for the extent of production in excess of TMER and the resulting reduction in ultimate recovery.

[20] It is possible that resources allocated to exploration may have substituted for inventories of crude 'wasted'. There may be no apparent fall in O/L and O/W if a sufficient number of new pools are discovered and are produced at a rate above TMER in the future.

Such Soviet managerial behavior can be rationalized in terms of success indicators that stress heavily current and physical criteria. Petroleum producers in the U.S.S.R. have had no rule of capture to encourage their production above TMER, but they have had substantial incentives for fulfilling taut plans. It is doubtful that the cost of producing beyond capacity is considered systematically, if at all, in Soviet calculations, and there may even be a tendency for managers to regard future inventories of crude oil as something close to a free good. When, in spite of the growing availability of reservoirs requiring less water injection per unit output, the program for constructing facilities for pressure maintenance fell behind schedule, operators apparently met planned targets by imprudently permitting pressure to drop, that is, by producing above capacity and at the expense of future efficiency and of reduced ultimate recovery.[21] While the practice makes much sense to the operators, it is clearly dysfunctional from the viewpoint of the rest of society, including the top policy-makers.

Although some quantitative limits can be set, it is difficult to appraise accurately the extent of Soviet production above TMER. First, it is technically difficult to make a judgment. And second, Soviet operators almost certainly attempted to hide the facts from the state control apparatus which in turn undoubtedly was not anxious to report details of unfavorable performance to the rest of the world.

At any rate it seems highly probable that in the Soviet Union production was exceeding capacity, while in the U.S. it was at substantially less than the optimal rate. Adjustment to capacity output in both countries conceivably could in some years eliminate, or even reverse, the large disparity in O/W. This is a fairly interesting result in itself, but it also tends to undermine use of output per well as evidence to support the argument that Soviet resources have been more favorable than those in the U.S.[22]

4. *Soviet lags in surface technology*

In spite of the very high $(O/W)_R$ compared with $(O/W)_U$, $(O/L)_R$ has consistently amounted to only a fraction of $(O/L)_U$. Why?

The disparity between $(W/L)_R$ and $(W/L)_U$, itself the result of

[21] It should be noted that the apparent predilection in the 1930s for flush production with its dire consequences for ultimate recovery may be rationalized in some degree by the particularly high discount rate appropriate for that period. With the decreasing scarcity of capital in the post-World War II period this argument may have become less appropriate.

[22] Some analysts have used national average O/W as an indicator of the contribution of natural resources.

differences in substitution for labor of surface capital, K, embodying new technology, would seem to contribute much to the answer. The number of wells per worker in the U.S.S.R. was generally less than a tenth of that in the U.S. during 1939–57. In the period 1958–60, firms in the U.S. may have been innovating surface technology, or bringing it up to date, at an even faster rate than Soviet firms were adapting it, as by 1960 $(W/L)_U$ had grown to something on the order of 15 to 17 times as great as $(W/L)_R$.[23] Soviet calculations suggesting comparatively short recoupment periods for telemetering and control equipment, if not extremely biased by distorted prices, indicate significant sluggishness in adjusting to new techniques made available by research and development departments of Western firms.[24] Thus we may have here another example of the tendency to implicitly discount very heavily the value of future output and to neglect the long-term interest of the enterprise. Presumably attainment of the American level of wells per worker could have raised $(O/L)_R$ by a factor of as much as 11 to 17 at various times during the period 1939–60, even if there had been no increase in O/W.

V. CONCLUSION

What may be concluded from the foregoing analysis? First, public policy has substantially and measurably affected performance in

[23] As shown in the following tabulation both $(W/L)_U$ and $(W/L)_R$ have grown rapidly during the period under consideration.

Year	$(W/L)_U^a$	$(W/L)_R$
1929	N.A.	0.15
1940	4.1[b]	0.34
1950	4.5	0.33
1960	7.1	0.45

[a] Data are approximations probably understating the level and growth of $(W/L)_U$. See [6, pp. 56–57].
[b] Datum refers to 1939.

[24] To some extent, of course, the comparatively large $(W/L)_U$ might be explained by Soviet and American factor endowments. But it seems that other variables, possibly technology, may have been important, since very rapid growth in capital per man in aggregate would suggest also a rise in the number of wells per man in the U.S.S.R. relative to the U.S. In fact the reverse occurred. This evidence is also consistent, however, with an alternative hypothesis. That is, the Soviet authorities may have found it administratively convenient to limit proposals involving substitution of capital for labor to a few sectors of the economy where the possible savings of labor were relatively large [13, p. 202]. Petroleum production with its small labor force may have offered little possibility for releasing labor, and therefore had not as yet crossed the threshold to be included among sectors from which such proposals were entertained.

production of crude petroleum both in the U.S. and the U.S.S.R. The outstanding example is the relation between productive capability and actual output in the two countries. It is clear beyond reasonable doubt that American regulations have resulted in surplus capacity at the national level, in some years apparently on the order of 25 to 40 percent. These paradoxical policies simultaneously stimulate creation of productive facilities while restricting their output *especially from the superior natural resources*. As a result excess capacity at the more prolific pools was even greater than the national average. On the other hand, there are clear signs that Soviet policy has encouraged production at above the optimal rate with detrimental effects on ultimate recovery of proved reserves.

These deviations from capacity output affect strongly the relative performance of the Soviet and American industries as measured by such commonly used indicators as output per unit input of labor and of capital. Unadjusted for differences in the degree of capacity utilization output per well in the U.S.S.R. has amounted to 3 to 14 times that in the U.S. Since rates of creation and utilization of capacity are strongly influenced by the government's rules, it might be said that at least in some periods it was principally because of differences in public policy that the large disparity in output per well was observed. Calculations suggesting levels of output per well adjusted to capacity in both countries show that the disparity would be very substantially reduced. Indeed during some years in the 1950s and 1960s American output per well could have exceeded that in the U.S.S.R.

Second, it seems that Soviet policy may have exerted a negative influence on efficiency in petroleum extraction in another way. It is clear that for some reason automation of the Soviet activity, while proceeding rapidly, has not kept pace with that in America. As a result the number of wells operated per man has been much higher, 11 to 17 times as high, and in recent years growing faster, in the U.S. Primarily for this reason, and despite relatively low output per well, output per man in the U.S. has generally amounted to 2 to 5 times that in the U.S.S.R. While one might argue that Soviet planners found it administratively convenient to ignore the possibilities for factor substitution because of the relatively small amounts of labor available for release to other sectors, it is also quite possible that failure to innovate, or even to adapt available western techniques, may have been an example of the well-known tendency for Soviet managers to neglect the long-term interests of their enterprise.

Third, sources of intertemporal and interspatial differences in output per unit input undoubtedly include important factors other than policy. Nevertheless, review of the possible operation of such factors[25] does not reduce our confidence that substantial disparities in performance do stem from differences in the rules of the game. Particularly where excess capacity is concerned the impact of other factors apparently does not vitiate our conclusions. Differences in *capacity* output per unit input may be the net result of a number of important factors, but differences in *actual* output per unit input appear to be enormously and unequivocally affected by deviations from optimal capacity utilization, such deviations being in both countries unintended consequences of public policy.

Thus this comparative analysis of Soviet and American experience lends additional confidence to the conclusions of those investigators who have argued that American performance in petroleum production could be improved markedly by altering the rules of the game toward the competitive compulsory unit model. Apparent shortcomings in American performance compared with the Soviet appear to be related to the fact that Soviet reservoirs have all been developed as units, while the American reservoirs have not.

Similarly, it seems that deficiencies in Soviet performance may have been related to operation under the national plans in a predominantly command economy without the discipline of market pressures. Soviet oil field operators have tended to treat costly underground inventories as a free good, and they may have failed to adapt at least some new techniques as rapidly as they were introduced in the West. Thus a substantial amount of relevant quantitative evidence supports the assertion that efficiency could be improved by shifting toward the complete competitive compulsory unit model in the U.S.S.R. as well as in the U.S.

UNIVERSITY OF WISCONSIN

REFERENCES

[1] M. A. ADELMAN, 'Efficiency of Resource Use in Crude Petroleum', *So. Econ. Jour.*, October 1964, **31**, 116–22.

[2] ——, 'Trends in Cost of Finding and Developing Oil and Gas in the U.S.', in S. H. Hanks & S. L. Gardner, eds, *Essays in Petroleum Economics*. Colorado School of Mines, 1967.

[25] In addition to the direct effects of public policy a host of other variables in all probability have contributed to greater or lesser degree to the observed disparities in factor productivities. Among the more important are factor endowments, historical stage of development, the scale and rate of growth of the industry, quality of inputs, technology and land. With the quantitative evidence available to date, however, it has proven possible to do little more than speculate about their effects. For a more detailed discussion of these factors see [6].

[3] American Petroleum Institute, *Petroleum Facts and Figures*. New York, 1959.
[4] ——, *Petroleum Facts and Figures*. New York, 1961.
[5] A. N. Basov *et al.*, 'K voprosu o klassifikatsii neftei po kachestvu i differentsiatsii raschetnykh tsen na nikh', *Khimiia i tekhnologiia topliv i masel*, 1962, No. 11.
[6] E. R. Brubaker, *Productivity in Extraction of Petroleum in the U.S. and in the USSR*. Ph.D. dissertation, University of Washington, 1964.
[7] M. G. de Chazeau and A. E. Kahn, *Integration and Competition in the Petroleum Industry*. New Haven, 1959.
[8] P. Davidson, 'Public Policy Problems of the Domestic Crude Oil Industry', *American Economic Review*, March 1963, **53**, 85–108.
[9] F. F. Dunaev, *Ekonomika i planirovanie neftianoi promyshlennosti SSSR, chast'I*. Moscow, 1957.
[10] *Ekonomicheskaia gazeta*, November 30th, 1963.
[11] W. Galenson, *Labor Productivity in Soviet and American Industry*. New York, 1955.
[12] D. Granick, 'An Organizational Model of Soviet Industrial Planning', *Journal Pol. Econ.*, April 1959, **67**, 109–30.
[13] ——, *Soviet Metal-Fabricating and Economic Development*. Madison, 1967.
[14] G. Grossman, 'Notes for a Theory of the Command Economy', *Soviet Studies*, October 1963, **15**, 101–23.
[15] ——, 'Scarce Capital and Soviet Doctrine', *Quart. Jour. Econ.*, August 1953, **67**, 311–43.
[16] Independent Petroleum Association of America, *Report of the Productive Capacity Committee*. Midyear meeting, April 1963.
[17] Interstate Oil Compact Commission, *A Study of Conservation of Oil and Gas in the United States*. Oklahoma City, 1964.
[18] O. E. Kiessling *et al.*, *Technology, Employment, and Output Per Man in Petroleum and Natural Gas Production*. Work Projects Administration Report No. E-10. Philadelphia, 1939.
[19] W. F. Lovejoy and P. T. Homan, *Economic Aspects of Oil Conservation Regulation*. Baltimore, 1967.
[20] D. I. Maslakov, *Toplivnyi balans SSSR*. Moscow, 1960.
[21] J. W. McKie and S. L. McDonald, 'Petroleum Conservation in Theory and in Practice', *Quart. Jour. Econ.*, February 1962, **76**, 98–121.
[22] E. V. Rostow, *A National Policy for the Oil Industry*. New Haven, 1948.
[23] H. Steele, 'Public Policy Problems of the Domestic Crude Oil Industry: Comment', *American Economic Review*, March 1964, **54**, 119–25.
[24] Ts Su, *Narodnoe khoziaistvo SSSR v 1961 godu*. Moscow, 1962.
[25] ——, *Narodnoe khoziaistvo SSSR v 1965 godu*. Moscow, 1966.
[26] ——, *Promyshlennost' RSFSR*. Moscow, 1961.
[27] ——, *Promyshlennost' SSSR*, Moscow, 1964.

[28] U.S. Bureau of the Census, *The Soviet Mineral–Fuels Industries, 1928–58: A Statistical Survey*, by D. B. Shimkin, International Population Statistics Repts., Series P. 90, No. 19. Washington, 1962.

[29] U.S. Geological Survey, Conservation Division, *Annual and Accrued Mineral Production, Royalty Income, and Related Statistics, Calendar Year 1957*. Washington, 1960.

[30] Vsesoiuznyi neftegazovyi nauchno-issledovatel'skii institut, *Ekonomika neftedobyvaiushchei promyshlennosti*. Moscow, 1963.

[31] ——, *Voprosy ekonomiki neftedobyvaiushchei promyshlennosti*. Moscow, 1960.

[32] L. W. Weiss, *Case Studies in American Industry*, New York, 1967.

COST FUNCTIONS FOR THE WATER INDUSTRY*

by J. L. Ford and J. J. Warford

I

This short paper presents some results of an attempt to derive a suitable function to explain unit costs in the water supply industry in England and Wales. The data we used were the latest available at the time of writing. The data, in effect, were for the year 1965–66. It was not possible, because of lack of data, to carry out a time-series analysis to supplement our cross-section findings. At the moment the industry is composed of some 331 undertakings; our sample, which is based on data provided by I.M.T.A.,[1] covers 162 of those undertakings. In effect, it covers: 67 local authorities; 75 water boards; and 20 water companies.[2]

Estimation of a cost curve for an industry on the basis of cross-section data for a given year could be regarded as the estimation of the long-run cost curve, of the 'envelope' variety, so familiar to us from elementary economic theory. However, to so regard the estimated cost curve we should have to suppose that any undertaking could jump from one short-run cost curve to any other, as the textbooks argue. This means that everything connected with the production conditions in any one undertaking is exactly the same as in any other undertaking except for the *size of 'plant'*. So that if we are to regard any estimated cost curve as the long-run one we must further suppose that we have a 'homogeneous' industry.

As far as the water industry is concerned we do not have the ideal textbook situation[3]—but this does not bother us. The product of the industry is, of course, more or less homogeneous. But for the greater part the production conditions are not so. By production conditions we mean those conditions that are necessary to provide water ready for distribution to industry and to the public. For some undertakings these production conditions consist simply of natural reservoirs;

* This paper is a substantially revised version of a chapter originally prepared for a book on the water industry, and based on part of Warford's Ph.D. thesis.

[1] See, *Water Statistics*, 1965–66, published by The Institute of Municipal Treasurers and Accountants.

[2] For details of these undertakings and for details of the data used in this study consult *Water Statistics*, op. cit. It would take far too much space for us to list all details here—remember we have 162 observations.

[3] This is not true of other public utilities, e.g. electricity. It is possible to estimate an envelope curve for the latter industry that could be reasonably regarded as the long-run cost curve of the textbook's perfectly competitive industry. See, for example, K. S. Lomax, 'Cost Curves for Electricity Generation', *Economica*, May 1952, pp. 193–7.

in others, such as the Manchester C.B.C. undertaking, the service reservoirs are fed by aqueducts from two large lakes; in yet others such as Leicester, they consist of several small reservoirs, as well as numerous wells, boreholes and springs.[4]

As water undertakings wish to expand their output, over time, and have to provide new means of doing so, we cannot say that they will do so merely by expanding the size of 'plant'—nor indeed that they will operate from an entirely new 'plant'—and so move along the conventional textbook envelope cost curve But this does not mean that there cannot be the *kind* of relationship between unit costs and output in the water industry that is presented in the textbooks.

We have implied that production costs are composed of three main items: (1) expenditure on sources of supply,[5] (2) transmission of water and (3) treatment of water. But such costs play only a small part in the total unit costs of most of the water undertakings. Since the industry adopts an average total cost pricing system, there does not seem much point in merely considering the relationship between costs of production and some output or size variable; especially is this so if the present study is to be used as a—tentative—guide to some of the policy problems concerned with the water supply industry. A large part of average total costs, or unit costs, in the industry is taken up by distribution costs. The latter are fairly uniform throughout all the undertakings in the industry. Other important costs, which do vary between undertakings, are 'capital' costs, in effect, 'debt charges, dividend and interest payments, etc.'. Here we have a cost item which should be regarded as an overhead cost, a cost directly related to the production conditions, and productive capacity, of a given undertaking.[6]

In this paper then we are concerned with the derivation of an industry average cost curve, or function. Although the resulting curve could be similar to the envelope curve, or to part of the envelope curve, as we know it, it will differ from the usual conception of that curve because of the nature of production conditions in the water supply industry. Furthermore, the cost functions that we shall

[4] We could argue further that production conditions differ because of the treatment that must be given to the water in given undertakings before it can be allowed to be distributed to the public. That is, the quality of water varies from area to area and to make the final product more or less homogeneous filtration and treatment costs have to be incurred, in varying degrees, by all undertakings. In effect: turbidity; colour; taste; suspended solids; acidity; salinity; hardness; the presence of certain salts, dissolved gases and micro-organisms; must all be tested for and dealt with appropriately.

[5] Expenditure on maintaining reservoirs and on major catchments.

[6] To give some idea of the costs incurred by a typical undertaking we have composed Table I which is for our own area, the Manchester C.B.C. undertaking. The costs are on the basis of pence per thousand gallons; so the output figures used to express average total costs, or unit costs, is one thousand gallons. The unit cost for the Manchester C.B.C. undertaking in our sample year being 23.75. (*See Table I on page 55.*)

be concerned with will be related to average *total* costs. Even if we had felt that it was worthwhile—or indeed possible—to separate out the costs of the given undertakings into production costs, etc., we could not have estimated, for example, the relationship between production costs and *capacity*; we would have had to use actual output figures as we have done here, adequate figures for capacity just cannot be constructed. There are some details on the capacity of reservoirs: but such information only covers a portion of the total means of supply of the industry.

The rest of the paper is organized as follows. Section II notes the type and characteristics of the four cost functions we have fitted to the data. Section III briefly presents and assesses the statistical results obtained from using those functions. Section IV then makes some comments on the major issue of amalgamation in the light of the statistical results.

II

If we are to judge whether or not some kind of envelope curve is relevant in the water supply industry,[7] we must make some statistical estimates based on *parabolic* functions. Suppose, for the sake of

Footnote 6 contd.

TABLE I

	pence per thousand gallons
Sources of supply	0.69
Transmission of water:	
Maintenance of aqueducts	0.57
Pumping boosters	0.08
Treatment of water:	
Filtration and treatment	0.66
Examination of water	0.10
Distribution:	
Pumping	0.10
Service reservoirs and water towers	0.28
Repairs, maintenance of mains/sewers	1.97
Meters	0.22
Meter reading	0.68
Waste prevention	0.79
Other	1.10
Rents and rates	2.19
Management and general expenses	2.24
Total working expenses	11.07
Debt charges, dividend and interest payments, etc.	12.68
TOTAL	23.75

[7] We should add formally, of course, 'for the year 1965–66'.

argument, that we have unit costs (C) as a function of output (Q). Then the simplest form of the parabola for estimating purposes where least squares can be used is a polynomial.[8] The latter should preferably be of low degree. In fact, the ideal polynomial is the quadratic equation, which is of the lowest degree possible if we are to have a parabola. Thus, in the present case, this is the best equation:

$$C = a\,Q^2 + b\,Q + d, \quad a \neq 0 \tag{1}$$

Equation (1) is particularly useful because it allows us, when statistically estimated, to judge the position and shape of the parabola. The sign of a indicates the position of the parabola: if $a > 0$, the axis of the parabola points upwards, if $a < 0$, the axis points downwards. Thus, if we follow convention by measuring C on the y-axis of a Cartesian diagram and Q on the x-axis, if $a > 0$ the parabola is of the U-shaped variety; if $a < 0$ the parabola is umbrella-shaped, i.e., an inverted U-shaped curve. The value of a is also significant: if a is large the parabola is elongated, i.e. really U-shaped, if a is small the parabola is flat, i.e. more envelope-like, or saucer-like, in shape.

In fitting equation (1) and other equations to the empirical evidence on costs we would apply the usual tests employed in multivariate analysis to assess the reliability of the equation. That is to say, the estimates of the coefficients would be assessed in the usual way by means of their F-values, and the goodness-of-fit would be indicated by the value of $\bar{R}^2$ (the coefficient of multiple determination adjusted for degrees of freedom). In estimating (1) we would suppose as usual that it contained an error or disturbance term, u. We would then use the value of the Von Neumann ratio to test for autocorrelation of the disturbances.

We tried a simple form of (1) and we also tried extensions of it introducing two independent variables so giving us a somewhat complicated parabola for estimating purposes.

It may well be the case that costs are related to output but not as indicated by an equation such as (1). We may find that as output increases C decreases, at a decreasing rate, but that it decreases for ever, i.e. for all values of output. Or, we may say, that if an equation such as (1) is of little value this could be because over the sample period the relevant part of the resulting cost curve is just the left-hand half of the U. So we should use an equation of this form:

$$C = K\,Q^n \tag{2}$$

To estimate equation (2), of course, we have to resort to logarithmic transformation of it.

[8] See, for example, J. Johnston, *Econometric Methods*, New York, 1963, pp. 50–2.

Again if we consider the simple function $C = F(Q)$ we can, if we wish, take a semi-log transformation of that function which would produce this type of equation:

$$C = \alpha + \beta \log_e Q \tag{3}$$

From (3) it follows that with $\beta < 0$ the slope of the curve relating C to Q is negative and it decreases as Q increases. We have a downward-sloping cost curve which cuts both the y-axis and the x-axis.

One other function that we could use is an exponential function which when transformed for estimating purposes into logarithms yields a semi-log equation with the dependent variable being 'logged'. Thus we may hypothesize that:

$$C = a\, e^{b\,(Q)} \tag{4}$$

In (4) we expect $b < 0$ and $a > 0$: b is the slope of the curve relating $\log_e C$ to Q; and a is the intercept on the y-axis. So the curve approaches the x-axis asymptotically.

Enough has been said about the basic nature of the four types of cost functions we have used. To decide which one best explains costs in the water supply industry we use the conventional methods of comparing their $\bar{R}^2$s, etc. But as a further test of the value of the semi-log and double log equations we have estimated the same relationship by means of straightforward linear equations.

III

Let us take the functions in Section II, *seriatum* and consider their empirical qualities. We begin then with the parabola. Our equivalent of equation (1) would be:

$$C = a\, DS^2 + b\, DS + d \tag{5}$$

where DS, daily supply, in thousand gallons, represents 'Q'. Because our C was total average cost we would not expect to find a good fit from using (5). In fact, the result obtained was as follows:

$$\begin{aligned} &\qquad\; * \qquad\quad * \qquad\qquad\qquad * \\ C &= 31.17 - 0.00014\, DS + 0.000000000036\, DS^2 \\ \bar{R}^2 &= 0.018,\; d = 2.13 \end{aligned} \tag{6}$$

We have written (6) in the usual way with the constant term first. In equation (6) the estimates of all parameters are highly significans and they all have the correct sign.[9] Also, the value of d is satisfactory at the 5 per cent level. However, the $\bar{R}^2$ indicates that equation (6) can account for only 1.8 per cent of costs. But the value of $\bar{R}^2$ for equation (6) is not statistically significant: we must test for the significance of the $\bar{R}^2$ since we have only a sample of water undertakings as the basis of our enquiry into industry cost functions. So it is obvious that the parabola represented by (5) provides no fit to the data.

But some other form of (5) might provide a good fit: indeed, some other type of parabola might provide a good fit. We tried this equation, a simple adjustment of equation (5):

$$C = a \text{ Area}^2 + b \text{ Area} + d \tag{7}$$

Here Area is the size of each undertaking in square miles: thus (7) would be *more* appropriate to estimates of C based solely on distribution costs. It would not be completely appropriate because the size of some areas will have a direct bearing on production costs, especially on 'transmission costs'.

This is the statistical counterpart to (7):

$$\overset{*}{C} = 26.8 + 0.012 \text{ Area} - 0.0000031 \text{ Area}^2 \tag{8}$$
$$\bar{R}^2 = 0.024, \; d = 2.10$$

In (8) the Area coefficient has the correct sign but it is not statistically significant; the value of d is satisfactory at the 5 per cent level. The value of $\bar{R}^2$ is better than that obtained from (6): but it is not greatly different from zero; and is, statistically speaking, equal to zero.

The two main variables that should be employed to explain costs in this study are DS and Area: the former relates partly to the production costs[10] of the textbooks and the latter relates *partly* to distribution costs. So we estimated a parabola that was slightly more complicated than the quadratic equation, which included DS and Area. The result was really no different from the two previous ones. However, we can include both DS and Area in a quadratic equation by simply taking the independent variable to be (DS/Area). Ideally the latter should then explain unit costs here: as the ratio gets bigger

[9] We have followed our usual procedure here in that we have omitted the standard errors of the coefficient, indicating the statistical significance or insignificance of the estimates of the coefficients by a system of asterisks. Thus: one asterisk over the estimate of a coefficient indicates that it is significant at the 1 per cent level or better; two asterisks that it is significant at the 5 per cent level or better; and three asterisks that it is significant at the 10 per cent level or better. d is δ^2/S^2, the Von Neumann ratio.

[10] As we implied earlier for us these costs would include most of the item 'capital costs'.

unit costs should fall. So, substituting $(DS/\text{Area})^2$ and (DS/Area) in (7) for Area^2 and Area, we obtained this result:

$$C = \overset{*}{33.3} - \overset{*}{0.035}\,(DS/\text{Area}) + \overset{*}{0.0000049}\,(DS/\text{Area})^2 \qquad (9)$$
$$\bar{R}^2 = 0.116,\ d = 2.09$$

In (9) all the estimates of the parameters are significant at the 1 per cent level or better; the value of d is satisfactory at the 5 per cent level; the coefficient of (DS/Area) has the correct sign; the value of the constant suggests that the parabola would be saucer-like, as hitherto, and its sign says that the saucer is right-side up, as required. However, once again the goodness-of-fit is quite poor. Nevertheless the R^2 is an improvement, as was to be expected, over previous values of $\bar{R}^2$. Equation (9) explains 11.6 per cent of the variation in unit costs in the water supply industry; furthermore, the $\bar{R}^2$ is significant at the 10 per cent level or better.

As can be seen we had no success with the parabola. Given that the variables we used were the most important ones we must conclude that for our purposes the parabola, envelope curve, of the textbooks is of no value. But to be able to conclude that parabolic functions as such, as distinct from the variables we have used, are of no value, we need to compare the use of other functions employing those variables with the previous results. To do so it is probably best if we simply catalogue the results obtained from using the power function, the semi-logarithmic transformation and the exponential function. This is done in Table II, in which we have indicated the three results based on the parabola. The fifth group of equations in Table II represent the simple linear equivalents of the non-parabolic functions. What clearly emerges from Table II is that statistically speaking equations (12), (13), (16) and (17), provide the best results. In all of them the estimates of the coefficients are highly significant, and they have the correct signs; the Von Neumann ratio is satisfactory; the $\bar{R}^2$s are higher than for other equations, and they are all highly significant.

The results tabulated above rely solely upon the use of variables DS, Area, and (DS/Area). It could be argued that a variable likely to affect total average costs is *population*; or better still a variable reflecting density of population, e.g. (Population/Area). However, no real success was obtained from employing such variables; and so we omit any consideration of results based on them.

But from the best results in Table II we must conclude that there is some tendency for there to be a 'cost curve', of, as it were, half of the envelope variety, for the water supply industry for our sample year. However, the relatively low values of $\bar{R}^2$ for our best equations means that some other explanatory variables must be included in them if

TABLE II

Equation Number	*Equation*	$\bar{R}^2$	d
(6)	$C = \overset{*}{31.17} - \overset{*}{0.00014}\,DS + \overset{*}{0.000000000036}\,DS^2$	0.018	2.12
(8)	$C = \overset{*}{26.8} + 0.012\ \text{Area} - 0.0000031\ \text{Area}^2$	0.024	2.10
(9)	$C = \overset{*}{33.3} - \overset{*}{0.035}(DS/\text{Area}) + 0.0000049(DS/\text{Area})^2$	$\overset{***}{0.116}$	2.09
(10)	$\log C = \overset{*}{3.76} - \overset{**}{0.05}\log DS$	0.020	2.07
(11)	$\log C = \overset{*}{2.91} + \overset{*}{0.83}\log \text{Area}$	0.094	1.62
(12)	$\log C = \overset{*}{3.84} - \overset{*}{0.13}\log (DS/\text{Area})$	$\overset{*}{0.219}$	2.06
(13)	$\log C = \overset{*}{3.78} + \overset{*}{0.133}\log \text{Area} - \overset{*}{0.124}\log DS$	$\overset{*}{0.214}$	2.06
(14)	$C = \overset{*}{52.8} - \overset{*}{2.63}\log DS$	0.058	2.1
(15)	$C = \overset{*}{19.75} + \overset{*}{1.99}\log \text{Area}$	0.045	1.43[1]
(16)	$C = \overset{*}{46.58} - \overset{*}{4.23}\log (DS/\text{Area})$	$\overset{*}{0.206}$	2.09
(17)	$C = \overset{*}{53.37} + \overset{*}{3.92}\log \text{Area} - \overset{*}{4.82}\log DS$	$\overset{*}{0.21}$	2.10
(18)	$\log C = \overset{*}{3.3} - 0.000000014\,DS$	−0.006	2.11
(19)	$\log C = \overset{*}{3.23} + \overset{*}{0.00034}\ \text{Area}$	0.057	2.14
(20)	$\log C = \overset{*}{3.32} - 0.000067\,(DS/\text{Area})$	0.004	2.11
(21)	$\log C = \overset{*}{3.23} + \overset{*}{0.00034}\ \text{Area} - 0.000000043\,DS$	0.052	2.14
(22)	$C = \overset{*}{29.49} - 0.0000011\,DS$	−0.0056	2.11
(23)	$C = \overset{*}{27.31} + \overset{**}{0.084}\ \text{Area}$	0.028	1.55[1]
(24)	$C = \overset{*}{29.8} - 0.0022\,(DS/\text{Area})$	0.004	2.11
(25)	$C = \overset{*}{27.3} + \overset{*}{0.0086}\ \text{Area} - 0.0000018\,DS$	0.024	2.11

[1] Unsatisfactory at the 5 per cent level.

Notes: Since we have only a sample of water undertakings we must test for the significance of $\bar{R}^2$. Three asterisks over the value of the latter indicate that it is, in fact, significant at the 10 per cent level or better; two asterisks that it is significant at the 5 per cent level or better; and one asterisk that it is significant at the 1 per cent level or better. No asterisks over the value of an $\bar{R}^2$ indicate that it could have arisen purely by chance: i.e. statistically $\bar{R}^2 = 0$.

Here, we have some negative value of $\bar{R}^2$. To some this may seem odd—but not to econometricians! R^2 will always be positive, but once *we* begin to adjust for degrees of freedom we can obtain negative $\bar{R}^2$s, especially, of course, as in the present case, if R^2 is very small.

we are to obtain a satisfactory explanation of variations in costs: and if we are to be in a position from which we can definitely decide what kind of shape cost curve we do have we would have to add the new independent variables to all the equations that lie behind Table II.

But it would seem to us that we could never derive a cost function for the water supply industry which had an $\bar{R}^2$ of say, 0.75+. Variables such as Area, Population, Daily Supply, etc., must be the only major *quantifiable* variables that one can use to explain average total costs. Since they yield such poor results we may hazard two conclusions: either (a) we should attempt to break down costs into the production costs of the textbooks and seek to explain these by using our independent variables; or (b) the technological and natural differences that do exist between the various water undertakings in the industry—the unquantifiable variables—must be such as to rule out the existence of a so-called long-run cost curve for the industry; such technological, etc., differences between areas must swamp the independent variables we have used.

In no way was it possible to include a 'technological or natural' independent variable in our equations. We tried to set up experiments with dummy variables or with proxy variables, such as the number of sources of supply over gallons supplied per day for each area of supply, but we did not make much headway, either because there was not adequate data or because the basic ideas could not be put into testable variables without our pre-judging the results.

Also, we had hoped to study costs in the water industry in the conventional manner of first estimating the industry production function and then deriving from it the industry cost curve[11] under the assumption of perfectly competitive market conditions. We could not even attempt this because of lack of data. In any case such a procedure is fraught with difficulties. But if we had been able to make some preliminary estimates along those lines we would probably have found that we could not obtain an industry production function and hence an industry cost curve again probably because of the complete lack of homogeneity of the undertakings in the industry.

IV

Our results are not so completely negative as one would think, *prima facie*. Given the significance of the relationships epitomized in such equations as (12) and (13), and in view of the significance of

[11] On this see, for example, the brilliant survey by A. A. Walters: 'Production and Cost Functions: An Econometric Survey', *Econometrica*, January–April 1963, pp. 1–66.

the estimates of the given parameters, we can make some useful comments on a major policy issue, namely, that of the amalgamation of water undertakings.

Already a great deal of amalgamation has taken place: in 1955 there were 1000 water undertakings in England and Wales; by 1966 there were only 331, 162 of which form our present sample. There is a widespread belief that such regrouping will enable costs to be lowered. Thus it has recently been argued that: 'The advantages of this (i.e., of amalgamation) are not merely the larger planning unit but economies of management and operating costs and more scope to even out fluctuations in demand within an area.'[12]

We would agree with part of these remarks, for a great deal of savings in cost would come about as a result of *rationalization* of operations in a new combined area, via the bigger planning unit. That is to say, not only could there be a spreading of management costs, etc., over a bigger supply, but there would be scope for the reduction in management, etc., as a result of simple economies of scale.

But there is no evidence to suggest that, as far as *existing* costs, etc., are concerned, amalgamations will lead necessarily to a lowering of average total costs. We may legitimately use equations such as (12) and (13) to show this. Strictly speaking, we can only use the coefficients in those equations to give us a *qualitative* guide to what would happen if two areas were amalgamated. But we could use the values of the coefficients as an approximate estimate of the effects of amalgamation on costs. Although we see from equation (12) that a 10 per cent rise in (*DS*/Area) would result in a 1.3 per cent fall in *C*, we cannot conclude that amalgamations that raised (*DS*/Area) for a given undertaking would necessarily lower costs in a combined area. This can readily be seen by means of a simple example constructed on the basis of equation (13). The latter shows more clearly the two conflicting tendencies here.

On the one hand, if we hold *DS* constant and increase Area, costs rise, but at a decreasing rate. The diseconomies associated with a larger area could be explained by additional transport costs and labour time required to deal with such matters as meter reading, waste prevention and detection, and by rising general building, repair and maintenance costs. The diminishing rate of growth in costs as area increases could be explained by the greater feasibility of decentralized supply and maintenance depots as areas become larger. As an offset to the general tendency of rising average costs,

[12] C. I. Jackson and P. A. Bird, 'Water Supply—The Transformation of an Industry', *Three Banks Review*, March 1967, p. 25.

certain economies of administration and management could be realized.

On the other hand, we see from equation (13) that if we hold Area constant as we increase *DS*, average costs fall, but at a decreasing rate. This can be explained in terms of elementary theory. Thus, the provision of a reservoir which doubles existing supplies will not be matched by a parallel increase in all other inputs.

The amalgamation of undertakings will, however, increase *both* Area and *DS*. The effect of amalgamation will then depend upon the circumstances of every case. As we said earlier we can show that the effect of amalgamation, in terms of its effect on *C*, can be favourable or unfavourable by means of a simple numerical example. Thus, let us suppose that equation (13) can be used to predict the effect of changes in Area and in *DS* on costs. Case 1 below shows a situation in which amalgamation of two undertakings, *A* and *B*, increases the average total cost of water supplied by them; Case 2 shows the opposite to be the case.

Case 1. *Before Amalgamation*

Undertaking	Area (sq. miles)	*DS* ('000 galls)	*C* (pence)
A	400	10,000	31.12
B	500	15,000	30.48
		Weighted average *C*	30.73
	After Amalgamation		
A+*B*	900	25,000	30.97

Case 2. *Before Amalgamation*

Undertaking	Area (sq. miles)	*DS* ('000 galls)	*C* (pence)
A	400	50,000	25.53
B	500	60,000	28.38
		Weighted average *C*	27.10
	After Amalgamation		
A+*B*	900	110,000	25.76

If a better equation to explain costs in the water supply industry than equation (13) is discovered it will almost certainly yield the same qualitative effects of amalgamation as equation (13) does. Also, its quantitative effects, based on a log–log equation, are not likely to be far removed from those suggested by equation (13).

THE NEW UNIVERSITY OF ULSTER
THE UNIVERSITY OF MANCHESTER

THE WATER SUPPLY SYSTEM UP TO A.D. 2001

by Douglas Wood

By the end of the century the capacity of the present public water supply system will be between 2000 and 2500 million gallons per day (m.g.d.) short of conservatively estimated water requirements. A minimum investment of approximately £1000m. will be needed to provide sufficient capacity to meet the shortfall.

In planning the increase, however, more than financial considerations are involved. If the deficit were to be met by conventional catchment schemes, between 50 and 70 new reservoirs would need to be constructed, a high proportion of which would inevitably have to be sited in national parks or similar high amenity areas.[1] The public resistance to the Ullswater and Windermere schemes of Manchester Corporation and to the Cow Green and Forndale schemes indicates that a programme ten to twelve times larger could only be achieved at the expense of a great deal of social and environmental upheaval.

Even so it is obvious that water resources to support an improved standard of living for an expanding population must be forthcoming, even where this involves the imposition of some social costs on the community. At the same time it is equally necessary that social as well as financial costs should be reflected in the choice of investment made.

This is particularly true at the present time when a number of schemes with widely differing specifications are available to meet given economic requirements. Whereas the social losses brought about by damming one valley rather than another are broadly similar, allowing a choice between them to be made on strictly financial grounds, the social costs and benefits of conventional conservation schemes, barrages schemes and nuclear desalination are so disparate that they must necessarily receive explicit attention in investment planning.

THE DEMAND FOR WATER

Domestic demand

The main determinants of the level of domestic water consumption at constant prices are the size of the population, its standard of living

[1] About 20 per cent of the total precipitation of England and Wales falls on National Parks and Areas of Outstanding National Beauty.

and its mobility. Up to the end of the century a population growth in the range 1.1–1.3 per cent p.a. would add a little over half to present water requirements of 1500 m.g.d. If income per head rises at 2 per cent p.a. in real terms over the same period it would almost double by A.D. 2000. Directly this would in itself add little to the growth of domestic water consumption but indirectly should contribute to continued rapid growth in the demand for water for industrial purposes.

Quantifying the implications of population movements for water demand is more difficult. Schemes for new towns have a high mortality and progress is slow. Urban renewal too proceeds at a leisurely pace. In principle a rapid population movement would require new water supplies in developing areas whilst making redundant capacity in the declining areas. A slow movement on the other hand, which merely transferred growth from the existing centre to some new areas would involve no duplication in water supply facilities. At the present time it appears that additional demands on capacity from contemplated new town development would be minor, but any increase would inevitably lead to an upward movement in demand.

Industrial demand

In recent years industrial demand for water has been increasing at over 5 per cent p.a.[2] However, since private sources of water provide around two-thirds of total industrial consumption this growth has not placed an undue strain on public water supplies. Whether private sources can continue to meet this fraction of total industrial demand in future must be an open question. Certainly the increasing size of production units may eliminate some marginal sources of supply exploitable at present. Even if the assumption were justified, a continuing growth of 5 per cent p.a. would increase demand from 1000 m.g.d. to around 3000 m.g.d. by A.D. 2001.

Agricultural demand

Crop irrigation has been a significant new element in water consumption in recent years. The response to irrigation seems, at existing prices, to make it worthwhile irrigating crops during the summer months on 1–1½ million acres. This would entail a peak demand of 2–3000 m.g.d.—virtually the present total output of existing statutory authorities. A further aspect of irrigation use is that

[2] Central Advisory Water Committee (1962), Subcommittee on the Growing Demand for Water, Final Report H.M.S.O.

it is a 'net loss' to the water system, whereas water in other uses—domestic and industrial—usually can be re-cycled and re-used.

Total demand

The Water Resources Board[3] estimate that by A.D. 1981 an additional supply of 425 m.g.d. will be needed in the Northern half of England and 405 m.g.d. in Southern England. By A.D. 2001 the respective estimates are 1200 m.g.d. and 1090 m.g.d. Resources have already been committed to provide about 225 m.g.d. of this.

However, even with minimum assumptions of growth of 1.2 per cent p.a. in population and 2 per cent in *per caput* income it seems likely that these requirements would be exceeded: and that 2750–3000 m.g.d. was a more reasonable estimate of the prospective increase. Despite this it is necessary to use the Water Resources Board's regional estimates of shortfalls. Nevertheless the fact that their estimate represents the lower bound of prospective demand increase has important implications for the selection of investments.

PROSPECTS FOR THE SUPPLY OF WATER

Meeting the Water Resources Board demand estimates would conventionally involve the construction of up to 70 reservoirs. The capital and running costs associated with development of this type are best illustrated by a currently authorized scheme in the south-east.[4] To secure an increment in supply of 130 m.g.d. an expenditure of £32.5m. has been approved. With due provision for depreciation and at an interest rate of 7 per cent the expected cost at net present value of an immediate supply from this should lie between 22–26d.[5] per 1000 gallons at the post treatment stage. Up to A.D. 1980 a further 300 m.g.d. of conventional capacity could be installed at this same price range, or perhaps slightly more, as less advantageous sources have to be brought into use. In any event it seems unlikely that the maximum cost at the current prices would rise above 30d. per 1000 gallons.

Since water catchment schemes are usually some distance from the consumption area they are intended to serve, a trunk delivery cost has to be added to this. Since no systematic procedure seems to be in operation to minimize distribution costs there is unfortunately no way of judging whether the costs are unrealistically high—the mini-

[3] Water Resources Board, *Morecambe Bay and Solway Barrages*, Report on Desk Studies. Water Resources Board (1966) H.M.S.O.

[4] Water Resources Board, *Water Supplies in S.E. England* (H.M.S.O. 1966) Table N—p. 66.

[5] The anticipated costs depend on the period by which full capacity becomes available.

mum appears to be 4d. per 1000 gallons but 6d. or 8d. is common and the costs can be as high as 1s. per 1000 gallons. In the southern half of England a typical delivered cost would be 32–36d. per 1000 gallons.[6]

The schemes at present proposed by the Water Resources Board together supply about 400 m.g.d. by A.D. 1981. This is still some 100–120 m.g.d. less than estimated minimum requirements, the difference being met by re-use of water after a purification process. Under certain conditions this is the cheapest of all sources—with typical costs for purification of a polluted source amounting to only about 12d. per '000 gallons, when operating on a reasonable scale. In itself, however, this is something of a problem since unit costs are likely to be twice as high for an installation serving 10,000 people as for one serving 100,000.

A further limitation on the re-use of water exists because down some rivers the process of extracting, purification and re-use has occurred so many times that salts build up in the water makes further processing impossible.

In practice these restrictions limit re-cycling to use in an urban area close to a source of relatively unpolluted water, conditions that limit prospective output from this source to 215 m.g.d. by A.D. 2000.

Apart from conventional catchment schemes and the limited use of recycling two further sources of water are under consideration—barrages and nuclear desalination. The barrage proposals receiving active consideration are those for the Solway and Morecambe estuaries and for the Wash. The main specifications are outlined in Table I.

Although the cost estimates for the barrages are based on the desk studies and not on full feasibility studies there is good reason to believe that the promises of low costs offered by the Morecambe and Solway barrages is likely to be fulfilled. The cost estimates for the work proposed are fairly conservative compared with those incurred in performing similar work elsewhere in Europe, and the figures are based on the higher estimates made by the consultants. The scheduled output too is probably lower than the extraction which could and would normally be made. As a result it seems unlikely that in real terms at least the cost estimate made would be exceeded. This leaves the Solway and Morecambe proposals with a distinct cost advantage over the conventional alternatives, even when the higher costs of trunk delivery into the relevant consumption areas are considered.

However, the advantage of the barrage proposals over alternative

[6] Water Resources Board. Ibid., Table J—p. 57.

conventional sources is subject to qualification on two counts. First the social costs imposed by barrage schemes differ to such a degree from those occuring under conventional schemes that they possibly override the strictly financial considerations. Secondly any proposed scheme must be integrated into an established water supply system. It is possible that the size of a scheme, its location, or some other factor could make in-system contribution of an investment differ from the expected contribution evaluated in isolation. These problems might best be resolved by a brief consideration of the physical specification of the Solway and Morecambe barrages.

TABLE I

SPECIFICATIONS FOR THE MORECAMBE, SOLWAY AND WASH BARRAGES

	Morecambe		*Solway*		*Wash*
	1st Stage	*2nd Stage*	*1st Stage*	*2nd Stage*	
Output, m.g.d.	250	500	380	580	380
Capital cost £m.	40	56	35	45	170
Annual costs, capital and operating £m	4.1	6.0	4.8	5.5	17.3
Cost at capacity, d./'000 gall.	10.8	8.0	8.3	6.8	45.1
Trunk delivery cost, d./'000 gall.	10	10	12	12	16
Total delivered cost, d./'000 gall.	20.8	18.0	20.3	18.8	61.1
Earliest completion date	1975	1977	1975	1976	1980

Sources: Water Resources Board, *Morecambe Bay barrage*: desk study; report of consultants. (H.M.S.O. 1966, 22s 6d.) Section V pp. 20–3.
Water Resources Board *and* Scottish Development Department, *Solway barrage*; desk study; report of consultants. H.M.S.O. 1966.
Water Resources Board. Ibid., Table J—p. 57.
The figures have been adjusted to provide comparability—the Morecambe estimates were provided within a range.

The Solway barrage is designed initially to raise the estuary water level some 15 feet above mean sea level, providing a storage capacity of 20,000m. gallons and a water surface of 16.2 square miles. At a later stage this storage capacity could be increased to 48,000m. gallons. Obviously a scheme of this size cannot be implemented without influencing the environment in which it is made and the nature of the changes imposed need to be evaluated to provide a measure of the harm or benefit brought by them.

One immediate loss brought about by the barrage would be to eliminate sea fishing in the Solway estuary. It is impossible to value this loss before the barrage is built, but it is fair to point out that a freshwater lake of larger dimensions is to replace the lost sea area.

The main use of this lake would be for recreational and associated commercial developments. It has been demonstrated[7] that the yield

[7] T. Burton and G. P. Wibberley (1965), *Outdoor Recreation in the British Countryside*, Wye College, University of London.

from recreational use of land is fairly competitive with the agricultural alternative, and that access to water is one of the primary determinants of recreational expenditure. Even valuing the enclosed estuary at half agricultural price produces a capitalization of £2m. Of course, part of this sum would represent a benefit transfer from the present sea fishermen, to tourists and those making a living from the tourist trade, but this transfer would be greatly outweighed by the net gain element.

In addition, under the scheme, around 3000 acres of agricultural land would be released for cultivation by virtue of the barrage's flood control potential, and this would have a value of £600,000. In addition substantial but less specific benefits would be felt all up the river valley through this flood control.

Another large social benefit would accrue because it is proposed to construct a roadway across the barrage, shortening the coast route between the North West of England and South West of Scotland by about ten miles. Since many of the existing roads in this area are subject to acute congestion it follows that the barrage route would be well used. The maximum value of the barrage from this source would be the additional cost of building an alternative dual carriageway road over the cheapest alternative route. This could be as high as £20m. A minimum value would be produced by valuing the savings made by motorists using the new route over the barrage. Even assuming only a low utilization rate of 40 vehicles per hour the shorter route should produce savings of £300 a day, representing a capitalized benefit of about £1½m. Together with the estimate for the value of the development to agriculture and recreation this provides a minimum estimate for the social benefits brought by the barrage at something over £4m.

A similar situation would result from the construction of the Morecambe barrage, though the prospective social benefits seem to be even higher. Under the proposed scheme around 15,000 additional acres of agricultural land will be brought into production, and the surface area of the new freshwater lake would be 30 sq. miles. Calculated on the same basis as the benefits from the Solway Barrage their value would be about £7m. Since the barrage is closer to the Lancashire urban complex it follows that even this estimate is probably too low. For the same reason the value of a coastal traffic artery would also be rather higher, so that total benefits arising from the Morecambe barrage would be at least £8½m. on completion of the entire scheme.

On the issue of social costs/benefits it appears that a barrage has a clear advantage over any conventional scheme. Although no estimate has been made for the social costs/benefits of traditional reservoirs it cannot be denied that usually they involve loss of amenity where existing lakes are concerned, and no gain when agricultural land is submerged.[8] It follows from this that the Solway or Morecambe barrages would be preferable to any equivalent cost conventional scheme.

Because the cost of long distance transport is prohibitive the Morecambe and Solway output is necessarily restricted to serving the Northern half of the country. The Southern area deficit has to be met from other sources. The only barrage project proposed in this area would be the Wash barrage. Although the social benefits derived from a new roadway and freshwater lake are as high as for Solway or Morecambe, the high costs of output from the barrage make it so uncompetitive that social costs or benefits scarcely affect the issue.

The fact that the Wash barrage is uncompetitive by present standards does not, of course, eliminate it from future consideration. The marginal cost of new water supplies will no doubt continue to increase to the point where these are comparable with the cost of water from the Wash barrage. It is, however, unlikely that this would occur before 1990.

The final current option is thermal desalination. At the present time this alternative is most often proposed in the form of nuclear desalination, with a dual purpose nuclear plant powering both generating and water purifying installations.

Unfortunately, the assessment of a nuclear desalination project depends on the analysis of production alternatives in not one but two markets—water and electricity. The reason the proposal is presented in this form is because, on theoretical grounds at any rate, a joint output installation is more economical than producing the same outputs from two separate establishments. The economies arise because the water purification process employs some of the waste heat from the electricity generation process and replaces some of the cooling equipment which would otherwise be necessary, thus lowering both the running and capital costs of the electricity generation process.

In practice, however, not all theoretical benefits are likely to materialize. The first difficulty is that for both electricity and water, delivery costs are a substantial proportion of total cost, and since few sites are going to minimize transport costs simultaneously for both water and electricity, extra delivery costs will be incurred for the

[8] Access to, and activities within, reservoir area are severely limited. Only a handful of reservoirs offer sailing facilities, for example.

tandem operation. Secondly, the availability of a dual operation is likely to fall short of that for two single purpose plants—it would no longer be possible to conduct maintenance in off-peak periods, since the summer water peak would coincide with the summer electricity slack.

Theoretical considerations apart, one immediate practical problem arises when an investment in a dual purpose plant is considered as an addition to the water supply system, that of allocating the costs between the two outputs. Although a number of artificial and rather arbitrary methods exist for doing this, the only valid economic technique is to use as a guideline the opportunity cost of securing an equivalent production from the best alternative source. If the combined alternative costs exceed the joint cost of the dual operation then some benefit must have accrued and the project is worthwhile. So far the only supply of water has been considered—a correct evaluation of the desalinization project requires an equivalent study of the supply of electricity.

THE SUPPLY OF ELECTRICITY

The 1967 Fuel Policy White Paper gives some indication of the relative costs of increments to generating capacity from alternative fuel sources. The output from Dungeness B and Hinckley Point nuclear station is estimated to cost 0.52 and 0.48d./kWh respectively, compared with the 0.532d./kWh costs of output from Cottam and Drax coal fired stations and about 0.42d./kWh from comparable oil burning installation.

These costs, of course, are for currently installed capacity, whereas the nuclear desalination plant, if adopted, could scarcely be running before 1975. There seems to be little question that between the present time and 1976, or even by 1970, costs of both commercial and nuclear electricity generation will fall. The best estimate currently available for the fast breeder reactors likely to come into service by the late 70s are as low as 0.32 or 0.25d./kWh.[9] The cost of conventional power should also be declining too, one estimate placing them at 0.42d./kWh by 1970,[10] using 50 per cent utilization and 6.4 per cent interest charges.

One further factor to be considered, apart from the direct costs of operating each installation is the impact of alternative types of investment on the operating costs of the rest of the generating system. Because nuclear fuelled power sources have low variable costs they

[9] R. McKinney, *Review of the International atomic programmes of the United States*, Report to the Joint Committee on Atomic Energy, U.S. Congress, Oct. 1960, p. 46.

[10] *Financial Times*, Wednesday, Nov. 15th, 1967, p. 13, col. 2.

are able to maintain a place high in the merit order and are usually on base load for most of their expected life, whereas conventional stations, with lower capital costs but higher variable costs, gradually slip down the merit order as more efficient replacements are introduced, until they are used for peak demand only. Lifetime utilization of only about 40 per cent is common for this type of investment.

It follows that to date a base load nuclear plant has greater ability to reduce the operating costs of the rest of the system than a similarly rated conventional station which is gradually phased out of use and so that usually between equal cost alternatives the nuclear station is to be preferred.

By 1975, then, it should be possible to provide electricity from sources other than the nuclear desalination process for about 40d./kWh, so that the same value should be used for calculating the benefit for the electricity supply for a dual purpose plant. In the event that a non-nuclear fuel service were to be prepared, a rather lower benefit would be relevant because of its inferior base load characteristics.

TABLE II

COSTS OF THE U.K.A.E.A. NUCLEAR DESALINATION PROPOSAL

Capital	Complete construction and equipment excluding land and site costs	£66.5m.
	Annual capital charges at 8.7 per cent p.a. including amortization	£5.3m.
Operating	Fuel costs	£2.1m.
	Operation, maintenance, insurance	£1.4m.
		£8.8m.

Source: U.K.A.E.A.: Research Group. A.E.R.E.; Chemical Engineering Division, *Freshwater from sea water*, by I. H. Newton. (A.E.R.E.—M1504) H.M.S.O. 3s. 6d. 1965.

THE PROPOSED NUCLEAR DESALINATION PLANT

The immediate proposal for a dual purpose nuclear desalination plant has a rated output of 40 MW of electricity and 60 m.g.d. of water. The Atomic Energy Authority has provided the cost estimates detailed in Table II.

The benefits to set against these costs are an output of 2.98×10^6 MWh of electricity and 52 m.g.d. of water.[11] Using the derived value of the electricity output at 0.40d./kWh gives a value of £4.4m. for the annual electrical production. To cover the remaining costs of the installation, neglecting for a moment any social costs or benefits

[11] Assuming 85 per cent utilization.

involved, the water output must have a value of 55s. 6d. per 1000d. gallons, exclusive of land or site costs.

Since the equivalent cost for water from barrages costs from 10d. to 40d. per 8000 gallons this figure seems high. Even if the nuclear desalination plant is sited so that no trunk delivery is necessary, the cost is still almost double that from conventional sources or from the Solway or Morecambe barrages, although it is not very different from the cost of a supply from the Wash.

One further argument used in favour of building a nuclear desalination plant is that the knowledge so gained would open the door to a large world market for similar installation. One estimate has put world capital expenditure on water resources investment at £1,000,000m. by 1984,[12] with presumably a similar investment in the following two decades. It seems unlikely that nuclear desalination would supply much of this market, for several reasons. First, the expense makes it a less preferable scheme than conventional or barrage schemes where these alternatives are available. Of the remaining areas many of the best market prospects enjoy good indigenous supplies of oil so would not consider a nuclear fuelled desalination plant in any case. In the areas with no alternative schemes and no indigenous fuel resources the high price of desalinated water would restrict consumption to such a degree that the minimum population necessary to absorb the output of a nuclear desalination plant operating on a reasonable scale would be as high as 20m. in some areas. This consideration also eliminated as prospective customers those isolated or island communities that are already paying high water prices.[13] The resulting market, split amongst the five or six countries likely to be interested, could scarcely justify the investment in excess cost of £2–£3m. per annum over the next 25 years that would be incurred for each desalination plant built.

CONCLUSION

After establishing the incremental costs from alternative supply sources the problem comes in choosing amongst them to maximize or minimize some objective function. In this context the economist's objective and the Water Resources Board's objective are rather different. The economist wants water resources to be supplied up to a point where the marginal incremental social cost is just equal to the amount people would be willing to pay for the additional supply. The Water Resources Board on the other hand is trying to meet

[12] M. Batisse, (1965), 'Learning the value of water', *The World in 1984* (Penguin 1965).

[13] *Sea Water Desalination for Developing Countries* (1964). Department of Economic and Social Affairs, Resources and Transport Division, United Nations.

prospective demand, taken as fixed, at minimum cost. Fortunately in this case there is no significant practical difference between these two objectives because the supply increments generated by the proposals studied offer costs closely similar to those of the existing supply. Since in addition water is sold at average cost it would not be too inaccurate to claim that consumers were being offered water at the incremental cost of supplying it.

This being so it is possible to accept, with reservations, the Water Board criteria and find the minimum cost method of fulfilling it. The costs of four alternative schemes for meeting demand in the Northern half of the country as soon as they occur are given in Table III.

TABLE III

NET PRESENT COSTS £1968M. OF ALTERNATIVE WATER SUPPLY STRATEGIES

	I	*II*	*III*	*IV*
Total Expenditure, £m.	1126.28	895.97	919.80	925.10
Net Present Cost £1968m. exclusive of social costs and benefits	264.53	232.02	245.71	244.50
Net Present Cost £1968m. inclusive of social costs and benefits	264.53	228.38	241.81	241.10

I All Conventional.
II Conventional to 1975, then Morecambe I, II, Solway I, II.
III Conventional to 1975 then Solway I, Morecambe I, II, Solway II.
IV Conventional to 1975, then Solway I, II, Morecambe I, II.

An inspection of the table reveals that the introduction of the two barrages in any order is a better investment than conventional schemes, whether social benefits and costs are considered or not. The best scheme amongst the barrages assuming the forecast growth in in demand, is to introduce the Morecambe barrage in 1975, complete the second stage by 1983, and finally to introduce the first part of the Solway barrage in 1989. There is no way in which either conventional or nuclear sources could be introduced into this programme to lower costs, unless the rate of growth was considerably lower than that anticipated, in which case a package of conventional installations is more economical. However, sensitivity analysis of the results in Table IV shows that this would not occur unless the growth rates were one-fifth of those expected—i.e., about 0.5 per cent p.a. Since that implies a declining *per caput* consumption of water it can be dismissed.

In the Southern half of the country the package of conventional schemes offered by the Water Resources Board up to 1981 is easily the cheapest method of meeting demand, even after considering social costs. Since current prices for water are at or about the incremental costs of these schemes it would clearly be beneficial to proceed.

On the other hand there would seem to be no case for proceeding either with the Wash barrage or with nuclear desalination. The cost of either of these schemes is so much out of line with existing water supplies that it would be a fiction to maintain that present consumption patterns would demand them at realistic prices. In fact if the demand elasticity for water is assumed to be around -0.4[14] the social losses incurred by doing absolutely nothing to increase water supplies and rationing existing supplies through price would be only about £300m. in net present value, compared with the £250m. net present cost of meeting demand at existing prices. To install either the Wash barrage or nuclear desalination is not only far more expensive than conventional schemes, but more expensive, in social terms, than doing nothing at all.

The conclusion must be that if consumers were offered water at Wash or nuclear desalination plant prices the demand would be so small that existing water supplies would satisfy them well into the 1990s. To ignore this would lead directly to the Californian paradox, where nuclear desalination, alleged to cost $88 per acre ft. as opposed to $24.30 from available conventional resources (72d. per 1000 gallons as against 20–25d.) has to be heavily subsidized in order to dispose of the output.[15]

As to the future, developments in nuclear technology are unlikely to benefit the competitiveness of dual purpose nuclear desalination since the reference price for valuing the electricity output is necessarily affected in exactly the same way by the same developments in single purpose stations. The only possibility seems to be to combine a nuclear distillation plant with a purification recycling operation to produce water at about 42d. per 1000 gallons. Intuitively it would seem that a dual purpose nuclear plant would become competitive as a source of process heat, or community heating (hot water having a value many times that of pure cold water) long before it becomes competitive as a source of water.

MANCHESTER BUSINESS SCHOOL

[14] J. Hisshleifer and J. W. Millinian (1967), p. 175, *American Economic Review*, vol. LVII, May, 1967, No. 2.
[15] Ibid., p. 177.

AN EMPIRICAL INVESTIGATION OF ADVERTISING AND CONCENTRATION: COMMENT

by ROBERT B. EKELUND, JR. and CHARLES MAURICE*

IN a recent issue of this *Journal*, H. M. Mann, J. A. Henning, and J. W. Meehan, Jr. (hereafter Mann, *et al.*, the Mann test, or the Mann study) have, in their words, attempted to '. . . . present additional evidence' on the hypothesis that product differentiation—measured by advertising expenditures as a percentage of sales revenue—is positively correlated with seller's concentration.[1] In a study of fourteen consumer goods industries, the authors found significant positive correlation between advertising and industrial concentration. Our comment focuses upon and questions the statistical significance of their test.

The hypothesis that advertising promotes the concentration of economic power has been forcefully promulgated by Kaldor[2] and subjected to various tests by, among others, Stigler,[3] Bain,[4] and Telser,[5] as well as by Mann, *et al.* The Bain study supported the hypothesis, while those of Stigler and Telser did not. In fact, Telser, using forty-two, three-digit census classification industries, found the correlation coefficients for the 1947, 1954, and 1958 data 'unimpressive'.

In contrast, the Mann study employed the four-digit SIC (Standard Industrial Classification) industry data on concentration rather than the broader three-digit data because of 'considerable doubt that the broad I.R.S. (Internal Revenue Service) industries correspond to economically meaningful markets' and in order to minimize measurement error in the independent variable.[6] That study assigned forty-two firms chosen from the list of advertisers compiled by *National Advertising Investments* to fourteen, four-digit industries. The average amount of advertising of the selected firms, all of which

* We would like to thank William P. Gramm and Russell Thompson for helpful suggestions on earlier drafts of this paper. We would also like to thank D. M. Barton and A. J. Hebert for computational assistance.

[1] H. M. Mann, J. A. Henning, and J. W. Meehan, Jr., 'Advertising and Concentration: An Empirical Investigation', *The Journal of Industrial Economics*, November, 1967, p. 34.

[2] Nicholas Kaldor, 'The Economic Aspects of Advertising', *The Review of Economic Studies*, 1950, particularly pp. 13–16.

[3] George J. Stigler, 'The Economies of Scale', *Journal of Law and Economics*, October, 1958, p. 66 *et passim.*

[4] Joe Bain, *Industrial Organization*, (New York: John Wiley & Sons, Inc., 1959), particularly pp. 221–37.

[5] Lester Telser, 'Advertising and Competition', *The Journal of Political Economy*, December, 1964, pp. 537–62.

[6] Mann, *et al.*, *op. cit.*, p. 35.

were among the dominant firms in their respective industries, as a percentage of their sales revenue for 1952–56, 1957–61, and 1962–65 was considered the average for the designated industries. These figures were related to the concentration ratios (as reported by the Bureau of the Census) of the respective industries for 1954, 1958, and 1963. Linear regression was run on all of the data, and significant positive correlation (coefficients of 0.59, 0.72, and 0.68 for 1954, 1958, and 1963) was found in all three years. The same technique was used for the same firms and industries in 1954 and 1958, and for thirty-one of the forty-two firms in twelve of the fourteen industries in 1963, using *Printers' Ink* and *Advertising Age* data, which included more media than did *NAI*. Significant positive correlation was found in all three years in this part of the study also (0.41, 0.56, and 0.54 for 1954, 1958, and 1963).[7]

Mann, *et al.*, without noting certain more fundamental difficulties did specify one limitation about the interpretation of their tests—the size of the sample—but this caveat, while important, in our view is not the most significant one which their analysis warrants. Rather, certain other, possibly more crucial, problems appear to be inherent in the test itself, primarily in the composition of the sample—i.e., in the way in which the tested firms and hence the industries were chosen.

The industries in the Mann study were basically consumer goods industries, the selected firms in which employed advertising as their principal means of sales promotion and were chosen, as noted above, from lists in *NAI*, *Printers' Ink*, and *Advertising Age*.[8] The very nature of the population from which these firms were selected indicates a strong bias toward extremely large national advertisers. *Printers' Ink* and *Advertising Age* during the period of the sample listed only the top 100 advertisers in the United States. In the sample of forty-two firms, thirty appeared on their list during all three periods, eleven appeared in two periods, and one appeared in one period. Obviously, only absolutely large firms should be able to spend absolutely large amounts on advertising. Thus, by excluding firms which spend absolutely little on advertising, small firm industries would be systematically excluded from the sample. Since, as appears likely, firm size is positively related to concentration ratios, one would suspect that relatively few industries with low concentration ratios

[7] In the *Printers' Ink–Advertising Age* study the levels of significance were 0.15, 0.04, and 0.08 respectively; in the *NAI* study they were 0.03, 0.01, and 0.01 for 1954, 1958, and 1963. Ibid., p. 37. Because some of the firms which were among the largest 100 advertisers in the 1950s were not so placed in the 1960s, the sample was reduced from 42 to 31 firms and from 14 to 12 industries for 1963.

[8] Ibid., p. 35.

would be included in such a sample, even had it been randomly selected from the same sources. This perhaps explains why in the Mann study nine of the fourteen industries had concentration ratios over fifty percent in all three years and one more had a ratio over fifty percent in two of the three years.[9]

Although the sample is, in all likelihood, strongly biased toward industries with relatively high concentration (it is certainly biased toward industries whose dominant firms are absolutely large advertisers with absolutely large sales), it is not apparent that the correlation between concentration and advertising-sales ratios must necessarily be biased upward. Conceivably, of course, a low correlation between concentration and advertising-sales ratios might occur. The nature of the products of the firms sampled, however, gives reason to suspect some upward bias. In eleven of the fourteen industries (excepting pens, liquor, and tires and tubes) much of the sales, and in several, practically all of the sales take place in grocery stores. Given their type of product, one would expect the leading firms which commanded a very large part of the market to rely more upon advertising competition among themselves than upon price competition. On the other hand, in this same situation where the leading firms enjoyed a relatively smaller share of the market and in many cases where they had to compete with chain store or local brands (e.g., meat, baking, canned fruits and vegetables), *ceteris paribus* more price competition would be expected. Thus the product makeup of the sample could be one reason for upward bias.

But, the reason for the upward bias (if any) in the sample is not the primary point at issue. The fundamental point is whether or not a group of industries with all of the characteristics discussed above is a representative cross section of the economy. One wonders how significant the correlation would have been had the sample included such low concentration industries as perfumes and drugs (which in the Telser test for 1958 ranked first and second in advertising-sales ratios and thirtieth and twenty-eighth in concentration) and possibly some consumer goods industries whose dominant firms were not large advertisers, for example, sugar (which ranked fifth in concentration but forty-first in advertising-sales ratio in the 1958 Telser test).[10]

[9] Bain, whose conclusions the Mann study claimed to support, was much more guarded in interpreting his own results due to a similar, but acknowledged bias in his sample: 'The indications on this issue from our sample of manufacturing industries are not necessarily conclusive, since the sample is heavily weighted with industries of high or moderate seller concentration and does not give us much chance to observe the varying importance of product differentiation in industries of relatively low seller concentration.' *Op. cit.*, pp. 235–6.

[10] See Jules Backman, *Advertising and Competition* (New York: New York University Press, 1967), Appendix Table E-4, p. 220.

One further feature of the Mann study which might indicate the possibility of bias is the absence of any significant positive correlation between changes in advertising intensity and changes in concentration. Since the correlations between concentration and advertising-sales ratios were significant and since the regression coefficients are so close for both sets of data, significant correlation between changes would appear likely also. This expectation appears particularly warranted in view of the fact that the advertising-sales ratios were not those of the industries but those of the leading firms in the industries—i.e., those very firms whose sales, in large measure, determine the concentration ratios of the industries. Significant positive correlation between first differences was not the case, however. Using the Mann data, we computed linear regressions between

TABLE I

REGRESSIONS RELATING CHANGES IN CONCENTRATION (Δy) TO CHANGES IN ADVERTISING-SALES RATIOS (Δx)

Period	*Regressions*	*Correlations*	*Means*	
			Δy	Δx
NAI data				
1963–1954	$\Delta y = -3.47 + 1.70\ \Delta x$	0.19	−3.214	0.152
1963–1958	$\Delta y = -1.91 + 2.85\ \Delta x$	0.28	−1.857	0.021
1958–1954	$\Delta y = -1.24 - 0.93\ \Delta x$	−0.13	−1.357	0.131
Printers' Ink and *Advertising Age* data				
1963–1954	$\Delta y = -8.43 + 1.79\ \Delta x$	0.42	3.583	−2.000
1963–1958	$\Delta y = -3.70 + 0.83\ \Delta x$	0.19	−1.500	2.658
1958–1954	$\Delta y = -2.21 + 1.53\ \Delta x$	0.34	−0.786	0.936

Source: Computed from data in Tables I and II in H. M. Mann, *et al.*, pp. 40–5.

changes in advertising to sales ratios and changes in concentration ratios for both *NAI* (for fourteen industries) and *Advertising Age–Printers' Ink* (for twelve industries) figures for the intervals 1963–1954, 1963–1958, and 1958–1954 (see Table I). In no case was significant correlation indicated (testing at the five percent level); the largest positive coefficient was 0.42. For the *NAI* data, which included the larger number of observations, two of the coefficients of correlation were quite small (0.19 and 0.28) and, indeed, one was negative (−0.13). Moreover, in all six tests the mean change in advertising intensity was of the opposite sign from the mean change in concentration. Thus, while the results of the first differences computation do not by themselves give sufficient evidence for rejecting the Mann test, they by no means give added evidence for accepting the Mann conclusions.[11]

In summary, the results presented by Mann *et al.*, irrespective of the relative merit in their modified approach, seem unconvincing. Unfortunately, as the authors themselves note, the relevant advertising and sales data were unavailable for a larger—and we might add a more representative—sampling. Certainly the four-digit classification may well be as advantageous as the Mann study contends and the use of firm data in estimating advertising intensity is not without merit. However, should a reporting source for the advertising data with a very large number of observations at the higher SIC classification continue to be unavailable, future attempts at a test of the hypothesis must apparently trade off some (as yet unsettled) accuracy for greater and more representative coverage. In short, while the method proposed by Mann, Henning, and Meehan to correlate advertising and concentration may not be without some merit, we do not believe that, owing to inherent defects in the sample, the authors have successfully overturned previous, contrasting empirical conclusions, or that the test necessarily indicates valuable policy implications.

TEXAS A & M UNIVERSITY

[11] Telser, *op. cit.*, p. 546, used the results of his first difference test to corroborate his findings of no significant correlation. In that case the results of both types of tests pointed in the same direction.

TESTING HYPOTHESES IN INDUSTRIAL ECONOMICS: A REPLY

by H. M. MANN, J. A. HENNING, and J. W. MEEHAN, JR.*

ROBERT B. EKELUND, Jr. and Charles Maurice (hereafter E & M) raise four statistical points in their comment on our paper. Our immediate aim will be to defend our statistical analysis with respect to the question of the relation between concentration and advertising intensity. But because of the nature of the data available for the statistical analysis of problems in industrial economics, there is no doubt that much of past, present, and future research is open to challenge on exactly the same grounds as those on which our own study has been challenged. Therefore, we believe that the vulnerability of such research to the objections raised by E & M, whether sustained in the present instance or not, should be carefully assessed now, in order to avoid as much unnecessary mischief in the future as possible.

First, E & M attempt to demonstrate that our sample is '... strongly biased towards industries with relatively high concentration ...'.[1] It would be interesting to discuss the steps in their argument, several of which are highly questionable. But the entire discussion is totally irrelevant; it has no bearing whatsoever on the question of bias in our estimation of the correlation between concentration and advertising intensity. Since E & M themselves admit that their argument says nothing about such bias, there is little point to our continuing the discussion, except to express curiosity as to why the issue was raised in the first place.

Second, we take the liberty of quoting E & M's contention with respect to upward bias in our correlation between concentration and advertising intensity.

> In eleven of the fourteen industries (excepting pens, liquor, and tires and tubes) much of the sales, and in several, practically all of the sales take place in grocery stores. Given their type of product, one would expect the leading firms which commanded a very large part of the market to rely more upon advertising

* Professors Mann and Meehan thank J. A. Henning for assuming the primary responsibility in drafting this comment.

[1] E & M cite Bain in their footnote 9 as acknowledging a similar bias while we did not. But Bain was not commenting on bias, as is clear from the context from which the quotation was taken. Bain laments the limited variability in his sample. To identify the issues of variability and bias can only be based on a misconception of the statistical concept of 'bias'.

> competition among themselves than upon price competition. On the other hand, in this same situation where the leading firms enjoyed a relatively smaller share of the market and in many cases where they had to compete with chain store or local brands (e.g., meat, baking, canned fruits and vegetables), *ceteris paribus* more price competition would be expected. Thus the product makeup of the sample could be one reason for upward bias.

E & M are saying here quite unequivocally that for products distributed through grocery store outlets they accept *a priori* the hypothesis that concentration and advertising intensity are positively associated. But this, of course, is precisely the hypothesis we are testing for all products! The standard statistical tests we employed hypothesize *no* relationship (the null hypothesis) between concentration and advertising intensity. The source of bias to which E & M refer is their *own* acceptance of the hypothesis under test for a subset of our sample. If one accepts *a priori* that fathers' and sons' heights are positively associated, then any test of the hypothesis that the heights of fathers and their offspring are positively associated will be biased upward if the sample contains any male offspring, according to E & M's logic. The absurdity of their position can be seen perhaps even more clearly by observing that had our sample consisted only of the eleven industries whose products are distributed through grocery stores, there would be no point to an empirical test since, as the quotation above makes quite explicit, for these eleven industries E & M are quite prepared to accept *a priori* the hypothesis of a positive association between concentration and advertising intensity.

Third, E & M appear to question the randomness of our sample. As is so often the case, our sample was in effect selected for us by the compilers of the data. In research of this type there is little choice to do otherwise. To the extent that judgement may be involved, as for example when data collected from diverse sources must either be reconciled and made consistent or else excluded entirely from the sample, objectivity must be maintained to avoid 'preselecting' or biasing the results to favor or disfavor the hypothesis under test. Granted this much, there is no reason not to treat such a collection of data as a random sample. Indeed, since it is possible only to *disprove* the hypothesis of randomness, the burden of disproof is on those who doubt. This can be done by demonstrating a systematic bias with respect to the hypothesis in the original collection of data, in the selection of the sample by the researchers, or both. We do not see on what grounds E & M doubt the randomness of our sample.

At one point, they seem to imply that our sample should have included the presence of a number of observations for which concentration ratios and advertising/sales ratios were negatively related. But this is exactly the kind of 'preselecting' that one must guard against. Perhaps this is too harsh an interpretation; they may be merely saying that if our sample had been different (perhaps only larger) the results might have been different. That this point is valid goes without saying, but the new conclusion with respect to the hypothesized relationship could go either way; there is just as much reason to expect that a different sample would confirm our original conclusions as to expect the reverse to happen.

We strenuously reject as irrelevant casual empiricism the citation of a number of industries whose inclusion in our sample, had data been available from our sources, would very likely have led to statistically insignificant results; we can find at least twice as many industries whose inclusion in our sample, again had data been available, would almost certainly have *strengthened* our conclusions considerably. It is no more absurd and no less relevant for us to make this observation than it is for E & M to make theirs.

Fourth, E & M find poor correlations between changes in concentration and changes in advertising intensity, whereas our original study had found statistically significant correlations between the *levels* of these variables. This type of analysis, originally applied by Telser,[2] can be applied to any research where the data consist of a series of cross-section samples, taken at more or less regular intervals over time from industrial censuses (to take the most common source of such data as an example). The case against this technique can be stated very simply: In taking first differences of successive cross-sections *they permit to vary variables that had been held constant for each cross-section*. In particular, they permit variation in variables which as they vary over time have a differential impact among industries; in each cross-section, of course, these variables are held fixed. Criticism based on a technique that does this is completely unacceptable; it is formally identical to attempting to verify significant results from a controlled experiment by replicating the experiment *without the experimental controls*. The application of this specious 'test' will lead to results that are at best impossible to interpret and, at worst, positively misleading.

We would be among the first to admit the fragile nature of statistical conclusions in industrial economics. We are well aware of the short-comings in our own study, in particular sample size and the

[2] Lester G. Telser, 'Advertising and Competition', *The Journal of Political Economy*, December, 1964, p. 546.

effect of diversification on measurement of the independent variable. Criticism is welcome, of course, for it is often the basis of progress. Unfortunately, we find each of the criticisms advanced by E & M to be uncontrovertedly in error. About all we can concede is that some of these errors are quite subtle. Nonetheless, it may be counted as a contribution to progress that a discussion has been provoked where a number of important methodological issues have been cleared up once and for all. Finally, whether our findings have 'successfully overturned contrasting empirical findings' is something each reader can only decide for himself.[3] But we do suggest that there is nothing in E & M's comment that would warrant reconsidering such a decision made on the basis of reading our original paper.

BOSTON COLLEGE
SYRACUSE UNIVERSITY
NORTHEASTERN UNIVERSITY

[3] We remind the reader that there exists evidence which supports our results: Joe Bain, *Industrial Organization*, 2nd edition, *op. cit.*, pp. 249–50; P. K. Else, 'The Incidence of Advertising in Manufacturing Industries', *Oxford Economic Papers*, March, 1966, pp. 88–110.

ANOTHER LOOK AT ADVERTISING AND CONCENTRATION

by L. G. TELSER[1]

A RECENT article in this Journal presents new evidence that allegedly supports the view that 'the degree of product differentiation will be positively associated with seller concentration'.[2] The degree of product differentiation is measured by the ratio of advertising outlays to sales and seller concentration is measured by the ratio of sales of the four leading firms to total sales of the industry. It is claimed that this new evidence directly refutes my earlier work, which found little if any relation between concentration and advertising intensity.[3]

The new 'evidence' is nothing more than a badly biased sample which seriously distorts the true state of affairs. In fact, when properly corrected, the new evidence, far from overturning my previous findings, lends them strong additional confirmation. I shall show how the impressive correlation between advertising intensity and concentration falls from 0.6 to virtually zero when the hypothesis is tested fairly and, moreover, the initial positive association turns into an insignificant negative association. Since I have dealt with the economic issues elsewhere, I shall confine this note to a sequence of statistical tests which clearly establish the misleading nature of the new 'evidence' presented by my critics.

The critics claim that my failure to find a strong positive correlation between advertising intensity and concentration is due to the presence of excessive measurement error in the concentration figures brought about by the use of 3-digit instead of 4-digit groupings. Thus the 3-digit concentration figures are weighted averages of their 4-digit components. If the advertising intensity varies within the 4-digit components of the 3-digit class, then, it is claimed, the result is a downward biased estimate of the true positive association between concentration and advertising intensity. Hence to overcome these difficulties it is proposed to use data by 4-digit industry classes. The advertising outlays are estimated from published trade sources

[1] This note would not have been possible without the able help of my research assistant, Harry Bloch, who is, however, not responsible for any errors herein. The financial support of the National Science Foundation is gratefully acknowledged.

[2] H. M. Mann, J. A. Henning and J. W. Meehan, Jr., 'Advertising and Concentration: An Empirical Investigation', *Journal of Industrial Economics* (1967), 34–45. Hereafter I shall refer to these gentlemen as 'critics'.

[3] L. G. Telser, 'Advertising and Competition', *Journal of Political Economy* LXXII (1964), 537–62. Actually the critics deal with only part of the empirical evidence I present in my article. In particular they ignore the evidence on the stability of brand shares and the regressions that relate ΔC and $\Delta(A/S)$.

by company and the companies are classified into 4-digit industries according to the composition of their output.

Actually, this procedure introduces two additional sources of measurement error. First, as is well known, the published advertising figures are derived from list prices and refer only to certain measured media. The former biases the figures upward and the latter, by omitting certain kinds of advertising expenditures, biases them downward. It was to avoid these difficulties that I chose to base my previous work on the advertising figures by 3-digit industry classes which are reported by the Internal Revenue Service. These figures are taken from the corporate tax returns of the companies themselves and are, presumably, more reliable than the published estimates of advertising outlays in the trade journals. In a few cases it is possible to compare the I.R.S. figures with the trade estimates. In these cases, large differences appear and the trade estimates may be as much as 60 percent higher than the I.R.S. figures.

In addition the use of company data introduces a source of error in the concentration figures. This error depends on the company's degree of specialization. Therefore, there is no theoretical argument to support the view that an analysis based on company data and 4-digit concentration ratios is less prone to measurement error than one based on weighted averages of the 4-digit concentration ratios and on the advertising figures reported by the I.R.S.[4]

My tests of the hypothesis relate only to the concentration figures for 1958. This is sufficient because there is a high degree of autocorrelation in both concentration and advertising intensity so that consideration of two other census years would not yield much independent new evidence.

The first task is to see whether the regressions for 1958 using the data published by the critics can be replicated. Two sets of advertising data are given. The first covers three advertising media as reported in *National Advertising Investment* (*NAI*). The results for my replication are as follows:

$$(1) \qquad C = \underset{4.25}{32.44} + \underset{4.23}{12.11}(A/S)_1 \qquad R^2 = 0.60, n = 14$$

[4] The critics also argue that their choice of companies is guided by the principle that advertising should constitute 'a principal means of influencing consumer preferences'. No evidence is given to support the choice of companies or industries in terms of this principle. As shown in Table I, a number of industries are omitted although the ratio of advertising outlays to sales is quite high. Since nothing is known about the magnitude of expenditures on methods of promotion other than advertising, it is hard for me to understand why these industries should be excluded from the study. The effect of averaging company figures on the regression is more subtle than the critics seem aware of. I refer them to Yule and Kendall, *An Introduction to the Theory of Statistics*, 14th ed. (London: Charles Griffin & Co. 1950), esp. pp. 310–15, the discussion of the 'attenuation effect'.

(The figures shown below the regression coefficients are always the t-ratios.)

My critics report the following for the same data:

$$(1c) \qquad C = 36.23 + \underset{3.64}{10.80}\,(A/S)_1 \qquad R^2 = 0.58,\ n = 14$$

where C = 4-digit concentration ratio, 1958

$(A/S)_1$ = (unweighted?) average of the ratio of advertising outlays to sales for the period 1957–61 using *NAI* advertising data.[5]

The second set of data is obtained from *Printers' Ink* and *Advertising Age*. These cover more advertising media and, therefore, give a higher ratio of advertising to sales. Thus the average $(A/S)_2 = 4.72$ percent while the average $(A/S)_1 = 2.24$ percent. Using the second set of data I obtain

$$(2) \qquad C = \underset{3.34}{37.81} + \underset{2.20}{4.59}\,(A/S)_2 \qquad R^2 = 0.29,\ n = 14$$

For precisely the same data my critics report the following:

$$(2c) \qquad C = 37.05 + \underset{2.36}{4.81}\,(A/S)_2 \qquad R^2 = 0.31,\ n = 14$$

$(A/S)_2$ = (unweighted?) average of advertising outlays to sales for the period 1957 to 1961 from *Printers' Ink* and *Advertising Age*.

Although the agreement is tolerably good, in principle it should be possible to obtain precisely the same results as my critics when I use *their* data to replicate *their* results.

These results deserve additional comment. Observe that the coefficient of advertising intensity is lower for the more inclusive measure of advertising, $(A/S)_2$, than it is for the less inclusive measure, $(A/S)_1$. If the excluded advertising data were strictly proportional to the included data, then the ratio of the coefficients of the advertising intensity in (1) and (2) would be inversely proportional to the ratio of the advertising intensity. This assumes that the advertising in the various media are strictly complementary. However, if the advertising in various media were substitutes, then the use of the more inclusive measures of advertising outlays would result in a coefficient of advertising intensity that is larger than the one

[5] I cannot tell from the critics' article whether they calculated the ratio of total advertising outlays to total sales, which would be a weighted average, or an average of the ratios of the company's advertising outlays to sales, which would be an unweighted average. This may account for the difference in results.

predicted on the basis of strict complementarity. Actually, the coefficient of $(A/S)_2$ is too low to be explained by the complementarity hypothesis, and, therefore, it surely cannot be explained by the substitutability hypothesis. It is explained by a third hypothesis, namely, that the measurement error of the advertising outlays excluded from the *NAI* figures exceeds the measurement error of the included figures. Hence although my critics do not comment on the differences between the results for the two sets of data, one should entertain no illusions about the accuracy of the advertising figures in the published trade sources.[6]

Still using the data published by the critics, it is instructive to calculate the regressions by *company* as well as by industry averages. This shows how the dispersion of the advertising intensity among the companies within a 4-digit industry class affects the results. The results are as follows:

(3) $$C = \underset{8.94}{40.21} + \underset{5.01}{8.45}\,(A/S)_1 \qquad R^2 = 0.39,\ n = 42$$

(4) $$C = \underset{7.09}{42.60} + \underset{2.89}{3.28}\,(A/S)_2 \qquad R^2 = 0.18,\ n = 41$$

Thus the dispersion of the ratio of advertising outlays to sales among the companies reduces the coefficient of advertising intensity to about 70 percent of the coefficient of the corresponding variable for the industry average.

To demonstrate the sensitivity of the results to the choice of companies and industries, it is necessary to collect data for advertising outlays and sales not only for the companies in the critics' sample but also for additional companies both within the industries they have chosen to study as well as within other industries in which advertising is an important method of sales promotion. The industries and other pertinent data are given in Table I. The first problem we encounter is how to treat the federal tax on certain products, notably beer, distilled liquor and cigarettes. These taxes are paid by the manufacturer. In addition there are federal excise taxes paid by manufacturers of tires, radio and television sets, cameras, pens, and certain

[6] The average *NAI* advertising to sales ratio is 2.24 percent and the average *Printers' Ink* advertising to sales ratio is 4.72 percent. If all forms of advertising were complementary, the product of the advertising intensity by the regression coefficients would be the same for both sets of data. If the various advertising media were substitutes then the product of the advertising intensity and the regression coefficients would be higher for the *Printers' Ink* data. Actually, this product for the more inclusive measure of advertising is 80 percent of the value for the less inclusive measure. This result is consistent with the view expressed in the text that there is a larger measurement error in those media included in *Printers' Ink* and excluded from *NAI.*

TABLE I

CONCENTRATION RATIOS IN 1958 AND THE RATIO OF ADVERTISING OUTLAYS TO SALES, 1957–59, BY SELECTED 4-DIGIT INDUSTRIES

SIC	*Industry Name*[a]	*C* (*percent*)	*A/S′ including excise tax*			
			Unweighted	*Weighted*	*Critics′*[b]	
2011	Meat packing 6	34	0.44	0.43	0.42	4
2023	Concentrated milk 2	50	2.00	2.06		
2033	Canned fruits and vegetables 8	29	3.06	2.42	1.43	3
2041	Flour[d] 3	75	3.09	3.66	5.05	2
2043	Cereal 3	83	7.57	5.95	6.20	2
2051	Baking 5	22	2.60	3.06	2.75	2
2052	Biscuits 2	65	2.28	2.62	2.35	2
2073	Chewing gum 3	88	7.26	6.91	9.25	2
2082	Beer[c] 9	28	3.35	3.46	5.40	4
2085	Distilled liquor[c] 9	60	3.19	3.15	6.87	4
2095	Soft drinks 5	55	8.02	5.17	5.13	3
2111	Cigarettes[c] 5	79	3.85	3.87	5.75	4
2121	Cigars 3	54	5.60	5.09		
2834	Pharmaceuticals 13	27	6.40	4.95		
2841	Soaps 4	90	10.17	8.07	7.70	2
2842	Cleansers 4	24	19.84	15.3		
2851	Paints and varnishes 3	25	0.50	0.42		
2893	Toiletries 16	29	16.67	12.5		
3011	Tires 6	74	0.79	0.71	0.72	4
3141	Shoes 3	27	0.79	0.79		
3581	Laundry machines 3	71	0.93	0.72		
3621	Electrical appliances 3	43	2.13	1.45		
36512	Radio and television 4	55	1.16	1.13		
3861	Photographic equipment 3	65	1.47	1.35		
3951	Pens 2	51	6.80	6.88	7.03	3
3982	Hard surface floor covering 3	79	3.08	2.22		
Means		53.1	4.73	4.01	4.72	
Std. Dev.		22.5	4.80	3.65	2.75	

Sources: C: Concentration Ratios in Manufacturing Industry 1958 Part I. Washington: U.S. Govt. Printing Office, 1962.
A: Printers' Ink.
S: Moody's Industrials.

[a] Numbers following the industry name give the number of companies.

[b] These ratios apparently exclude excise taxes. Numbers to the right give the number of companies in the industry for the critics' sample.

[c] The figures *excluding* excise taxes are as follows:

	Unweighted	*Weighted*
Beer	4.91	5.00
Distilled liquor	8.73	7.66
Cigarettes	6.60	5.88

[d] This is the concentration ratio for flour mixes, 2045. The concentration ratio for flour is 38. We ran the regressions with both figures and found the results to be about the same.

other consumer appliances. The problem is whether or not to include these taxes with sales. The critics exclude these taxes from the sales figures but this is not justified on theoretical grounds. The tax constitutes a cost to the manufacturer and ultimately to the consumer like any other cost. Hence it raises the product price. For a given advertising outlay the higher the price the less effective the advertising. This suggests that advertising intensity should be calculated as a ratio of advertising outlays to sales including the tax. Unfortunately, this cannot be done in all cases because the companies do not always report the tax as a separate figure. It can be done for the three industries where it is of greatest importance, beer, liquor and cigarettes. To show the importance of the tax treatment on the results, it is, therefore, advisable to calculate the advertising intensity in two ways, one excluding the tax and the other including the tax with the sales. As we shall see, the regressions are better if the taxes are included.[7]

To calibrate my results with those of my critics for the new data, I estimated the regression relating the concentration ratio and the advertising intensity for nearly the same sample of companies.[8] It should be noted that the concentration figure refers to the year 1958 while the figure for the advertising intensity is an average for the years 1957 to 1961. Hence it includes figures for three years following the year of the concentration ratio. Though there may be something to be said for averaging the advertising figures, it is not obvious why the average should include three years following the year for which the concentration ratio is measured. Hence I have calculated the advertising ratios as an average for the years 1957 to 1959 using *Printers' Ink* advertising data. The resulting regression, which is comparable to (4), is as follows:

$$(5) \qquad \underset{}{C} = \underset{7.19}{43.79} + \underset{2.95}{3.45}\,(A/S) \qquad R^2 = 0.19,\ n = 40$$

[7] The issue of excise taxes is important only for those industries where the tax constitutes a large fraction of sales. These industries are beer, liquor and cigarettes. In a few industries excise tax figures are not available for all of the companies in the sample but all companies available are included in the sample anyway since the tax does not make much difference. An example of an industry for which this is true is radio and television. For the tire industry figures are available only for sales excluding excise taxes. For convenience I refer to all of these taxes as federal excise taxes. However, the taxes have different origins and legal requirements. Thus the tax on liquor, beer and cigarettes is a federal tax paid by the manufacturer and is proportional to measures of physical output. The excise tax, strictly speaking, is an *ad valorem* tax paid by the manufacturer and levied on certain consumer items. The tax on pens, television sets and tires is an example of the latter.

[8] There are a few differences between my sample and my critics' sample in this replication. In the chewing gum industry the critics' sample excludes Beechnut for 1958 (but not in 1954 and 1963) while their sample includes Scripto in pens. My sample includes Beechnut and excludes Scripto, the latter for lack of data. In addition my sample excludes Pabst. However, in the sample which *includes* the excise tax, Pabst is included while Schlitz is excluded. This is because we lack data on the excise tax separately for these two companies and the Pabst sales figures include the tax while the Schlitz figures exclude the tax.

A/S = ratio of advertising outlays to sales averaged over the years 1957–59 where sales exclude the federal excise tax.

The results when excise taxes are included are as follows:

(6) $$C = \underset{7.81}{44.12} + \underset{3.20}{4.11}\ (A/S)' \qquad R^2 = 0.21,\ n = 40$$

$(A/S)'$ = advertising intensity including excise taxes.

It is also desirable to calculate the regressions by industry average with and without excise taxes. The results are as follows:

(7) $$C = \underset{3.24}{39.09} + \underset{1.92}{4.43}\ (A/S) \qquad R^2 = 0.235,\ n = 14$$

(8) $$C = \underset{3.57}{39.45} + \underset{2.10}{5.00}\ (A/S)' \qquad R^2 = 0.269,\ n = 14$$

Equation (7) should be compared with (2). Although the R^2 is lower by more than 20 percent, the agreement is tolerably good. By including the excise taxes with sales, the regressions show a stronger relation between concentration and the advertising intensity.

Comparison of the results for the industry averages with those by company shows the effect of aggregating the company data. It is hardly surprising that the coefficients of the advertising intensity are higher with the industry averages but the difference is not very large when excise taxes are included as can be seen by comparing (6) and (8). In these results with industry averages, all of the companies receive equal weight. It is also desirable to see what happens if companies are weighted according to size as measured by sales.[9]

(9) $$C = \underset{3.24}{39.74} + \underset{1.92}{4.32}\ (A/S)_w \qquad R^2 = 0.205,\ n = 14$$

and the weighted average included the excise tax gives

(10) $$C = \underset{3.42}{39.97} + \underset{1.92}{4.90}\ (A/S)'_w \qquad R^2 = 0.235,\ n = 14$$

For a random sample of 14 observations and 12 degrees of freedom the t-ratio for a two-tailed test at the 5 percent level is 2.18. Since the sample is not a random one drawn from the population of consumer

[9] The weighted average corresponds to my original regressions in 'Advertising and Competition' *op. cit.* It may be helpful to display the algebra that relates the two measures. Let w_i denote the weight given company i in an industry. Then

$$w_i = S_i/\Sigma S_i$$

where S_i denotes the sales of company i. The unweighted index of advertising intensity is as follows:

$$(A/S) = \Sigma(A/S)_i/n$$

where n denotes the number of companies in the industry. The weighted average is given by

$$(A/S)_w = \Sigma(A/S)_i\, w_i = (\Sigma A_i/\Sigma S_i).$$

goods industries, the standard statistical tests do not apply. Hence it is safe to conclude that an even larger t-ratio is necessary to take these results seriously. Observe also that the effect of using a weighted average of the advertising intensity is to lower the correlation (cf. (7) with (9), and (8) with (10)).

The next step in my analysis is to show what happens if other companies, that can be classified as operating in the same 14 industries chosen by my critics, are included in the analysis. Since all of the results are better if excise taxes are included with sales, that is, better in the sense of showing a stronger positive association between concentration and the advertising intensity, I shall only give the results when excise taxes are included. There are 30 companies that can be included with the original sample of 40 companies. For the expanded sample of companies where excise taxes are included with sales, the regression using companies as the unit of observation gives the following results:

$$(11) \qquad C = \underset{10.74}{42.73} + \underset{3.53}{2.72}\,(A/S)' \qquad R^2 = 0.155,\ n = 70$$

Compare this result with (6). The coefficient of the advertising intensity is 66 percent of its value in (6) and there is a decrease of the R^2 from 0.21 to 0.155.

In addition to these results by company for the expanded sample, it is necessary to calculate the regressions by industry average weighted and unweighted including the excise tax. The results for the unweighted average are as follows:

$$(12) \qquad C = \underset{3.95}{42.07} + \underset{1.94}{3.90}\,(A/S)' \qquad R^2 = 0.239,\ n = 14$$

and for the weighted average the results are as follows:

$$(13) \qquad C = \underset{3.29}{38.87} + \underset{1.99}{5.12}\,(A/S)'_w \qquad R^2 = 0.249,\ n = 14$$

Comparing (8) and (12) we see that the regression for the industry average advertising intensity is slightly poorer if all companies receive the same weight and the sample is expanded. However, comparing (10) and (13) shows a slight improvement using the weighted average. This pattern of results is not surprising because it is the smaller company that tends to be overlooked and that tends to be different from the larger one. This effect shows up more strongly in the regression where all companies receive the same weight.

There is no reason to accept the critics' choice of 14 industries where they allege advertising is a significant factor. Actually, they exclude several industries for which the advertising intensities are very high such as cleansers and toiletries and several with moderately high advertising intensities such as cigars and pharmaceuticals. To demonstrate the critical effect of the choice of industry, it seems both wise and fair to expand the sample by 12 industries for which advertising is an important means of sales promotion. At the very least it is instructive to see how the choice of industry affects the results. However, to maintain the suspense a bit longer, I first present the results by company for the expanded sample of 26 industries. These are as follows:

(14) $$C = \underset{20.97}{49.75} - \underset{1.97}{0.48}\,(A/S)' \qquad R^2 = 0.029,\ n = 130$$

This regression should be compared with (11). The R^2 drops from 0.155 to 0.029 and the coefficient of the advertising intensity from 2.72 to -0.48. There is now an inverse relation between the advertising intensity and the concentration ratio!

Now consider the regressions for the industry averages. These are as follows:

(15) $$C = \underset{8.70}{55.22} - \underset{0.46}{0.44}\,(A/S)' \qquad R^2 = 0.009,\ n = 26$$

(16) $$C = \underset{8.11}{54.72} - \underset{0.31}{0.39}\,(A/S)'_w \qquad R^2 = 0.004,\ n = 26$$

On the basis of these results I can maintain my earlier conclusion that the correlation between the concentration ratio and the advertising intensity is unimpressive. It is certainly true that a judicious choice of industries from these 26 can raise the R^2 from an anemic 0.01 to a healthy 0.6. All this really proves is that there is a considerable variation in the sampled relation between concentration and advertising intensity.[10]

[10] There is another measurement error problem connected with the sales figures. Some companies in the sample have large foreign sales which are reported together with their domestic sales. Since the advertising figures refer only to advertising in the U.S., the effect is to understate the advertising intensities for these companies. To correct for this it is necessary to calculate the advertising intensity with respect to domestic sales alone. Unfortunately, this cannot be done in all cases. However, we can calculate two regressions by company, one for the companies with a noticeable amount of foreign sales and the other for companies with domestic sales. There are 87 companies with primarily domestic sales. Including excise taxes we obtain

$$C = \underset{16.32}{46.71} - \underset{1.08}{0.42}\,(A/S)' \qquad R^2 = 0.0147,\ n = 81$$

There are 49 companies with non-negligible foreign sales. For these the results are as follows:

$$C = \underset{12.96}{55.72} - \underset{1.94}{0.65}\,(A/S)' \qquad R^2 = 0.0745,\ n = 49$$

On the basis of these results I can see no harm in combining the two sets of companies.

Certain aspects of the role of advertising do not emerge in either my regressions or in those of my critics. Some of these have to do with the dispersion of the advertising intensity among companies within an industry. For example, in pharmaceuticals there is an especially large dispersion of the advertising intensity among companies. Those companies with a high advertising intensity tend to specialize in proprietary remedies while those with low intensities specialize in ethical drugs (sold by a physician's prescription). The latter tend to rely more on salesmen and as a result the ratio of total promotional outlays to sales is higher relative to advertising outlays divided by sales for the ethical than for the proprietary producers. However, since several large firms make both kinds of products it would be inadvisable to separate the pharmaceutical industry into two industries, proprietary and ethical. It would be better to relate the concentration ratio to the total promotional intensity to see whether or not outlays to 'differentiate the product' raise concentration. The large dispersion of the advertising intensity among firms is present also in toiletries and in cleansers. The explanation here lies in the high turnover of firms and brands which makes for a higher proportion of new products in these categories. In order to gain consumer acceptance, the producers tend to invest heavily in advertising. Thus the high advertising intensity indicates strong competition within the industry and a low concentration ratio. One firm in the toiletries industry nicely illustrates the diversity in methods of promotion—Avon. This firm has a low advertising intensity because it relies heavily on door-to-door salesmen just like producers of ethical drugs.

In conclusion I wish to remind the reader that the theoretical argument for an inverse relation between advertising intensity and the concentration ratio has attracted far less attention than it deserves. Everyone knows the contention that advertising is a source of monopoly and, therefore, expects a positive association between the two. But intensive advertising is often an instrument of competition as well. The entry of new firms and the offering of new brands is frequently accompanied by high advertising expenditures. Hence advertising can enhance competition. Even if advertising does reduce competition in some cases, it can increase it in others. The net effect reveals itself by the absence of a dependable relation between the advertising intensity and the concentration ratio.

UNIVERSITY OF CHICAGO

STATISTICAL TESTING IN INDUSTRIAL ECONOMICS: A REPLY ON MEASUREMENT ERROR AND SAMPLING PROCEDURE

by H. M. Mann, J. A. Henning, and
J. W. Meehan, Jr.

Professor Telser's opening paragraphs betray a curiously scholastic view of research. He sees our original paper as an attempt to refute his earlier work on the association between concentration and advertising intensity. Finding that our 'badly biased' sample '. . . seriously distorts the true state of affairs', he promises to test 'fairly' the hypothesis at issue. We believe that the term 'refute' is more suitable to a discussion involving issues of deductive rather than inductive inference. It is inappropriate as a synonym for 'disagree with', especially when the disagreement is one of degree. What we did, of course, was simply to uncover a statistical relationship between concentration and advertising intensity that was stronger than that uncovered earlier by Telser. It may be that Telser has tested the hypothesis fairly, though we shall present some comments on this below. But it is not clear to us how Telser knows what the true state of affairs is. Further, since Telser nowhere even attempts to demonstrate bias in a statistical sense, we wonder whether his conclusion that our sample is badly biased might have been developed from a chain of reasoning somewhat as follows. If one were in a position to know that the true correlation between concentration and advertising intensity was zero, then he might be tempted to conclude that any sample yielding a strong non-zero correlation must be badly biased. We turn now to the specific issues raised by Telser.[1]

[1] Professor Telser points out that we ignored evidence in his original article '. . . on the stability of brand shares and the regressions that relate ΔC and $\Delta(A/S)$'. As we note above, our purpose was not to comment on Professor Telser's paper, but to present some other findings on the relationship between concentration and advertising intensity.

We do point out, however, that we have commented on the relationship between ΔC and $\Delta(A/S)$ in our 'Testing Hypotheses in Industrial Economics: A Reply', in this number *The Journal of Industrial Economics*. In addition, it is not clear to us what the evidence on brand-share stability has to do with firm market shares, the relevant variable. There may be a relationship, but, to our knowledge, there has been no empirical demonstration.

Professor Telser also replicates our 1958 equations and concludes: 'Although the agreement is tolerably good, in principle it should be possible to obtain precisely the same results as my critics when I use *their* data to replicate *their* results.' The mistakes are as follows: Telser is correct with respect to his replication of our *NAI* regression, his equation (1). The mistake was ours. We recorded an average advertising-to-sales ratio for biscuits in the regression program which was lower than the one computed from our Table 1. His result, therefore, is not only correct, but *strengthens* the relationship between advertising intensity and concentration.

The regression for 1958, using the *Printers' Ink—Advertising Age* data, is correct in the

MEASUREMENT ERROR

Professor Telser finds that '... there is no theoretical argument to support the view that an analysis based on company data and 4-digit concentration ratios is less prone to measurement error than one based on weighted averages of the 4-digit concentration ratios and on the advertising figures reported by the Internal Revenue Service'. Interpreting this statement strictly, we find that we must agree. There can be no doubt that in avoiding one type of measurement error of unknown dimensions we may have introduced others, also of unknown dimensions. Indeed, we recognized this and in our original paper we listed three sources of measurement error in our data. Obviously, under the circumstances of total ignorance concerning the size of either type of measurement error, it would be impossible to prove unequivocally that our data are less prone to measurement error than are Telser's data. We think our original language was sufficiently qualified and sufficiently modest to make it quite clear that we were making no such categorical claim.

Having said this, however, we persist in the view that Telser's 3-digit data are subject to more serious measurement error than our 4-digit data. This view is based partly on an admittedly subjective and unquantifiable evaluation of the 4-digit data underlying Telser's 3-digit aggregates, and partly on the simple fact that the 4-digit data turn out to be considerably more highly correlated than the 3-digit data are—a result that one would expect if Telser's measurement error were more serious than ours.

We are tempted to press Professor Telser for some of the details of his argument that our data are not free of measurement error. But since this would contribute nothing to our knowledge of the relative size of the measurement error in our data, and since we have already acknowledged the *existence* of measurement error in our data, we see little point in inviting further unnecessary discussion. We do wish to object, however, to Telser's analysis of the significance of the regression coefficient ratio. The fact that 'the coefficient of $(A/S)_2$ is too low' can be explained by hypotheses other than the one selected by Telser—the presence of measurement error in our data. It can also be explained by the perfectly plausible hypotheses (a) that the strict complementarity relationship among the various media is not

article. The source of Telser's mistake, which may well be our fault, is that the advertising-sales-ratio for Pabst Brewing (Table II) in 1958 should be 4.5 percent, and in 1954, 6.0 percent, the opposite of Table II's presentation. We recorded the correct percentages in our regression program.

We thank Professor Telser for discovering these errors, although fortunately the interpretation of our findings does not change.

identical for all firms; or (b) that the relationship among the various media is something less than that of strict complementarity. Thus, though we are as anxious as Telser is not to entertain any illusions about the accuracy of our data, we find this particular line of argument unsound.

To summarize the measurement error discussion to this point: Telser argues (a) that there exists measurement error in our data, and (b) that therefore we cannot prove that our data are less prone to measurement error than his own. We acknowledged (a) in our original paper and agreed with (b) implicitly in our original paper and explicitly above. What little evidence Telser offers does not lead us to change our view, however, on the relative accuracy of the two sets of data. Nevertheless, we are prepared to admit that we may be quite wrong in this view.

The central question, however, is whether the measurement error issue raised by Telser amounts to a substantive criticism of our findings. We do not believe so. In fact, Telser focuses so much on a demonstration that our 4-digit data cannot be proven to be more accurate than his aggregated 3-digit data[2] that he loses sight of the purpose of the statistical tests: Is there an association between concentration and advertising intensity? In our own study, the suspicion that Telser's 3-digit data may have led him astray suggested to us that it might be worthwhile testing the same hypothesis using less aggregative data. Our conclusion, namely, that we found statistically significant correlations between concentration and advertising intensity, depends in no way on whether our data are more or less prone to measurement error than is Telser's data. Indeed, in arguing that our data are subject to greater measurement error than we appear to believe it is subject to, Telser is providing evidence that our correlations are serious *under*estimates of the strength of association between concentration and advertising intensity. We do not know if that was his intention.

TELSER'S STATISTICAL TESTS

What are we to make of the battery of tests that Telser advances? We think a few simple comments, the last of which we wish particularly to stress, will be sufficient.

[2] Telser states that trade estimates of advertising expenditures '. . . may be as much as 60 percent higher than the IRS figures'. In the case of cigarettes, IRS figures are considerably higher than the trade estimates. See Staff Report on the Bureau of Economics, Federal Trade Commission, *A Report on Cigarette Advertising and Output*, 1964, Table I, p. 3. The trade data used by the FTC is equivalent to the *NAI* data used in our original article. A computation from *Printers' Ink* for 1959 gives $172.4 million for the six major cigarette companies versus $232.6 million from the IRS data. One case does not prove that Telser's statement is generally mistaken, but he cites no instances to support his contention.

First, there is the relatively minor issue of whether excise taxes should be included in measuring sales. We have excluded them, using revenue net of taxes; Telser argues that taxes should be included since the higher the tax the higher the price and the less effective the advertising. But such a tax will have a great or small effect on price depending on the extent of forward shifting that is possible. In any event, it is the effect on *net* revenue that would be crucial to the firm.

Second, we observe that except for the last three regressions, Telser finds correlations that are consistently positive and consistently statistically significant at or close to the 5 percent level. Though r^2 (proportion of variance explained) is always smaller than our own, we think it is permissible to take these results of Telser as further confirmation of our own original conclusions. Again, we do not know if this was Telser's intention. His last three regressions, dealing with the 130 firms in 26 industries from his new sample, give negative and statistically insignificant correlations. We discuss these below.

Third, an inspection of scatter diagrams of Telser's data suggests that his correlations are as relatively low as they are because of a few extreme observations ('because' in the sense that if they were removed the fit improves dramatically). A Spearman rank correlation analysis[3] (which does not place as much weight on extreme observations as does the Pearson r) was applied to those data which generated the negative correlations reported for Telser's equations (15) and (16). In both cases, the rank correlations were *positive*, 0.161 and 0.149, respectively, though not statistically significant. They were, however, markedly different from the Pearson coefficients suggesting the presence of outliers unfavorable to the hypothesis of positive association. A similar analysis on our data gives almost identical Pearson and Spearman coefficients. This indicates that *our* results are not due to a small number of outlying observations. We do not argue, of course, that this provides a basis for excluding such unfavorable observations. What we do suggest is that many of them would be excluded if strict criteria, discussed immediately below, were followed in selecting the sample.

Fourth, Telser makes much of the point that the choice of industries can have a significant effect on the results. This is a point we would make much of, too. We submit that Telser's relatively weaker cor-

[3] We believe that rank correlation analysis is sufficient to test the hypothesis of positive association between concentration and advertising intensity. It has the further practical advantage of reducing the effect of extreme observations. Rank correlation analysis applied to Telser's 1964 JPE data gives the following rank correlation coefficients: 1947, 0.292; 1954, 0.362; 1958, 0.300; all statistically significant at about 5 percent or less.

relations are due to the presence of a substantial number of 'industries' that correspond very poorly or not at all to economically meaningful markets. It is in principle possible to establish a grading or scaling of 'industries' as defined in official statistics according to the degree of correspondence to such theoretically meaningful markets.[4] It seems clear that a researcher using this data must decide and make explicit how far down this scale he is willing to go, given the quality and availability of his other data. We were quite explicit on the criteria which we used in our original paper. The result was that our samples were quite small. Telser, on the other hand, appears willing to dig as far down into the barrel as mere data availability will permit.

For instance, Telser selects pharmaceuticals, cleansers, and toiletries on the basis that their advertising intensities are very high and berates us for failure to include these cases. Our exclusion of pharmaceuticals was grounded on two considerations. First, it is true that pharmaceutical companies have large advertising budgets, but advertising is not the most important means of sales promotion, representing only about 40 percent of the total spent. Therefore, pharmaceutical companies did not meet one of the criteria we explicitly set forth in our article.[5] Second, pharmaceuticals is not a theoretical industry, that is, an industry whose boundaries include all sellers producing substitute products and selling them to a common group of buyers and exclude all others. The Census 4-digit industry lumps together groups of ethical drugs which do not have the same therapeutic purpose, as well as drugs for veterinary use. The Census concentration ratio, therefore, dramatically understates the concentration ratios for the theoretical industries within the Census category.[6]

Our exclusion of cleansers and toiletries rested on the fact that the Census 4-digit industry lumps together nonsubstitute products, as an examination of the 5-digit product classes will attest.[7] The well-known effect of such overinclusion, as indicated above, is to understate the concentration ratio for the theoretical industries within the Census grouping.[8]

[4] Joe Bain, *Industrial Organization*, New York, John Wiley & Sons, Inc., 1968, pp. 124–33.

[5] Subcommittee on Antitrust and Monopoly, Committee in the Judiciary, U.S. Senate, *Administered Prices Drugs*, Washington, D.C., 1961, p. 157.

[6] *Administered Prices Drugs*, *op. cit.*, chart 8, p. 67. Sub-committee on Antitrust and Monopoly, Committee on the Judiciary, U.S. Senate, *Concentration Ratios in Manufacturing Industry 1958*, part 1, Washington, D.C., 1962, Table 4, p. 132.

[7] *Concentration Ratios in Manufacturing Industry 1958*, *op. cit.*, Table IV, pp. 132–3.

[8] Bain, *op. cit.*, pp. 130–2. Also see Dean A. Worcester, Jr., *Monopoly, Big Business, and Welfare in the Postwar United States*, Seattle, Washington, University of Washington Press, 1967. Worcester states: 'An important thesis of this book is that the actual degree of concentration is substantially higher in the United States than shown in previous studies'. (p. 5). He uses cleansers as an example later in the book, pp. 60–1.

Telser's willingness to include the above industries increases sample size, but at the expense of adding individual industries which correspond poorly to a market in the economic sense. It seems obvious to us that adding more and more poorly corresponding industries to the sample is more and more akin to adding as bona fide observations numbers drawn from a table of random digits, making the null hypothesis more and more difficult to reject. It is therefore not surprising that Telser has had such great difficulty with his large samples in finding an impressive correlation between concentration and advertising intensity. We think the moral in all this for research in industrial economics is that by lowering the selection criteria (taking poorer and poorer data) in order to increase sample size, we may be diminishing, rather than increasing, the power of the standard statistical tests to reject the null hypothesis. It is our view that empirical testing of the hypotheses of micro-economics requires the satisfaction of stringent theoretical conditions.[9] This inevitably reduces sample size, but the gain is greater confidence in the validity of the statistical results.

CONCLUSION

As we see it, what Telser has contributed is not, as he would have it, a refutation of our work, but rather another piece of evidence bearing on the issue we all share a common interest in. The only thing that we (the authors) are certain about is that no one has said the last word on this issue.

BOSTON COLLEGE
SYRACUSE UNIVERSITY
NORTHEASTERN UNIVERSITY

[9] On a different microeconomic problem than that discussed above, but making the same point, see J. Johnston, *Statistical Cost Analysis*, New York, McGraw-Hill Book Company, 1960.

PUBLICATIONS RECEIVED

Business Finance and the Capital Market, by Kenneth Midgley and Ronald G. Burns, Macmillan & Co. Ltd., May, 1969, 55s. (hardcover) 25s. (Papermac).

Business Strategy, edited by H. Igor Asnoff, Penguin Modern Management Readings, April, 1969, 10s.

Capital Gains Taxation: Issues in Perspective, by Martin David, The Brookings Institution, 1968, (Paper) $2.50 (Cloth) $6.75.

The Case for Floating Exchange Rates Reconsidered, by Anthony M. Lanyi, No. 72 Essays in International Finance, International Finance Section of the Department of Economics at Princeton University, February 1969.

Collective Bargaining, edited by Allan Flanders, Penguin Modern Management Readings, April, 1969, 10s.

Company Policy and Taxation, by John Treasure, Industrial Educational and Research, June, 1969, 5s.

Costs of Urban Infrastructure for Industry as Related to City Size in Developing Countries—India Case Study, a joint study by Stanford Research Institute, School of Planning and Architecture, Small Industry Extension Training Institute under contract with the Agency for International Development, Stanford Research Institute, January, 1969, $8.00.

Criminal Liability of Corporations in English Law (an L.S.E. Research Monograph), by Leonard Leigh, Weidenfeld & Nicolson, July, 1969, 56s.

Criteri di Analis Della Dinamica Degli Aggregati del Conto dell Produzione, by Carlo Ferreri, Collana di Stude de Statistica Economica Abbaco, Palermo, December, 1968.

Distribution Channels: Behavioural Dimensions, by Louis W. Stern, Houghton Company, 1969, $4.25.

Doncaster—an Area Study, prepared by the Humberside Planning Council and Board, West Riding County Council, County Borough of Doncaster, H.M.S.O., August, 1969, 25s.

Economics: Britain and the E.E.C., by H. G. Johnson, J. Pinder, D. Swann and M. A. G. van Meerhaeghe, Longmans, Green & Co. August, 1969, 25s. (Paper). A hard back edition of this will be available later in the Autumn for 40s.

Economic Survey of Denmark, 1969, prepared by the Economic Secretariat of the Government, Royal Danish Ministry of Foreign Affairs.

The Economics of Wages and Labour, by L. C. Hunter and D. J. Robertson, Macmillan & Co. Ltd., June, 1969, 80s. (Hardcover) 45s. (Papermac).

Essays in Modern Economic Development, edited by R. L. Smyth, Gerald Duckworth & Co. Ltd., June, 1969, 50s.

External Surpluses, Capital Flows, and Credit Policy in the European Economic Community, 1958 to 1967, by Samuel I. Katz, No. 22, Princeton Studies in International Finance, International Finance Section of the Department of Economics at Princeton University, 1969.

The Federal Budget: Its Impact on the Economy, a research report from the Conference Board, planned by Michael E. Levy, Fiscal Edition 1970, price to NICB Associates & Government Agencies $2.50, to students and teachers $2.50, price to all others $10.00.

Federal Support to Universities and Colleges, Fiscal Year 1967, Prepared by the National Science Foundation for the Office of Science and Technology, National Science Foundation, December, 1968, $1.00.

The Fund Agreement: Living Law and Emerging Practice, by Hans Aufricht, International Finance Section of the Department of Economics at Princeton University, No. 23, Studies in International Finance, 1969.

Gold: A Forward Strategy, by Jack L. Davies, International Finance Section of the Department of Economics of Princeton University No. 75, Studies in International Finance, May, 1969.

History of Trade Unionism in Australia, by J. T. Sutcliffe, Macmillan & Co. Ltd., May, 1969, 32s. 6d.

Huddersfield and Colne Valley: An Area Study, a Report by the Yorkshire and Humberside Economic Planning Council and Board, H.M.S.O., June, 1969, 17s. 6d.

Industrial Relations and the Personnel Specialists, by Peter Anthony and Anne Crichton, B. T. Batesford Ltd., May, 1969, 55s.

Kenricks in Hardware, A Family Business 1791–1966, by R. A. Church, David & Charles, July, 1969, 63s.

Low Income Groups and Methods of Dealing with Their Problems, Papers for a Trade Union Seminar, International Seminars 1965–68, Organization for Economic Co-operation and Development Manpower and Social Affairs Directorate, Social Affairs Division, 1969.

Management in the Textile Industry, The Textile Institute, Management Studies Series, Longmans, Green & Co. Ltd., May, 1969, 120s.

Managerial Economics, Analysis for Business Decisions, by D. C. Hague, Longmans, Green & Co. Ltd., August, 1969, 45s. (This book is concerned with the wide range of practical decision problems that fall to management, including topics usually studied separately under such titles as managerial economics, management accounting and operations research. It is aimed at two types of reader: those studying for degrees or diplomas in business studies or in management, and managers who are attending management courses after some years in business.)

Manufacturing Employment by Type of Location, An Examination of Recent Trends, by Daniel Creamer, assisted by Walter B. Brown, a research Report from the Conference Board. Studies in Business Economics No. 106. Price to N.I.C.B. Associates and Government Agencies, students and teachers $2.00; price to all others $10.00.

The Modern British Economy, by K. S. Reader, Longmans, Green & Co. Ltd., May, 1969, 45s.

Modern Financial Management, edited by B. V. Carsberg and H. C. Edey, Penguin Modern Management Readings, April, 1969, 10s.

Modern Management Methods, by Ernest Dale and L. C. Ichelon, Penguin Books Ltd., May, 1969, 7s.

Natural Gas in Western Europe, a Case Study in the Economic Geography of Energy Resources, by Dr. Peter R. Odell, Haarlem, De Erven F. Bohn N.V., 1969.

Objective Tests in Economics, By G. Stanlake, Longmans, Green & Co. Ltd., June, 1969.

On the Process of Planning, by Peter O. Steiner, Training-Seminar Series, Center of Planning and Economic Research, Athens 1968. (An extended essay concerned with the process of planning, the assumption being that the process is important and the substance vitally affected by the way it is approached. It is a stimulating general and theoretical analysis, to be read alongside—or before undertaking—specific development plans for a country or region.)

Ownership, Control, and Ideology, by Theo. Nichols, George Allen & Unwin Ltd., August, 1969, 55s. (No. 8 in the Studies in Management series, an enquiry into certain aspects of modern business ideology, this is a sociological approach to controversial questions raised by the 'managerial revolution' in industry.)

Political Bargaining, Systematic Analysis, and Federal Budget Decision, Highlights of the Politics and Economics of Public Spending, by Charles L. Schultze, Brookings Research Report 95, The Brookings Institution. Cloth $4.95, Paper $1.95.

Principles of Data Processing, by J. E. Walsh, N. E. Williams, E. E. Barnett and R. H. Collyer, Sir Isaac Pitman and Sons Ltd., 40s.

Private and Official International Money: The Case for the Dollar, by Ronald I. McKinnon, International Finance Section of the Department of Economics of Princeton University, Essays in International Finance, No. 74, April, 1969.

The Proceedings of the Fourth International Conference on Operational Research, edited by David B. Hertz and Jacques Melese, John Wiley & Sons Ltd., July, 1969, 235s. (Mainly in English, with summaries in French, this important volume is a collection of papers presented at the Conference held in 1966. There are contributions from experts from 12 nations, giving the latest developments of interest both in the theory and application of operations research.)

R. & D. and Small-Company Growth, a Statistical Review and Company Case Studies, by Wm. J. J. Smith and Daniel Creamer, a Research Report from the Conference Board, Studies in Business Economics No. 102, 1968, $3.00.

Scientists Engineers, and Physicians from Abroad, Fiscal Years 1966 and 1967, Surveys of Science Resources Series, National Science Foundation, NSF 69-10.

Speculocracy and the International Monetary System, by Xenophon Zolotas, Victor Papazissis Publishers, 1969.

Studies in Accounting for Management Decision, edited by A. M. Bourn, McGraw-Hill Ltd., 1969, 70s. (A collection of papers, developed from seminars on management accounting at the University of Liverpool School of Business Management, which reflect the conviction that business is a dynamic process and that accounting practice should be modified to take account of the dynamic element of continuing change in business activity.)

Systems Thinking, edited by F. E. Emery, Penguin Modern Management Readings, April, 1969, 10s.

Technical Forecasting and Corporate Strategy, edited by Professor Gordon Wills, B. Taylor, D. J. L. Ashton, Management Centre, University of Bradford, The Bradford University Press in association with Crosby Lockwood, August, 1969, 90s.

The Theory of Imperfect Competition, a Radical Reconstruction, by Donald Dewey, Columbia University Press, 1969, $7.50. (An attempt to present a unified theory of imperfect competition out of the various pieces of earlier theorizing about oligopoly, mergers, product differentiation etc., with some attention to policy implications. The author is concerned with a multi-plant, freedom of contract situation which leads him to an equilibrium solution in terms of rationalization of production, minimization of cost, and entry-limit pricing.)

Toward Limited Exchange Rate-Flexibility, by George N. Halm, International Finance Section of the Department of Economics of Princeton University, Essays in International Finance, No. 73, March 1969.

Twenty Years of Nationalisation, The British Experience, by R. Kelf-Cohen, April, 1969, 70s.

The U.S.S.R. in Today's World, The M. L. Seidman Memorial Town Hall Lecture Series, Edited by Dr. Festus Justine Viser, Memphis State University Press, Tennessee, 1969, $2.50.

Values and the Future, The Impact of Technological change on American values, edited by Kurt Baier and Nicolar Rescher, 1969.

Wage Policy Issues in Economic Development, edited by A. D. Smith, Macmillan & Co. Ltd., July, 1969, £6.

Woolwich Economic Papers No. 15, *Invention and Monopoly*, by W. Kingston; No. 16, *Economic Constraints in the Third World*, by J. B. Wilmshurst; 3s. 6d. each, November, 1968.

PROJECT EVALUATION OF MULTINATIONAL PLANTS IN AFRICA

by R. Robson

1. As is well known most African countries are too small to provide an adequate market for large-scale industry and the only way in which such plants can be economically established is through two or more countries combining so as to offer a common market. Since the common market is only large enough for one plant, however, the country in which this is located will derive the main benefit unless special measures are taken to avoid this. These measures are discussed in the first part of this paper. The alternative, discussed in the second part, is when feasible to divide the manufacturing process into two parts so that two or more countries can share in producing the final product.

2. SINGLE MULTINATIONAL PLANT

Little[1] has discussed the case of a single plant located in the 'host' country supplying a number of markets in 'non-host' countries and has shown that provided each non-host country contributes to the capital cost in proportion to its takings of the product and that earnings are fully paid out, then each non-host country will benefit equitably irrespective of the price at which the product is sold. The benefit to the host country is not calculated, but it is implicitly recognized that this will be greater than that accruing to the non-host country and it is proposed that in principle this can be adjusted by arranging that the host country contributes its own share of the capital required while the non-host countries' contributions are assisted by aid in the form of low interest loans.

It is important, however, that this should be spelled out in some detail since it is precisely this higher advantage to the host country which is the main obstacle to a market agreement. The calculations will be made in the ensuing paragraphs of this part of the paper for the particular case of an iron and steel plant supplying two countries and located in one of them.

3. The case may be illustrated by the two African countries (A) and (B), the former having rich deposits of iron ore suitable for establishing an iron and steel industry while the latter has a larger

[1] I. M. D. Little, 'Regional International Companies as an Approach to Economic Integration', *Journal of Common Market Studies*, December 1966.

market for the finished product. It has been estimated[2] that by 1983 (A) will be able to consume 72,000 tons of bar and light sections per annum while (B) will consume about 216,000 tons. (B) has a scrap melting unit—the first steel making activity normally established in a developing country—using locally available scrap and its capacity can be expanded to supply about 48,000 tons of sections so that the net demand on the integrated works in 1983 is for 240,000 tons. It is assumed that the plant will come into operation in 1974 when demand is 100,000 tons rising by 10 per cent per annum. The details of the plant to be erected in country (A) are estimated[3] as follows:

		$ *million*
	Capital investment	100.0
	Capacity	240,000 tons per annum
Operating cost:	Imported materials	8.1
	Local materials	7.9
	Wages and salaries	3.0

Transport on finished steel from (A) to (B)—$10 per ton.
C.I.F. price of imported bar and sections—$125 per ton.

It will be further assumed that the plant is operated as a state concern in order to reduce payments abroad as much as possible and that the expatriate staff required to operate it accounts for half the wage bill and can remit half of this abroad. It will be noted that from 1983 onwards when the plant is working to capacity, import prices can be met and there will be a reasonable profit, for operating costs amount to $19.0 million and revenue to $28.3 million, i.e. a surplus of $9.3 million. In 1974, however, the first year of operation, this will be much smaller; assuming that material costs are proportional to output and that wages and salaries fall to $2.5 million it amounts to only $2.5 million. Over the whole life of the plant taken at 20 years the return may be obtained by discounting cash flows and comes to 3 per cent over and above amortization. To obtain the commercial minimum of 5 per cent prices would have to be raised to $133 per ton.

4. The object of the exercise is to ascertain what contribution should be made by (B) to the capital cost of the plant and at what price steel should be sold to (B) so that both countries obtain the same benefit to their national economies, benefit being taken to include the gain to the balance of payments and to the gross national product.

[2] These estimates have been made by the Economic Commission for Africa in respect of Liberia (A) and Ghana (B).

[3] From an engineering study prepared for the Government of Liberia, on behalf of UNIDO, by W. S. Atkins and Partners.

(a) The contribution to the balance of payments of country (B) in 1983, ignoring for the moment the question of which country undertakes the transport of the steel, will be:

$100.r.y+0.168(125-10-p)$ where r is the return paid on capital, y the proportion contributed by (B), and p the ex-works price of steel sold to (B).

(b) The contribution to the balance of payments of country (A) will include the following elements:

(i) Import saving—72,000 tons at \$125 equals \$9.0 million less imported materials \$8.1 million.
(ii) Exports—168,000 tons at $\$p$ per ton.
(iii) Less wages remitted abroad \$0.75 and profit distributed to (B), i.e. $100.r.y$, r being constant.
(iv) During the construction of the plant imports of machinery will be required amounting to \$60 million.

On the assumption that the countries can borrow at 5 per cent these flows may be discounted at this rate for the twenty years ending 1993 giving the following 1973 values:[4]

$$\left.\begin{array}{l}\text{For country (B)}: 1246.r.y+188.6-1.64.p\\ \text{For country (A)}: -8.3-1246.r.y+1.64.p-60\end{array}\right\} \qquad (1)$$

The contributions will be equal after subtracting the original capital contribution if

$$3.28.p = 2492.r.y-200.y+357$$

Illustrating this by a numerical example let $y = \frac{1}{2}$ and $r = 0.05$, then $p = 97$, so that (A) sells steel to (B) at \$97 per ton ex-works compared with an imported delivered price of \$125. The net gain to the discounted balance of payments is in both cases \$10.2 million so that the project is in fact a capital gain and costs nothing.

5. The contribution to the gross national product is exactly the same as that to the balance of payments during the operation of the plant, but during construction (A) obtains an increased benefit of \$13.3 million, namely, one-third of the value added in construction which in total is estimated at 40 per cent of the value of the project, i.e. \$40 million. To include this in the benefit it seems reasonable to introduce the conception of opportunity cost and to assume that normally an increase of \$100 in gross capital formation will give an increase of \$20 approximately in GDP which discounted as before

[4] See annex.

amounts to \$250. The above equation slightly modified to take account of this contribution then becomes:

$$3.28.p = 2492.r.y.-200.y+341$$

and using the same numerical example p = \$92 per ton.

6. It is now necessary to see how the plant will operate from a commercial point of view. Gross profit in 1983 will be in \$ million:

$$0.168.p+0.072\,p_1-19$$

where p_1 is the price at which (A) sells steel in the domestic market. Discounting at 5 per cent, i.e. taking a profit of 5 per cent per annum over and above amortization as the commercial minimum we get[5]

$$1.64p+0.703p_1 = 291.8 \qquad (2)$$

i.e. if $p = 92$ then p_1 would have to be as high as \$200. It is therefore not practicable to equalize the benefit and to earn a minimum margin of profit except by charging excessive prices in A's home market.

The situation can be improved in two ways. First if country (B) is allowed to undertake the shipment of steel thus gaining \$10 per ton to her economy then B's price can rise to \$98, and A's domestic price can fall to \$187. Secondly, following the suggestion of Little, if B's contribution to the capital cost is facilitated by being granted a soft loan at, say, 2 per cent interest, then B's price can rise to \$102 and A's price could be reduced still further in view of this and the increased profitability of the project to \$156.

7. DIVIDED MULTINATIONAL PLANT

In many industries it is technically feasible and affects costs only slightly to begin the manufacturing process in one country and complete it in another. This is true primarily of the assembly industries of which engineering is the typical example, e.g., wheels and axles for railway wagons can be forged in one country and the wagons constructed and assembled in another country to supply the joint market or an automobile assembly plant may be located in one country and supplied with one or two simple components manufactured in adjacent countries. In such cases to ensure co-ordination of production and ready acceptance of components it is desirable that the same firm should control the various national plants involved. Similarly, the production of cloth can be readily divided into spinning and weaving and the production of steel rod into the casting of billets and

[5] See annex.

the subsequent rolling. This usually involves a small addition to transport costs, but these are internal and while affecting slightly the commercial profitability of the project do not affect the gain to the national economy.

The following calculations relate to the iron and steel plant previously considered as a whole. Country (A) now produces in 1983 254,000 tons of cast billets which are exported to country (B) and rolled into 240,000 tons of bar and sections (and 14,000 tons scrap) of which 72,000 are then exported to country (A). Since billets are transported at a slightly lower cost than finished steel and since there will be some economy on return traffic it will be estimated that transport costs each way are reduced to \$7.5 per ton as compared with \$10 previously so that total transport costs in 1983 will be \$2.45 million as against \$1.68 million previously. There are probably certain administrative losses in dividing the plant, but, on the other hand, it is necessary in any event for country (B) to have a rolling works in order to effectively use available scrap.

8. The details of the divided plant are as follows:

		Country (A)	*Country (B)*
		(*\$ million*)	
	Capital investment	70.0	30.0
Operating cost:	Imported materials	7.5	0.6+ billets
	Local materials	6.0	1.9
	Wages and salaries	1.8	1.2

and the gain to the balance of payments and gross national product in 1983 from the operation of the plants, assuming no profit passes from one to the other, is:

Country (A) $125 \times 0.072 - 0.072(p_2 + 7.5) + 0.254p_1 - 7.5 - 0.45$ (wages)

Country (B) $0.168 \times 125 - 0.254(p_1 + 7.5) - 0.072p_2 - 0.6 - 0.30$ (wages) $+ 0.42$ (scrap)[6]

where p_1 is the ex-works price of billets and p_2 that of rod.

Discounting over the life of the plant as before at 5 per cent interest and taking account of contributions during the construction of the plants the benefit to both countries will be equal if

$$4.958p_1 - 1.406p_2 = 232 \qquad (3)$$

[6] Scrap valued at \$30 per ton.

so that, for example, if (A) sells billets to (B) at \$90 per ton, then (B) will sell rod to (A) at \$152 per ton.

9. The actual prices will depend on the level of profit required which as before will be taken at the commercial minimum of 5 per cent over and above amortization. To obtain this we have for the two works since no profit passes:

$$\left.\begin{array}{l}\text{For (A)}: 2.479p_1 = 223 \text{ or } p_1 = \$90 \text{ per ton.}\\ \text{For (B)}: 0.703p_2 - 1.64p_3 = 291 \text{ where } p_3 \text{ is the ex works}\\ \qquad\text{domestic price in country (B).}\end{array}\right\} \quad (4)$$

These equations give the result $p_3 = \$112$ and $p_2 = \$152$ which is a considerably less differential than in the case of a single plant. If further, (B) undertakes shipment as before, then selling prices come still nearer to \$120 and \$135, respectively.

The equations may be readily modified to include the situation, which would be more typical of engineering activities, in which the same firm operates both plants and profits of the order of 15 per cent over and above amortization are expected and of this perhaps a rate of 10 per cent remitted abroad. Applied to the present example however such profit rates would raise prices by about one third while the remittances abroad would heavily reduce the gain to the National Economy.

10. SUMMARY

The technique of project evaluation has been used to equalize the benefits to two countries co-operating in the establishment and operation of an iron and steel works to supply the joint market. It is shown that because of the advantage derived from the use of local materials and wages in the host country the benefit cannot be equalized, in the absence of special measures, except by maintaining relatively excessive prices there. Such special measures include in particular the granting of a low interest loan to the non-host country. This situation may be largely avoided by dividing the manufacturing process at a suitable stage between the two countries.

UNITED NATIONS ECONOMIC COMMISSION FOR AFRICA

ANNEX

1. Discounting at 5 per cent, \$1 has the following values:

1973	\$1.0000
1974—$1/1.05$	0.9524
1975—$1/(1.05)^2$	0.9070
....	
1983—$1/(1.05)^{10}$	0.6139
1993—$1/(1.05)^{20}$	0.3769
Total	12.46[a]

If in addition flows are reduced by 10 per cent per annum from 1983 to 1973 then the contribution from 1974 to 1982, inclusive, is reduced from 7.11 to 4.41[b] and the total from 12.46 to 9.76.

2. Discounted flows (1) for B: $100.r.y \times 12.46 + 0.168(115 - p) \times 9.56$

for A: $0.9 \times 9.76 + 0.168 \times 9.76 \times p - 0.75 \times 5.35 - 0.69 \times 7.11 - 100.r.y \times 12.46 - 60.$

3. Equation (2) $0.168 \times p \times 9.76 + 0.072 \times p_1 \times 9.76 - 16 \times 9.76 - 3 \times 5.35 - 2.75 \times 7.11 = 100.$

$$(a) = \sum_{n=1}^{n=20} \frac{1}{(1.05)^n} = \frac{(1.05)^{20} - 1}{0.05\ (1.05)^{20}}$$

$$(b) = \sum_{n=1}^{n=20} \frac{1}{(1.1)^{10-n}(1.05)^n} = \frac{(1.1)^9 - (1.05)^9}{0.05 \times (1.1)^9 \times (1.05)^9}$$

ADDIS ABABA

THE CONCENTRATION OF PATENT OWNERSHIP IN CORPORATIONS*

by Donald Stevenson Watson and Mary A. Holman

A neglected dimension in the measurement of concentration is the ownership of patents by business corporations. Although there have been published data for some time, they have not entered into the continuing discussion of concentration. The usual measures of concentration are such things as assets, sales and employees; other measures have included research and development. In what follows we shall present and analyze quantitative evidence on the concentration of patents in American industry.

There has been no lack of strong opinion on the concentration of patents in large corporations. Wilcox refers to it as a 'monopolization of patent monopolies'.[1] Edwards maintains that patent accumulation '. . . comes to be a substantial monopolization of the industry itself'.[2] Stocking and Watkins write about the evils of patent accumulation and its tendency to 'assure a perpetual monopoly'.[3] Machlup holds that the 'accumulation of patents in the hands of large corporations may secure them an almost unlimited monopoly power'.[4]

Kaysen and Turner say that patent accumulation can be 'something much larger than the sum of its parts'. Patent concentrations can be a barrier to entry; it increases the burden of 'inventing around' the technologists of accumulating firms; it puts patent blankets over areas of technology; and it has further oppressive effects, given the risks and costs of patent litigation. That Kaysen and Turner believe patent concentration to be a problem deserving solution is shown by their suggestions for reform, which include the strengthening of the antitrust laws to deal directly with patent accumulation (there is nothing now illegal about large patent holdings) and tentatively a tax per patent varying with the size of a corporation's holdings.[5]

Consisting only of number of patents, our quantitative evidence

* The research underlying this paper was supported in part by a grant (NsG 425) from the National Aeronautics and Space Administration to The George Washington University.

[1] Clair Wilcox, *Public Policies Toward Business* (Homewood, Illinois: R. D. Irwin, 1966), p. 172.

[2] Corwin, D. Edwards, *Maintaining Competition* (New York: McGraw-Hill, 1949), p. 224.

[3] George W. Stocking and Myron W. Watkins, *Monopoly and Free Enterprise* (New York: Twentieth Century Fund, 1951), p. 468.

[4] F. Machlup, *The Political Economy of Monopoly* (Baltimore: Johns Hopkins Press, 1952), p. 284.

[5] Carl Kaysen and Donald F. Turner, *Antitrust Policy* (Cambridge, Mass.: Harvard University Press, 1959), p. 165 ff.

cannot be adduced to analyze monopoly power as a direct function of patent concentration. Clearly, much depends on degrees of monopoly from the uses of individual patents and groups of patents. But our evidence does, we think, put the whole matter of patent concentration into better perspective.

THE DATA

The data we shall deploy are the 17-year patent portfolios of all domestic corporations with portfolios of 200 or more patents in 1938, 1955 and 1962. The data for 1938 were prepared by the Patent Office for the Temporary National Economic Committee (T.N.E.C.);[6] patents assigned to 193 corporations were counted for the period from January 1st, 1931, to June 30th, 1938, and their numbers were estimated by the Patent Office by extrapolation for the rest of the 17-year period. For 1955, the data for 195 corporations were prepared by P. J. Federico of the Patent Office.[7] For 1962, we made the count for the 234 corporations with 200 or more patents. For each period, the patent portfolios of a corporation contain the patents of its subsidiaries, including those acquired before the end of the period. To add the patents of subsidiaries to parents' portfolios probably exaggerates the degree of concentration of control, at least for corporations with diversified product lines and with decentralized patent management systems. On the other hand, our measures of concentration do not change significantly when the patents of subsidiaries are included or excluded.

The data for the three periods are patents assigned, at the time of issue, to domestic corporations. We make no adjustment for sales of patents or for purchases from individual inventors and from other corporations after patents issue. So far as we can tell, the relative numbers of patents bought and sold by corporations are small. In the study made for the T.N.E.C., it is shown that only about 2 per cent of the patents issued to individuals in 1931–38 were acquired by corporations. Using the files of the Patent Office, we made a test of purchases and sales for 30 of the 234 corporations (the first, middle, and last 10, by size of patent holdings) for the period 1937–62. Here too the numbers are small—the 30 corporations sold 1.8 per cent of the patents assigned to them and bought a number equal to 3.4 per cent.

[6] U.S. Congress, Hearings before the *Temporary National Economic Committee*, 76th Cong., 1st Sess., Part 3, Patents, January 16–20th, 1939, pp. 1127–8.

[7] P. J. Federico, *Distribution of Patents Issued to Corporations, 1939–1955*. Study No. 3 of the Senate Committee on the Judiciary (Washington, D.C.: U.S. Government Printing Office, 1959).

Our data, to repeat, are numbers only. For the 216,078 patents in, for example, the portfolios of the 234 corporations with 200 or more in 1962, we have no information on their values, on the incomes attributable to them, or on the fields of technology they cover. We do have, however, an estimate of the industry distribution, which we shall deal with later.

MEASURES OF CONCENTRATION

We have two measures of concentration, conventional concentration ratios and the slope coefficient of a simple Pareto distribution.[8] The ratios shown in Table I display the concentration of assigned patents among all domestic corporations that were assigned one of more patents in each of the three 17-year periods. Table I also

TABLE I

CONCENTRATION RATIOS FOR CORPORATE PATENTS IN THREE PERIODS AND FOR RESEARCH AND DEVELOPMENT PERFORMANCE IN INDUSTRY IN 1955

Number of Corporations	*First 4*	*First 8*	*First 20*	*First 40*	*First 100*	*Total*
Patents, 1921–38						
Number	27,785	44,512	64,178	80,796	113,263	320,121
Per cent of Total	9	14	20	25	35	100
Patents, 1939–55						
Number	34,757	53,819	80,043	104,390	137,832	317,726
Per cent of Total	11	17	25	33	43	100
Patents, 1946–62						
Number	35,329	58,387	95,863	125,324	172,076	373,513
Per cent of Total	9	16	26	34	46	100
R & D Performance 1958						
Per cent of Total	20	33	54	68	81	100

Sources: Patent data for 1921–38 from U.S. Congress, *Hearings before the Temporary National Economic Committee*, 76th Cong., 1st Sess., Part 3, Patents, January 16–20th, 1936, pp. 1127–8. Patent data for 1939–55 from P. J. Federico, *Distribution of Patents Issued to Corporations, 1939–1955*. Study No. 3 of the Senate Committee on the Judiciary (Washington, D.C.: U.S. Government Printing Office, 1957). Patent data for 1946–62 compiled from records of the U.S. Patent Office. Research and Development data from the National Science Foundation.

contains concentration ratios for total performance in 1958 of research and development, as reported by the National Science Foundation. We take the R & D data for 1958, because it is the earliest year for which N.S.F. published concentration ratios; the

[8] We use this form of Pareto's law: $C = AP^{-\alpha}$, where C is the cumulative number of corporations with P or more patents and A and α are the parameters. The smaller the absolute value of α, the greater is the concentration.

lag between R & D and patents seems to average about five years, most of the lag being the period of pendency in the Patent Office. It seems almost certain that the first 100 of the performers of R & D in industry are not identically the same corporations in the 1946–62 column for patents. But we are fairly sure that the two lists contain, with only few exceptions, the same names.

Table I shows little change in concentration among the first 4, 8, and 20 corporations. For the first 40 of the first 100, however, there was a decided tightening of patent concentration between 1938 and 1955. The enormous growth of R & D in the postwar period and the high concentration of that R & D have had astonishingly little impact on the concentration of patents.

The total number of corporations to which patents were issued in any of the three periods are not known. Federico believes that in 1955 the number was 'considerably over 20,000'. For the 7½ year period ending on June 30th, 1938, the number of corporations was 21,257.[9] Whatever their right number might be, it seems certain that the corporations with patents are a small minority of even all manufacturing corporations. Few patents are assigned to corporations not engaged in manufacturing.

The Pareto alphas in Table II give a different measure of patent

TABLE II

PARETO ALPHAS FOR PATENTS IN THREE PERIODS, FOR RESEARCH AND DEVELOPMENT IN 1958, AND FOR ASSETS IN 1962

Patents Assigned to Domestic Corporations	*Pareto Alphas*	*Standard Error*	R^2
1921–38, 193 Corporations	1.1118	0.0214	0.993
1939–55, 195 Corporations	1.0096	0.0109	0.998
1946–62, 234 Corporations	1.0396	0.0194	0.992
R & D Performance in Industry 1958			
1958, 200 Corporations	0.6503	0.0073	0.998
100 Largest Patent Holders:			
1946–62 Patents *vs.* 1962 Assets			
1962 Assets, 100 Corporations	0.6529	0.0292	0.836
1946–62 Patents, 100 Corporations	1.2576	0.0182	0.980

Sources: Patent data and Research and Development data, see notes to Table I. Assets from *Fortune Directory of 500 Largest Industrials.*

concentration. They show the inequality, or concentration, among the corporations with 17-year portfolios of 200 or more patents. The Pareto distribution fits the data well. The fit is also good when the coverage is extended to corporations with 100 or more patents.

[9] Federico, *op. cit.*

The Pareto coefficients tell the same story as the concentration ratios. Concentration increased from 1938 to 1955, but not from 1955 to 1962—the coefficients for these two years are not significantly different.

We do not know the shape of the distribution for all corporations

TABLE III

DISTRIBUTION OF R & D IN 1958 AND OF PATENTS BY INDUSTRY IN 1968 AND CONCENTRATION RATIOS (1st 4 FIRMS)

	Distribution		*Concentration Ratios for First Four Companies*	
Industry	*Funds for Total R & D*[a] *1958 Per cent of Total*	*Patents Assigned to U.S. Corps.*[b] *1962 Per cent of Total*	*R & D 1958*[c]	*Patents 1962*[b]
Food and kindred products	1.0	1.3	35	37
Textiles and apparel	0.2	1.0	47	[d]
Lumber, wood products and furniture	0.2	1.0	35	[e]
Paper and allied products	0.6	2.3	41	32
Chemicals and allied products:				
Industrial chemicals	6.6	9.9	60	61
Drugs and medicines	1.6	3.2	44	33
Other chemicals	1.3	2.9	28	22
Petroleum refining and extraction	2.9	7.9	48	47
Rubber products	1.1	1.7	69	51
Stone, clay and glass products	0.8	2.2	51	42
Primary metals:				
Primary ferrous metals	0.8	1.7	61	41
Nonferrous and other metal products	0.7	1.8	54	67
Fabricated metal products	1.5	5.4	50	17
Machinery	9.5	16.5	43	17
Electrical equipment and communication:				
Communication equipment and electronic parts	11.4	8.1	65	47
Other electrical equipment	12.3	10.0	88	49
Motor vehicles and other transportation equipment	10.3	5.3	92	78
Aircraft and missiles	30.1	5.2	46	38
Professional and scientific instruments:				
Scientific and mechanical measuring instruments	1.9	2.3	74	43
Optical, surgical, photographic and other	1.6	2.5	69	55
Other	3.6	7.8	20	9
Total	100.0	100.0		

[a] National Science Foundation, Funds for Research and Development in Industry 1958, NSF 61–32 (Washington: GPO, 1961), p. 22.

[b] Estimated from a 6.3 percent random sample of all patents assigned to U.S. corporations in 1962. Patents were classified by the major 2-digit (or 3-digit) number of the assignee.

[c] National Science Foundation, Funds for Research and Development in Industry 1958, NSF 61–32 (Washington, D.C.: GPO, 1961), pp. 18 and 61.

[d] No companies were assigned 200 or more patents.

[e] One company was assigned 200 or more patents.

with one or more patents. It is quite enough to know the upper tail. Neither analytical interest or concern over policy can be bestowed upon corporations that are poor as owners of patents, particularly when, as in this study, nothing is said about the values of patents.

Patent portfolios are much less concentrated than assets. A comparison of the two stock variables must face the fact that the largest manufacturing corporations include some with great assets and few patents (e.g., food, tobacco, lumber, even steel and nonferrous metals) and others with modest assets but with fat patent portfolios (e.g., instruments). For the 100 largest industrial corporations in 1962, the Spearman coefficient of rank correlation for assets and patent holdings was only 0.5256. For the 100 largest patent holders in 1962, the coefficient was 0.6652. In any event, there is substantial difference between the Pareto alphas for assets and patents; this difference is shown in the last two lines of Table II.[10]

DISTRIBUTION BY INDUSTRY

Table III contains data on the distribution of R & D in 1958 and of patents in 1962 by industry, the classification of industries being that of the National Science Foundation. The R & D data are from N.S.F.; the patent data are our estimates from a sample. The figures in the table throw additional light on our general finding on the much smaller degree of concentration in patents than in R & D. Except for industrial chemicals, all of the industries with substantial amounts of R & D had, on a first-four-firms basis, much less concentration in patent acquisitions than in R & D performance.

SUMMARY

It is apparent from both Tables I and II that there is a large difference between the concentration of patents and of R & D. Both patterns of concentration seem to be stable in the 1950s and early 1960s. The concentration ratios and the Pareto alphas say about the same thing, namely, that the large corporations' share of R & D is about twice their share of patents.[11]

THE GEORGE WASHINGTON UNIVERSITY

[10] Only 81 of the 200 largest nonfinancial corporations in 1963 are on our list of domestic corporations with patent portfolios of 200 or more patents in 1962. The list of the largest nonfinancial corporations comes from R. J. Larner, 'The 200 Largest Nonfinancial Corporations', *American Economic Review*, September 1966, (Vol. 56), pp. 777–87.

[11] For example, the 20th corporation in 1962 had a calculated 4.7 times as many patents as the 100th, but a calculated 8.9 times as much R & D in 1958. In 1962, the 20th patent holder was Honeywell, with an actual 4.0 times as many patents as Boeing, the 100th.

SHORT-RUN COST FUNCTIONS OF A MULTI-PRODUCT FIRM

by Ronald S. Koot and David A. Walker

I. INTRODUCTION

In discussions of the neoclassical theory of the firm in economic theory textbooks, short-run average and marginal cost curves of a firm are U-shaped. However, U-shaped curves derived from the principle of diminishing returns is only one of many hypotheses about the forms of cost functions to be subjected to empirical verification. An alternative hypothesis is that of constant short-run marginal cost. In at least four industry studies without critical shortcomings, marginal costs have been found to be constant in the short-run.[1] Three of these are Dean's[2] studies of a furniture factory, a hosiery mill, and a department store. Another study is of a multi-product food processing firm by J. Johnston.[3] Although the results of these studies differ from what is predicted by the traditional theory of the firm, A. A. Walters concludes that '. . . the evidence in favor of constant marginal cost is not overwhelming. Certainly the revision of theory to include this phenomenon is not an urgent matter'.[4]

In this paper, linear, quadratic, and cubic cost functions are tested for a multi-product manufacturing firm. It is found that the short-run total cost functions are linear for each product and for the firm as a whole. The implication is that marginal and average variable costs are constant over the observed range of outputs.

According to the management of the firm, several observations on output are at more than 90 per cent of 'full-capacity' output. There are no observations at 'full-capacity' output. Marginal and average variable costs do rise at some output level. However, the data employed in this paper do not allow a conclusion as to whether costs rise sharply but smoothly between 90 per cent capacity and

[1] A comprehensive review of the literature on cost functions is given in A. A. Walters, 'Production and Cost Functions: An Econometric Survey', *Econometrica*, Vol. 31 (January–April, 1963), pp. 39–52.

[2] Dean, Joel, 'Statistical Determination of Costs with Special Reference to Marginal Costs', *Studies in Business Administration*, Vol. 7, No. 1, 1936.

Dean, Joel, 'Statistical Cost Functions of a Hosiery Mill', *Studies in Business Administration*, Vol. 14, No. 3, 1941.

Dean, Joel, 'Department Store Cost Functions', *Studies in Mathematical Economics and Econometrics*, ed. Oskar Lange (London: Cambridge University Press, 1942), pp. 222–54.

[3] Johnston, J., *Statistical Cost Functions* (New York: McGraw-Hill Book Co., Inc., 1960), pp. 87–97.

[4] Walters, *op. cit.*, p. 51.

'full-capacity' or whether the average variable cost curve is L-shaped with costs rising vertically at 'full-capacity'.

Finding additional evidence to support the conclusion of studies by Dean and Johnston on linear cost functions is not a useless exercise. The current interest in optimal decision-making for the firm hinges on applications of linear programming. These models rely on maximizing or minimizing a linear function subject to a set of constraints. For the firm that cannot readily influence its demand, as is the case for most manufacturing plants, the goal of the firm is usually to minimize costs. If the firm's total cost function is linear, linear decision models can often be constructed, since there are numerous mathematical approaches to forming an appropriate constraint set.[5]

The data and estimation technique used in this paper are described in section II. The regression results for each product are presented in section III. In section IV, cost interrelationships are discussed. It is shown that the relationship between cost and output for any product is independent of the cost–output relationships for all other products. In section V, two aggregated cost–output relationships are estimated using different indices to find a measure of aggregate output for the firm.

II. THE DATA AND ESTIMATION TECHNIQUE

Data have been obtained from a major American firm engaged in producing ten types of plastic containers. Monthly observations for the period January 1966 to September 1967, are reported on (a) physical production of each product and (b) direct per-unit costs for labor, machinery, and materials. No attempt is made to allocate indirect or overhead costs among the ten products. Such methods of allocation are arbitrary and, in any case, changes in indirect costs during the 21-month period are not substantial. During the period under study, plant capacity is fixed, and all factor prices are fixed by contract.[6] Furthermore, wide variations in output occur during the observed 21 months. Several observations are over 90 per cent of 'full-capacity' output level as defined by the management of the

[5] For example, see Ijiri, Yuji, *Management Goals and Accounting for Control* (Amsterdam: North Holland Publishing Company, 1965).

[6] Although wage rates were fixed by contract, the labor contract did contain an escalator clause adjusting wages for changes in the Consumer Price Index. To remove the influence of factor price changes in the cost–output relationships, labor costs need only be deflated by the same price index. In any case, the wage changes were not substantial and, according to management, did not lead to the varying of factor proportions in the production process. The nature of the factor price data eliminates one potential source of linearity bias. See Johnston, *op. cit.*, pp. 170–6.

TABLE I

REGRESSION RESULTS FOR PRODUCTS

Product	Hypothesis	b_0	b_1	b_2	b_3	R^2	d-Statistic	$\hat{\rho}$	Coefficient of Variation (%)
1	I	648.909 (1031.979)	425.938 (10.603)**			.988	1.60		120.1
	II	−403.776 (1117.349)	503.406 (41.507)**	−.403 (.209)		.990	1.59		
	III	123.063 (1122.618)	405.169 (72.342)**	1.157 (.980)	−.0055 (.0034)	.992	1.73		
2	I	−665.256 (746.712)	277.961 (7.681)**			.986	1.81		112.4
	II	364.924 (550.305)	199.407 (17.121)**	.436 (.090)**		.994	2.24		
	III	76.664 (546.585)	258.380 (37.379)**	−.330 (.446)	.0024 (.0013)	.995	2.05		
3	I	2856.548 (3038.692)	420.655 (41.010)**			.847	2.39		64.4
	II	480.967 (3738.013)	538.344 (116.188)**	−.912 (.843)		.856	2.42		
	III	−562.838 (4517.404)	662.324 (309.203)**	−3.088 (5.085)	.0096 (.0220)	.858	2.38		
4	I	318.179 (728.914)	258.084 (5.250)**			.992	1.63		90.7
	II	396.455 (834.334)	255.095 (15.112)**	.012 (.057)		.992	1.61		
	III	−38.490 (874.589)	301.431 (36.933)**	−.407 (.311)	.0009 (.0007)	.993	1.62††		
5	I	−2138.314 (3299.575)	419.421 (26.864)**			.928	1.65		96.6
	II	136.973 (3352.630)	246.706 (97.797)**	.873 (.477)		.939	1.49††		
	III	−40.471 (3576.918)	300.903 (309.280)	.171 (3.821)	.0022 (.0116)	.939	1.49††		

TABLE I (*cont.*)

Product	*Hypothesis*	b_0	b_1	b_2	b_3	R^2	d-*Statistic*	$\hat{\rho}$	*Coefficient of Variation* (%)
6	I	6384.367 (8059.923)	322.886 (34.903)**			.818	.94†		51.5
	II	−4184.877 (9949.536)	487.871 (103.847)**	−.440 (.262)		.843	.86†		
	III	−508.584 (10806.340)	300.425 (233.162)	.828 (1.435)	−.0022 (.0024)	.850	.80†		
6′	I	−28438.648 (5707.139)**	316.993 (23.440)**			.910	1.80	.4730	
	II	−34877.798 (7465.759)**	412.629 (76.865)**	−.224 (.172)		.919	1.57	.4421	
	III	−28041.474 (8638.585)**	162.184 (188.252)	1.273 (1.047)	−.0023 (.0016)	.928	1.65††	.4715	
7	I	1752.642 (4132.142)	292.316 (18.906)**			.926	1.17†		78.5
	II	7676.778 (5290.321)	164.599 (78.068)*	.340 (.202)		.936	1.39††		
	III	1833.758 (5478.575)	443.659 (144.788)**	−1.768 (.972)	.0039 (.0018)*	.951	1.58††		
7′	I	−643.819 (4337.019)	302.151 (20.615)**			.918	1.21††	.0757	
	II	6707.732 (6517.810)	172.106 (89.557)	.326 (.222)		.928	1.33††	.0146	
	III	−3116.019 (7071.263)	511.587 (163.296)**	−2.042 (1.016)	.0042 (.0018)*	.943	1.54††	.0197	
8	I	172.060 (2388.007)	411.653 (12.211)**			.984	1.18†		48.7
	II	−804.875 (3418.820)	430.477 (47.763)**	−.061 (.150)		.984	1.26††		
	III	790.569 (5131.953)	365.045 (161.528)*	.448 (1.208)	−.0011 (.0025)	.984	1.27††		

TABLE I (*cont.*)

Product	*Hypothesis*	b_0	b_1	b_2	b_3	R^2	d-*Statistic*	$\hat{\rho}$	*Coefficient of Variation* (%)
	I	1046.867 (1442.133)	403.568 (11.064)**			.986	1.74	.4009	
8′	II	1582.522 (2096.132)	387.696 (43.690)**	.055 (.139)		.985	1.61	.3635	
	III	2193.395 (2934.418)	347.517 (138.009)*	.369 (1.027)	−.0007 (.0021)	1.61††	1.61††	.3621	
	I	645.323 (1345.056)	486.013 (14.948)**			.982	1.11†		87.3
9	II	−472.476 (1950.177)	531.914 (59.080)**	−.249 (.310)		.983	1.23††		
	III	342.594 (2541.533)	462.825 (146.842)**	.824 (2.103)	−.0040 (.0078)	.983	1.17††		
	I	400.452 (921.523)	480.334 (10.991)**			.990	1.88	.4257	
9′	II	190.671 (1221.817)	497.441 (49.194)**	−.089 (.261)		.989	1.79	.3594	
	III	1117.046 (1439.237)	363.782 (129.721)**	1.963 (1.885)	−.0077 (.0070)	.989	1.68	.3853	
	I	1615.229 (1920.127)	351.875 (21.693)**			.966	1.89		131.9
10	II	1000.417 (1545.855)	545.735 (49.417)**	−1.010 (.244)**		.966	1.53††		
	III	143.965 (1384.346)	320.789 (91.652)**	1.972 (1.094)	−.0090 (.0033)*	.976	1.66††		

* Indicates significance at the 5 per cent level.
** Indicates significance at the 1 per cent level.
† Indicates autocorrelation at the 5 per cent level.
†† Indicates test for autocorrelation inconclusive at the 5 per cent level.

firm. Therefore, the cost–output relationship is not observed for only a narrow range of outputs well below the 'full-capacity' level.

Ideally, an investigation of the relationship between costs and outputs should be part of a model which includes a description of the firm's decision to produce at a given level of output. Hence, the econometric problem is one of simultaneous-equation estimation techniques. However, output can be treated as an exogenous variable in the cost function, and the technique of single-equation least squares can be employed if one of two conditions exists: (1) the disturbance terms in the output-determination equations and the cost functions are independent, or (2) the differences between planned and actual output are small and have little effect on the disturbance term in the cost-function.[7] Data are also reported by the multi-product firm for planned production for each of the 21 months. The differences between planned production and actual production are small. Thus, single-equation least squares is used to test the following three hypotheses about the cost–output relationships for each product and for the firm as a whole:

$$\text{I} \quad C_t = \beta_0 + \beta_1 Y_t + \varepsilon_t$$
$$\text{II} \quad C_t = \beta_0^1 + \beta_1^1 Y_t + \beta_2^1 Y_t^2 + \varepsilon_t^1$$
$$\text{III} \quad C_t = \beta_0^{11} + \beta_1^{11} Y_t + \beta_2^{11} Y_t^2 + \beta_3^{11} Y_t^3 + \varepsilon_t^{11}$$

where Y_t is current output, and C_t is total direct costs and is the sum of labor, machine, and materials costs. Estimates of the coefficients of the variables are tested for statistical significance using the t-test, and tests for autocorrelated disturbances are made using the Durbin–Watson d-statistic.[8]

III. REGRESSION RESULTS FOR PRODUCTS

Table I presents regression results of hypotheses I–III for each of the ten products. For each product, the coefficient of variation is calculated to determine if the observations on output have a range great enough to justify regression analysis. The coefficients of variation have a range of 48.7 per cent to 131.9 per cent. These coefficients compare favorably with other studies.[9] In Table I, b_0 is the estimate of the intercept, and b_1, b_2, and b_3 are the estimates of the coefficients of Y_t, Y_t^2, and Y_t^3, respectively. R^2 is the coefficient of determination, and the standard errors of the coefficient estimates are in parentheses.

[7] Johnston, *op. cit.*, pp. 37–43.
[8] Significance points of the d-statistic for alternative sample sizes and probability levels are given in J. Durbin and G. S. Watson, 'Testing for Serial Correlation in Least Squares Regression', *Biometrika*, 38 (1951), Parts 1 and 2.
[9] For example, see Johnston, *op. cit.*, p. 88.

The d-statistics indicate that there is autocorrelation at the .05 probability level in regressions I–III for Product 6 and regression I for Products 7, 8, and 9. To eliminate the autocorrelated disturbance in any regression, a transformation is applied to the cost and output variables by assuming a first-order autoregressive scheme, $\varepsilon_t = \rho\varepsilon_{t-1} + \mu_t$. An estimate of ρ, $\hat{\rho}$, is found by applying ordinary least squares to this first-order scheme. The value $\hat{\rho}$ is then used to calculate the transformed variables $C_t - \hat{\rho}C_{t-1}$ and $Y_t - \hat{\rho}Y_{t-1}$, $t = 2, 3, \ldots, 21$, and these transformed variables are used to re-run the regressions. Since tests for autocorrelation in regressions II and III for products 7, 8, and 9 are inconclusive, this method of transformation is also applied to the variables in these regressions. The regression results of the transformed variables are given as products 6′, 7′, 8′, and 9′ in Table I. Also given in Table I are the values of $\hat{\rho}$ used in transforming the variables in each regression. The transformations improve the d-statistics for each product except product 7. The tests for autocorrelation in each of the regressions for product 7′ is inconclusive.

Table I shows that Hypothesis I, a linear total cost function, can be accepted for each product. The coefficient estimates of Y_t^2 are significant only for Hypothesis II for Products 2 and 10. In Product 2, the inclusion of the variable Y_t^2 explains only an additional .8 per cent of the variation in costs, and the coefficient estimate loses significance when the variable Y_t^3 is added. In Product 10, the inclusion of Y_t^2 adds nothing to an explanation of the variation in costs, and again, the coefficient loses significance when the variable Y_t^3 is added. The coefficient estimates of Y_t^3 are significant at the .05 level for Products 7′ and 10, but the inclusion of Y_t^3 explains only an additional 2.5 per cent and 1 per cent of the variation in costs for Products 7′ and 10, respectively. For all cases except Product 6′, the intercept estimates are not significantly different from zero. This implies that average variable direct cost is constant and equal to the constant marginal costs for the observed range of outputs. For Product 6′, b_0 is not an estimate of β_0, but of $\beta_0(1-.473)$ because of the transformation employed. However, the transformation of the variables does not destroy any of the relationships found for Product 6, and an intercept coefficient not different from zero can probably be accepted for Product 6′ also.

IV. COST INTERRELATIONSHIPS

In a multi-product firm, several products are produced simultaneously, and the cost–output relationship for each product might depend upon or be influenced by the levels of output of other products. Such cost interrelationships are likely to have consequences

TABLE II

COST INTERRELATIONSHIPS

Products	$r_{CI.Y}$	d-*Statistic*	$\hat{p}$	r_{IY}
1	−.1509	1.64		−.1984
2	.1105	1.86		.3030
3	.0164	2.31		.0350
4	−.3155	1.32**		−.1080
5	.0254	1.64		.1905
6	−.0715	1.83		.2765
7	−.0854	1.16**		−.0845
7′	−.2184	1.55	.0903	−.0881
8	−.1695	1.10*		−.2002
8′	−.2598	1.64	.4320	.1046
9	−.2777	1.13*		.1774
9′	−.2523	1.74	.4232	.1556
10	.3102	1.96		.3451

* Indicates autocorrelation at the 5 per cent level.
** Indicates test for autocorrelation inconclusive at the 5 per cent level.

for the conclusion made in the previous section that average variable direct costs are constant and equal to marginal costs. If there are cost interrelationships, the firm is unlikely to be able to operate over wide ranges of output under conditions of constant average variable cost for each product.

If cost interrelationships exist among products, larger outputs of all products but one should increase the cost of producing a given output of that one product. The first-order correlation coefficients, $r_{CI.Y}$ show the relationship between the cost of producing a given level of one product and the output levels of all the other products. None of the values of $r_{CI.Y}$ for Products 1–10 in Table II is significant at the .05 level. The simple correlation coefficients, r_{IY}, indicate the relationship between the output of one product and the outputs of all other products. Again, none of these coefficients is significant at the .05 level. The d-statistics indicate that there is autocorrelation in the regressions for products 8 and 9 at the .05 probability level. Although the test for autocorrelation in the regression for product 7 is inconclusive, the d-statistic barely falls into the inconclusive range. When the variables C_t, Y_t, and I_t are transformed by assuming a first-order autoregressive scheme for products 7, 8, and 9, the results are those given as 7′, 8′, and 9′ in Table II. None of the values of $r_{CI.Y}$ or r_{IY} is significant at the .05 level, and the d-statistics for products 7′, 8′, and 9′ indicate that there is no autocorrelation at the .05 probability level. Thus, the existence of cost interrelationships among products is ruled out, and the firm can likely operate over wide ranges of output under conditions of constant average variable costs for each product.

V. REGRESSION RESULTS FOR THE AGGREGATE COST–OUTPUT RELATIONSHIPS

Hypotheses I–III are tested for the firm's aggregate cost–output relationship. The cost data are aggregated by summing all product costs in each period. The data on physical output are aggregated by using base period product prices as weights and by finding the sum

$$Q_t = \sum_{j=1}^{10} P_{jo} Y_{jt} \quad t = 1, \ldots, 21$$

for each of the 21 monthly periods. The results of regressing aggregated costs, $\sum_{j=1}^{10} C_{jt}$, on aggregated outputs are presented in Table III.

The coefficient of variation is 28.5 per cent and indicates a range

TABLE III

REGRESSION RESULTS FOR THE AGGREGATE COST–OUTPUT RELATIONSHIPS

Hypothesis	b_0	b_1	b_2	b_3	R^2	d-*Statistic*	*Coefficient of Variation* (%)
I	56392.870 (27690.867)	3.368 (.270)**			.891	1.88	28.5
II	−22343.057 (99367.413)	4.993 (1.992)**	.0000		.895	1.92	
III	−80182.433 (353436.282)	6.874 (11.193)	.0000	.0000	.895	1.93	

* Indicates significance at the 5 per cent level.
** Indicates significance at the 1 per cent level.

of observations great enough to justify applying regression analysis. The d-statistics indicate that there is no autocorrelation at the .05 probability level. The only coefficient estimate that is statistically significant is the coefficient of Q_t, and it is significant at the .01 level. Again, the same hypothesis that is accepted for each of the individual products is accepted for the aggregate cost–output relationship—total direct costs are linearly related to output.

Following Johnston,[10] an alternative method of aggregating

[10] Johnston, *op. cit.*, p. 96.

physical outputs is also used. This output index employs average variable costs as weights where average variable costs are taken as the coefficient estimates of b_1 from Hypothesis I for each product in Table I. The output index is:

$$Q'_t = \sum_{j=1}^{10} b_{1j} Y_{jt} \quad t = 1, \ldots, 21$$

where the subscript j refers to the jth product. Defining Q'_t in this manner permits a joint test of the constancy and independence of the average variable costs of the individual products. Johnston says that Q'_t is

> . . . in fact, an estimate of what aggregate variable costs would be if average variable cost were constant for each product and independent of the outputs of the other products. Correlating the actual aggregate variable cost with this index should then give a correlation coefficient and a regression slope which both approach +1 the more perfectly the two assumptions are realized.[11]

The results from regression aggregate variable costs on Q'_t are:

$$\sum_{i=1}^{10} C_{jt} = \underset{(22270.944)}{5897.821} + \underset{(.058)}{1.026}\, Q'_t.$$

The regression slope does not differ significantly from 1 and r = .971. It is concluded from this test that the average variable costs of the individual products are constant and independent of each other. Similar results are derived from both aggregated relationships even though different sets of weights are used in the aggregation procedure. Also, the results and conclusions that are reached in this section and section IV are the same even though the tests of interrelationships among products are different.

VI. CONCLUSIONS

In this paper, short-run cost functions are estimated for a multiproduct firm. Contrary to what is expected from the traditional theory of the firm, the average variable cost curves estimated in this paper do not have the familiar U-shape. For each individual product and for the aggregate cost–output relationship, total direct costs are linearly related to current output. Average variable costs are constant and equal to constant marginal costs. No cost interrelationships

[11] *Ibid.*, p. 96.

among products are found, and it is concluded that the constant average variable costs of the individual products are independent of each other. If subsequent short-run cost curve studies arrive at similar results, perhaps the phenomenon of constant marginal cost should be incorporated into the mainstream of neoclassical theory.

THE PENNSYLVANIA STATE UNIVERSITY

ON THE SALES REVENUE MAXIMIZATION HYPOTHESIS

by C. J. HAWKINS*

A. INTRODUCTION

FEW recent theories of the firm have aroused more interest than Professor Baumol's Sales Revenue Maximization Hypothesis. His hypothesis was put forward in an attempt to derive a determinate solution for oligopoly[1] along the lines that some firms may aim to maximize total sales revenue subject to the constraint that they make profits at a level they deem to be the minimum necessary to keep shareholders satisfied and to make possible the raising of funds for future investment for growth.

Baumol's hypothesis proved interesting in that it seemed to be determinate for oligopoly, it could explain price changes in response to changes in fixed costs, and it gave considerable weight to advertising and customer service forms of competition, which are known to be prevalent in most oligopoly markets.

In 1962, however, W. G. Shepherd's critique[2] of Baumol's theory seemed to narrow down the fields in which it might be useful to a limited number of not very prevalent forms of competition. In particular, Shepherd's article aimed 'to dispel any lingering notion that sales maximisation can explain the behaviour of the firm in conditions of oligopoly as this term is customarily defined, that is, where inter-dependence in decision-making is present in a group of rival firms'.

The purpose of this paper is to reconsider the Baumol model in the light of Shepherd's critique to see whether any firm conclusions can be drawn, even in inter-dependent oligopoly—the case that Shepherd mainly considers. The relevant sections of Shepherd's critique are quoted below after a brief restatement of Baumol's basic model.

B. OUTLINE OF BAUMOL'S MODEL

Figure 1 shows the results of the basic Baumol hypothesis. The profit maximizer selects output A while the sales revenue maximizer

* An earlier version of this paper appeared in The Southampton Series of Discussion Papers in Economics and Econometrics, January 1969.

[1] W. J. Baumol, 'On the Theory of Oligopoly', *Economica*, Vol. XXV (1958); and in *Business Behaviour, Value and Growth* (New York, 1959); and in *Economic Theory and Operations Analysis* (London, 1961).

[2] W. G. Shepherd, 'On Sales Maximising and Oligopoly Behaviour', *Economica* (1962).

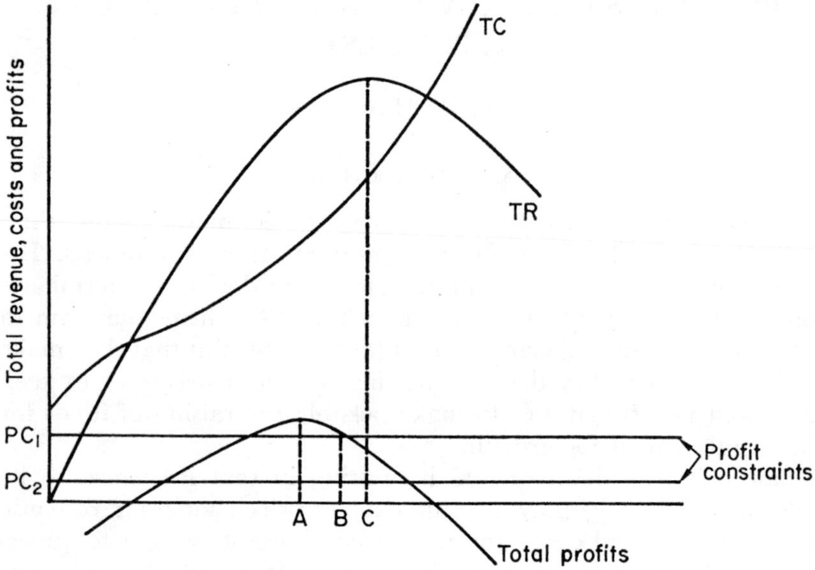

Fig. 1

selects output B if its profit constraint (minimum acceptable profit level) is at the level PC1 in the diagram. If, however, its profit constraint were only at the level PC2 it would be able to maximize total revenue before its profits had fallen to this level, i.e. it is unconstrained by profit requirements and chooses output C where revenue is maximized.

C. THE SHEPHERD CRITIQUE

Shepherd's analysis uses severely kinked demand curves, to show that output will usually be the same for both the revenue and profit maximizer.

The relevant passage from Shepherd is:

> If the kink is very definite—and it will seem to be so under conditions of strong inter-dependence—the range of discontinuity of the marginal revenue curve will extend below the *x*-axis, and the total revenue curve will reach its peak at the level of output where the kink occurs. Then, as shown in diagram 2 *A* will coincide with *C*, and the firm will stay at the output level of the kink no matter which motivation is followed. In this situation, then, the sales maximisation approach does not add to our understanding of inter-dependent oligopoly situations.

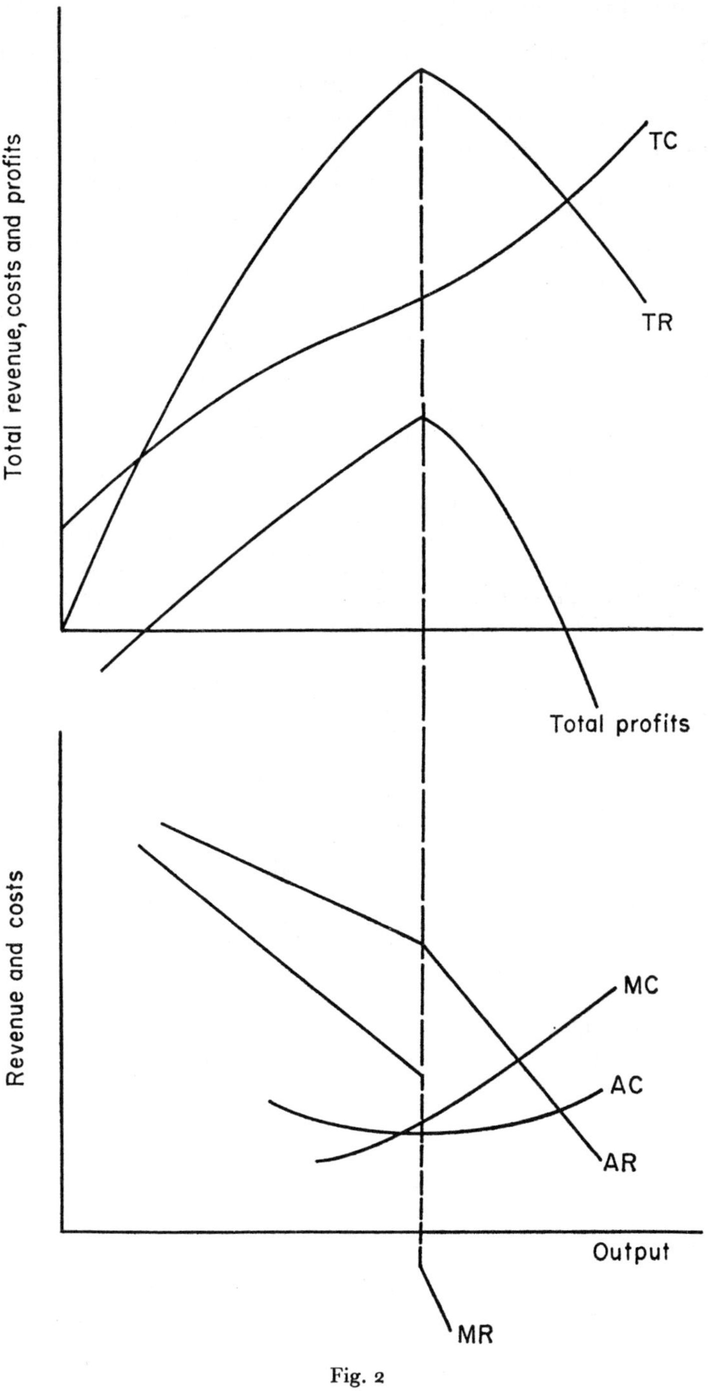
Total revenue, costs and profits
TC
TR
Total profits
Revenue and costs
MC
AC
AR
Output
MR

Fig. 2

Shepherd continues:

> If the kink is less pronounced the foregoing argument must be qualified in degree, but its essential point still stands. Thus, even if—in the case of weak inter-dependence—the discontinuity in marginal revenue does not extend below the *x*-axis, *B* and *C* will remain close to *A*; that is, sales-maximisation will make only a slight difference. One can put it in more general terms: the more there is of oligopolistic inter-dependence, the less will sales-maximisation affect or explain output decisions. Baumol's approach therefore turns out to be a possible theory for almost every market situation *except* inter-dependent oligopoly, and, of course, except perfect competition. This is not to deny that the approach may prove useful for non-collusive, non-inter-dependent firms whose access to ample profits permits them the luxury of maximising something else instead of profits. For example, Baumol's conclusions about product-mix decisions, *advertising*, and the role of changes in fixed costs in influencing output decisions, are not challenged at all by the arguments in this article, *except in their relevance to firms whose rivals react to their decisions*. [The italics are mine.]

D. ANALYSIS OF THE SHEPHERD CRITIQUE

It is important to note that Shepherd accepts Baumol's conclusions about advertising and so on '*except in their relevance to firms whose rivals react to their decisions*'. While Shepherd's critique is accepted in full where competition takes the form only of price changes, its validity seems doubtful in the typical oligopoly situation where advertising and other forms of non-price competition also take place.

The validity of Shepherd's critique is doubted because once advertising is included the SRM (Sales Revenue Maximizing) and PM (Profit Maximizing) firms are no longer choosing where to settle on a total revenue curve, rather they are deciding which of the many total revenue curves open to them should be chosen in the first place. Since advertising, etc. *shifts* a demand curve (whether or not it is kinked) there must be a new total revenue curve corresponding to each shift in the average revenue schedule. The fact that total revenue is at a peak at the kink where maximum profits occur does not mean that both firms will choose the same level of output unless we can prove that they must necessarily choose to operate on the same total revenue schedule. Certainly both firms may operate at the maximum profits position of their chosen total revenue curve (at the kink) but they may have each chosen *different* curves. It is perhaps not the movement along a curve that needs to interest us most, so much as the shifts in the curves themselves, which can be induced by advertising and other non-price forms of competition.

While avoiding the problems of 3-dimensional diagrams and the complications of mathematics around curves involving kinks, we can analyse the choice of output, advertising outlay, etc., by means of one simple diagram. Figure 3 shows the maximum total revenue

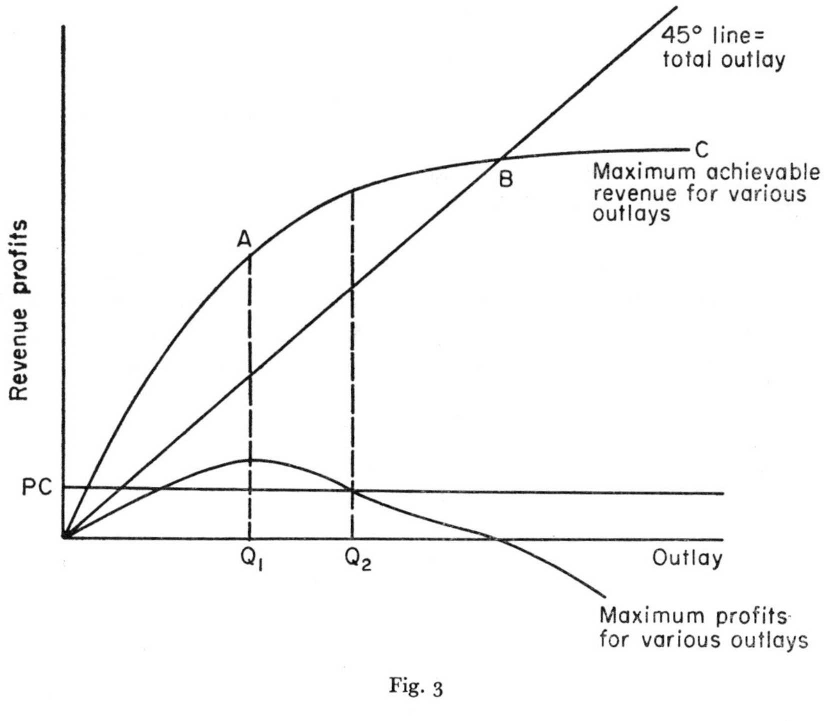

Fig. 3

possible (line OABC) for all possible levels of outlay on optimum mixtures of production and advertising costs. If profits were identically equal to zero at all levels of outlay then (OABC) would be a 45° line. The gap between (OABC) and the 45° line shows the maximum total profits possible at all levels of outlay on optimum combinations of advertising and production costs. This information is then translated on to a maximum total profits curve. The SRM firm's profit constraint is shown as PC.

The PM and SRM firms choose outlays Q_1 and Q_2 respectively. The only case where one can get identical outlays is where the profit constraint happens by coincidence to be identically equal to maximum achievable profits. In all other cases the SRM firm will choose a different outlay from the profit maximizer. This does not of course necessarily mean that it would choose a higher or even a different level of *output*.

Since the two firms choose different outlays we can now consider what this implies in terms of advertising and *output*. Assume, as in the Shepherd analysis, that the kink is sufficiently severe that

(a) the range of discontinuity in marginal revenue extends through the horizontal axis, and

(b) the marginal cost curve intersects marginal revenue within the range of discontinuity.

Assume that these conditions are met at all levels of advertising and output that yield profits equal to, or greater than, the profit constraint.

Since both firms must choose different levels of outlay (shown above) the following conclusions can be drawn:

(a) As both firms are assumed because of the nature of the kink to have no inducement to change price, both must operate at the kink in one of the average revenue curves open to them. They both operate at a kink but, since they choose different levels of outlay, they operate on different demand curves due to shifts induced by different levels of advertising.

(b) Since the price charged is the same by both firms—due to the nature of the kink—it follows that increased advertising can only be used to achieve greater demand at the same price and not to gain higher prices for the same or smaller quantities.

(c) It follows from (b) that in response to advertising, the kink in the average revenue curve (which reflects a given price) must move horizontally to the right as advertising increases.

(d) Hence the sales revenue maximizer under these conditions can only achieve more revenue by choosing a greater output level and by advertising more to achieve it.

(e) The sales revenue maximizer can always achieve greater revenue than the profit maximizer chooses, in all cases except where its profit constraint happens to be identically equal to maximum achievable profits.[3]

[3] This conclusion holds even without Baumol's assumption that the marginal revenue of advertising is always positive. In practice it is not necessary to assume demand increases for ever as advertising is raised. The PM firm cannot go to the point where advertising no longer raises sales since at this point its MR from advertising is zero but the MC of advertising is positive which clearly conflicts with PM. It is therefore always possible for the SRM firm to get more output at the same price as the PM firm simply by advertising more. This would only not be true if sales were not responsive to any level of advertising at all, or if one were prepared to accept a freak case such that total revenue responds to

Under the conditions stated above, we can conclude that wherever advertising and/or other non-price forms of competition are possible (almost everywhere in oligopoly?), the sales revenue maximizer will choose to produce a greater output and, in order to gain demand for it, will advertise more than the profit maximizer. Both firms will charge the same price.

Far from weakening Baumol's arguments, kinked demand curves lead us to far stronger conclusions than Baumol could draw, i.e. the only tenable major conclusion from Baumol's model without kinked demand curves was that sales revenue maximizers would in general advertise more than profit maximizers. No conclusions about price or output were possible. The reason for this is that the SRM firm may find it beneficial to use the extra demand created by higher advertising to enable it to charge a higher price for smaller quantities.

In fact, once we drop the assumption of a markedly kinked demand curve, all that we can say about the SRM firm is that it can choose between many combinations of levels of prices, advertising outlay and output. About the only combinations it cannot choose are the same or less advertising than the PM firm allied to higher prices (whether it chooses the same, a greater or a lower output), since these cases directly imply either that it makes higher profits than the PM firm or that the PM firm is not operating on its demand curve.[4]

If Shepherd is right in believing that markedly kinked demand curves are typical of oligopoly, a serious problem emerges for empirical testing of whether revenue maximization is a dominant motive of some firms. Even armed with detailed knowledge of a firm's total revenue and total cost curves, its selling price, levels of output and profits, one could not say whether it was operating at the point of maximum profits. The reason for this is that both SRM and PM firms will operate where MC = MR on their chosen cost and revenue schedules.

To prove the firm is revenue maximizing involves proving that it could have chosen to operate on a more profitable demand curve at a different cost level, i.e. the level of its advertising, etc. is non-optimal from the profit maximization point of view.[5]

advertising up to a particular level (which happens to yield maximum profits) but that it then abruptly declines as advertising rises, i.e. the TR curve is kinked along the advertising outlay axis.

[4] It is also obviously true that the SRM firm cannot choose a lower price and a lower output since this clearly implies non-maximization of revenue. The equilibrium conditions for the revenue maximizer when the demand curve is not kinked have been developed in a forthcoming article by the present author: 'The Revenue Maximization Oligopoly model: a Comment', *American Economic Review*, June 1970.

[5] This conclusion may add still further to the problems recently raised concerning the difficulties of empirically testing the hypothesis. See *Journal of Industrial Economics*, (a)

REVENUE MAXIMIZATION IN A MULTI-PRODUCT WORLD

1. *General*

It is stressed that all the foregoing applies to a one-good model where the firm is only concerned with production of one commodity. Once the SRM firm is faced with a multi-product choice some further conclusions emerge.

Since Sales Revenue Maximization can lead to results different from profit maximization in a one-good model, it is worth considering whether general economic conclusions about firms' behaviour in a multi-product world may now need to be modified. Sales Revenue Maximization is examined below both in and out of equilibrium, bearing in mind the opportunities that may be open to a particular firm in industries other than its own.

Clearly the more money shareholders lend a firm the higher will be the absolute profit constraint. The profit constraint (as Baumol himself accepts)[6] can therefore be expressed as a minimum average rate of return on capital employed. If we are talking about the long-run behaviour of a firm it is clearly more sensible to talk of rates of return than of an absolute profit level since vastly different amounts of capital employed may be involved over long time-periods. It is assumed that in no case will shareholders accept a rate of return below 'normal'.

2. *Equilibrium Conditions*

In equilibrium profits are assumed to have dropped to 'normal' in all industries. Faced with this situation the SRM firm can do nothing except maximize profits, since any other policy must involve making sub-normal profits. To make sub-normal profits clearly conflicts with the need to meet a constraint level rate of return—which it can hardly be argued could be less than the 'normal' rate. In equilibrium, therefore, a divergence between profit maximization and Sales Revenue Maximization, subject to a profit constraint, is not possible since the constraint must be identically equal to maximum profits in this case.

3. *Non-Equilibrium Conditions*

One can now consider whether Baumol's model significantly alters our conclusions about firms' behaviour at times when all industries are not in equilibrium, i.e. when the rate of return on capital is in some cases in excess of normal. Since so many econ-

M. Hall, 'Sales Revenue Maximization: An Empirical Examination', April 1967; (b) L. Waverman, 'Sales Revenue Maximization—A Note', November 1968; (c) M. Hall, 'Sales Revenue Maximization—A Reply', November 1968.

[6] *Business Behaviour, Value and Growth*, p. 68.

omists believe that many industries spend much of their time out of equilibrium (but possibly en route towards it), Baumol's model would still be of value if it had predictive powers under non-equilibrium conditions. Assume some or all industries are out of equilibrium (including the SRM firm's own industry). The SRM firm will simply invest money raised from shareholders wherever it can obtain, in any industry, a return greater than the constraint rate. It will invest in its own industry and in all others that meet this condition. Its revenue will rise, so will its profits. Nor will it stop there. It will then borrow non-equity funds at the market rate and continue investing in its own industry and in others. So long as there are industries out of equilibrium where it is possible to make supernormal profits, the SRM firm will keep on investing in them. This, however, does not make the SRM firm any different from a normal profit maximizing firm. Once we postulate out of equilibrium positions with supernormal profits, the profit maximizer would be investing there anyway. Both firms invest wherever there is a profit. We can therefore say that wherever there are some industries out of equilibrium with supernormal profits possible the SRM firm cannot logically do anything different from a profit maximizer. In most growth economies this situation must cover most firms for most of the time.

If at any point in time the SRM firm had established plant at maximum profits output to produce every single product which allowed supernormal profits, it still need not resort to investing at a loss to gain revenue. It could now begin to take over or merge with other firms: it would continue to do so until no takeover was profitable (above 'normal'). Only when the revenue maximizer had entered every industry where it could invest at a profit and only when it had taken over every firm that it could buy at an expected future profit could it behave differently from a profit maximizer. The problem then becomes that if a large number of firms are investing in every profitable venture they can find (as revenue maximizers must—and so of course must profit maximizers) then one must clearly expect profits to decline to normal—at which point the revenue maximizer's profit constraint will prevent it from expanding any further.

There is, however, a special case where the SRM firm can be different from the PM firm. No profitable investments must exist for the SRM firm anywhere in the economy; for example, all industries open to the SRM firm as a potential new entrant must be in equilibrium making only normal profits; at least one of the industries in which the SRM firm operates must be out of equilibrium—profits must be supernormal and all other firms must be excluded from entering, and thereby reducing profits to normal. Since the SRM firm's profits are supernormal and since no profitable new investments are open to it anywhere, it could in this case expand output beyond the maximum profits position. It should be noted however that the SRM firm would incur a loss on the marginal investment since it would be passing the maximum profits position. The SRM firm would, in addition to the already stringent conditions, need to be immune to a takeover bid—since if it expands past maximum profits it could be acquired and run more profitably. Even other revenue maximizers would want to acquire it since they could gain extra revenue *and* extra profit.

It seems to be extremely difficult to construct a plausible case where profit and revenue maximization can yield different results.

In its present form Sales Revenue Maximization seems hardly to modify our predictions about firms' behaviour in a multi-product world. For revenue maximization to yield different results in general from profit maximization it is necessary to reformulate the hypothesis and suggest that some firms are aiming at Sales Revenue Maximization for a particular product. Instead of merely wanting a large total turnover they must want, for example, to be the biggest producer of cars in their country. If that is all that they want then one could apply Baumol's single-product analysis. Sales Revenue Maximization for a particular product would yield different results from profit maximization even where demand curves were heavily kinked.[7] It does not seem implausible that such a motivation might be relevant to particular firms or even to sections of multi-product groups. But the welter of diversification by takeover, mergers and other means in recent years seems to conflict with such a hypothesis being of general application.

E. SUMMARY AND CONCLUSIONS

1. *Single-good model*

Shepherd's critique of Baumol's model, that when demand curves are markedly kinked the SRM firm and PM firm will necessarily have the same price/output equilibrium, holds only when advertising and all other forms of non-price competition are either completely ineffective or impossible.

In the typical oligopoly situation where advertising and service competition are a dominant feature the SRM and PM firms' equili-

[7] As has already been shown above, non-price forms of competition, such as advertising, enable Revenue Maximization to be different from profit maximization despite the presence of kinked demand curves.

bria are likely to be different even where demand curves are heavily kinked. Both firms will operate where MC = MR on their chosen total revenue and total cost curves, which poses an interesting problem for empirical testing of Baumol's hypothesis. But each firm will choose to operate on different revenue and cost curves, made possible by varying expenditure on non-price competition. With heavily kinked demand curves SRM firms will advertise more and produce a bigger output but will charge the same price as PM firms.

Without heavily kinked demand curves, one can say little definite about the SRM firm except that its advertising outlay[8] will in general (but not always) be higher. Having so engendered extra demand for its product the SRM firm may choose the same, higher or lower prices than the PM firm, with consequent variations in output.

2. *Multi-good model*

That Baumol's model can be shown to differ substantially from profit maximization in a one-good model does not mean it has predictive powers for firms in practice, since the typical 'real world' situation is where firms can produce in a range of industries.

Wherever a profitable investment exists it pays the revenue maximizer to undertake it, since it gains revenue at no loss of profits. Therefore so long as it is possible to invest somewhere in the economy at a profit, the SRM firm cannot differ from the PM firm which also invests wherever there is profit. Under these conditions the SRM firm cannot expand beyond the point of maximum profits in its own industry, since this would clearly reduce total profits and the new investment involved in expansion would have been undertaken at an absolute loss.

If to remove the possibility of profitable investments, we assume the whole economy is in equilibrium the SRM firm still cannot differ from PM firms. Profits will everywhere have fallen to 'normal' and the SRM constraint, which cannot be below normal, will preclude any further expansion.

The SRM firm can only behave differently from the PM firm under highly restricted conditions. No profitable investments may exist anywhere in the economy, i.e. all industries must be in equilibrium where freedom of entry exists. In addition, one must assume that the SRM firm's industry is not subject to free entry (otherwise profits would decline to normal and the profit constraint would prevent it from expanding). If there is no possibility of investing at a profit anywhere in the economy and if the SRM firm is so free

[8] And/or outlay on other forms of non-price competition.

from competition as to be able to make supernormal profits in the long run in its own industry, only then could it choose to expand output past the point of maximum profits. This special case however needs to meet such severely restrictive conditions that it can only be of rather limited applicability in practice.

Baumol's SRM hypothesis may add much to our understanding of firms' motivation, some of whom may well *aim* to maximize revenue in a desire to be 'big'. Fortunately, however, it seems that if we want only to predict their economic behaviour, we can do so equally well in most cases by assuming that they are trying to maximize profits. Baumol's hypothesis about *motives* may well be correct; the conclusions for economics about *actions* do not seem to be upsetting. It must be stressed that this conclusion about revenue maximization only holds for the hypothesis in its present formulation. It is possible that the revenue motive works in a different way; it is possible that some firms are driven not by a desire to maximize revenue from whatever source it comes (i.e. to maximize the aggregate of sales of many products) but that some are interested specially in achieving 'size' in a particular field—in revenue maximization for a particular product. Some may prefer to expand sales of their brand of motor car if that is their prime interest rather than to invest more profitably in scrap metal trading. If the revenue motive does sometimes apply in this formulation, then Baumol's formal single product analysis can be applied, as has been shown above, to yield significantly different results from profit maximization even in the case where demand curves are markedly kinked.

UNIVERSITY OF SOUTHAMPTON

EFFECTIVE COMPETITION IN THE TELEVISION RENTALS INDUSTRY: A NOTE

by J. F. Pickering

INTRODUCTION

Many public policy decisions concerning aspects of the structure and behaviour of particular industries depend, in some degree at least, on the view that is taken of the extent and nature of competition that exists in those industries. With the current preoccupation of such bodies as the Monopolies Commission, Prices and Incomes Board and Restrictive Practices Court with these problems this becomes a matter of some importance in answering such questions as: 'Can the forces of the market be relied upon to keep prices and profits reasonable?'; 'Will a merger significantly affect competition in an industry?'; 'Do information agreements inhibit competition?'

There is, however, a problem in deciding just what is meant by competition and identifying whether the necessary conditions do, in fact, exist to a significant and sufficient extent in a particular market for it to be classed as competitive. It has long been recognized that the textbook extreme of perfect competition is neither a necessary nor a desirable condition for a competitive situation. Instead various commentators have chosen to talk in terms of workable or effective competition.[1]

Two recent investigations by different bodies into aspects of the British television rentals industry have served to highlight the importance of assessing the present and future strengths of competitive forces in an industry and the difficulties involved in so doing. The first was carried out by the National Board for Prices and Incomes (N.B.P.I.) whose terms of reference required it to examine the question of costs and charges in the industry.[2] The second was an investigation by the Monopolies Commission to determine whether a proposed merger between the two companies with the largest shares of the television rental market would be expected to operate against the public interest.[3] Both the N.B.P.I. and the Monopolies

[1] E.g. J. M. Clark, 'Towards a Concept of Workable Competition', *American Economic Review*, Vol. XXX (1940), pp. 241–56; J. M. Clark, *Competition as a Dynamic Process* (Brookings), 1961; C. D. Edwards, *Maintaining Competition* (New York), 1949; J. S. Bain, *Industrial Organisation* (Wiley), 2nd edition, 1967.

[2] National Board for Prices and Incomes Report No. 52, *Costs and Charges in the Radio and Television Rental and Relay Industry* (H.M.S.O.), January 1968. Cmnd. 3520 (to be referred to as *Rental Charges*).

[3] The Monopolies Commission, *Thorn Electrical Industries Ltd. and Radio Rentals Ltd. A report on the proposed merger* (H.M.S.O.), July 1968 (to be referred to as *Thorn/Radio Rentals*).

Commission decided that the industry was competitive and the majority of the Monopolies Commission held that it would still remain competitive after Thorn and Radio Rentals had merged. This was a crucial factor in leading the majority of the Monopolies Commission to approve the proposed merger.[4] The N.B.P.I., however, found that, notwithstanding the degree of competition it thought existed in the industry, certain price increases which had occurred in 1966 had not been justified in relation to changes in the level of costs.

The purpose of this note is to examine briefly the information contained in the two reports on competition in the industry and to attempt to assess whether it does, in fact, justify the conclusion that the industry was competitive.

CRITERIA FOR EFFECTIVE COMPETITION

It is clear that in stating that the industry was competitive, the N.B.P.I. and Monopolies Commission were not suggesting that conditions for perfect competition existed. Presumably some concept of effective competition was implied. Unfortunately, however, neither report is specific on this matter and no information is provided on the criteria used in reaching such a conclusion. The first task in this note must therefore be to indicate some objective criteria by which to assess the situation. Recognizing the importance of considerations with regard to both structure and conduct, the requirements for effective competition might be specified as follows:

1. There are a sufficient number of firms either in the market or able to enter the market easily and quickly as a result of low barriers to entry that customers have a wide range of choice between alternative suppliers of the same or readily substitutable products.

2. The market is free of collusion, price leading and predatory practices. Each firm makes its own price and output decisions independently of its rivals but in the awareness that failure to prevent its prices rising above those of its rivals (after allowing for compensating quality differences) will lead to loss of sales revenue as a significant proportion of consumers switch to alternative suppliers. Price and cost changes in the industry are closely related to each other.

[4] Professor T. Barna dissented. He argued that although the industry was competitive while Thorn and Radio Rentals remained independent, the merger would significantly reduce competition and so harm the public interest. The evidence referred to by Professor Barna to justify his own conclusions appears, in certain critical respects, to be at variance with that contained in the majority report. This note is particularly concerned with the majority view of the facts since this carried the necessary two-thirds majority to allow action to be taken on the report. At appropriate points the majority and minority views will be contrasted.

3. Consumers are sufficiently well informed and 'mobile' that they choose rationally between alternative suppliers. There is no significant tendency on the part of consumers to be attached to any particular supplier for reasons of excessive product differentiation, goodwill or inertia.

4. A spirit of competition exists in the industry in which each firm attempts to increase its own market shares and profits through price and product changes and other forms of marketing effort.

In an effectively competitive market certain consequences in terms of performance will follow: prices will tend to be close to average costs and in the long run profits will be reasonable in relation to the degree of risk in the industry, the industry will be progressive with emphasis on product and process innovations, the enterprising and efficient firms will gain at the expense of the unenterprising and inefficient, firms will tend to be close to optimum size and significant excess capacity or insufficient reserve capacity will be avoided.

If these criteria are acceptable, the question we have to try to answer is, how far are they satisfied by the situation reported on in the television rentals market? Not all the conditions would necessarily have to exist together but it is reasonable to suppose that a substantial proportion would be satisfied in a competitive industry and similarly that if the reverse conditions were found to exist in large measure this would suggest that non-competitive or monopolistic pressures predominated. It is convenient to consider the N.B.P.I. and Monopolies Commission reports together since they contain information that is complementary and the Monopolies Commission drew on the findings of the N.B.P.I. in reaching its own conclusions. The information is best considered under the separate heads of structure, conduct (supplier and customer) and performance.

EFFECTIVE COMPETITION AND TELEVISION RENTALS

1. *Structure*

The first problem in identifying the structure of a market is to arrive at a satisfactory definition of that market. This depends on the extent to which there is close substitutability between alternative products. In the case of television rentals the term 'product' refers to the distributive service in making television sets available to the public. Consumers have a choice of three main ways of acquiring a television set; they may purchase a set from a retailer, or they may rent a set from a retailer, or they may rent a set from a specialist rental company.

The Monopolies Commission advanced cogent reasons for the advantages of the specialist rental companies, explaining that servicing was free and reliable, it avoided paying the high cost of replacement picture tubes and that if the customer intended to change his set in under four or five years (which is likely as a result of the rapid technical progress in the industry) renting was probably cheaper than outright purchase. Although the new, cheap black and white transistorized sets were likely to be bought rather than rented, the Commission expected that with the growth of colour television renting would be even more important. The Commission thought there was some competition between the specialist rental companies and electrical goods retailers who were also prepared to rent sets but appeared to recognize that this was of limited significance. The N.B.P.I. thought the level of hire-purchase instalments on bought sets exercised some control over specialist rental charges but also recognized that the competitive restraint was weak. There was therefore agreement that the specialist rental market is well insulated and there can be no suggestion that a high elasticity of substitution with other forms of supply of television sets exercises a significant competitive restraint.

We must next consider the structure of the specialist rental market alone. The N.B.P.I. reported that eighteen companies were responsible for 90 per cent of the specialist rental business and 80 per cent was in the hands of ten companies. The Monopolies Commission listed eleven separate organizations,[5] which it stated had about 90 per cent of the market. In addition, we know from the Commission's report that the two largest companies, Radio Rentals and Thorn, had 45 per cent of the market between them. It appears that after the Thorn/Radio Rentals merger had taken place, between two-thirds and three-quarters of the market would be in the hands of the four largest companies.[6] Neither body offered any comment to indicate whether they considered such a degree of concentration was high, medium or low for a competitive industry. In fact, such a concentration ratio is quite high by any standards and particularly so when compared with other sections of the distributive trades which tend to have low concentration. In terms of structure, therefore, it appears the market is best described as oligopolistic. This does not necessarily invalidate a conclusion that the industry is competitive, it does, however, emphasize the need to confirm this in the light of conduct and performance criteria. Even when account

[5] That is after allowing for the fact that several of the companies listed were owned by other rental organizations (see *Thorn/Radio Rentals*, para. 31).

[6] This note is not concerned with the market for relay services which was more highly concentrated and consisted of a series of local monopolies.

is taken of the rather lower degree of concentration at the time of the rental charges investigation, it does not appear that the N.B.P.I. was justified in reporting: 'There are many hirers of sets in any one locality and most customers can choose between several national firms as well as a variety of local suppliers. . . . The rental business, *therefore*, is highly competitive.'[7]

Low barriers to entry into an industry will increase the threat of potential competition and may help to preserve an effectively competitive situation. The Monopolies Commission considered this possibility and decided that any new entry was likely to come from successful electrical retailers diversifying into the specialist rental market. The Commission did not appear to place much reliance on this aspect and in view of the large minimum optimum size of rental outlets (estimated by the N.B.P.I. to be one renting 3000–4000 sets) the likelihood of new entry does not appear to offer a significant competitive restraint.[8]

2a. *Supplier Conduct*

There is certainly no suggestion that any form of collusive practice existed in the market and yet much of the evidence indicates that the competitive restraints on the independent conduct of suppliers were not strong. In a competitive situation prices charged by individual suppliers would be expected to be more or less in line with each other except where the differences were explicable in terms of real variations in the quality of the product offered by a particular supplier. Significant departures from this principle would suggest a substantial degree of freedom to individual suppliers in setting prices without regard to the level of prices set by rivals and would indicate a strong element of monopolistic protection surrounding each firm due to excessive product differentiation, goodwill, customer inertia, etc.

The N.B.P.I. produced a table showing a range in September 1967 of nearly 20 per cent in the annual rental charges of the specialist rental companies.[9] At one point it seemed to accept that this variation was explicable in terms of differences in the appearance of the set and the quality of services offered,[10] but later implied that

[7] *Rental Charges*, para. 9 (italics added).

[8] There is no direct indication whether significant additional economies from the ownership of multiple rental outlets were considered to be available. If they did exist this would constitute a further barrier to new entry. The Monopolies Commission view that there would be significant savings in distribution costs from the Thorn/Radio Rentals merger seems to confirm this. On the other hand, the N.B.P.I. reported that a sizeable minority of the rental trade was carried on by local shops. This seems to suggest that such economies might not be so important.

[9] Expressed in terms of the difference between the highest and lowest charges as a proportion of the lowest.

[10] *Rental Charges*, para. 9.

this was not the case and suggested that 'Many customers could save a considerable sum of money without losing satisfactory servicing by choosing the cheapest contract.'[11]

Thorn told the Monopolies Commission it did not accept the N.B.P.I.'s figures and supplied an alternative table showing a range of 8 per cent.[12] Thorn also suggested that in comparing rental charges it was necessary to bear in mind differences in servicing arrangements and the value of special offers given with the sets. For instance D.E.R., Thorn's main rental company, had been offering free magazine racks to its subscribers. The Monopolies Commission did not offer any view on Thorn's arguments except to say that it seemed to illustrate the difficulties that customers would face in trying to make a true comparison between different rental companies.

The immediate cause of the N.B.P.I. investigation into the question of costs and charges in the industry was public concern at certain increases in charges which occurred in 1966 as a result of the introduction of Selective Employment Tax and revision of the Control of Hiring Order. The N.B.P.I. found that the effect of the cost changes had not been sufficient to justify the increases in charges which the companies imposed. Although some firms with low profits would have been expected to raise charges, the N.B.P.I. decided that other companies which were earning much higher profits also increased their charges when they could well have absorbed costs. Again, we would expect that in an industry in which competition really did exist there would have been every incentive to the more profitable firms to hold their charges steady and so reduce their relative charges in order to gain market shares. The only economic reason for not doing so is if the demand curve facing the individual firm is inelastic. If this is the explanation in this case it would indicate either an absence of competition between suppliers or that there was oligopolistic interdependence in the market.[13]

It seems clear that each company was able to exercise a considerable degree of independence in setting its rental charges without much regard to those set by its rivals and that this took place in an environment where real differences in the quality of the product were not important. A further example of this independence is to be found in the variation in depreciation policy adopted by Thorn and

[11] *Rental Charges*, para. 19.
[12] *Thorn/Radio Rentals*, Appendix 4, p. 71.
[13] The fact that charges were reduced again in 1967 is explained by the N.B.P.I. in terms of sluggish consumer demand and a relaxation in the Control of Hiring Order. There is no suggestion that competition between suppliers contributed to the reduction. See *Rental Charges*, para. 41.

Radio Rentals. Thorn depreciated its sets over five years and Radio Rentals over seven years. According to Professor Barna's note of dissent it appears that this could be equivalent to a difference of as much as 10d. per week, or 10 per cent, in the rental charges between the two groups.[14] In a truly competitive market it is hardly likely that such a significant variation in policy could persist indefinitely.

While not attempting to explain or account for the price differences that existed, the Monopolies Commission held that competition tended to be on the speed and quality of service rather than price. Although this may be a very important source of competition in the supply of some producer and consumer goods it hardly seems adequate evidence of a competitive market in television rentals. The N.B.P.I. reported that the majority of customers were satisfied with the service they received and presumably there was therefore little scope for much competitive improvement in the service offered. The Monopolies Commission's view of service competition was essentially the passive one that an alternative supplier exists to take advantage of any failings in service. This is again very close to reliance on the structural existence of alternative suppliers without any evidence from the conduct of the firms in the industry that a competitive spirit does prevail.[15]

2b. *Customer Conduct*

Competition is made effective when consumers actively exercise choice between alternative suppliers in a rational and informed manner. This means that *ceteris paribus* the cheapest supplier will be patronized, but the *ceteris paribus* conditions may include a wide range of non-price considerations (including, where appropriate, considerations of quality and service, ability to make other acquisitions from the same supplier, differential costs of reaching alternative suppliers, etc.) and so the rational exercise of consumer choice will not necessarily force all prices to equality where there are other compensating advantages. The information we have on consumer behaviour in the television rentals market suggests that it did not contribute to a competitive situation. It also appears that the N.B.P.I. and Monopolies Commission were aware that it was in

[14] *Thorn/Radio Rentals*, para. 227.

[15] In fact, the *Thorn/Radio Rentals* report does contain some reference to price competition. The Monopolies Commission reported (para. 72) that Radio Rentals Ltd. had recently reduced its charges in an attempt to improve its competitive position. Presumably the Commission did not consider this a significant piece of information, it certainly did not allow it to influence its view on the nature of competition in the industry. In his note of dissent Professor Barna drew attention (para. 225) to further evidence the Commission had received from Radio Rentals that there was keen competition between themselves and D.E.R. and that market shares changed as relative charges were adjusted.

conflict with their general view that the industry was competitive but failed to make the appropriate adjustment to their conclusions.

The N.B.P.I. conducted a survey of consumers and found that more than half the renters of sets chose their initial supplier without 'shopping around' to discover the charges set by other firms. The Monopolies Commission also quoted the results of this survey and both bodies used it as an indication of the weakness of consumer purchasing power in the market.[16] According to the N.B.P.I., even in 1966 when charges rose generally, there were still sufficient outlets holding or reducing their charges to enable many, if not all, customers entering into new contracts to avoid the increased charges.

There was a problem of ensuring that the right information was made available to consumers, as both the N.B.P.I. and Monopolies Commission noted. The advertising of weekly rental charges was not altogether helpful since it tended to obscure important differences in charges over longer periods of one, three or five years which were also relevant to a rational decision. Even if improved information was made available there was doubt whether it would be acted upon by consumers since customers did not seem to be particularly sensitive to differences in rental charges and they appeared unwilling to 'shop around' for the cheapest contract to meet their needs.

Even when existing rental customers renewed their contracts the Monopolies Commission found that there was a strong tendency to renew as a matter of course with their existing suppliers if satisfactory service had been given. According to the N.B.P.I. the majority of customers reported themselves satisfied with the servicing provided by their suppliers and so it appears that here too there was little incentive for active consideration of possible alternative suppliers.

3. *Performance*

The information contained in the reports on performance is limited. From the N.B.P.I. report it is clear that the 1966 price increases bore little relation to the increase in direct costs that had been incurred. The Monopolies Commission's view that any cost savings arising out of the proposed merger between Thorn and Radio Rentals would not be passed on to the public also confirmed the impression that the actual relation between price and average

[16] The use made of this information is interesting. Other commentators have suggested that a much smaller proportion (may be as low as 10 per cent) of consumers comparing prices and acting rationally on the information would be sufficient to create a competitive market, see P. W. S. Andrews, *On Competition in Economic Theory* (Macmillan), 1964, pp. 101–2. The N.B.P.I. and Monopolies Commission might therefore have used this to support their general argument that the market was competitive.

costs is too tenuous and remote to satisfy considerations for effective competition, particularly as improvements in the quality of the 'product' offered by the rental companies were unlikely.

The snapshot picture of profits for one or two years only given in the reports does not allow much opportunity to comment on the long-run reasonableness of profits. The Monopolies Commission described the profits earned by Thorn and Radio Rentals as 'comfortable' and it appears that Thorn's profits had risen between 1965 and 1967 at the same time that D.E.R.'s charges had also risen relative to those of Radio Rentals and most of the other rental companies. Again, it is unlikely that higher relative charges and higher profits could go hand in hand in a competitive market.

If the N.B.P.I.'s calculations that the optimum size of individual rental outlet was one with at least 3000–4000 customers[17] was correct the whole industry appeared to be well below optimum size and to have considerable excess capacity. The average number of sets rented per outlet according to the N.B.P.I. was 1550, while for Thorn and Radio Rentals it averaged respectively 1933 and 2275.[18] The forces of competition do not therefore appear to have been particularly strong in leading to optimum plant size and it is relevant to note in this respect that there was little intention that the Thorn/Radio Rentals merger would lead to a significant rationalization of the number of outlets in an attempt to achieve economies of scale in distribution.

CONCLUSION

The factual information referred to in this note is taken solely from the reports of the N.B.P.I. and Monopolies Commission. Far from confirming the view that the television rentals industry was competitive it suggests that significant features were to be found which indicated a situation quite different from that which criteria for effective competition would require.

To summarize, we find the specialist rental market was insulated from other competition and was itself quite highly concentrated. Barriers to entry appeared to be high. Wide price variations without compensating real product variations suggested a greater degree of independence in price-making than is acceptable. Non-price forms of competition did not appear to be important. The failure of the more efficient firms to hold charges stable when the opportunity presented itself in 1966 suggests the absence of a spirit of competition

[17] *Rental Charges*, para. 44.
[18] *Thorn/Radio Rentals*, paras. 89–90 and 60.

in the industry. The information on consumer behaviour indicates that consumers were insufficiently mobile in placing initial contracts or in renewing them to make an effective choice between alternative suppliers. Costs and prices did not appear to be directly related to each other and there was little evidence of an attempt to reduce excess capacity in the industry.

The surprising feature is that the N.B.P.I. and the Monopolies Commission appeared to recognize that much of this information pointed to a conclusion different from the one they reached. How then did they come to decide that the industry was competitive? It appears that the N.B.P.I. looked only at the structure of the industry, found that there were numerous alternative suppliers and did not consider it necessary to continue the analysis further. The Monopolies Commission emphasized non-price competition on the speed and quality of service. Both of these were essentially passive elements in the situation and do not appear strong enough to offset sufficiently the non-competitive factors.

The moral of this note must be that before a market is considered to be competitive a much more rigorous analysis of the evidence is required in the light of some acceptable criteria for effective competition. It is necessary to look beyond the structural data to evidence on conduct and performance before a valid conclusion can be drawn with confidence.

UNIVERSITY OF SUSSEX

A NOTE ON ADVERTISING AND UNCERTAINTY

by Ira Horowitz*

I. INTRODUCTION

The 'economics of advertising' has been a source of varied and frequent, if unresolved, academic debate. Recently, the discussion has moved onto one of its more controversial and fascinating planes: namely, the implications of advertising for market structure and profitability. It is rather tempting to seek to clarify these implications by recourse to the traditional 'look at the data'; but, either the latter may not be an available option or the results might not be unequivocal. In the first place, the U.S. experience is necessarily going to dominate any such analysis. Whereas in the U.S. marketing *per se* has long been treated as a respectable academic discipline, and academic respectability has undoubtedly encouraged wider dissemination of such marketing data as advertising expenditures, the rest of the academic world has not exactly clamored to let the marketing people in.[1] Second, it is even somewhat disconcerting to 'have the look' at the U.S. data, for the same data have not necessarily carried the same message to different observers.[2]

Still further, one of the prerequisites for building a valid empirical model and correctly interpreting its results is a sound theory. As will be indicated, neither the neoclassical theory of the firm nor its variants has been quite up to the mark.

The fact that there are discordant views of the causes and effects of advertising takes on an especially significant posture when questions of market power enter the picture; specifically, questions of whether advertising is compatible with, or is undertaken because of, competitive pressures, or whether advertising is symptomatic of, and enhances, market power. The resolution of the issue has important macroeconomic implications, and as far as the ladder of questions to resolve is concerned, this helps to place the matter a rung or two above many others about which economists might disagree.

* With the traditional disclaimer, support from the International Business Research Institute, Indiana University, is gratefully acknowledged.

[1] For an extensive bibliography and discussion, see Peter Doyle, 'Economic Aspects of Advertising: A Survey', *Economic Journal*, Vol. LXXVII, No. 311 (Sept. 1968), pp. 570–602.

[2] In particular, see the conflicting inferences drawn by Lester G. Telser, 'Advertising and Competition', *Journal of Political Economy*, Vol. LXXII, No. 6 (Dec. 1964), pp. 537–62, *vis-à-vis* William S. Comanor and Thomas A. Wilson, 'Advertising, Market Structure and Performance', *Review of Economics and Statistics*, Vol. XLIX, No. 4 (Nov. 1967), pp. 423–39. Also see Joe S. Bain, *Barriers to New Competition* (Harvard University Press: Cambridge, 1956), ch. 4, pp. 201–3.

The purpose of the present paper is to offer some theoretical arguments that serve to alter the perspective with which the role of advertising should be viewed. These arguments are derived from a pair of comparatively simple models of the firm. These differ from the neoclassical model 'only' in so far as uncertainty is permitted to rear its mischievous, if ever-present, head. The injection of this most significant ingredient endows the traditional model with a degree of realism that it has heretofore lacked, and leads to the conclusion that *attitudes towards risk* will be extremely important in determining the firm's preferred level of advertising. Moreover, the effects of risk preferences appear in a quite systematic way. This conclusion in turn implies that the interpretation of, say, positive correlations between advertising expenditures and either profitability or measures of industrial concentration as reflecting causality, may indeed be spurious; and this can be the case even in a complex regression analysis, so long as other variables related to risk and risk preferences are neglected.

II. THE MODELS

Consider a single product firm producing output Q in accordance with the known continuous cost function c(Q). Uncertainty enters the picture through the demand schedule $Q = d(P, A) + u$, where u is a continuous random variable with density f(u) such that $\int_{\alpha}^{\infty} uf(u)du$ = the expected value of u = 0, and $\int_{\alpha}^{\infty} u^2 f(u)du$ = the variance of $u > 0$; α is the lower bound of u and is assigned to assure that $Q \geqslant 0$ for all P and A. The actual demand during some time period T is thus a random variable Q with density f(u), and the *expected* demand is given by $\int_{\alpha}^{\infty} Qf(u)du = \bar{Q}_{PA} = d(P, A)$; that is, expected demand is a continuous function of the price P and advertising expenditures A. One can think of f(u) either as being *estimated* via the mechanical manipulation of data, or as being *assessed* by individual decisionmakers in light of their personal judgments, experience, and insights. In either event, the probability that a given price and advertising policy pair will result in a given level of demand, will ordinarily reflect some judgment or set of assumptions with respect to both *competitors'* policies and the impact that these will have on the firm, and the many other potentially influential variables that are traditionally *ceteris paribus*ed into the background. The advantage of this simplistic framework is that it provides a mathematically tractable setting from which one can draw some interesting suggestions that contribute to a better understanding of real world behavior.

(a) *The Quantity-Setting Price-Taker*

Within this basic setting then, let us first consider a firm akin to that of the purely competitive model. This firm must accept the market price of P in order to remain a viable competitor, but it must produce some quantity Q^* in advance of knowing its actual demand Q.[3] The firm's marginal cost curve is assumed to rise in the relevant range. The firm must also determine a level of advertising A^*, for the latter can influence the demand at P. In particular, it is assumed that $\partial Q/\partial A \geqslant 0$ and $\partial^2 Q/\partial A^2 < 0$. That is, increases in advertising expenditures cannot hurt sales and can ordinarily be presumed to increase sales, but at a decreasing rate.

It is supposed that management's attitudes towards risk are summarized in a von Neumann–Morgenstern risk preference schedule solely in terms of profits π, such that $V = v(\pi)$ is the utile equivalent of π.[4] To avoid unfruitful and unnecessary complications, it will be assumed that all unsold output must be scrapped after the time period of T has elapsed without the firm's incurring additional cost or receiving any revenue therefrom. Profits will thus be given by $\pi_1 = PQ - c(Q^*) - A^*$ for demand of $Q \leqslant Q^*$, and by $\pi_2 = PQ^* - c(Q^*) - A^*$ for demand of $Q > Q^*$. Hence, the expected utility associated with the policy (Q^*, A^*) is given by

$$E[V] = {}_{\alpha}\int^{u^*} v(\pi_1) f(u)du + v(\pi_2)\, {}_{u^*}\int^{\infty} f(u)du, \tag{1}$$

where $u^* = Q^* - d(P, A^*)$. To maximize expected utility we require $\partial E[V]/\partial Q^* = \partial E[V]/\partial A^* = 0$, given that the second-order conditions are satisfied, and we shall so presume them to be.[5]

The $\partial E[V]/\partial Q^* = 0$ condition is readily shown to imply that, for a given advertising expenditure, the preferred output level of risk-evading firms will be less than that of firms linear in risk producing under similar cost conditions and reacting to similar probability assignments; the output of 'linear' firms will in turn be less than that of firms that are risk-takers.[6]

[3] For an extensive discussion of this model, see Saul H. Hymans, 'The Price-Taker: Uncertainty, Utility, and the Supply Function', *International Economic Review*, Vol. 7, No. 3 (Sept. 1966), pp. 346–66.

[4] See John von Neumann and Oskar Morgenstern, *Theory of Games and Economic Behaviour* (Princeton University Press: Princeton, 1953), particularly pp. 15–31.

[5] Interestingly enough, however, when V is a strictly convex function of π (i.e., the case of the risk-taker) the second-order conditions will not *necessarily* obtain even though they might hold for V a linear function of π. In this case they can, nonetheless, be shown to hold for V a strictly concave function of π (i.e., the risk-evader).

[6] See Hymans, *op. cit.* Also see Ira Horowitz, *Decision-Making and the Theory of the Firm* (Holt, Rinehart & Winston: New York, 1970), ch. 13, for related discussion. In particular, the $\partial E[V]/\partial Q^* = 0$ condition leads to the equilibrium condition

$$E[v']/v'^* = P\, {}_{u^*}\int^{\infty} f(u)du/(dc/dQ^*),$$

where $v'^* = v'(\pi_2)$.

The second of the first-order conditions is given by

$$\frac{\partial E[V]}{\partial A^*} = {}_{\alpha}\!\int^{u^*} v'\left(P\frac{\partial Q}{\partial A^*}-1\right)f(u)du - v'^*\,{}_{u^*}\!\int^{\infty} f(u)du = 0, \qquad (2)$$

where $v' = \partial v(\pi_1)/\partial\pi$ and $v'^* = \partial v(\pi_2)/\partial\pi$.

Writing $E[v'] = {}_{\alpha}\!\int^{u^*}v'f(u)du + v'^*\,{}_{u^*}\!\int^{\infty}f(u)du$ = the expected 'marginal utility' associated with the optimal advertising and production policy, (2) may be rewritten as

$$P\frac{\partial Q}{\partial A^*} = \frac{1}{1-\dfrac{v'^*}{E[v']}\,{}_{u^*}\!\int^{\infty} f(u)du}. \qquad (2')$$

For a firm linear in risk, $v'^* = E[v']$ since $\partial v/\partial\pi$ = a constant. For such a firm, (2′) implies that advertising monies are spent to the point at which $P(\partial Q/\partial A)({}_{\alpha}\!\int^{u^*}f(u)du) = 1$; that is, until the *expected* additional revenue generated exactly equals the cost of generating that increment, *given an output of Q^**. In risk-evading firms 'marginal utility' is a nonincreasing function of π, Q and u; hence $v'^* < E[v']$. *At the previous Q^** then, the risk-evader seeks to operate at a *lower* $P(\partial Q/\partial A)$; i.e., at a given level of output, risk-evading firms will prefer to spend more on advertising than do linear in risk firms. The increased spending is required in order to effect the reduction in $P(\partial Q/\partial A^*)$, by the assumption that $\partial^2Q/\partial A^2 < 0$. Analogously, $v'^* > E[v']$ for the risk-taking firm, and the latter therefore prefers to spend less on advertising—in order to sell a given Q^*—than does the firm that is linear in risk. It is important to recognize, however, that the values of Q^* and A^* will be determined *jointly*, and we are unable to demonstrate that, irrespective of the degree to which risk is preferred or eschewed, the risk-evading management will *necessarily* spend more on advertising than does the risk-taking management.[7] What we can say, however, is that for *given* output levels risk aversion leads to greater advertising, in effect to raise the probability of selling what has already been produced and reduce the profit variance. Further, and unlike the traditional model, once we admit uncertainty into the picture, even in a purely competitive atmosphere the firm finds advertising to be an attractive weapon.

[7] It is, however, interesting to note that by substituting the first-order equilibrium condition as given in the previous footnote into (2′), the latter reduces to: $\partial Q/\partial A^* = 1/(P-dc/dQ^*)$. Since P is fixed, the lower is the marginal cost at the point at which the firm chooses to produce, the lower is the value of $\partial Q/\partial A^*$ that management will seek to achieve. Thus the management of a given firm that prefers the lower output also prefers the higher advertising. It is not apparent, however, that given the advertising option the risk-evading firm will *always* prefer the smaller output.

(*b*) *The Price-Setting Quantity-Taker*

As a second variation on the basic theme, we next consider the price-setting firm selecting a price of P^* to quote to the market. This firm supplies all that the market demands at P^*, subject to the qualification that when marginal costs are increasing, the maximum quantity the firm will produce is Q_M, where Q_M is the output at which $P^* = \partial c/\partial Q$, or price equals marginal cost. This firm's profit also depends upon actual demand: $\pi_1 = P^*Q - c(Q) - A^*$ for $Q \leqslant Q_M$ and $\hat{\pi}_2 = P^*Q_M - c(Q_M) - A^*$ for $Q \geqslant Q_M$. Expected utility will therefore be given by[8]

$$E[V] = {}_{\alpha}\int^{u_M} v(\hat{\pi}_1)f(u)du + v(\hat{\pi}_2)\,{}_{u_M}\int^{\infty} f(u)du, \qquad (3)$$

where $u_M = Q_M - d(P^*, A^*)$. To maximize expected utility we require $\partial E[V]/\partial P^* = \partial E[V]/\partial A^* = 0$, again assuming that the second-order conditions are satisfied (and with the remarks of footnote 5 once again holding).

The $\partial E[V]/\partial P^* = 0$ condition is readily shown to imply that, for a given advertising expenditure, the preferred price of risk-evading firms will be less than that of firms linear in risk producing under similar cost conditions and reacting to similar probability assignments; the price of 'linear' firms will in turn be lower than that of firms that are risk-takers.[9]

The second of the first-order conditions is given by

$$\frac{\partial E[V]}{\partial A^*} = {}_{\alpha}\int^{u_M} v'\left(P^*\frac{\partial Q}{\partial A^*} - \frac{dc}{dQ}\frac{\partial Q}{\partial A^*} - 1\right)f(u)du - v'^*\,{}_{u_M}\int^{\infty} f(u)du = 0. \qquad (4)$$

As before, writing $E[v'] = {}_{\alpha}\int^{u_M} v'f(u)du + v'^*{}_{u_M}\int^{\infty} f(u)du$ = the expected 'marginal utility' associated with the optimal advertising and price policy, (4) may be rewritten as

$$\frac{\partial Q}{\partial A} = \frac{E[v']}{{}_{\alpha}\int^{u_M} v'\left[P^* - \dfrac{dc}{dQ}\right]f(u)du}. \qquad (4')$$

For a firm linear in risk, $E[v'] = v'$ and (4′) implies that advertising monies are spent to the point at which $P^*(\partial Q/\partial A)({}_{\alpha}\int^{u_M} f(u)du) = 1 + (\partial Q/\partial A)({}_{\alpha}\int^{u_M}(dc/dQ)f(u)du)$; that is, until the *expected* additional

[8] If marginal cost is a nonincreasing function of Q, the firm will always choose to satisfy *all* demand at the quoted price, so that $Q_M = \infty$ and the second term disappears.

[9] For a discussion, see Horowitz (*op. cit.*). In particular, the $dE[V]/dP^* = 0$ condition leads to the equilibrium condition

$$E[Q] = (-\sigma_1 - (dQ/dP^*)\,{}_{\alpha}\int^{u_M} v'(P^* - dc/dQ)f(u)du)/E[v'],$$

where σ_1 is the covariance between Q and v′. The statement holds except for the equivocal case of decreasing costs.

revenue generated exactly equals the cost of generating that increment plus the *expected* additional cost required to satisfy the additional demand encouraged by the advertising, *given a price of* P^*. In risk-evading firms, $E[v'] \leqslant v'$ for all v′ such that $Q \leqslant Q_M$. Hence, *at this same* P^*, since $P^* \geqslant dc/dQ$ the risk-evading management will choose to operate at a point such that $\partial Q/\partial A$ has a lower value than that maintained by the management that is linear in risk; that is, the risk-evading firm prefers to advertise more; reasoning analogously, the risk-taking firm prefers to advertise less than the firm linear in risk.

As in the first situation, however, the optimal price and advertising levels will be determined simultaneously, and the actual relative differences between advertising expenditures, given the option of selecting different prices, is not apparent. Nevertheless we can state that at any *given* price risk aversion encourages the firm to take greater advantage of the advertising option than would otherwise be the case. In effect, the firm is willing to buy more advertising than can be economically justified in the 'fair bet' sense, in order to raise its expected demand at the quoted price, and reduce the variance in revenues and costs.[10]

III. THE IMPLICATIONS

In a recent empirical study, Comanor and Wilson infer as their 'primary finding . . . that advertising has a statistically significant and quantitatively important impact upon profit rates which provide a measure of market performance as well as indicate the existence of market power'.[11] Even if one were to agree that a causal link had been established between advertising and profit (without necessarily accepting the ensuing arguments), agreement will not necessarily come with raised eyebrows. Assuredly, many a marketing manager will welcome such statistical support; but, as Telser has commented: 'To say that business firms advertise because they find this to be profitable, although true, does not necessarily advance our understanding of the subject.'[12] In a world of uncertainties the 'profitability' motive is equivocal; it is neither very well defined,

[10] It can be shown that risk aversion leads the price-taking quantity-setter to policies which reduce the revenue and profits variances, whereas those of the price-setting quantity-taker reduce the revenue and cost variances, but not *necessarily* the profits variance. The latter result somewhat offends one's prior prejudices; but, the offense is ameliorated by the readily admitted, if oft-neglected, realization that a decision maker can be influenced by other moments of the profits distribution, beyond the first two.

[11] *Op. cit.*, p. 423.

[12] Lester G. Telser, 'Some Aspects of the Economics of Advertising', *Journal of Business*, Vol. 41, No. 2 (April 1968), p. 168.

nor the unique stimulus of behaviour. As the present analysis emphasizes, attitude towards risk and management's lack of omniscience will affect both the firm's level of advertising *and* the firm's long- and short-term profits. Specifically, risk-evading (taking) managements will tend to advertise to a greater (lesser) extent than is economically justified in the sense of maximizing the firm's long-term (i.e., expected) profitability. There is certainly nothing novel in the notion that some firms might advertise 'too much' or 'too little'. The Baumol–Williamson type of analysis, for example, suggests that managements seeking to maximize sales revenue, or some corporate utility function, subject to a minimum profits constraint, will spend a greater amount on advertising than will the strict profit-maximizer.[13] Still, and while the analyses provide useful insights into real world behavior, like the traditional model they too are carried out in a rather dull world of certainty wherein each action will have a *determinate* and known result.

The fact that the overwhelming majority of sophisticated economic models completely neglect uncertainty, whereas decision makers must live with it every day, is readily explained. Only recently have economists become adequately equipped to deal with uncertainty in anything more than a casual manner; they are just now getting around to making risk and attitudes towards risk integral parts of their theoretical constructs.

Thus, the notion that some firms might advertise more than others in order to reduce the risks associated with the inability to perfectly forecast demand is quite simple and appealing. Yet, it tends to enter discussions of the 'economics of advertising' almost in the nature of a brief afterthought—if it enters at all.[14] The present analysis suggests, however, that the risk-reducing potential of advertising is one of its very important attributes. Further, other things such as firm size being equal, the fact that the policies followed by firms linear in risk result in the maximization of expected profit, would lead one to anticipate that a graph of long-term average profits (which can be taken as an approximation of expected profits if the term is long enough) versus advertising expenditures *by firm in a given industry*, to be $\cap$-shaped with $E[\pi]$ the ordinate and A the

[13] See W. J. Baumol, *Business Behavior, Value and Growth* (Harcourt, Brace & World, Inc.: New York, 1967), pp. 60–70; and O. E. Williamson, 'Managerial Discretion and Business Behavior', *American Economic Review*, Vol. LIII, No. 5 (Dec. 1963), pp. 1032–57.

[14] Doyle (*op. cit.*, p. 596), for example, when chatting about research and development and technical progress, notes *en passant* that 'if advertising was not the instrument it is probable that less palatable ways could be found for reducing risks, such as collusive agreements or cartel arrangements'. When placing advertising in a theoretical, if admittedly oversimplified setting, however, he falls back on the traditional approach ('Advertising Expenditure and Consumer Demand', *Oxford Economic Papers*, Vol. 20, No. 3 (Nov. 1968), pp. 399–401).

abscissa. Implicit in this is the suggestion that in fact the advertising potential of presumably smaller and similar price-taking competitors will, in general, not be sufficiently great so as to lead to an alteration in their relative output preferences; and the price quotes of price-setters will, in general, lie in a sufficiently narrow range such that the previous results obtain. This effects an optimal level of advertising as far as maximizing long-term average profits is concerned, but risk-evaders (takers) will *consciously* choose to spend more (less) than this optimum.[15]

Differing attitudes towards risk provide only one uncertainty-related factor through which differing advertising preferences can be explained. Additionally, when information is of an imperfect and limited nature, different managements in ostensibly parallel situations can act on the basis of different sets of probability assignments. Even when managements hold precisely the same attitudes towards risk, then, they need not concur on the optimal level of advertising; and, in the sense that a set of probability *judgments* will neither be 'correct' nor 'incorrect', there can be quite rational differences in expenditure preferences. Once we further admit, as we properly should, the possibility of non-profit related interests on management's part, the analysis of the impact of advertising on the firm, and whether 'too much' or 'too little' is being spent, becomes a most complex matter.

Unfortunately, the available data have encouraged inter*industry* studies of advertising rather than inter*firm* studies within a given industry. In order to question the conclusion that a positive *inter-industry* statistical relationship between advertising and profits implies that advertising abets and is symptomatic of market power, and that it enhances profitability, one need not argue that the direction of causality is the reverse (i.e., advertising is financed out of profits). Instead, we would suggest that there are other factors, such as uncertainty, indigenous to the industries themselves which both encourage advertising *and* lead to higher profit rates (and

[15] Clearly, items such as research and development expenditures can be subjected to a similar analysis. It might also be noted that the introduction of, say, a minimum expected profits constraint can force the policies of managements holding different attitudes towards risk into greater coincidence. It can also be shown that the introduction of a perfect loss offset profits tax, or an increase in such a tax, will tend to draw otherwise differing policy preferences together. Finally, and in light of the remarks in footnote 5, it should be noted that when the first-order conditions in the previous models lead to a unique solution, and the second-order conditions obtain for one linear in risk but not for the risk-taker, the latter will want to move *away* from this point (and policy). This implies that the advertising policy, say, of a risk-taking management may very well lie on one of the two extremes of 'no' or 'infinite' expenditures. The impracticality of the latter would suggest that, for the risk-taker, when the second-order conditions for an expected utility maximum are not satisfied, the solution to the first-order conditions is not likely to be unique (see Horowitz, *op. cit.*).

perhaps greater industrial concentration as well). One could argue, for example, that greater profit is the entrepreneurial reward for accepting the risks of doing business in a highly uncertain industry; and 'higher than average' advertising expenditures are maintained by firms in the industry in an effort to ameliorate these risks. Indeed, on an interindustry basis and using the Comanor and Wilson data, a quadratic regression of profits on advertising[16] yields the equation

$$A_i = 2.63 - .37\pi_i + .05\pi^2_i + e_i \qquad (R^2 = .255)$$
$$(1.00) \quad (2.05)$$

where the subscript denotes the ith of 41 three-digit industries, e is the residual term, and the t-ratios for the regression coefficients are in parentheses. Ultimately, greater profits and greater advertising do go hand in hand, but this does not necessarily imply direct causality. Further, both in Telser's work ('Advertising and Competition,' pp. 541–6), and Comanor and Wilson's work (p. 433) with U.S. data, as well as in Doyle's work ('Advertising Expenditure and Consumer Demand', pp. 410–12) with British data, the correlation between advertising and concentration (or changes in concentration) although positive is only slightly so. Indeed, using Stigler's concentration estimates, the *partial* correlations between concentration (in the immediately preceding period) and advertising, with profits held constant, are actually negative, although negligible.[17] The merits of the concentration ratio as a measure of market power are certainly questionable. In and of themselves, however, they generate no evidence whatsoever of a relationship—causal or otherwise—between market structure and advertising. Additionally, and irrespective of the underlying motivation, there is nothing in the data to suggest that advertising promotes concentration, or that it might not in fact be one of the more scrupulous options available to management whereby risk can be reduced.

The dangers of drawing inferences about microbehavior on the basis of macroeconomic data are well known;[18] but, in the absence of the requisite microdata these dangers are often overlooked. If we really want to learn more about factors affecting advertising, as well as learn more about the effectiveness of advertising (and in particular

[16] Profits are after-tax as a percentage of stockholders' equity; advertising is the advertising to sales ratio (1954–57).

[17] George J. Stigler, *Capital and Rates of Return in Manufacturing Industries* (Princeton University Press: Princeton, 1963), pp. 214–15. Specifically the partial correlation between the four-firm concentration ratio in 1954 and the 1954–57 advertising to sales ratio is −.023; that between the ratio of the 1954 to 1947 concentration ratios and the advertising to sales ratio is −0.117 (π^2 held constant).

[18] For a useful discussion see Edwin Kuh, *Capital Stock Growth: A Micro-Econometric Approach* (North-Holland Publishing Co., Amsterdam, 1963), pp. 189–203.

its impact on profits), the appropriate place to begin would be with an interfirm analysis within individual industries. Then, depending upon attitudes towards risk, the previous theoretical discussion would lead one to expect a ∩-shaped curve to emerge. It also encourages the rather unprofound observations that the advertising *preferences* of *firms* can differ, and that the advertising *potential* of *industries* can differ. It is important for these theoretical observations to receive empirical validation; it is at least equally important that we understand just what it is that our analysis is validating.

CATHOLIC UNIVERSITY OF LOUVAIN

A SURVEY INTO THE R&D EVALUATION AND CONTROL PROCEDURES CURRENTLY USED IN INDUSTRY

by J. M. Allen

1. SUMMARY

This paper consists of an account of an enquiry into the methods and procedures used in industry for the evaluation and control of R&D (Research and Development) carried out by the R&D Research Unit at the Manchester Business School.* The organization of a questionnaire survey, and the methods of analysing the return by industry group are set out in (2) the Introduction and (3) the Presentation of Results. The different techniques and procedures which the questionnaire survey showed to be in use are set out in parts (4) to (9), and the information obtained from visits to organizations made concurrently with the survey in part (10). Some conclusions drawn from the work are advanced in (11).

2. INTRODUCTION

A great deal of material has been published recently on the evaluation and control of research and development (R&D), some of it being accounts of how it is carried out in a given organization, and some being outlines of possible evaluation models and techniques. However, this literature gives little indication as to how widely used are the techniques described. The most recent large-scale survey in Britain to discover the evaluation techniques which were in use at the time was the 1959/60 Federation of British Industries survey amongst its members, published in 1960 under the title of 'Research in Manufacturing Industry'. It was considered valuable by the R&D Research Unit to organize a survey to gain some indication of the evaluation and control procedures at present in use: first to gain knowledge of the current situation, and secondly as an indication to where research into methods and procedures could be of most practical use.

A questionnaire survey, supplemented by some personal visits and a certain amount of correspondence was considered the best way to obtain the required information. After discussion within the Unit, and with people from organizations in contact with the Manchester Business School, a questionnaire was formulated. The questionnaire

* The work of the R&D Research Unit is jointly sponsored by The Ministry of Technology and the Atomic Energy Authority.

(Appendix) was designed to obtain information on R&D procedures which could not be derived from other sources.

The sample decided upon as being the most useful and accessible was the 'Times 300' for 1967, plus the major nationalized concerns and several large organizations in contact with the Business School, but not included above. This gave a total sample of 316. It is estimated that the 'Times 300' account for not less than 80 per cent of private sector R&D expenditure, and that they employ about 23 per cent of the working population.[1] The range of goods and services provided by the '300' and the nationalized industries is extremely wide, and using them as a sample covers most of the fields of commercial R&D.

The questionnaire was posted, with a covering letter, to fifty companies randomly selected from the '300' on November 25th, 1967 and, following minor modifications in wording suggested by the replies, to the remainder on January 6th, 1968. The nationalized industries were contacted using the same questionnaire and covering letter, but with a further note requesting assistance, if possible, beyond the completion of the questionnaire. The questionnaire introduction invited respondents to qualify their answers with any clarifying material they wished to add.

The return from this sample, to June 30th, 1968, has been 167 completed replies, which break down as follows:

Completed questionnaires returned	112
Organizations carrying out no R&D	19
Organizations not prepared to co-operate with the Unit on this work	36[2].

From the sample of 316, this represents an overall reply of 53 per cent, and this paper is based on the information given by the 35 per cent of the sample who returned questionnaires.

With the completed questionnaire many organizations enclosed standard, or specifically compiled, information sheets, or copies of documents used in the evaluation procedure. This information, and the qualifying remarks added to answers on the questionnaires, has been taken fully into account when analysing the replies. A number of invitations to visit the organization and discuss the topics under investigation with R&D staff accompanied questionnaires.

[1] R&D expenditure calculated on the Federation of British Industries estimate that 90 per cent of R&D expenditure amongst its membership is within firms with more than 2000 employees. This proportion is assumed to hold throughout the private sector, and in any case, most of the '300' are FBI members.

Proportion of the working population estimated from personnel figures of the '300' and Annual Abstract of Statistics data.

[2] A number of these organizations were involved in amalgamations, etc., during the course of the survey, and offered this as their reason for being unable to co-operate.

3. PRESENTATION OF RESULTS

The following results are not necessarily representative of the R&D procedures of British industry as a whole, and are only interpreted with regard to the organizations who were good enough to co-operate in providing them.

For purposes of analysis the industrial groups represented in the return were ranked in an order of 'rate of increase of applicable technical knowledge' within the industrial field in which the greater part of the operations of the group fell. By consultation with R&D staff from a number of organizations, and the formulation of a numerical measure based on the ratio of qualified scientists and engineers (QSE) to capital employed, the groups were ranked in the following manner.

CONTINUUM OF RATE OF INCREASE OF APPLICABLE TECHNICAL KNOWLEDGE

Lowest rate of increase of applicable technical knowledge	*Number of organizations in section*
Section 1 Service industries[3] Sand and Gravel Extraction Brewing and Tobacco	19
Section 2 Paper, Textile manufacture Shipbuilding, Steel production, Construction engineering, Building materials Motor industry and allied engineering Heavy Chemicals	59
Section 3 Fine chemicals and Dyestuffs Pharmaceuticals and Electronics	30
Highest rate of increase of applicable technical knowledge	

Different industrial groups on the same level on the continuum are considered to have the same rate of increase of applicable technical knowledge. Four companies were considerably smaller than the rest in their respective industrial groups, and it was considered that their answers to certain questions could not be justly assessed with the rest. This point is made in the text wherever it occurs. The organizations represented in the questionnaire return are divided into three sections only, as many of them have diversified interests which would have caused a great deal of overlap in a

[3] Service industries are defined as industries which exist to give a service, and any machinery (in the widest sense) used is purchased as the products of other industries' research—new vehicles, dry cleaning apparatus, etc. If any organization carries out technical research on the machinery of the service—GPO electronics research, British Rail rolling stock research, for example—it is included in the continuum, not as a service industry, but where appears appropriate from the type of research being undertaken.

continuum with a larger number of divisions. Industrial groups not represented in the questionnaire return are not included in the continuum. The frequency Tables I and II show the distribution of R&D budgets and numbers of qualified scientists and engineers amongst the organizations which returned questionnaires. Table II contains data from companies in the top 100 of the 'Times 300' which are in sections 1 or 3 of the continuum. These companies are randomly distributed throughout the top 100, but companies in continuum section 3 consistently expend more effort on R&D than do those in section 1. This illustrates that the greater the rate of increase of applicable technical knowledge in an industry, the greater the R&D expenditure which companies in that industry must make to keep abreast of current developments.

TABLE I

FREQUENCY TABLE OF 109 ORGANIZATIONS, ACCORDING TO R&D BUDGET SIZE, AND NUMBER OF RESEARCH STAFF

R&D Staff has been entered against R&D Budget by number of organizations. Questionnaire data only has been used, and three of the 112 returns contained no R&D Budget figures, and are omitted from the Table.

R&D Budget \ R&D Staff	0 to 20	20 to 40	40 to 70	70 to 100	100 to 150	150 to 250	Over 250
Over £2,000,000						2	10
£2,000,000 to £1,000,000		1	1	1	2	7	1
£1,000,000 to £500,000		2	3	9	2	2	1
£500,000 to £100,000	9	13	10	2	1	1	
£100,000 to £60,000	9	1					
£60,000 to £30,000	6						
£30,000 to £0	13						

The results are not presented in terms of replies to questions, but as an outline of how organizations are operating in certain fields of R&D evaluation and control.

4. PROPOSAL OF R&D PROJECTS

About two-thirds of the return had a formal system for proposing R&D projects to be submitted for evaluation. The proportion of organizations using a formal system increased along the continuum outlined above, from under half in section 1, to over three-quarters in section 3. Most of these systems consisted of the use of structured proposal forms requesting standard information. The trend is towards organizations which have a formal proposal system having a formal procedure for evaluation and control throughout the complete lifetime of each project. This is to be expected, as systems

TABLE II

THE ABOVE FREQUENCY TABLE REPEATED, BUT CONTAINING ONLY DATA FROM ORGANIZATIONS IN SECTIONS 1 AND 3 OF THE CONTINUUM CLASSIFICATION

The companies in this Table are all from the top 100 of the 'Times 300'. The asterisk * indicates that the companies are in section 3 of the continuum.

R&D Budget \ R&D Staff	0 to 20	20 to 40	40 to 70	70 to 100	100 to 150	150 to 250	Over 250
Over £2,000,000						2*	10*
£2,000,000 to £1,000,000			1*		1*	1*	1*
£1,000,000 to £500,000			1	1*	1*		
£500,000 to £100,000	2	1					
£100,000 to £60,000	2						
£60,000 to £30,000	2						
£30,000 to £0							

using, for example, selection models or project indices, require uniform information on all projects if they are to be correctly assessed. A formal proposal system is one way of obtaining much of this information.

A frequently used system, outlined by several organizations, and implicit in the replies of others, is as follows:

A proposal form is completed by the person who has the idea for the project, with the assistance of other people with knowledge on particular aspects, say, costing. This is submitted to an evaluation committee, who may reject the project or, up to a certain estimated cost, allow it to proceed. Large-scale projects which the evaluation committee considers worth while are referred to the executive board for financial authorization and policy decisions as to whether the project, though financially viable, is in the long-term interests of the organization. Evaluation appears to be carried out at a high level, the research head frequently being a member of the executive board. This greatly facilitates communications between the R&D department and the other functions of the organization.

About three-fifths of the return had provision to allow research workers a certain amount of 'spare time' to work on project ideas of their own, with a view to submitting them to the organization evaluation procedure if they appear feasible. That this spare time is intended to be very strongly oriented towards the research programme of the organization concerned is shown by the way in which its use is controlled, and by remarks made about it by some organizations.

Only eleven organizations put the use of spare time at the discretion of the individual research worker. The spare time of a further sixty-two was at the discretion of the R&D Director or project leader. A formal money or time limit on the value of resources which could be used on a project before it must be submitted to the evaluation procedure was specified by thirty-eight organizations. Projects commenced in the worker's spare time, which on evaluation were considered worth continuing, would be formally made a part of the organization's programme of on-going research. Except for one company which used a top expenditure limit of £2000, the expenditure limits were all between £200 and £500, and the percentages of time varied from $1\frac{1}{2}$ to 15 per cent. (Nationalized industries and small companies excepted from these figures.) With the exception of seven companies the use of these resources was at the discretion of the R&D Director or project leader, and in these cases his permission had to be requested, and could presumably be withheld.

In the other cases no formal resource limits were specified, and how much should be spent on a given spare time project was at the discretion of the head of the R&D department. This, and the fact that thirty-three organizations with fixed resource quotas to allocate to spare-time research put their administration into the hands of the R&D Director/project leader, implies that most projects from the R&D department are informally assessed before they enter the formal proposal system, or are indeed tested to discover whether they are worth a formal evaluation. That is, a 'one-man committee' is in a position to reject them with no appeal mechanism against the decision, before their technical feasibility has been assessed, and probably before a proposal form has been completed. This by-passing of the formal channels may speed up the project selection process, but it may result in a number of good projects being rejected, as the research worker's immediate superior is unlikely to be in possession of all the data necessary to evaluate a project.

Many scientists claim that they are so busy with current work that they have no time to take up the 'spare time' which they are officially allotted within their working hours.

5. EVALUATION OF R&D PROJECTS

The information requested about evaluation falls under two heads: evaluation procedures in use, and information required to implement these procedures.

Only sixteen organizations did not use either net present value, payback period or average rate of return on capital invested methods when assessing the commercial viability of projects. As fourteen of these estimated 'probability of commercial success' of the end-products of research, it is assumed that other cash-flow forecasting techniques are used.

Estimates of the probability of commercial success, technical feasibility, and probable development costs were made by ninety-nine organizations as a part of their project evaluation procedure. About one-third of the return used mathematical models and/or weighted checklist or project ranking indices as a part of their project assessment procedure.[4] Though a number of organizations may all find the same probability estimates, mathematical models or project ranking indices useful, the data inputs will be specific to the organization concerned, as the availability and quality of information at each stage of a project's evaluation will differ between organizations.

About one-third of the return had a proposal and evaluation system which was used to assess all projects, and several others had one system for basic and applied research, and a further one for development projects. A number of other organizations had a standard system which applied to all categories of projects, but which could be by-passed by a number of projects which were considered to be mandatory, because they had been assessed as desirable elsewhere inside or outside the organization. About two-fifths of the return had no formally defined evaluation procedure, and it is assumed that evaluation was carried out by the *ad hoc* method most suited to the project under scrutiny.

Twelve organizations had a numerical weighting system on their standard evaluation forms which could be used to form a picture of the weak and strong points of a project by drawing a profile line connecting the weights given to the project attributes. This profile procedure draws attention to the weak points of a project and indicates where further work is needed to ascertain whether the project can be made feasible. The weighting figures from such a profile can be incorporated into a project ranking index, and five organizations

[4] All the ranking and checklist methods found to be in use are based on procedures briefly described in 'R&D Project Selection—Where We Stand', by Baker and Pound, *Engineering Management*, November 1964.

said that this was done with information on projects whose profile indicated that they were feasible.

Development projects in industry utilize far more resources than do basic and applied research projects, and involve departments within an organization other than the R&D department.[5] By definition, once a project has reached the development stage, plans for the production and distribution of the end-product of research need to be made. Thus in some respects the future profitability and survival objectives of the organization are best met by developing only projects from basic and applied research which are 'good' from a production and marketing point of view. It was hypothesized that these factors would mean that the evaluation of development projects would be at least as rigorous as the assessment of basic research. This was found to be the case in three-quarters of the organizations represented in the return.

Twenty-seven organizations were unable to assess the comparative rigour of evaluation between basic research and development. Five of these said that the nature of their basic research made a comparison extremely difficult as entirely different types of information were used in the two evaluations. This condition can be assumed to apply in many of the other cases. A further five stated that because of the nature of their business they carried out little basic and applied research in any case.

Only seven organizations said that basic research was more rigorously evaluated than was development, and so further information was requested from them as to why this should be so. The replies indicate three reasons:

(a) Basic research projects generate development projects leading to marketable end-products of research. Thus basic research, if rigorously assessed at a high level within the organization with regard to its matching of organization objectives, is only likely to lead to development projects which are in keeping with corporate product policy.

(b) By the time a project has got to the development stage it can be easily seen whether it is economic to carry through the development. Therefore there is less need for it to be rigorously assessed. Basic research involves considerably more uncertainty, and thus requires more work to ascertain its viability.

(c) A development project may well need no prior basic research

[5] Most industrial groups are spending 8 or 9 per cent of their research budgets on basic/applied research, and there are usually more basic/applied research projects in existence at a given time than development projects. [Source: *Research in Manufacturing Industry*, FBI, 1960.]

within the organization. It may be a project initiated in the production department based on existing knowledge (previous research work in the organization, licences, etc.), and for the reasons expressed in (b), can be assessed comparatively easily.

'More rigorously' has been interpreted by these organizations as meaning more difficult, more time-consuming, more necessary, and at a higher level in the organization.

6. PERIODIC REVIEW OF PROJECTS

About two-thirds of the return review their basic research projects at least once in every period of six months, and several companies review each project monthly. A common practice is frequent but sporadic reviews: the reviews come at 'natural breaks' between stages in the project's evolution. In two-thirds of the return the reviews are carried out by the same body which carried out the original evaluation. Many of the rest use a system where the evaluation and review are carried out by different bodies, but the same body carries out each review that a project undergoes. The second system appears to obtain where greater formal authority is needed to allow a project to commence, than to allow it to continue. That is, the review considers changes in the technical and commercial feasibility of the project, and probably, fewer categories of information are taken into account at the review than at the original evaluation.

Important review criteria are changes in the chances of technical success and commercial potential, and estimates of further development and completion costs. Nearly all organizations took all of these into account at the review stage, and only eight considered just one. In seven of these cases it was the chance of commercial success. As five of these seven came from section 1 of the continuum—the least research-oriented sectors of industry—it is advanced that technical success should have a high probability, and can be taken into account at the informal level, without the need for its formal assessment.

7. R&D TIME SCALES

All the organizations in section 3 of the continuum—the most research-oriented organizations in the return—attempted to set time scales and completion dates to their basic/applied research. This practice was not common in groups 1 and 2. Many organizations making extensive use of network methods for development projects in groups 1 and 2 made no attempt to fit completion dates to basic research. This may be because the pressure of technological change and product technical obsolescence is not great enough to produce an urgent need for the results of basic research in many cases.

As would be expected, the determinants of both research and development time scales were the factors most relevant to the organization's market situation. Marketing was prominent in consumer goods, and R&D for consumer durables and industrial goods, in organizations where the R&D departments appear to have a reasonable lead time over the immediate requirements of the market served. Constraints such as contractual liabilities and availability of resources were mentioned in a number of cases as having a large part to play in the setting of time scales for specific projects.

Twenty-six organizations in the return did not use networks, bar-charts or graphs to specify time scales for some part of their R&D programme. These included ten companies from section 1 of the continuum, and a number of organizations whose research can be considered to have insufficient different aspects to make the use of networks worth while. One company stated that its research could be considered in terms of sequential short-term problems. There is a relationship between the use of the more complex methods of time allocation and an organization's position on the continuum. Programme Evaluation and Review Technique (PERT) and/or Critical Path Analysis (CPA) are used by approximately 40 per cent of section 1, 60 per cent of section 2, and 90 per cent of section 3. This tendency may be because the more rapidly changing and complex the technology, the greater is the need to allocate resources to meet completion dates, and the complexity of research means that highly structured methods are needed to organize it.

Five organizations have tried network procedures and have found them to be unsatisfactory in many respects, but only one has abandoned their use altogether. Another organization would have given up comprehensive networks and used only bar-charts and graphs were it not for the fact that many of the contracts it received specified the use of overall time scale networks. Two organizations using PERT stated that they originally updated the charts by computer, but that this had been discontinued, because its advantages over manual updating did not justify the cost of the system. Four other organizations said they had experienced difficulty with computer time allocation models. One had discontinued, on cost grounds, a Linear Programme for resource allocation, and three others had discontinued resource allocation models, designed for them by external consultant bodies, because they could not suitably perform the work they were intended for.

8. SOURCES OF RESEARCH INFORMATION

A total of ninety-four different Research Associations (RA's), Government Establishments, Research Institutes, Consultants and University Departments were named by the return as bodies from whom research information was purchased. About half of these were mentioned by one organization only, and the research organizations mentioned more than five times in the return are limited to thirteen of the larger RA's whose work spans the requirements of a wide range of industrial applications. E.g. The Welding Institute or the Rubber and Plastics R.A. Though there is a wide range in the numbers of organizations consulted (see Table III), the typical 'modal' industrial organization, representing about one-quarter of the return, is a member of three or four RA's and commissions private work from at least one, sponsors a certain amount of university research, and at times brings in consultants to deal with specific problems.

TABLE III

Number of organizations	*Number of research organizations consulted*
10	0
18	1
8	2
20	3
16	4
8	5
5	6
3	7
3	8
2	9
3	10
2	11
2	12

Twelve is the maximum number of research organizations consulted on a continuing basis, with the company being a member of the research organization, or keeping it on retainer.

There appears to be a tendency for the larger, and often more diversified, organizations in an industrial group to regard the RA's as an information service. Research Associations are commissioned to carry out specific research for the larger companies because the spin-off from their work for the industry at large is often too general in nature. The majority of the membership of the RA's is composed of companies well below the level of about £12½ million capital employed which marks the bottom of the 'Times 300' list, and thus it can be expected that much of the routine work of the RA's will not be technically suited to large organizations. Certain leaders in industrial groups have little to do with RA's carrying out research into the main field of their business. Instead, they use a large number of RA's doing research into the 'fringe technologies' of the company's activities. This enables the company to direct its own research effort into the main line of its interests and maintain its competitive position, without losing sight of important developments where the company expends only a small proportion of its productive effort.

Three companies stated that their sponsorship of university research had no strings attached, and that, though useful information was gained, it was too sporadic in appearance to be of competitive use. Buying research in this manner was considered to be buying goodwill, and useful information appears to be considered an incidental benefit. Department of Scientific and Industrial Research (DSIR) and Federation of British Industries (FBI) information for 1960 indicates that the universities expenditure on basic research was almost double that of the private sector of industry. Thus the universities should be a good source of basic research information.

Organizations were asked about their sources of data retrieval, patents information and abstracting services: were these facilities available within the organization, purchased from outside sources, or a mixture of both? All save seventeen organizations had some internal information system, and it appears that information is only purchased to supplement this, as by far the most frequent purchase is information on patents, which fifty-one organizations bought. Of the organizations which had no internal information system, sixteen had research departments of twenty QSE (qualified scientists and engineers) or less, and it is assumed that it is not economic to run an information system for a department of this size. Four of these organizations also said that they purchased no information of this type. Three were in section 1 of the continuum, and one was a small company, and it is assumed that the rate of increase of knowledge, and thus the rate of increase of available information, is small enough to be handled informally.

There appears to be no trend in respect of the types of information purchased by industrial groups. Ranking the industrial groups in the order of the mean number of information sources consulted per company within that group produces an order which agrees well with the ranking put forward in the continuum above. That is, the greater the increase of applicable technical knowledge, the greater the number of information sources consulted to keep abreast of the increase.

9. 'TROUBLE SHOOTING'

Only nine organizations stated that research projects were never temporarily suspended to free personnel to work on 'trouble shooting'. Two of these explained that different categories of personnel were engaged for the research stages and development through to production stages, and that it was part of the work of the second group to deal with any snags which occurred in the production stage of any operation. Two other organizations said that it was not company policy temporarily to reduce or cease the volume of effort applied if basic and applied research were to be fitted to a time scale.

Of the organizations who did use research staff for 'trouble shooting', twenty-two, mostly from section 3 of the continuum, qualified their replies to indicate that they would be most grateful if this were not the case. The borrowing of staff from research projects varied from very frequently—every time anything went wrong—to only in serious operational emergencies. Only one organization stated that there was any formal mechanism to ensure that research projects were kept on schedule after being interrupted by 'trouble shooting' by having the overall man-hours allocated to the project during that time period made up at the expense of the department whose pressing problems had been dealt with.

10. INFORMATION FROM PERSONAL VISITS

During the course of the questionnaire survey personal contact was made with R&D staff from about one-third of the organizations represented in the questionnaire return. Members of the R&D Research Unit staff visited certain organizations to investigate specific aspects of their R&D activities, and personnel from other organizations visited the Business School. Some points brought out by these interviews concern (a) the definition of objectives, (b) the generation and assessment of ideas, (c) co-ordination with other departments, and (d) finance and costing of R&D.

(a) The establishment of a single objective for R&D within an organization is extremely difficult, because the term embraces a wide variety of long- and short-term activities. What constitutes R&D varies between organizations: in most, 'trouble shooting' is included, and in others quality control and technical services to the organization and its customers also falls under this heading. Save in routine development, the establishment of objectives for individual projects is not always easy, and in fundamental research it is frequently not seriously attempted. It was stated by a number of people that the inadequate definition of project objectives often leads to difficulties in carrying out the research work, and subsequently to the termination of the project, as no objectives based criteria of success existed on which to judge it. The establishment of such criteria is not easy, but it was generally agreed that without such measures it is impossible to realistically assess the progress of a project.

(b) In a number of organizations in which formal project proposal methods are in use there do not appear to be sufficient ideas being submitted to the evaluation mechanism to give the organization a wide enough range of potential projects from which to select its portfolio. When the number of proposed projects is only slightly larger than the resources available to the research department will permit to be carried out, there is a danger that several inferior projects will be undertaken, in default of anything better being available to occupy the resources allocated to research. Some organizations have attempted to remedy this by setting up small departments whose specific task is to encourage and assess ideas which are relevant to the organization's long-term policy objectives. These departments are designed to match the technical capabilities of the R&D department to the forecast needs of the market. Other organizations have attempted to widen the area from which ideas can *easily* flow by instituting a project ideas suggestion system throughout all departments of the organization, the originators of all suggestions incorporated into research projects being paid for their idea, whether or not they take any part in its further development.

Where attempts have been made to introduce analytically based selection models into organizations, these have generally been developed and adapted within one department, and no attempt has been made to force their use on to other departments of the same organization. This is seen as an indication that there is insufficient evidence to date to demonstrate that the advantages of the method outweigh its possible disadvantages.

The major areas of difficulty encountered in evaluation were generally considered to be the formulation of an estimate of the probability of technical success at an early stage in a project's life, and accurate forecasting of the potential benefits to the organization if the project were to be successful.

(c) Virtually all organizations are aware of some problems in the co-ordination between R&D and other functional areas of the organization. The degree of co-ordination and co-operation varies considerably, and appears to be a function of the individuals concerned and the organization's structure. The formal structure of the organization to a large extent determines the communications channels between R&D and the rest of the organization. Several examples were found of cases where the research department was geographically separated from the production and marketing functions of the organization, but was always fully aware of their actions and opinions because effective channels of communication existed in the organization's formal structure. Cases were found where R&D and production operated in the same building, but communications were poor because there were inadequate formal channels, and though the informal communications network operating in the plant could provide information, decisions could not be taken on the basis of this information because of its unauthorized origin.

Most of the R&D staff interviewed by the Unit expressed great interest in the overall activities of their organization, and a genuine desire to see a successful end-product following the completion of the research work. Dissatisfaction was expressed with the attitude of certain organizations who do not consider it necessary to make research staff aware of the market potential or general usefulness of the end-results of the research work on which they are engaged.

In many cases, the market situation was not assessed in sufficient detail to enable the potential benefits to be accurately quantified, and in particular the changing needs of the market were not always noted. In several organizations this has resulted in technically good research not being used because when it was completed, further market research indicated that the market situation had altered, and that the end-product of R&D was not a commercially viable proposition. Had sufficient attention been paid to the changing requirements of the market, and information on this communicated to the research department, the work could have been discontinued, rather than completed, and the resources committed to it used on other projects. Cases were also met where the research department had produced new products or processes which were not commercially exploited because they were technically too advanced for the organization, or the industry which it served, to accept at that time.

Discussion with scientific personnel suggests that they prefer to work on projects which have well-defined, and reasonably precise, objectives, and this is particularly so when they have been involved in the process of deciding the objectives, and have been fully informed about the commercial implications of the research. In general, they did not object to having their research planned, and working within controls of time and expenditure, provided that these controls could be seen to be of benefit to the R&D department as a whole. The amount of control which should be applied appears to depend upon the type of project and the type of person who is handling it. Some scientists given considerable freedom of action, and not working to precise objectives, found that their apparent rate of progress was slow. As the research objectives were not precise, there was no means of accurately gauging progress, and the apparent lack of results caused dissatisfaction. On the other hand, instances were found where the emphasis on the allocation of effort on a time basis led to opposition, because research staff disliked filling in weekly time sheets, and saw no reason why management should need to know exactly how each hour of the working week had been spent. It is advanced that in the latter cases, 'time booking' systems could be detrimental to the organization in the long run, because they are causing dissatisfaction in the research department which will encourage individual members of staff to falsify their time sheets and allocate their time as they see fit.

Many organizations considered their R&D departments to be good recruiting grounds for people who are potential management personnel, and considered that the training and experience which personnel received during their time in R&D could be of great use in other parts of the organization. Scientists can make a satisfactory career in research, but there are management career opportunities for scientific personnel in other parts of the organization, and a number of people who have successfully moved from R&D into general management have been involved in the Unit's discussions. However, in most organizations there are no formal procedures to facilitate or encourage such transfers.

(d) Few cases were met where the organization's R&D department carried out the costing of its own research. Usually the authority for determining the R&D budget, and how the research should be financed, rested outside the R&D department, many organizations considering the annual research budget as a single item whose size was fixed as being a given percentage of turnover or operating profits of the organization. Individual projects are usually costed on a total-cost basis, with provision for overheads to be added by a well-defined, but sometimes very arbitrary, method.

Costs are often accumulated using a system of booking time to projects by the scientists involved, and some form of control system is operated which is usually based on a comparison of estimated costs against actual expenditure in each time period. It appears to be difficult to include in these control systems a measure of the technical achievement to date, and without such a measure, though the variance between forecast and actual expenditure can be calculated for each time period, it will be difficult to estimate what the total cost of the completed project is likely to be.

II. CONCLUSIONS

From the results of the questionnaire survey and information drawn from personal visits, it seems that most of the 'textbook' methods of evaluation and control are currently in use amongst large organizations, if only on a limited scale. The evidence we have points to an interest in formal procedures for research evaluation and control amongst organizations, and to their increasing use. Many instances were found of organizations not using certain techniques, but currently employing staff on organizing their introduction. This is a process taking several months, and the staff concerned were assessing the techniques and modifying them to suit the organizations' requirements. Once in operation, the performance of the techniques are examined, and their benefit to the organization evaluated. Also, as a number of organizations expressed dissatisfaction with resource allocation and scheduling procedures, and several have discontinued these procedures, it is advanced that formal techniques are being carefully examined, rather than uncritically adopted. This examination and evaluation of techniques, combined with the difficulty of adapting theoretical ideas to fit the real situation of the organization may account for much of the time lag between the exposition of a method in the literature and its subsequent widespread adoption by industry.

MANCHESTER BUSINESS SCHOOL,
UNIVERSITY OF MANCHESTER

APPENDIX. THE QUESTIONNAIRE

A. RESOURCES EMPLOYED ON R&D

1 How many qualified scientists and engineers (graduate *equivalent* and above) has the organization currently engaged on Research and Development? Please indicate one of the following:

20 or less	...
21 to 40	...
41 to 70	...
71 to 100	...
101 to 150	...
151 to 250	...
Over 250	...

2 Please indicate within which of the following ranges the total cost to the organization of R&D falls:

£30,000 or less	...
More than £30,000, but less than £60,000	...
More than £60,000, but less than £100,000	...
More than £100,000, but less than £500,000	...
More than £500,000, but less than £1 million	...
Over £1 million, but less than £2 million	...
Greater than £2 million	...

B. ORIGINATION OF R&D IDEAS

3 When a person has an idea for a new R&D project, are there formal channels for presenting the idea for assessment, such as filling in a proposal form or checklist, or presenting the idea plus some supporting evidence to a committee?

Yes ... No ...

If 'Yes', please specify the system very briefly, giving the names of any committees, or assessment boards.

4 Are R&D staff allowed any time within their working hours to work on their own projects, and investigate ideas of their own, rather than work on the research programme which the organization has under way?

Yes ... No ...

If 'Yes', at whose discretion is the allocation of this 'spare time'

The individual worker	...
The section head/project leader	...
The R&D Director/Manager	...

5 What expenditure limits are placed on the use of facilities and materials by R&D workers to test their own ideas before they must be submitted for assessment? ....

6 Does the organization consider projects for assessment which are not directly connected with current products or processes?

Yes ... No ...

7 Does the organization use the services of Research Association(s)?

Yes ... No ...

If 'Yes',

(i) Are the Associations services used primarily for basic research ..., or for development problems ...? (Please tick as applicable.)

(ii) Does the organization commission private work from the Research Association(s)?

Yes ... No ...

(iii) Please name the Associations whose services are used, in the order of their usefulness to the organization.

8 Does the organization purchase research information in any of the following ways?

(i) Rights to use patented processes ...
(ii) Rights to manufacture under licence ...
(iii) Services of consultants ...
(iv) Sponsoring of university research ...

9 Does the organization sell research information, by selling 'know-how' ..., or by licensing its patents to other organizations ...? (Please tick where applicable.)

10 Do the R&D staff have access to the following services? Please indicate whether these are available from the organization's service departments, or are purchased from outside sources.

	Within organization	*Outside sources*
(i) Data retrieval services	...	...
(ii) Patents checking services	...	...
(iii) Abstracts reading services	...	...

Please specify any other information services, for example, a library, and indicate whether it is within the organization, or purchased from outside sources.

C. EVALUATION OF PROPOSED PROJECTS

11 Is there a standard procedure used for the evaluation of proposed R&D projects?

Yes ... No ...

If 'Yes', is this procedure used to assess all proposed R&D projects?

Yes ... No ...

If 'No', please specify the type of project which it is used for.

....

12 Is there a standard proposal form, such as a checklist?

Yes ... No ...

If there is a standard form, are numerical weightings given to the items listed so that one project can be compared to another?

Yes ... No ...

13 Below are some criteria for evaluating the commercial feasibility of proposed projects. Could you please tick any currently used by your organization:

(i) Period taken to pay back capital invested ...
(ii) Average rate of return on capital invested ...
(iii) Discounted cash flow methods (e.g. The DCF yield, or Net Present Value) ...

14 Are the following considered when a project is at the evaluation stage?

(i) Estimation/probability of commercial success ...
(ii) Estimation/probability of technical feasibility ...
(iii) Estimation of development costs ...

15 Does the organization make use of mathematical models in the selection of projects? (e.g. Decision Trees, Mathematical Programming).

Yes ... No ...

If 'Yes', please name the techniques used. ....

16 Could you name, or briefly outline, any criteria or methods which are in use within the organization, but *not covered in questions* 13 *and* 14, for estimating the feasibility of proposed projects.

If *none*, please tick here ...

17 If there are any criteria or decision-making techniques which the organization has tried, and then discarded as unsuited to its needs, could you name them below, and give the reason why they were discarded (e.g. Too unwieldy; Requiring unavailable information; Did not justify additional cost).

18 Are the criteria which the organization uses to evaluate projects applied to development projects with the same ..., greater ..., or less ... rigour than they are applied to basic research projects? (Please tick where applicable.)

D. REVIEW AND CONTROL

19 Is a completion date assigned to a basic research project when it is commenced?

Yes ... No ...

If 'Yes', by whom is the time scale determined? ....

20 How frequently are basic research projects reviewed? Every three months ..., every six months ..., annually ..., or sporadic-

ally ... at 'natural breaks' in the projects lifetime. Please tick where applicable, or give frequency of reviews ....

21 Are the assessors at these reviews the same assessors who originally evaluated the project?

Yes ... No ...

If 'No', who is responsible for the periodic reviews? ....

22 Are networks used to specify original time scales, and dates of review, when a project is first assessed to be feasible?

Yes ... No ...

If 'Yes', please tick any of the methods below which the organization uses, indicating the degree of use.

	Wide use	*Occasional use*
(i) Programme evaluation and review technique, PERT	...	...
(ii) Critical path analysis, CPA	...	...
(iii) Programme evaluation procedure, PEP	...	...

Are there any other methods used by the organization to specify time scales? e.g. Bar Charts.

Yes ... No ...

If 'Yes', please name or specify briefly. ....

23 Please name any network techniques which have been used and found unsatisfactory.

If none, please tick ...

24 Please indicate any of the following criteria which are used to decide whether to continue or discontinue a project in which the organization is currently engaged:

(i) Changed estimate/probability of commercial success ...
(ii) Changed estimate/probability of technical feasibility ...
(iii) Changed estimate of development costs ...

25 What factors determine the completion dates assigned to development projects? e.g. Marketing considerations, R&D considerations, Contract obligations.

26 Are basic research projects occasionally 'suspended' in order to free staff to work on pressing short-term projects, such as, for example, production snags in a new product?

Yes ... No ...

PUBLICATIONS RECEIVED

Accounting: A Modern Approach, by R. W. Wallis, McGraw-Hill Publishing Co., 1970.

Balance-of-Payments Policy, by B. J. Cohen, Penguin Modern Economics, September, 1969.

The Causes of Graduate Unemployment in India, by M. Blang, P.R.G. Layard and M. Woodhall, L.S.E. Studies on Education, Allen Lane, The Penguin Press, December 1969, 105s.

Company Organization: Theory and Practice, P.A. Management Consultants Ltd., M. C. Barnes, A. H. Fogg, C. N. Stephens and L. G. Titman, George Allen & Unwin, 1970, 70s.

The Competition for Savings, Determinants of Deposits at Commercial Banks, Mutual Savings Banks and Savings and Loan Associations, by George K. Kardouche, Studies in Business Economics, No. 107, National Industrial Conference Board, 1969.

Constructive Conflict, by N. S. Ross, Oliver & Boyd, January 1970, 25s.

Continuing Education for R. & D. Careers, prepared for the National Science Foundation by Social Research, Inc., June 1969, $1.75.

The Contribution of Local Subsidies to the Economic Development of West Virginia, by Carl W. Hale, West Virginia University Economic Development Series, No. 12, January 1969, $2.50.

The Economics of Agriculture, by David Metcalf, Penguin Modern Economics, September 1969, 7s.

Economics of Ocean Freight Rates, by Esra Bennathan and A. A. Walters, Pall Mall Press, September 1969, 125s.

Economics and Sociology of Industry, by P. Sargant Florence, C. A. Watts & Co., second edition, 1969, 40s.

The Economics of Technological Change, by Edwin Mansfield, Longman Group, December 1969, 50s.

Elements of Regional Economics, by Harry W. Richardson, Penguin Modern Economics, September 1969, 7s.

The Future of Manufacturing Industry in Johannesburg and the Demand for Industrial Land, by Professor G. Marais, Bureau of Market Research, University of South Africa, 1969.

Gaps in Technology, Plastics, a report by the OECD, Paris, 1969.

Geographical Mobility and The Brain Drain, A case study of Aberdeen University Graduates 1860–1960, George Allen & Unwin.

The Gold Money Rift, A Classical Theory of International Liquidity by P. R. Brahmananda, Bombay Popular Prakashan, 1969, Rs. 36.00.

Government and The Exporter, A Study of the Effectiveness of Official Export Services and Incentives in West Germany and The United Kingdom, The Export Research Group, December 1969, 25s.

Highlights of the Dilemma of Freight Transport Regulation, by Ann F. Friedlander, Brookings Research Report 99, November 1969.

The Hop Industry of Eastern Europe and the Soviet Union, by David A. Strausz, Washington State University Press, June 1969.

Industrial Britain: The North East, by Professor John W. House, David & Charles Ltd., November 1969, 95s.

Industrial Demand for Water: A Study of South East England, by Judith Rees, Weidenfeld & Nicolson, November 1969, 65s.

Industrial Research and Technological Innovation, An Econometric Analysis, by Edwin Mansfield, Longman Group, 1969, 65s.
Industrialization in Nineteenth Century Europe, by Tom Kemp, Longmans Group, November 1969, 50s.
Industry and Empire, by E. J. Hobsbawm, Penguin Education, 9s.
Industry Production Behaviour: The Order Stock Distinction, by D. A. Belsley, North Holland Publishing Company, 1969, 105s.
Input–Output in the U.K. Proceedings of the 1968 Manchester Conference, edited by W. F. Gossling, Frank Cass & Co., 1970, 60s.
Inter-Market Food Cost Differentials: A Case Study of Honolulu and the San Francisco Bay Area, by John A. Jamison, Food Research Institute, Stanford University, 1969, $2.00.
The International Monetary System, by Herbert G. Grubel, Penguin Modern Economics, September 1969, 7s.
International Trade, by I. F. Pearce, Book I, The Balance of Payments, Adjusting Mechanisms, Trade Impediments and Customs Unions, Macmillan Student Editions, 1970, 45s.
International Trade, by I. F. Pearce, Book II, Factor Endowment and Prices, Factor Mobility, Factor Market, Imperfections, Growth and Control, Macmillan Student Editions, 1970, 45s.
Investment & Uncertainty, by Edward C. Townsend, Oliver & Boyd, January 1970, 45s.
Manpower in the Road Transport Industry, Survey of Manpower and Labour Turnover in the Road Transport Industry, 1968.
Managerial Economics, Analysis and Cases (revised edition), by W. W. Haynes, Business Publications Inc., July 1969, $10.50 college price.
Monetary Theory, by R. W. Clower, Penguin Education, 1969, 10s.
Nationalised Industries, by Graham L. Reid and Kevin Allan, Penguin Modern Economics, 1970, 7s.
The New Industrial State, by J. K. Galbraith, Penguin Education, October 1969, 8s.
The North West, Industrial Britain, by David M. Smith, David & Charles (Holdings) Ltd., September 1969, 95s.
Office Automation in Social Perspective, by H. A. Rhee, Basil Blackwell, 45s.
Organization Behaviour, by J. Kelley, Richard D. Irwin Inc., June 1969, $9.95.
Pay and Productivity Bargaining, A Study of the Effect of National Wage Agreements in the Nottinghamshire Coalfield, by R. G. Searle Barnes, Manchester University Press, October 1969, 45s.
Personal Income for Missouri Counties, 1950–1965, by Paul E. Junk, Brackston Hinchey, Robert W. Paterson and Lonnie Nickles, Research Center, School of Business and Public Administration, University of Missouri, Columbia, 1968, $3.50.
Perspective 1975, Sixth Annual Review, by Economic Council of Canada, September 1969.
Politics of De-control of Industry, by Susan Armitage, Weidenfeld & Nicolson, L.S.E. Research Monographs No. 4, September 1969, 55s.
Price Theory & Price Policy, by M. A. G. Van Meerhaeghe, Longmans Group, December 1969, 40s.
Profit in the United States, An introduction to a study of economic concentration and business cycles, by Howard J. Sherman, Cornell University Press, August 1969, 85.

Readings in the Concept and Measurement of Income, edited by R. H. Parker and G. C. Harcourt, Cambridge University Press, January 1970, 80s. (cloth), 21s. (paper).

Reformation to Industrial Revolution, by Christopher Hill, Penguin Education, 1969, 7s.

The Role of the Government in Research and Development, Hill Samuel, Occasional Paper No. 4, produced by Maxwell Stamp Associates Ltd., October 1969.

The Role of Structural Fire Protection: A Sample Survey and Case Studies of 56 Large Fires, by Merrett Cyriax Associates, Industrial Consultants, Cement and Concrete Association, November 1969.

Scientific Activities of Nonprofit Institutions, 1966 Survey of Science Resources Series, National Science Foundation, March 1969.

The Sources of Invention, second edition, by John Jewkes, David Sawers and Richard St. Ullerman, Macmillan & Co., November 1969, 70s.

Studies on the Strategy and Technique of Development Planning, edited by Azizur Rahman Khan, The Pakistan Institute of Development Economics, September 1969, $4.00.

Sweet Encounter: The Confectionery Resale Price Maintenance Case, by H. Crane, Macmillan & Co. September 1969, 160s.

The Tax System in Sweden, by Martin Nor, Claes Sandels and Nils G. Hornhammer, Stockholm's Enskilda Bank, November 1969.

The Times 500 Leading Companies in Britain and Overseas 1969–70, Times Newspapers, October 1969, 15s.

Wages, by B. J. McCormick, Penguin Modern Economics, September 1969, 7s.

Weather Economics, edited by James A. Taylor, 1970, Pergamon Press.

The Welfare State U.S.A., an Exploration in and Beyond the New Economics, by Nelrille J. Ulmer, Houghton Mifflin Company, November 1969, $4.95.

Workshop Wage Determination, by Shirley W. Lerner, John R. Cable and S. Gupta, Pergamon Press, November 1969, (hard cover) 45s. (flexi-cover) 35s.

COMPETITION IN THE SAUSAGE MARKET

by Dennis Lees and John Morley*

'Let them make sausages of me and serve me up to the students'
Aristophanes: *The Clouds*

INTRODUCTION

This work began as a study of the economic effects of advertising in the market for sausages but has developed into a more general analysis of competition in the sausage market. The reasons are 2-fold. Firstly the volume of advertising is small—only about £½ million a year in a £100 million market and almost half of that is accounted for by one firm. Secondly, the complex competitive structure of the market contrasts sharply with that of fast-moving package foodstuffs where there is often extensive competitive advertising between a few major brands. Broadly, the study is about competition between national brands, local brands and unbranded products in which advertising is only one and, as yet, a not very important influence.

The scope of the study is in two parts. Firstly, the collection and analysis of published data, research reports and government/industry market research agencies, supplemented by data from particular companies who kindly co-operated with us. This material is presented in Sections I and II. The second part involved a local shop survey carried out in the Nottingham area, which studied 100 outlets in four areas of the city, collecting information on brands, prices and types of sausages. The data are set out and interpreted in Section III.

SECTION I: THE PRODUCT

Apart from the fun value, there are a number of reasons why a study of sausages is of interest to economists. First, the product is highly perishable. An unwrapped sausage should normally be consumed within 2 days of production and, while wrapping extends this period, it seldom does so for more than a day. Thus rapid sale is essential, stock building is impossible, and production and distribution tend to be localized. Secondly, although techniques of production can be expensive and sophisticated, anyone with a mixing bowl, meat, grain and spices, a mechanical pump with a nozzle on the end, and a

* The authors are grateful to the Advertising Association for a grant that assisted the preparation of the study and to manufacturers' associations, local authorities and particular companies for their kind co-operation. The authors alone are of course responsible for use made of material and conclusions reached.

bundle of skins, can start production. So there are few if any financial or technical barriers to entry and elasticity of supply is virtually infinite. It is true that sausage and meat product manufacturers have to register with local public health authorities for purposes of hygiene and the like. This creates a *potential* legal barrier to entry but, in practice, it is of little significance, as evidenced by the fact, for example, that there are 374 butchers and meat product manufacturers in Nottingham alone.

Thirdly, although the product is essentially non-homogeneous (thick, thin, long, short, blotchy, pasty, spicy, bland, coarse, fine-cut *et hoc genus omne*), the competitive structure in local areas is such as to enable a bewildering variety of original empirical evidence to be grouped into that small number of categories crucial to any kind of analysis. Or, put the other way around, by treating non-homogeneous sausages within each category *as if* they were homogeneous, we get an explanation of observed phenomena that seems pretty satisfactory.[1]

This study is principally concerned with these three facets of the product—perishability, ease of entry and non-homogeneity—but there are one or two others worth noting.

Legislation

Like many other food products, the composition of sausages was controlled during the last war under Defence Regulations, which did not finally come to an end until March 1953. After then, however, attempts to enforce certain standards (particularly regarding the percentage meat content) by local food and drug authorities have run into difficulties, not least because there was no longer a statutory definition of a sausage. The Lord Chief Justice remarked with some asperity in one piece of litigation that 'the sooner it is seen that these cases lead to chaos and it is prescribed what a sausage is, the better'.[2]

Consequently, the Ministry of Agriculture, Fisheries and Food called on the Food Standards Committee (itself appointed in 1947 to advise on composition and labelling of food) to advise whether statutory standards, or some other form of compositional control, was

[1] Our most important sources of data were:
(a) Odhams reports on *Branded Food Products* (referred to simply as 'Odhams').
(b) *Domestic Food Consumption and Expenditure*, Annual Reports of the National Food Survey Committee, Ministry of Agriculture, Fisheries and Food, H.M.S.O.
(c) Our own sample survey of sausage distribution in Nottingham, Autumn, 1968. See Section III.

[2] Thrussell v. Whiteman (*The Times*, January 18th, 1956). See also Williams v. Hurrells Stores (*The Times*, May 6th, 1954) and Marston v. Longy (*The Times*, October 12th, 1955).

needed for sausages. The Committee[3] reported in 1956, recommending various proposals designed to set minimum meat contents and this led, 11 years later, to Statutory Instrument 1967 No. 862, 'The Sausage and Other Meat Product Regulations 1967', which came into force on May 31st, 1969.

The statutory instrument's definition of a sausage runs thus: 'a product of a shape usually known as sausage shape or part of that such product made of comminuted meat with or without the addition of cereal and other minor ingredients, whether contained in an edible or inedible casing or not, and including any chipolata, frankfurter, salame, saveloy and polony'. In broad terms, the 1967 legislation defines 'meat' and required a minimum meat content of 50 per cent for beef sausages and 65 per cent for pork.

Joint Products

For very few companies are sausages the whole source of revenue and joint, or complementary, products exist in the forms of hams, pies, sausage rolls and the like. For the butcher, equally, sausages are jointly demanded along with other meat products and jointly supplied, at least partially, in the form of processing of unsold meat.

Not all butchers' sausages are produced by the butchers themselves. and many obtain supplies either from other butchers of similar size who happen to specialize in sausages, or from local firms who either supply a number of outlets, or who produce products locally under their own brand and also sell the same item unbranded to butchers.

Raw materials form the biggest single item in total costs and it is therefore important for the manufacturer to utilize fully the meat he buys by producing a wide variety of meat products.

Packaging

One of the biggest developments in the marketing of sausages and pies over the past 10 years has been the development of wrapping and pre-packaging. This has increased the shelf life, enabled the retailer to handle it more easily, but, most important of all, enabled the manufacturer to put his brand name clearly and permanently on the product. Nevertheless, in some areas, including that in which we carried out our survey, there is still a good trade for loose-linked sausages. The development of the supermarket alongside this has meant that the meat processing company has been able to provide a whole range of meat products, all suitably packaged and branded for self-service display.

[3] *Food Standards Committee, Report on Sausages*, H.M.S.O., 1956.

Research

Apart from the research carried out by individual companies, collective research is undertaken by the British Food Manufacturing Industries Research Association based in Leatherhead, Surrey. Research reports are confidential to members of the R.A., who in turn, maintain overall control on the nature of research carried out, mainly through the technical committees which contain representatives from the technical staff of companies.

Current research is concentrated on both technical aspects of the product and its composition, for example, research into preservatives and additives, as well as into consumer acceptance properties, like cooking losses or colour fading during cooking.

SECTION II: THE MARKET

1. *Introduction*

The sausage market is more or less static in terms of both total value and volume of sales, with annual consumption close on £100 million at present-day prices.

TABLE I
ANNUAL CONSUMPTION OF SAUSAGES
(lb. per person per annum)

	1960	*1961*	*1962*	*1963*	*1964*	*1965*	*1966*
Pork	6.9	6.9	7.6	7.4	6.9	7.2	7.5
Beef	4.8	4.8	4.8	4.8	5.2	4.9	4.3

Notes:
(i) Volume calculated from data in *Domestic Food Consumption and Expenditure*, Min. of Ag., Fish, and Food, H.M.S.O. (annually).
(ii) The average national price is about 3*s*. a pound (*ibid.*) and prices rose slightly over the 6-year period: Pork 3s. 1d. to 3s. 5d. and beef 2s. 5d. to 2s. 10d.

Total sales of processed meat products are increasing but this increase is in products like meat pies and other meat and pastry products, rather than in sausages.

2. *Tastes*

Although it is convenient to talk of the national market for sausages, in fact, there is no national market in the sense of a reasonably homogeneous pattern of demand across the length and breadth of the country. Perhaps because of the historical development of the product, and the traditional qualities that it represents, the nature of the demand for sausages varies very considerably from region to region, and even area to area. Nor are these mere minor variations, detected only by statistical significance tests, but are fundamental determinants of the demand for sausages.

The national market is, in other words, only the aggregation of a number of regional and local markets, each with distinctive preferences in terms of meat content, type, size and various other attributes of the product. There is a sort of national market which transcends regional boundaries, but it is still relatively small and, in fact, represented in the main by the products of the major producer, Walls. With this exception, and the rising activities and national aspirations of some other brands, the market requirements are already fairly precisely defined and manufacturers succeed, or fail, to the extent to which they can meet the widely differing tastes of consumers. Whether these tastes are 'irrational' or 'traditional', bred in the local environments, or whether their existence reflects something intrinsically different about local palates is not a question we can answer. But it is abundantly clear[4] that these marked and persistent differences in consumer tastes are *not* the result of marketing activities, advertising or any other, and those who hold that the consumer in modern society is a puppet on an advertiser's string, here at least, have something to explain.

Regional Variations

We have seen that sausages can differ in very many ways but if we take only the broad distinction between pork and beef sausages, *regional* variations are revealed; these are shown in Table II. The

TABLE II

PROPORTION OF PORK/BEEF SAUSAGES BOUGHT IN DIFFERENT REGIONS *1965*

Region	*Pork : Beef*
North Midlands	9 : 1
Midlands/Eastern/South-east and South	8 : 2
East and West Ridings/South-West	7 : 3
North/North-west/Wales	6 : 4
Scotland	2 : 8

Source: calculated from data in *Domestic Food Consumption and Expenditure*, Min. of Ag., Fish, and Food, H.M.S.O. (annually).

differences are striking enough but, within these wide regional groupings, both casual observation and discussions with producers show that there are further substantial differences of local taste.

[4] See subsection on *Advertising and Vertical Integration.*

Household Variations

There are also significant variations of taste as between households and these can be explained in part at least by differences in the composition and income of households.[5] As to composition, households in Britain with children make up 40 per cent of all households but account for 56 per cent of total expenditure on sausages.[6] More significantly, households with children buy a higher proportion of beef sausages than households without children[7] and this may well be due to the fact that beef sausages are cheaper.

As regards income, calculations made for the years 1960, 1962 and 1965 in the *Domestic Food Consumption and Expenditure* reports show that households with high incomes buy more pork and less beef sausages than households of similar composition with lower incomes. Without wishing to predict the demise of the beef sausage, it would not seem to have a bright future in an expanding economy.

Market and Brand Shares

The product market is quite unlike that of the normal grocery item with which most marketing men are acquainted in that branded goods have a bare majority rather than a dominant situation. As Table III shows, unbranded sausages account for 40–45 per cent of the national market compared with 'national' brands who have some 30–35 per cent and 'local' brands with 20–25 per cent.[8]

Although a large number of different brand names of makes of sausages are known to consumers, very few brands can in fact claim more than 1 or 2 per cent of the national market.

Among the branded products, Walls is the outstanding exception with a market share over the last four years of between 14 and 18 per cent. Moreover, next to Walls, are two retail, rather than manufacturing organizations, the Co-op and Sainsburys with around 5 per cent each. They are followed by Richmond with some 3–5 per cent, but whose products are, again, aided to a large extent by their distribution through the retail outlets of its holding company, Allied Suppliers.

Outside of these, only four brands—Brazils, Harris, Drings and Marsh & Baxter can claim above 1 per cent, and a number of well-

[5] Unfortunately, the data do not exist or are not in a form amenable to statistical analysis, like multiple regression, which could enable differences in taste to be explained more precisely.

[6] Odhams reports on *Branded Food Products* and Registrar General's estimates of population.

[7] Odhams.

[8] The term 'national brand' is rather misleading, since only one company—Walls—has achieved something like nation-wide coverage, but we use it for want of a better term to distinguish brands like the first eight in the table from other brands more regionally/locally oriented.

known brands, like Bowyer and Palethorpes, achieve less than 1 per cent. However, these 'local' brands are so numerous that they make up around 20 per cent of the total market.[9]

On a regional basis, however, the importance of branded sausages and the importance of particular manufacturers shows more strongly. A brand share of less than 1 per cent nationally can be 15 per cent in the South-west as with Bowyer Ltd., of Wiltshire, or brand leadership in some areas, as with Pork Farms, a local manufacturer/retailer in Nottingham with distribution contained within the East Midland area.

In fact, even Walls's national coverage is not spread evenly, with strong areas centred upon their two main points of manufacture and distribution in London and Manchester, and weaker areas further afield.

TABLE III

MARKET SHARES OF SAUSAGES

(% national averages)	*1964*	*1965*	*1966*	*1967*
Walls	14	18	14	17
Co-operatives	8	4	3	5
Richmond	5	5	4	3
Sainsbury	3	3	5	5
Brazils	2	—	2	2
Harris	2	2	2	1
Dring	—	—	1	1
Marsh & Baxter	2	—	2	1
Other brands	20	20	20	20
Unbranded	40	44	41	43
No information	5	6	6	2
	100	100	100	100

Source: Odhams.

Advertising and Vertical Integration

Table IV gives the press and T.V. advertising expenditure for the five leading advertisers in the sausage market in the period 1963–66. *Total* expenditure was roughly £½ million in 1966.

It will be seen that one firm alone—Walls—accounts for 40 per cent of advertising expenditure and is the only firm to achieve national coverage for its brands. For other firms, advertising tends to be regional or even local.

We were unable to obtain data on 'below-the-line' promotional expenditure—special offers, point of sale, special discounts and bonus

[9] It should be noted that the latest figures available at the time of writing refer to 1967.

offers to retailiers—but one large firm disclosed that it spent about the same 'below-the-line' as above. Experience would of course differ from firm to firm but a very rough estimate of total selling or marketing expenditures by sausage manufacturers would be £1 million a year.

With total sales of sausages of £100 million a year, the ratio of advertising (above-the-line) expenditures to sales is very low compared with the generality of fast-moving consumer goods. And even when 'below-the-line' expenditure is added, marketing costs cannot be considered a major influence in consumer purchases.

TABLE IV

SAUSAGES AND ADVERTISING EXPENDITURE
(*£'000 p.a.*)

T.V. advertising	*1963*	*1964*	*1965*	*1966*
Walls	234.2	286.9	298.0	201.1
Richmond	46.1	39.0	18.2	—
Bowyers	24.7	47.2	45.0	48.0
Harris	34.5	60.2	65.0	49.0
Marsh	7.6	3.9	12.2	16.3
Press advertising				
Walls	54.7	36.3	21.6	4.6
Richmond	16.9	16.7	24.3	27.4
Bowyers	4.9	—	20.0	7.6
Harris	40.3	5.8	13.0	11.9
Marsh	8.6	3.3	10.6	5.9

Source: Legion Information Services Ltd.
Notes:
(a) Legion figures are based on rate card rates and therefore overstate the amounts spent by taking no account of discounts for bulk buying, etc. Conversely, the figures understate by being based on less than complete press and periodical coverage, particularly the provincial press. These imperfections in the data need not concern us here as our concern is with broad orders of magnitude and comparisons.
(b) In Legion quarterly reports, the product category is 'meat pies, ham, bacon, sausages', but discussions with manufacturers established that almost all expenditure was on sausages.

Advertising is in part a substitute for vertical integration, i.e. the ownership of retail outlets by manufacturers. Looked at in this way, it is not surprising that Walls, who own no retail outlets, and yet have achieved national coverage, should be heavy advertisers. An obvious and illuminating analogy is Guinness in the brewing industry; they advertise far more than brewers with tied houses but have at the same time achieved national coverage. Sainsbury's, who do not advertise at all, are an example of vertical integration on the 'national' level and, in Nottingham, there are Pork Farms and Parrs, whose advertising is minimal.

Retail Distribution

There are two quite separate channels of distribution for sausages with, on the one hand, the various types of grocery outlets dealing in the main with branded products, and, on the other, the butchers' shops or butchers' counters of large stores handling non-branded goods. In addition, a number of general stores, corner shops, off-licences, and bakeries, also sell limited quantities of both branded and unbranded products, national, regional, and local.

TABLE V

SALES OF ALL SAUSAGES BY RETAIL OUTLET (1964)

	%
Independent grocers	23
Multiple grocers	17
Co-operatives	15
Variety stores*	3
Butcher	35
Other	4
(No information)	3
	100

* including Woolworth, Littlewoods, etc.
Source: Odhams.

Since sausages are such a perishable commodity and should, ideally, be sold within 24 hours of delivery, manufacturers can have ready-made retail audit data on the level of sales by outlets from their own factory sales data within 2 or 3 days at the most. While this is useful for manufacturers, it does not help independent research since there has been little incentive to set up audit panels, as is routine with the whole range of fast-moving grocery products, and upon which we could draw. Since no comprehensive information is available, various independent estimates have been used in order to arrive at a general picture. This is useful as a rough guide to the relative importance of different retail outlets, although it throws little light on the changes, if any, in distribution over recent years.

Table V provides one breakdown, for 1964. It shows butchers with around 35 per cent, grocers 40 per cent and the Co-op taking the bulk of the remaining sales. Although quantities sold could not be collected for our Nottingham survey, casual observation leads us to suppose that, in Nottingham at least, the Co-op share is much smaller.

In addition, Table VI shows a more detailed breakdown of retail distribution of *branded* sausages derived from two separate estimates. The picture is roughly the same as that for *all* sausages, including butchers, though the regional manufacturer shows a markedly different pattern of retail distribution—more through independents and less through Co-ops.

TABLE VI

RETAIL DISTRIBTUION OF BRANDED (WRAPPED) SAUSAGES ONLY
(i.e. excluding butchers)
(*Percentage of total sales*)

	All manufacturers of branded sausages*	One regional manufacturer†
Independents	35	55
Multiples	29	25
Co-operatives	23	13
Variety stores	4	7
Other	5	—
No information	4	—
	100	100

* Odhams.
† Kindly supplied by the manufacturer.

Van Distribution[10]

For a company to aim for a regional or national distribution, while at the same time taking advantage of centralized production, a complex organization of physical distribution is required, involving bulk transport over longer distances, broken at depots into smaller van loads for local distribution.

The most effective, if not the only successful method, is that of van to retailer selling as practised, and pioneered, by Walls and now being steadily adopted by other major producers.

This technique of van selling requires the van driver/salesman to act as order taker, salesman and promoter of new lines, delivery man and cash handler. Orders are rung through to a depot each day; these are made up and loaded into the van that night for delivery the following morning. Depending on the position on the round, the goods will be on display between 24 and 48 hours following the order.

Up to 70 per cent of van sales can be for cash, and this is strongly encouraged for independent shops. If credit arrangements are requested by retailers, the decision is out of the driver's hand and usually left to more senior sales staff. It is reckoned that a salesman

[10] This section benefited greatly from *Notes on the Distribution of Sausages by Van Salesmen*, kindly made available to us by the Openheimer Casing Co. (U.K.) Ltd., as well as from companies operating the system.

can make approximately sixty calls per day, of which three-quarters are likely to involve delivery of goods.

The system clearly requires careful planning for it to work smoothly, but it is by the adoption of these methods that more widely based companies have been able to compete in terms of delivery with local suppliers, although the edge still remains with the latter in more widely dispersed, rural areas.

Retail Margins

Discussion with firms has established that standard retail margins are on average, around 14 per cent of the selling price (equivalent to a mark-up on the buying-in price of around 22 per cent). In money terms, this is something like 5d. to 7d. on a pound of wrapped sausages. These margins do vary a bit—between 12 and 15 per cent—but are not normally exceeded. The exceptions are to large stores with many branches who may obtain a maximum margin of around 22–23 per cent but, even here, most of the discounts are obtained on the basis of branch sales with relatively little discount given because of the overall quantity bought by the company, although this naturally varies with competitive conditions.

SECTION III: PRICES AND COMPETITION

Local Market Survey: Nottingham

(a) Scope and Method

A local market survey was carried out in the autumn of 1968 in certain areas of Nottingham in order to obtain detailed information on: number and types of shops selling sausages; types of sausage sold by brand; size (thick and thin); and price.

In order not to prejudice the response to these enquiries, no information was sought formally on sales, although this was given in certain cases.

It was decided to undertake a full population survey in a sample of areas, rather than a sample of the whole population of shops in Nottingham, in order to identify local shopping area competition, on the assumption that competition would be greatest between shops in the same area. On this basis, three areas were chosen. One of these was in a largely low-income area, the other two expecting to draw custom from all income groups. The central area of the city was also surveyed on the assumption that the choice for the customer would be between the area (or areas) in which they lived and/or worked and the central shopping area.[11] Reliable evidence on shopping habits at this level of detail is limited but the assumption would seem to accord with common experience.

The population of shops was obtained from the local planning authority, and the short questionnaire was sent to the appropriate shops with a covering note that we would call in 2 days' time. The shops were then approached by interviewers to collect, and in many cases to complete, the questionnaire. By this method, a virtual 100 per cent response was achieved. The questionnaire was sent to 100 shops of which 15 were no longer in existence (due to redevelopment and the like); one refused to co-operate, leaving a total of 84 completed.

Table VII gives details about the number and types of shops selling sausages, based on Census of Distribution classifications.

TABLE VII

Type of shop	*Area in Nottingham*				*Number of shops*
	A	*B*	*C*	*D*	
Multiple grocer	1	3	4	4	13
Independent grocer	8	2	4	1	14
Butcher	11	10	5	15	41
Others*	3	3	3	7	16
					84

* Co-ops, off-licences and variety stores.

(*b*) *Prices: 'National' Brands*

'National' brands were sold at full recommended manufacturers' prices in all outlets covered in the survey. The general picture for all manufacturers in the four survey areas was as follows:

Pork—thin: 4s. per lb.
Pork—thick: 3s. 6d. per lb.
Beef—thin: 3s. 9d. per lb.
Beef—thick: 3s. 1d. per lb.

There were minor price variations between different brands but discussions with manufacturers of 'national' brands suggested that they do not expect to get a larger market by cutting recommended prices at which their sausages are sold to the consumer. In view of the absence of price-cutting in the shops in the Nottingham Survey, the same would seem to be true of retailers, including supermarket chains with a reputation for price competition.

[11] For simplicity, these four areas are referred to from now on as, respectively, Areas A, B, C and D.

From this evidence, it can be inferred that the manufacturers' main sales effort goes *either* into advertising to the final consumer *or* into offering larger discounts and other incentives to retailers to stock their brands. Facts presented on advertising in the previous section suggests that the first alternative is not generally used in this market and this conclusion is reinforced by the fact that three of the market leaders—the Co-op, Sainsbury and Richmond—are in effect retailer brands.

TABLE VIII

Prices of Butchers' sausages sold in Butchers' shops
(Unweighted average price per pound—September 1968)

	Pork—thin	*Pork—thick*	*Beef—thin*	*Beef—thick*	*Other*
Area A, mean price	3s. 11d.	3s. 6½d.	2s. 8d.	2s. 1d.	3s. 6d.
Area B, mean price	3s. 10d.	3s. 6d.	2s. 6½d.	2s. 5d.	3s. 6d.
Area D, mean price	4s. 0d.	3s. 6d.	2s. 8d.	2s. 0d.	3s. 6d.

Notes:
(a) 25 per cent of shops sold pork (thick and/or thin) only.
(b) None sold beef only.
(c) The number of observations for beef (thick) was in all cases small, particularly in Area B, which may account for the mean price there being out of line with mean prices in other areas.
(d) Area C is not included as it contained only three independent butchers.

(*c*) *Prices: Butchers' Sausages in Nottingham*

The figures in Table VIII were derived from our Nottingham survey. They show that the average prices of butchers' sausages as between areas are remarkably similar. From these results, it is possible to deduce the existence of highly competitive conditions, particularly in view of differing locations, non-homogeneity of the product and incomplete knowledge on the part of the consumer. Coupled with virtually complete freedom of entry into the 'sausage industry' noted in Section 1, it looks as though we have here a close approximation to a perfectly competitive market.

(*d*) *Prices: Local Brands in Nottingham*

The two local firms with branded sausages are Pork Farms and Parrs. Both own shops (though they also sell to other retailers) and both sell mainly thin pork sausages through them. For Pork Farms, the price of these sausages was a standard 4s. 6d. a pound in all their own shops in the survey. The price of Parrs sausages varied a bit from shop to shop but 4s. a pound was the cheapest and generally prices lay between that and 4s. 6d. a pound.

(e) Prices: Pork and Beef Sausages

The survey showed that, for *pork sausages* both thin and thick, 'national' brands were 1d. or so dearer a pound than butchers' sausages *but* that the two local brands were up to 6d. a pound dearer. In other words, the local brands are the price leaders, with the prices of 'national' brands lower and very close to unbranded substitutes.

For *beef sausages* the picture is quite different: here 'national' brands are about 1s. (or one-third) dearer than local butchers' sausages. At first sight, this is both a contradiction and a puzzle, but two facts explain the divergent price experienced:

(i) Nottingham is predominantly a pork sausage area—see Table II in Section II, which shows the proportion of pork to beef as 9:1.
(ii) There are no local *brands* of beef sausage.

From all this it would seem reasonable to conclude that, for sausages at least, the existence of local products curbs or constrains the price behaviour of 'national' brands, and (less certainly) where local products do not exist on any substantial scale, 'national' brands may be able to command a price advantage.[12]

Brand Loyalties

In the case of sausages, these do not seem to be strong. Direct evidence is difficult to come by, but it seems a fair inference from the fact, established by our survey and associated observation, that many retail outlets change the brand of sausage they sell quite frequently. Also, we found by direct enquiry that manufacturers generally had no formal longish-term contracts with any retailer, not even with the large multiple grocers and, most important, that the initiative in this arrangement appeared to be on the side of the retailers. Further, some firms, like the Co-op and Sainsbury, retail mainly their own brands and, as has been shown,[13] this policy has given them a market share second only to the market leader.

Stocking of Brands by Retail Outlets

This apparent fragility of brand loyalty consequently reduces the effectiveness of direct appeals by manufacturers to the consumer and concentrates the focus of marketing activity on retail outlets.

We have seen that branded sausages account for more than half of total sales. Our Nottingham survey showed that individual branches

[12] For similar conclusions for other products in the United States, see Neil H. Borden, *The Economic Effects of Advertising* (Irwin, 1942).
[13] Table III, Section II.

of supermarket chains tended to stock just one brand (sometimes its own) and, less commonly, two or more competing brands. Furthermore, within the same supermarket chain, different policies were pursued, for example, with one store stocking one brand and another stocking four competing brands. Whether this is the outcome of central office or local strategy we have been unable to discover, but it would seem that there is a fair amount of managerial discretion at the regional and local level. This pattern of responsibility is matched on the manufacturing side by area sales managers who negotiate discounts and agree credit arrangements and followed up by salesmen, working on commission, who push their wares.

Chain stores like Woolworths and Marks & Spencers tended not to stock 'national' brands but either their own or unbranded sausages. This has the obvious effect of widening the market for producers of sausages by offering outlets for unbranded sausages other than through butchers' shops. The rationale of this stocking policy is that firms of this reputation, in effect, put their own brand on whatever they sell.

The perishability of sausages, already noted, means that salesmen and retailers are in close and very frequent contact. This leads to a continuous interchange of information which is an essential ingredient in the workings of a competitive market. It is a situation of many buyers and many sellers but, unlike the classical or conventional conception of competition, the buyers are not final consumers but other business firms in the form of retailers. If there is a balance of advantage between the parties, it probably lies with the retailers, since it is only through the retailer that manufacturers who are not vertically integrated can reach the ultimate market.

Retailers and the Consumer

It is beyond the scope of this study to examine this area in any depth but we would make the following observations. The choice within any one retail outlet is likely to be limited to the products of one or a very small number of manufacturers. The real choice for the consumer is between retail outlets, who themselves can choose between the products of a large number of manufacturers and, furthermore, revise those choices readily at frequent intervals. The range of choice available in an actual situation can be illustrated from our Nottingham survey where, in the City centre alone (Area D), there are twelve retail outlets offering the branded products of seventeen manufacturers (that is, over fifty different types of sausage), as well as ten independent butchers. Quite apart from offering evidence of very wide choice for the consumer, this situation is clearly one of intense competition between a variety of retail outlets.

In effect, then, the synoptic picture of competition in the 'sausage market' is that manufacturers compete for the custom of grocery retailers and they, in turn, compete against butchers and the traditional meat trade for the custom of final consumers.

UNIVERSITY OF NOTTINGHAM

THE DETERMINATION OF SELLING PRICES

by R. C. Skinner

INTRODUCTION

There seems to be little doubt that 'cost-plus' pricing is fairly widely used in British industry. About 80 per cent of the firms in the survey by Hall and Hitch [1] claimed to use it some or all of the time. In a survey recently carried out by me on Merseyside, 70 per cent of the respondents claimed to use it for some or all of their products or services.[1] The prevalence of the method, however, is not at all easy to understand. This is quite apart from difficulties over profit maximization or marginal-cost pricing; probably few people nowadays would put forward these principles as realistic generalizations about the behaviour of firms, however useful they may (or may not) be in macro-economics or welfare economics. It is not proposed to define cost-plus pricing at this stage; indeed, one of the main objects of the investigation reported here was to ascertain just what it does mean. As normally understood, cost-plus pricing has three obvious defects:

(*a*) It is difficult to believe that, as a general rule, sales volume can be estimated independently of price. If, however, sales volume depends on price, unit costs[2] must also depend on price, and so the method involves a vicious circle in attempting to use cost as a basis for price-fixing.

(*b*) Sales volume will almost certainly depend on customers' willingness and ability to pay for a firm's products, and these factors are not likely to be unaffected by the prices charged.

(*c*) Sales volume will also be affected by the behaviour, particularly the prices, of a firm's competitors, relative, of course, to the firm's own behaviour. It is difficult to believe that, as a general rule, sales volume can be estimated without taking account of competition.

These three difficulties would seem to imply that a firm which uses cost-plus pricing could well end up with no sales and no profit at all, and that it is therefore not a rational method for a firm with any interest at all in its profit. I know from first-hand experience of firms which employ (or used to employ) cost-plus pricing in a quite

[1] I am indebted to Mr. J. A. Banks, a distinguished sociologist, and Mr. W. T. Osborn an economic statistician, both of Liverpool University, for valuable advice on the design of the questionnaire used in the investigation.

[2] As used here, 'unit costs' means average total cost per unit, not just average variable cost per unit.

extreme form. Anyone with experience in industry will know that there are firms which seem to pay remarkably little attention to the likely effects of their prices on demand and on competition, and are unaware of the extent to which unit costs are affected by different assumptions about sales volume. There is, however, little evidence to indicate whether or not ignoring competition and demand is common. There is, of course, empirical evidence, particularly the studies by Edwards [2], Pearce [3], Fog [4], Haynes [5] and Lazer [6], of firms which adjust their prices to take account of competition and demand, even if initially they may be arrived at on a cost-plus basis. Joel Dean [7] has even distinguished this as a separate pricing method, and named it 'variable or flexible mark-up pricing'. Given sufficient flexibility, this would resolve the difficulties described above. It is not clear, however, how common flexible mark-up pricing is in Britain. The studies by Edwards [2] and Pearce [3] were very restricted in scope, and the firms involved may well not have been cost-plus pricers; after all, about 20 per cent of the Hall and Hitch sample [1] claimed not to use the method. The same criticism cannot be applied to the surveys by Fog [4], Haynes [5] and Lazer [6], but these studies are somewhat lacking in quantitative data, and it may well be that what is true of Scandinavian and North American industry is not true of British industry.

The investigation reported in this paper is an outcome of the work of Haynes [5] and Heflebower [8], and attempted to discover just what cost-plus pricing means. To anticipate: the main conclusion is that, although 70 per cent of the respondents in the survey claim to use cost-plus pricing, great weight is given in fixing prices to competition and demand, although not quite as much weight as to a firm's own costs and profit. The investigation was also designed to establish what proportion of firms can be described as profit-maximizers; it was found that not more than half, and possibly much less, could be described in that way. This possibly helps to explain the popularity of cost-plus pricing: prices arrived at in this way can perhaps be interpreted as being in some sense more 'fair' than prices not based mainly on costs.[3] Information was also sought as to how 'progressive' firms are in their accounting methods, and whether large firms are more progressive than small: the firms in the survey proved to be progressive in some ways but not in others, and firms with 100 or more employees proved to be, on the whole, more progressive than smaller firms. Progressive accounting methods are relevant to cost-plus pricing, in order to ensure that firms can earn even a reasonable profit.

[3] See Fog [4], pp. 112–14.

THE INVESTIGATION

The survey was carried out during the first half of 1968 by means of a postal questionnaire despatched to all members of the Merseyside Chamber of Commerce. The difficulties of the questionnaire method are well known, the main one being that of formulating questions whose meanings are precise, but not so precise as to make the questions unintelligible. The difficulties cannot be entirely overcome by means of interviews, as no one is ever then quite sure just what questions have been asked: it is very difficult for an interviewer to avoid leading questions. Several methods were used to overcome the difficulties. A covering letter was sent with the questionnaire, explaining the purpose of the investigation, promising anonymity to those who desired it, and offering to send all respondents a summary of the results. The covering letter was printed on the headed notepaper of the Liverpool and District Branch of the Institute of Cost and Works Accountants, replies were requested to be sent to me at the University of Liverpool, and it was stated that the questionnaire had been despatched by the Merseyside Chamber of Commerce.[4]

The questions were expressed at reasonable length, partly in order to avoid ambiguity, and partly so that the answers could be as brief as possible. The suggested answers were mostly either ticks, or marks on a scale from 0 to 4. The second type of answer was to indicate the importance of each of a number of factors in pricing decisions, and follows the work of Professor Shackle [9].[5] The respondents were invited to give supplementary information where they felt that the simple answer indicated was not adequate, but few did so. The questionnaire ran to seven 12 in. by 8 in. pages; it comprised 32 questions, some of which were in two or three parts, so that there were, in effect, 51 questions in all, calling for 83 items of information. However, some types of company (such as organizations providing services) were told that certain questions did not apply to them, and some respondents did not answer all the questions that did apply. On the other hand, some companies answered questions which were stated not to apply to them; these answers were accepted, as it was decided that the companies themselves were best able to judge what did or did not apply to them. Some care was taken that the significance of *individual* questions was not too obvious, and some cross-checking questions were inserted: in analysing the replies, contra-

[4] The questionnaire, covering letter, and summary of replies were produced at Liverpool University; they were printed and despatched by the Institute of Cost and Works Accountants, in a set of envelopes supplied by the Merseyside Chamber of Commerce.

[5] The interpretations suggested for the marks were as follows: 4—vitally important; 3—very important; 2—fairly important; 1—slight importance; 0—no importance.

dictory or ambiguous answers were treated as no answers. The respondents were asked if they would be prepared to amplify their answers in an interview, and of those who did so, telephone enquiries were made of a sample, partly in order to obtain clarification of ambiguous answers, and partly to ascertain how certain of the questions had been interpreted. The response rate was little more than 10 per cent, but this was probably not poor by British standards, in view of the length of the questionnaire and the low average size of the firms surveyed. The response was no doubt unrepresentative, but probably less so than any previous survey on the subject. Further details of the survey are given in Appendix A.

COST-PLUS PRICING

The questionnaire asked specifically whether or not the companies ever used cost-plus pricing, and whether they used it for pricing all products, for pricing new products only, for revising the prices of existing products (Question 12—those questions identified by their numbers here are reproduced in Appendix B). Seventy per cent of the respondents claimed to use cost-plus pricing. In practice, most pricing decisions are likely to be price revisions, and an idea derived from the work of Eitman [10] was that cost-plus pricing was more likely to be used for revising the prices of existing products than for pricing new products, or as a general pricing method. The survey gave no evidence for this hypothesis, as 57 per cent of the companies who used cost-plus pricing used it for pricing all products, and of the remainder, slightly more used it for pricing new products than for revising existing prices. Another hypothesis that was tested, and for which no evidence was found, was that firms which compute prices only on receipt of enquiries from potential customers (what can perhaps be called 'jobbing' firms) would be far more likely to use cost-plus pricing than firms which have a scale of fairly standardized prices or charges determined in advance of receiving orders. Seventy-five per cent of 'jobbing' firms (53 out of 71) claimed to use cost-plus pricing, compared with 67 per cent (68 out of 101) of firms which compute prices in advance; the difference between these proportions is not statistically significant.[6] In addition, the alternative uses of cost-plus pricing (all prices, new prices, revising existing prices)

[6] The chi-squared test was used for differences between proportions, including the proportions giving each answer in questions where alternative answers were indicated. The t test was used on differences between means, including the mean marks allotted in questions where marks were called for. 'Not significant' means not significant at the 5 per cent level. The levels of significance used were (in percentages): 5, 2.5, 2, 1, 0.5, and 0.1.

was very little different (statistically not significant) between the two types of company.

The cost-plus pricers were asked how often they reviewed their profit mark-up; 55 per cent said yearly, and a further 38 per cent said they reviewed it more frequently than yearly, or irregularly, as and when necessary. They were further asked whether, between reviews, they applied the same percentage mark-up to all products and orders, and 68 per cent (80) replied 'No'. Of those 80 companies, 81 per cent varied their mark-up according to the force of competition, 53 per cent according to the strength of demand, and 26 per cent to take account of other factors, mainly on the supply side (for example, the level of stocks or the existence of surplus capacity). A result that is surprising to accountants, but which is in accordance with the findings of Andrews [11], is the large proportion of cost-plus pricers (80 per cent) whose mark-up is designed to cover both profit and some overhead, rather than profit only; the telephone enquiry revealed, however, that a few respondents had interpreted the question (rather surprisingly) as asking whether they attempted to recover overhead in their prices. This finding on the use of composite mark-ups, together with that on flexibility in the application of mark-ups, provides some (rather weak) evidence for Fog's contention (4, pp. 97–100) that firms may well, in effect, adjust not only profit margins, but also unit costs, to take account of competition and demand. A somewhat disturbing (although not surprising) feature of cost-plus pricing is the small proportion of firms (11 per cent in this survey) which base their profit mark-up on a desired rate of return on employed capital; the great majority base it on a desired percentage profit on cost or sales value, or on a desired total profit for the year. (The results described in this paragraph are discussed further in the last section of this paper, dealing with accounting methods.)

The flexibility of prices which is likely to result from the comparatively frequent review of mark-ups by cost-plus pricers was not confined to 'jobbing' firms. Thirty per cent of those who issue list prices revise them yearly, and 54 per cent more frequently than yearly, or irregularly, as required. The main cause of a change in list prices was a change in costs (9 marks out of 10); the need for more or less profit was allotted 5 marks, as was a change in competitors' prices; a change in customers' ability or willingness to pay was given only 3 marks.[7] A point that is stressed by Oxenfeldt [12] in his study of steel prices is the comparative rigidity of list prices, but the frequent adjustment of dealers' margins. This practice seems not to apply generally:

[7] In reporting the results of questions where marks (out of 4) were asked for, the average marks allotted have been converted to a scale from 0 to 10 (see Appendix B).

of the firms in this survey who gave trade or quantity discounts on list prices, only 34 per cent varied them from time to time depending on trade conditions.

Further evidence as to the weight given to competition and demand in pricing was obtained by asking how important those factors were in computing prices generally (Q. 20) and in computing the price of a new or improved product or service (Q. 24). The former question was stated to apply only to 'jobbing' firms; the latter question was put to all the firms, but would obviously apply less well to 'jobbing' firms than to others. A firm's own costs and profit were allotted 9 marks (out of 10) in both questions, competition was given 7 marks in the former question and 8 in the latter, and demand was given 6 marks in both questions. The relative importance of these factors is consistent with what is widely believed about British industry—that it is rather less 'market-orientated' than is, say, American industry, and that within the marketing field it is somewhat less 'customer-orientated'.

The significance of these results for the interpretation of cost-plus pricing is that cost and profit is likely to be the most important factor in arriving at a price, but that it is by no means the only factor to which importance will be attached. To explain the use of the description 'cost-plus' in such circumstances, an analogy may be drawn with other aspects of management practice, such as work study, production planning, or incentive payments: a company may, for example, describe its remuneration system as a payment-by-results scheme, even if only a comparatively small part of its total wage payments (even to those under the scheme) is computed on an incentive basis. The investigation provided virtually no evidence for any extreme or pure form of cost-plus pricing. A 'pure' cost-plus pricer can perhaps be defined as one who: uses the method for all his prices (not just for revising existing ones); between reviews of his mark-up applies the same rate to all orders (irrespective of competition and demand); revises prices *upwards* if sales volume is lower than expected (since unit costs will be higher at the lower volume);[8] changes only his prices if he has a permanent change in his costs (rather than, for example, his profit or the design of the product); and bases his product cost calculations on sales volume in the previous accounting period or periods (rather than on a forecast for the next period). Of the companies in this survey, only 1 out of the 121 who claim to use cost-plus pricing does all these things. The picture that emerges fairly clearly is of considerable sensitivity to the effects of competition and demand, as well as to cost and profit, in setting prices.

[8] See Haynes [5], p. 31 of the book.

PROFIT POLICY

Price-determination is a very difficult subject to study in isolation, because it is often not possible to separate it from other elements in the marketing 'mix'. (One respondent felt unable to answer some of the questions for that reason.) For example, it cannot be isolated from other objective factors such as quality and delivery dates, from more subjective factors such as design and appearance, and from irrational factors such as the effects of persuasive advertising. If, however, the scope of an enquiry is widened beyond price alone, the investigator is then likely to become involved with everything that goes on in a company: if, say, a stable employment policy is followed, a firm may have to adjust prices to dispose of any excessive stocks it builds up. The questionnaire did in fact attempt to investigate the relationship between price and other elements in the marketing 'mix'.[9] Only one aspect of company-wide policies was enquired about, however, namely, profit policy.

Profit policy is even more difficult to study than price-determination. Businessmen seem almost as ready to quote profit maximization as their objective (or, less extremely, to state that they are 'in business to make a profit') as they are to describe their pricing method as being cost-plus. The difficulties are similar: it is notoriously difficult to attach any meaning to the phrase 'profit maximization'. No clarification of meaning emerged as regards this phrase, as it was desired to keep the survey to a manageable size by concentrating on pricing. The profit to be maximized is often interpreted as being the total amount of profit for a period of time. On this interpretation, little evidence was found for it: only 12 per cent of cost-plus pricing firms aimed for this, the majority (75 per cent) aiming for a given percentage profit on cost or sales value.

The firms who determined prices in advance were asked (in Q. 8) whether they could (if they wanted) increase their profit by changing their prices: 48 per cent of the respondents said 'Yes'. During the telephone enquiry, those who had replied in the affirmative were asked whether they had interpreted the question as applying to their firms' *long-run* profit, and they all said they had. Where an explanation was offered, it was that some or all of their products had a distinct competitive edge, of which further advantage could be taken in terms of price; a few respondents said that, within fairly wide limits, price was not important in securing sales. Those who could increase their profit by means of price changes are presumably not

[9] These results are not reported here.

profit-maximizers, but it does not follow that the remainder are: owing to competitive pressures they might not be able to change their prices, even if they wanted to. Those who answered in the affirmative were further asked whether their competitors would probably follow their price change, and 60 per cent said 'No'. Not surprisingly, in most cases (87 per cent) the price change involved would need to be upwards rather than downwards.

The topic of price changes was pursued further (in Q. 9), where it was asked whether the firm could estimate what effect a price change would have on its sales volume: 32 per cent said they could. The weighted average change in price (up or down) necessary to produce a noticeable effect (suggested as being 1 per cent or more) on sales volume was 6.7 per cent (the simple average of the price changes was 7.0 per cent).[10] The average price reduction necessary to increase sales volume was slightly greater than the average price increase that would reduce volume. There is an apparent anomaly between the number who gave the affirmative answer to this question (40) and to Q. 8 (62); in other words, some of the firms which thought that they could increase their profit by changing prices could not estimate the effect of a price change on sales volume. Some respondents who had originally answered 'Yes' to Q. 9, enquiring about the effect of a price change on sales volume, had altered their answer, presumably when they discovered that the second part of Q. 9 asked them to quantify their reply. This suggests a possible explanation of the anomaly: that demand is insensitive to price changes, but only within certain, not at all well-defined, limits. A company may, for example, be fairly sure that a price change of, say, 2–3 per cent would not affect sales volume (and would therefore affect profit), while not being at all sure whether or not a 5–6 per cent price change would affect volume. This explanation is to some extent borne out by a recent survey of *industrial* purchasing by Buckner [13], where it was found that, while price was the most important factor in determining a purchase, about 40 per cent of the firms surveyed would require a price difference of 5–9 per cent to induce them to change from their best supplier for an *identical* product, and about 20 per cent would require a difference of 10 per cent or more.

A further question relevant to profit policy was Q. 26, the first part of which enquired whether the firm had ever pioneered a new product or service: 71 per cent of the respondents said they had. This proportion certainly seems high: it is probably a result of the vast amount of product differentiation that exists nowadays, some of it highly artifi-

[10] These are averages of the four price-change figures quoted in the second part of Q. 9 in Appendix B.

cial, of course, but some of it due to the sophistication of modern technology. One of the 'new' products mentioned during the course of the telephone enquiry was a plant food designed specifically for rose bushes, which the company had developed as an improvement on the more general-purpose products previously used on those plants—not an earth-shattering invention perhaps, but one that can reasonably be called a new product. The second part of Q. 26 enquired about the alternative pricing policies for new products distinguished by Joel Dean [7]. Forty-six per cent of the respondents had initially charged a cost-plus price, 33 per cent a 'skimming' price, and 17 per cent a 'penetration' price. The cost-plus pricers were presumably not profit-maximizers, whereas the 'skimmers' probably were: the 'penetrators' may have been either.

A question which was relevant to profit policy, although not directly so, was Q. 27, which enquired about the phenomenon reported, in particular, by Fog [4, pp. 44–46]—the 'backward-sloping' demand curve. Thirty-nine per cent of the respondents claimed to have had experience at least occasionally of a given price generating a greater sales volume than a lower price would have done. This provides further evidence for the attention usually paid to demand factors, as presumably pure cost-plus pricers would not be aware of the phenomenon. It was assumed that such an experience would be far less common among firms selling only to other industrial and commercial organizations or to public authorities, than among firms selling only direct to the general public or to wholesale or retail distributors. This proved not to be so, however: 3 per cent of respondents in the first category (2 out of 71) had had frequent experience of a backward-sloping demand curve, and 31 per cent (22 firms) had occasionally experienced it. These proportions do not differ significantly from those for companies selling, directly or indirectly, to the general public.

Those parts of the questionnaire relevant to profit policy, while not providing support for profit maximization as a realistic generalization about the majority of firms, did provide more support for it than was originally thought would be the case. A possible explanation may lie in the comparatively low average size of the firms surveyed.[11] If competition is likely to be stronger for small firms than for large, a small firm may have to give major emphasis to profit earning, whether it likes it or not, in order to be sure of earning even a reasonable profit. A large firm, moreover, may, for a number of reasons, have a greater degree of social consciousness, and be less subject to pressures from shareholders. In view of the vagueness

[11] See Appendix A.

surrounding the whole idea of profit maximization, however, no attempt was made to test this hypothesis.

ACCOUNTING METHODS

Even if cost-plus pricing means only that cost plus profit is the most important factor out of a number in computing prices, 'progressive' accounting methods in computing cost and profit are likely to be important in order to ensure that firms achieve a reasonable sales volume, rate of growth, and profit. Four aspects of accounting methods were examined, and the practices of large firms were compared with those of the smaller.[12] All but the last of these four practices (variable costing) have already been briefly mentioned. Two definitions of large were used: respondents employing 100 or more (70 firms), and of these, those firms employing 1000 or more (15 firms). Firms with fewer than 100 employees will be described as 'small', those with 100 or more as 'large', and those with 1000 or more as 'very large'. There were too few very large firms to permit significance tests to be carried out on their results.

The cost-plus pricers were asked how their profit percentage mark-up was calculated initially and, as mentioned earlier, only 11 per cent (12 out of 106) of the respondents calculated it as a percentage on employed capital. The proportion for large firms, at 17 per cent (7 out of 41), was not significantly different from that for the small firms (8 per cent); the proportion for the very large firms was 29 per cent.[13] A number of respondents mentioned in their questionnaires, or during the telephone enquiry, that they were thinking of changing over to this basis. It is perhaps worth noting that, for a firm which is not growing in terms of either sales or net assets, the calculation of profit as an amount for the year, or as a percentage of cost or sales value, will give the same end result as the return on capital method.

The cost-plus pricers were asked whether, between reviews of their mark-up, they applied the same percentage to all products and orders. It is reassuring that 68 per cent (80 out of 117) said they did not, but usually varied it according to the force of competition and the strength of demand. In view of this quite high proportion, it is not too surprising that the proportion for large firms, at 76 per cent (34 out of 45), was not significantly different from that for the small (65 per cent); the proportion for the very large firms was 89 per cent.

All the firms were asked how they usually arrived at the capacity

[12] In making this comparison, the replies of 3 firms, which gave no information about their numbers employed, were ignored.

[13] Large firms in America may be more progressive in this respect than those in Britain: see Kaplan, Dirlam and Lanzillotti [14].

utilization figure on which their product cost calculations were based. Only 46 per cent (53 out of 116) forecast their usage for the next period.[14] It is perhaps worth mentioning, however, that for a firm whose capacity utilization does not vary from year to year, the usage figure for the previous period (or periods) will give the same result as a forecast. The proportion for large firms, at 67 per cent (36 out of 54), was significantly higher (at the 0.1 per cent level) than that for the small (26 per cent); 91 per cent of the very large firms forecast their capacity utilization.

The most surprising aspect of accounting methods revealed was the widespread use of variable costing.[15] The firms were asked (in Q. 18) whether they had analysed their costs into fixed and variable elements, and if so, whether they normally made any use of the distinction in setting selling prices. Seventy-three per cent (122 out of 166) of the respondents said they had made the distinction, and of these, 69 per cent used it in price-determination. The proportion of large firms who had made the distinction was even higher at 85 per cent (58 out of 68), which is significantly different (0.5 per cent level) from the proportion for the small firms (66 per cent); almost all the very large firms (93 per cent) had made the distinction. A separate question asked all the firms (whether or not they distinguished between fixed and variable costs) whether they were able to estimate the effects on their costs of an increase or decrease in sales volume; the number (and proportion) of affirmative answers to this question were, not surprisingly, almost the same as in Q. 18.[16]

The findings on variable costing are out of line with the results of other British investigations, which are described by Sizer [15].[17] The most recent of these was carried out in 1963, and they all showed very little use of variable costing. The findings are, however, remarkably similar to those of an American survey carried out by Early about 1955 [16]: about 90 per cent of his sample of 'excellently managed' companies had made the distinction between fixed and variable costs, and of those about 70 per cent made use of it in setting prices. A possible explanation of the discrepancy between the earlier British

[14] The remainder employed the utilization figure of the previous accounting period (24 per cent), or an average of several previous periods (30 per cent). The mean rate of capacity utilization reported was 84 per cent.

[15] As understood by accountants, variable (or direct or marginal) costing means the analysis of costs into fixed and variable elements, and the use of the distinction, primarily, to predict the effects on costs of changes in sales (or production) volume.

[16] In fact there were 3 more affirmative answers to Q. 18, which seemed somewhat anomalous, as it implied that some of those who had made the distinction did not use it. Two such firms were contacted during the telephone enquiry. One said that its difficulty arose over predicting the behaviour of costs which were neither strictly fixed nor strictly variable. The other reported that its accountants had made the distinction, but had not had occasion to use it to predict the effects on costs of a change in sales volume.

[17] They are also out of line with the findings reported in Haynes's book [5, pp. 43–45].

surveys and this one is that perhaps changes do occur in British industry after all, and perhaps more rapidly than is sometimes thought! Or it may be that firms on Merseyside are more progressive than those in other parts of the country. Neither of these explanations is particularly plausible. The reason is more likely to lie in the nature of the question asked. A non-accounting manager may well not understand the meaning of such a question as 'Do you use marginal costing?' Having never heard this description of the technique, he will probably reply 'No' to the question.

The results of the survey relating to accounting methods tend to confirm what is widely believed about British industry: that in this area (as no doubt in many others) it is 'patchy'. Firms generally are progressive in some accounting practices but not in others. Large firms are more progressive than small in some aspects of accounting, but not in others.

UNIVERSITY OF OTAGO,
DUNEDIN, NEW ZEALAND

APPENDIX A

THE SURVEY

Of the 1903 despatched, 179 completed questionnaires were returned. In addition, letters and telephone calls were received from 81 organizations giving various reasons for not participating. These were mostly non-trading organizations and professional firms. If one excludes Chamber of Commerce members in these categories (about 180), the response rate works out at 10.4 per cent. Some idea of how representative the respondents were can be obtained because they were asked to state how many people they employed, and 98 per cent of them did so. The average number employed by respondents in manufacturing industries only was 448, with a standard deviation of 1188.[18] The Report on the Census of Production for 1958 shows that the average size of manufacturing enterprise on Merseyside was then 146.[19] These two means are significantly different from each other (at the 2 per cent level). To put the difference in perspective, however, it should be remembered that, over manufacturing industry as a whole (in Britain in 1958), enterprises with 100 or more employees, while comprising less than 20 per cent of manufacturing enterprises,

[18] The average number employed by all the respondents was 337, with a standard deviation of 1017.

[19] Board of Trade (H.M.S.O., London, 1963), Part 134, Table 7. Similar data from the 1963 census are not yet available. No comparable information is available for service industries, apart from retail distribution.

accounted for over 80 per cent of both manufacturing employment and net output, and the average number employed by such enterprises was 689.[20]

Replies were received from all Order numbers in the Standard Industrial Classification except Gas, Electricity and Water (Order 18) and Public Administration and Defence (Order 24). Some Orders, however, had very few representatives, but it was possible to combine these with others without increasing the diversification already existing within each Order. On the other hand, replies were numerous in Transport and Communication (Order 19) and Distribution (Order 20); the former was therefore split into two industry groups, and the latter into three. In all, the replies were analysed into 17 industries, comprising 8 manufacturing industries (96 companies), 7 service industries (67), Construction (8), and a group of 8 companies which did not give their names or any information about their industries. The replies were examined for statistically significant differences between industries. In the case of many questions, however, there were too few replies in each industry to permit tests of significance. Where tests were possible, most of the differences were not significant. The significant differences that were revealed were of little interest, merely reflecting such facts as that Food, Drink and Tobacco is more of a consumer-goods industry than others. Manufacturing companies together and service companies together were tested to see if their results differed from those for all the respondents. Replies to all the questions were tested, which revealed 3 significant differences, the only one of interest being that firms in service industries were significantly less well able (2 per cent level[21]) to estimate the effects on their costs of changes in sales volume. This was no doubt partly due to the fact that fewer service firms (although not significantly fewer) had analysed their costs into fixed and variable elements; the questionnaire did not reveal, however, whether this was because they were not able to do so, or had not chosen to.

The respondents were asked to give the name of their organization, and 83 per cent (149) did so. All the respondents asked for a copy of the results summary.[22] Fifty-one per cent (92) agreed to discuss their replies at an interview. From these three pieces of information (as managers' names and posts were usually quoted), it was possible, in respect of most of the replies, to ascertain who had completed the questionnaire, and in all cases these were proprietors, directors, or senior managers. Telephone enquiries were made of 26 of the firms who had agreed to answer further questions; the basis of selection were firms who had given apparently ambiguous answers to some of the questions. In the case of 2 respondents, this enquiry revealed

[20] This average figure, and that quoted earlier for Merseyside firms, is based on the assumption that, for enterprises with fewer than 25 employees, each enterprise comprises only 1 establishment.

[21] Comparing the results for manufacturing and service industries with each other, the difference is significant at the 0.5 per cent level.

[22] It is assumed that this was so, as the number of requests was the same as the number of completed questionnaires: as the respondents did not have to quote their names in their questionnaires, it was possible for a firm to send in a request for the summary without submitting a questionnaire.

what could be classed as a mistake in answering a question, but in all the other cases it revealed complex situations that could not be simply described; if the ambiguity could not be finally resolved, their replies to those questions were ignored. The main object of the telephone enquiry, however, was to ascertain how some of the questions had been interpreted; these results are reported in the text. The enquiry was not carried further as regards the interpretation of questions, partly through lack of time, but mainly because it was felt that no further useful information would emerge: of the 5 questions enquired about, the interpretations of 2 (including Q. 8) were unanimous and emphatic, and there were very few departures from unanimity on the other 3 questions.

APPENDIX B

THE QUESTIONNAIRE

This appendix reproduces only those questions referred to by their numbers in the text. For each question the percentage and number of replies are stated; the percentages are of the replies to each question, unless otherwise indicated. The number of replies to each question seldom equals the total number of questionnaires, as some questions did not apply to all organizations, and some respondents refrained from answering all the questions that did apply to them. For questions where marks on a scale from 0 to 4 were asked for, the average marks allotted have been converted to a scale from 0 to 10 by multiplying each average by 2.5; this was done in order to make the marks more intelligible.

8. (i) Taking account of all relevant factors, including the reactions of your competitors, could you at present (if you wanted) increase your profit by changing your prices?
Yes *62 (48%)* No *68* (52%) (Tick one)
(ii) If so,
(a) Would your competitors probably follow your price change?
Yes *24 (40%)* No *36* (60%) (Tick one)
(b) Would the price change need to be upwards or downwards?
Up *52 (87%)* Down *8 (13%)* (Tick one)

9. (i) Are you able to estimate what effect a change in price would have on your sales *volume*?
Yes *40 (32%)* No *85 (68%)* (Tick one)
(ii) If so, what is the minimum percentage change in price that would have a noticeable effect (say, 1% or more) on your sales volume:—

	No. of replies
(a) Minimum *reduction* in price necessary to increase sales volume:	
(i) Assuming your competitors did not react *6.1% (mean)*	29
(ii) Assuming your competitors did react *9.8% (mean)*	19
(b) Minimum *increase* in price that would reduce sales volume:	
(i) Assuming your competitors did not follow your increase *5.3% (mean)*	31
(ii) Assuming your competitors did follow your increase *6.8% (mean)*	23

(The above two questions were stated not to apply to firms which 'normally quote a price only on receipt of enquiries from potential customers'.)

12. (i) Do you ever use cost-plus pricing?
Yes *121 (70%)* No *51 (30%)* (Tick one)
(If No, go on to Question 16)
(ii) If Yes, in what circumstances do you use it? (Tick one)

	%
(a) Pricing all products *62*	57
(b) Pricing new products *22*	20
(c) Revising the prices of existing products *19*	18
(Other uses *5*)	(5)

18. (i) Have you analysed your costs into fixed and variable elements?
Yes *122 (73%)* No *44 (27%)* (Tick one)
(ii) If so, do you normally make any use of the distinction between fixed and variable costs in setting selling prices?
Yes *82 (69%)* No *37 (31%)* (Tick one)

20. How important is each of the following factors in computing your prices? (Mark each out of 4)

	Mean mark (out of 10)
(a) Your costs and profit *76 (84%)*	9
(b) Competitors' prices *73 (80%)*	7
(c) Customers' ability and willingness to pay *71 (78%)*	6
(d) Other factors (Please specify and allot mark) *7 (8%)*	7

No reply: 88
(The percentages above are of the number of questionnaires, less no replies.)

(The above question was stated to apply 'to organizations which compute prices only on receipt of enquiries'.)

24. For a new product or service, how important is each of the following factors in deciding on its price? (Mark each out of 4)

	Mean mark (out of *10*)
(a) The prices of your competitors *134* (*90*%)	8
(b) The estimated costs of your competitors *109* (*73*%)	4
(c) Your estimated costs and profit *144* (*97*%)	9
(d) The probable effect of price on demand *120* (*81*%)	6
(e) Other factors (Please specify and allot mark) *9* (6%)	9
No reply: 30	

(The percentages above are of the number of questionnaires, less no replies.)

26. (i) Have you ever pioneered a new product or service?
Yes *113* (*71*%) No *47* (29%) (Tick one)

(ii) If so, how did you price it *initially*? (Tick one)

	%
(a) At the price which would probably prevail eventually when competitors had entered the market *18*	17
(b) At the highest price you thought you could get for your initial output *36*	33
(c) At cost plus a normal margin of profit *50*	46
(d) Other bases (Please specify) *4*	4

(The above two questions were stated to apply 'to new goods or new services; this includes improved ones, and the use of new methods or new techniques for existing ones'.)

27. Sometimes a higher price generates a *greater* sales volume than a *lower* price would. Has this happened to you? (Tick one)

	%
(a) Frequently *5*	3
(b) Occasionally *60*	36
(c) Never *100*	61

REFERENCES

[1] Hall, R. L. and Hitch, C. J. 'Price Theory and Business Behaviour', *Oxford Economic Papers*, No. 2, May 1939. Reprinted in T. Wilson and P. W. S. Andrews (Eds.), *Oxford Studies in the Price Mechanism*, Oxford University Press, 1951.

[2] Edwards, R. S., 'The Pricing of Manufactured Products', *Economica*, vol. 19, Aug. 1952.

[3] Pearce, I. F., 'A Study in Price Policy', *Economica*, vol. 23, May 1956.

[4] Fog, B., *Industrial Pricing Policies*, North-Holland, Amsterdam, 1960.

[5] Haynes, W. W., *Pricing Decisions in Small Business*, University of Kentucky Press, Lexington, Ky., 1962. Summarized in W. W. Haynes, 'Pricing Practices in Small Firms', *Southern Economic Journal*, vol. 30, Apr. 1964.

[6] LAZER, W., 'Price Determination in the Western Canadian Garment Industry', *Journal of Industrial Economics*, vol. 5, Mar. 1957.
[7] DEAN, J. *Managerial Economics*, Prentice-Hall, Englewood Cliffs, N.J., 1951.
[8] HEFLEBOWER, R. B., 'Full Costs, Cost Changes, and Prices'; in National Bureau of Economic Research: *Business Concentration and Price Policy*, Princeton University Press, Princeton, N.J., 1955.
[9] SHACKLE, G. L. S., 'Business Men on Business Decisions', *Scottish Journal of Political Economy*, vol. 2, Feb. 1955.
[10] EITMAN, W. J. *Price Determination—Business Practice v. Economic Theory*, Michigan University Press, Ann Arbor, Mich., 1949.
[11] ANDREWS, P. W. S., *Manufacturing Business*, Macmillan, London, 1949.
[12] OXENFELDT, A. R., *Industrial Pricing and Market Practices*, Prentice-Hall, Englewood Cliffs, N.J., 1951.
[13] BUCKNER, H. *How British Industry Buys*, Hutchinson, London, 1967.
[14] KAPLAN, A. D. H., DIRLAM, J. B. and LANZILLOTTI, R. F. *Pricing in Big Business*, The Brookings Institution, Washington, D.C., 1958. Summarized in R. F. Lanzillotti, 'Pricing Objectives in Large Companies', *American Economic Review*, vol. 48, Dec. 1958.
[15] SIZER, J. 'The Accountant's Contribution to the Pricing Decision', *Journal of Management Studies*, vol. 3, May 1966.
[16] EARLY, J. S. 'Marginal Policies of "Excellently Managed" Companies', *American Economic Review*, vol. 46, Mar. 1956.

DIFFUSION OF MAJOR TECHNOLOGICAL INNOVATIONS IN U.S. IRON AND STEEL MANUFACTURING

by Bela Gold, William S. Peirce and Gerhard Rosegger*

I. BASIC QUESTIONS AND APPROACH

The impacts of an innovation on an industry and on larger sectors of the economy clearly depend on how rapidly it comes into use. In appraising such effects, the initial decisions to be made concern the measures to be used and the level of aggregation to be studied. And the choices to be made among the wide range of possible alternatives obviously depend on one's purpose.

For example, Lynn's study [16] of the 'diffusion' of twenty major innovations was concerned essentially with the growth of *new* industries rooted in major innovations and hence used the absolute value of outputs and their percentage shares of Gross National Product as measures. In another study [17, pp. 133 ff.], Mansfield was concerned with how rapidly given innovations had spread from enterprise to enterprise in four industries, so he used the percentage of major firms introducing the innovation over a given period as his measure. Neither of these approaches seems to provide a generally applicable basis for assessing the extent to which innovations displace predecessor processes and facilities. Lynn's reliance on total output is clearly inappropriate for established, as differentiated from new, industries.[1] Mansfield's concern with how many have adopted an innovation clearly ignores the *extent* of dependence on the innovation, and his concentration on major firms may be open to the possibility of unrepresentativeness—not only because smaller firms may account for significant proportions of output, but also because larger and smaller firms may differ in their responsiveness to innovations [17, pp. 155 ff.].

The objective of this paper is to assess the rates at which production comes to be dominated by new processes or facilities. Hence, its focus is on the industry as a whole and the measure used is the proportion of total output accounted for by the innovation. In particular, the analysis is concentrated on the early rates of diffusion of fourteen

* The research for this paper was supported in part by a grant from Resources for the Future, Inc.

[1] It may be of interest to note, however, that expectations concerning the diffusion patterns of technologies constituting new industries tend to overlap conceptually with expectations concerning the growth patterns of such industries. For a review of the latter along with relevant empirical findings, see [9a]. For a more recent application, see [7a].

major innovations in the iron and steel industry and its raw material-supplying branches during the past 100 years. Answers are sought to such questions as the following: Is there a common pattern of diffusion or are there widely different patterns? How early in the diffusion experience of an innovation can effective prediction be made of its eventual importance and of its long-term patterns of adoption? In what respects, if any, are diffusion patterns in recent decades markedly different from those of earlier decades? In addition, efforts will be made to appraise the influence of some of the commonly assumed determinants of decisions involving the adoption of innovations.

The innovations studied were selected on the basis of: evidence in the literature that the industry regarded each as of 'major' importance in some sense; and the availability of statistics permitting differentiation of the output of the new technology from that of older technologies. It should be emphasized, however, that such concentration on major innovations cannot be regarded as adequate coverage of technological advances in view of the possibility of comparably significant contributions from the cumulation of numerous smaller improvements. By studying a sample of innovations within one industry instead of a scattering over several industries, it was hoped both that the already formidable array of variables to be confronted in diffusion analyses might be narrowed somewhat and that possible interactions among successive or overlapping innovations might be uncovered. Iron and coal mining and processing were included in recognition of the technological as well as the economic aspects of the extensive vertical integration in steel manufacturing.

II. ACTUAL RATES OF DIFFUSION

Chart I shows the percentages of total output accounted for by fourteen major innovations during the first 15 years of their industrial application. Selection of these starting points required judgment in some cases, due to the paucity of statistics and some uncertainty as to what constitutes 'commercial' application. But we believe that any errors in such judgments have had no major effects on observed differences in diffusion rates. Although selection of a 15-year period is arbitrary, the long lead times in the steel industry between a decision to invest in new technology and actual production from the completed project suggest that much shorter periods may be inadequate. On the other hand, our previous findings indicate that the economic benefits to innovating firms tend to be dissipated over longer periods [9, pp. 118 ff.], so that early assessment of the potentials of new technologies is of great importance, lest laggards be forced to adopt such innovations more to avoid serious penalties than because of continuing attractive benefits.

These findings show an extremely wide range of patterns. Very rapid diffusion took place in the case of four innovations, i.e. the

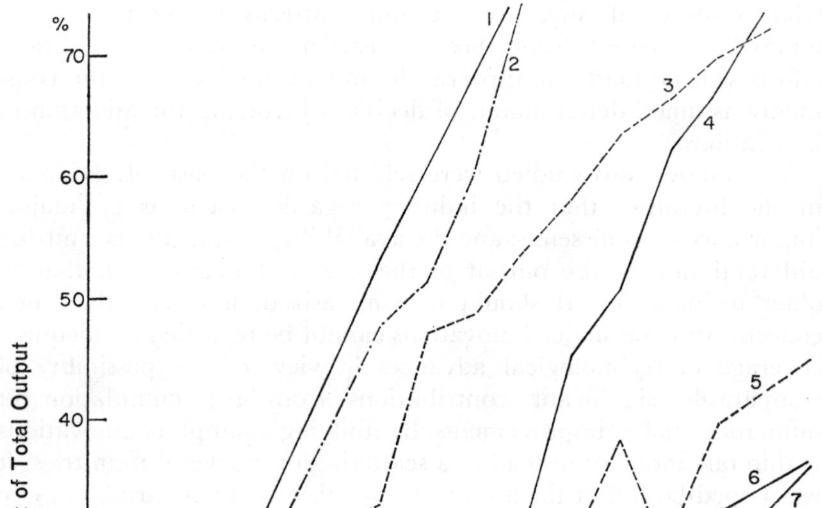

CHART I. Output by new technology as per cent of total output during first 15 years after indicated date of initial commercial use.

1. Bessemer Furnace (1865)
2. Cont. Cold Rolling, Sheets (1927)
3. Electrolytic Tinplating (1940)
4. Continuous Hot Strip Mill (1926)
5. Cont. Cold Rolling, Strip (1930)
6. Basic Oxygen Furnace (1954)
7. Pelletizing (1956)
8. Continuous Miner (1948)
9. Washing Coking Coal (1889)
10. Machine Loading, Coal (1923)
11. By-product Coking (1895)
12. Machine Cutting, Coal (1882)
13. Open Hearth (1870)
14. Strip Mining, Coal (1914)

Bessemer process, the continuous cold-rolling of sheets, electrolytic tin-plating, and continuous flat hot-rolling (the wide-strip mill); the first three accounting for over 50 per cent of total output only 10 years after their introduction, and all exceeding 70 per cent within the 15-year period. Another four innovations accounted for 30–50 per cent of output within 15 years: continuous cold-rolling of strip, the basic oxygen furnace, pelletizing, and the continuous miner. The remaining six innovations studied accounted for 22 per cent or less of output within 15 years.

In addition to revealing a wide disparity in average diffusion rates over the 15-year period as a whole, Chart I also shows that adoption rates during the first few years are often unreliable guides to estimating either subsequent adoption rates or ultimate levels of application. For example, five of the six innovations with the lowest average rates of adoption later came to dominate their respective segments of industry: the open-hearth; by-product coking; mechanical coal-cutting; mechanical coal-loading; and the washing of coking coal. Although hindsight suggests numerous possible explanations for such wide variations in early responses to the potentials of new technologies—some of which will be explored later—it is difficult to avoid the conclusion that the evaluations underlying initial decisions are not closely correlated with later demonstrations of worth. One might also note in this connection the potential bias in this and other studies which are concerned only with eventually successful innovations and thus neglect other innovations which may have been adopted more readily only to prove of less-than-expected value.

Three of the innovations in our sample (by-product coking, the continuous miner, and the continuous wide-strip mill) were also included in the Mansfield study. It is of considerable analytical significance that his 'rate of imitation', which is based on the percentage of (major) firms having adopted an innovation, is much higher in each of the three cases than our measure of the rate of diffusion. Thus, he reported that by-product coking had been adopted by almost 60 per cent of the major firms after 15 years, the continuous miner by 100 per cent in about 10 years, and the continuous wide-strip mill by 100 per cent in 12 or 13 years. Two factors may account for these differences: first, the fact that a firm has adopted an innovation need not imply that all of its output has been shifted over to the new technology; and second, by restricting his sample to major firms, Mansfield did not take into account the often considerable contribution made to total output by the many smaller enterprises about whose relative eagerness and ability to introduce innovations, both in terms of technological and financial criteria, empirical evidence is ambiguous.[2] In any event, if one is concerned with the impact of new technologies rather than with the pervasiveness of at least exploratory or partial involvements in them, results can be better appraised in terms of their bearing on total output.

It may also be of interest to relate our findings about the basic oxygen process to recent discussions in the economic literature. This process has been characterized as 'the only major technical breakthrough at the ingot level in the steel industry since before the turn of the century' [1], and the American industry has been castigated for being too slow to adopt it [2, 3].[3] Whatever the other merits of the case, our data show that the basic oxygen process was adopted at a rate which lies in the mid-range of our sample and much more rapidly than some other innovations which clearly also constituted 'major breakthroughs', such as the open hearth and by-product coking.

The difficulties of making early judgments which will eventually prove to have been correct is further illustrated by two major new processes currently in the development stage: the direct reduction of ore and continuous casting of steel. Work on these technologies has gone on for prolonged periods and some 'commercial', i.e. non-pilot or non-experimental, production has been reported. While experts seem almost unanimously convinced of the likelihood of ultimate success for these processes, such forecasts typically do not involve any commitment to a time scale or to a statement about the importance, measured in terms of the share of total output, of these new technologies. From the economic point of view, however, it is exactly these dimensions that would provide decision-makers with meaningful bases for their investment plans. At present, both the costs and benefits of innovating in these two areas are still clouded in uncertainty as are the specific forms of the innovations that will eventually prove most successful.

Similar uncertainties pervaded early evaluations of many other radically new technologies. Thus, for example, there existed considerable doubt about the quality of the open hearth's output, such a scrap-using process being regarded as a 'scavenger'. Similarly, the use of Connellsville (beehive) coke as a quality standard for metallurgical applications led to serious doubts about the suitability of by-product coke and a corresponding reluctance to invest in by-

[2] Mansfield himself has suggested that, in the iron and steel industry, the largest firms account for a smaller share of innovations than their share of the market [17, pp. 84 ff.; pp. 163–4].

[3] For a defense of industry decisions, see [8].

product facilities as long as high-grade Pennsylvania coke was plentiful [5].

Such fragmentary evidences obviously cannot suffice to explain the diversity of observed diffusion patterns, but they do indicate some of the inevitably judgmental elements in early managerial evaluations of new technologies which are likely to limit the potentials of purely mechanistic bases for forecasting eventual diffusion rates.

Turning to another of the questions raised at the outset, one may ask what conclusions are suggested by Chart I concerning whether diffusion rates are higher in recent than in earlier decades, as was found by Lynn in a somewhat different context. Not only is our sample too small to provide definitive support for any conclusions, but the results may be interpreted in several ways. First, seven of the eight innovations with the highest diffusion rates were introduced after 1925; and all but one in the 'slow' category were introduced before World War I. But it is also notable that diffusion rates of the four innovations adopted between 1926 and 1940 were higher than all those adopted in earlier or later years (except for the Bessemer process in 1865). Moreover, if the analysis is separated by sectors, we note that in basic steel-making the fastest rate was achieved by the Bessemer process (1865), the slowest rate by the open hearth process (1870) and the rate achieved by the basic oxygen process (1954) was roughly mid-way between these. In the coal sector, the washing of coking coal (1889) had a diffusion rate mid-way between the continuous miner (1948) and coal stripping (1914). In the face of such heterogeneity, much larger samples may be necessary before any reasonably consistent differences are likely to be discerned.

III. DIFFUSION RATES AND THE GROWTH OF OUTPUT

One intuitively appealing hypothesis suggests that diffusion rates are heavily influenced by variations in output levels, increasing during periods of expansion and decreasing during downturns. Such expectations involve associating the introduction of major innovations with significant additions to capacity, which are obviously more welcome during periods of growth, and with substantial investments, which are more likely to be made when output and profits are rising and capital markets are optimistic.

By way of exploring this hypothesis, the panels in Chart II present total physical output (with the 15th year after commercial introduction as the base) along with the comparable outputs of the 'new' and 'old' technologies for the first 15 years. The resulting wide variety of relationships may be summarized as in Table I by combining the earlier classification of diffusion rates in Chart I with output growth categorized as 'very rapid', if it increased several-fold during the 15-year period; 'rapid', if it roughly doubled; 'modest' if it increased by less than 50 per cent; 'fluctuating' if it varied with little net gain or loss over the period; and 'negative' if it declined throughout. Of the five innovations introduced during periods of modest or no growth, not one was diffused rapidly. But of the eight innovations introduced during periods of very rapid or rapid growth, three were diffused rapidly and four slowly. And one may also note that slow rates of diffusion were recorded for four of the eight innovations introduced during periods when output increased by 100 per cent or more and for two of the five innovations introduced during periods of little or no growth.

TABLE I

DIFFUSION RATES, GROWTH RATES AND RELATIVE INCREASES IN 'NEW' AND 'OLD' OUTPUT

	TOTAL OUTPUT GROWTH RATES				
DIFFUSION RATES	*Very Rapid*	*Rapid*	*Modest*	*Fluctuations No Growth*	*Negative*
Rapid (>70%)	Bessemer (A) Cold sheet (D)	Electro Tin (D)			
Medium (30–50%)	Cold strip (B)		Basic Oxygen (D)	Pelletizing (D)	Continuous miner (D)
Slow (<25%)	Open hearth (C)	By-product Coke (C) Coal cutting (C) Coal-washing (C)		Strip coal (B) Coal loading (D)	

Relative Increases in Output: (A) New > Old; (B) New = Old; (C) Old > New; (D) New+, Old−

Further analytical insight may be obtained by comparing the changes in output from 'new' and from 'old' technologies in Chart II. Of the seven cases in which output increased from both sources, the new increased by more than the old one in one (Bessemer), both increased by roughly equal amounts in two (cold strip and coal stripping) and the old increased by more than the new in four (open hearth, by-product coke, coal cutting and coal washing). In the remaining six cases, the new increased while the old decreased. These patterns are more understandably related to diffusion rates than to rates of increase in output. With respect to the former, it is obvious that rapid diffusion could occur only when new production is growing much faster than old, or when the latter is being displaced or replaced by the new. And it is equally obvious that slow diffusion would commonly involve increases in old production greater than, or equal to, increases in new production. But the weakness of the relationship between growth and diffusion rates is apparent from the fact that of the six cases involving increases in new production and decreases in old, two involve rapid diffusion rates, three medium and one slow. And findings are even less in accord with intuitive expectations when relative changes in new and old production are compared with the growth rates of total production. For example, all four cases of greater increases in old production than in new occurred when output was increasing rapidly or very rapidly. Moreover, the six cases of increases in new production accompanied by decreases in old production were spread almost uniformly among the five growth-rate categories.

Accordingly, it would seem useful to explore the possible factors underlying such disparate managerial responses to the availability of major innovations in processes and facilities.

IV. EXPLORATORY DIFFUSION MODELS

Exploratory models of managerial decisions concerning the adoption of major innovations may be divided into three types: those involving *additions* to available capacity; those involving the *displacement* of functioning facilities; and those involving the *replacement* of capacity withdrawals.

When expansion is deemed necessary, management must choose between adding facilities embodying established technologies (as modified by recent improvements) and those representing available major innovations. Under such conditions, the latter are likely to be preferred if they offer improved product potentials at little or no increase in costs, or equivalent product quality at even modest cost reductions, or more effective means of increasing output rapidly in the face of sharply expanding demand—providing that technological uncertainties relating to minimum acceptable performance have been eliminated. But diffusion rates might be expected to remain modest even during periods of expansion so long as such technological uncertainties are regarded as comparable to prospective gains, or if expansion is so rapid as to tax managerial capacity even without the added burden of learning how to use new methods effectively. Moreover, innovations often offer significant advantages only within limited sectors of the scale continuum, thus delaying adoptions by larger (or smaller) plants for however long it may take to develop effective adaptations to other levels of scale. And diffusion rates may also be slowed when innovations offer advantages for only part of the product range or require inputs in relatively short supply. Such rates would then be expected to rise sharply as output continues to expand, as cumulative practical experience dispels residual doubts about acceptable performance, and as further advances broaden the array of products and range of scales to which the innovation can be applied advantageously.

On the other hand, the adoption of major innovations to *displace* currently functioning facilities and capacity faces more serious obstacles. Even the production cost criteria tend to become more stringent, for innovative facilities yielding equivalent products might be required to produce at costs comparable to the variable unit costs of existing facilities instead of merely shading their average total unit costs. Such displacement would then involve writing off any remaining undepreciated investment in existing facilities—an especially unattractive prospect when major modernization or expansion programs have only recently been completed. Moreover, prospective displacements also tend to be confronted by high (often excessive) estimates of the change-over costs involved in effecting attendant adjustments in employment levels, job descriptions and skill requirements, production quotas and associated supervisory arrangements—in contrast to the relatively simpler process of establishing working arrangements for new kinds of processes and facilities in the absence of entrenched labor and supervisory personnel as well as habitual technical standards and production sequences. Even the actual gains realized from displacements may fall short of expected potentials when they are adopted within the constraint of not expanding capacity, because of the attendant tendency to utilize as much as possible of existing facilities and performance standards even if these are not optimally adapted to the new facilities. Under such conditions, the direct displacement of functioning facilities and capacity is likely to be substantial only when forced by shortages of input factors for which older facilities have heavier requirements and by increasing demands for product qualities not attainable via older facilities.

Attention should also be drawn to the possibility of *replacements* of the capacity represented by older processes and facilities without increases in the total capacity of the industry. These might be required because of: (a) shortages of capacity in some regions and product lines, while other sectors of capacity are under-utilized; and (b) declines in older capacity due to wear and breakdowns. In such instances, the bases for managerial choices are more likely to resemble the model relating to capacity additions than that relating to the displacement of existing facilities.

Although available data seldom permit decomposition of the foregoing diffusion rates into these three components, rough estimates of their relative proportions might be developed along the following lines. Changes in total output may be regarded as the sum of changes in 'new' and in 'old' production. Each of these, in turn, is determined, of course, by changes in that capacity and in its rate of utilization. By assuming that all 'new' capacity tends to be fully utilized during peak output periods, all gains in 'new' production can be attributed to capacity additions. Although variations in 'old' production may be due to changes either in its capacity or in the rate of utilization, certain limits tend to be applicable to each. For example, if utilization is assumed to approximate 85–90 per cent of capacity in peak periods of production, output gains exceeding the residual capacity would have to be attributable to capacity additions, either through the introduction of improvements which expand the capacity of existing facilities or through the acquisition of new facilities. Replacement rates might be regarded as not less than customary rates of capacity retirement (which might vary widely, of course, among different sectors of production). And decreasing trends in old production which exceed this replacement rate would represent evidence of displacement via progressive under-utilization and eventual withdrawal.

In short, even preliminary models such as the foregoing suggest that the diffusion rates of major innovations are likely to be influenced significantly by a variety of encouraging as well as discouraging factors, among which concurrent output trends constitute but one. They also help to enrich the analytical texture of relevant decision models by calling attention to the time basis for the merging of 'displacement' into 'replacement' and to the necessity for supplementing the polar categories of 'new' and 'old' technologies with an important intermediate group encompassing 'major improvements in the capacity of existing facilities'. The importance of the latter may be illustrated by the development of oxygen lancing in open hearth operations. Of the net capacity expansion of 39.6 million tons between 1950 and 1960, 29.9 million tons were derived from this means of upgrading the capacity of existing furnaces [8].

V. ILLUSTRATIVE APPLICATIONS

Of course, these conceptual models are still too embryonic to warrant serious testing, even if such efforts were not prevented as yet by the sheer inadequacy of available information. But useful indications of the wide variety of combinations of positive and negative influences to be encompassed by relevant analytical frameworks may be provided by a review of the factors associated with the diffusion of some of the major innovations studied in this paper.

Input shortages, for instance, were the prime movers behind the rapid initial growth of electrolytic tinplating during World War II, in the face of declining output; this growth was sustained after the war on the basis of strong demand forces. In a similar vein, heavy investments in beneficiating and pelletizing facilities were the result of developing shortages of high-grade iron ore; here, however, there was no marked expansion of total output, so that pellets appear in a replacement role.

The requirement for scale increases frequently, although not always, goes hand in hand with demand shifts. Thus, steelmaking before the advent of the Bessemer process was essentially a small-batch operation. The interaction between the rapid growth of steel output and industrial and transportation developments in the second half of the nineteenth century need not be recited here. But we find a similar pattern in the more recent growth of rolled flat products, which stimulated the rapid diffusion of continuous hot and cold rolling. On the one hand, the period after World War I saw a shift from heavy steel products used primarily in capital goods to the 'light' products entering into the rapidly expanding consumer durables industries. But continuous rolling not only revolutionized scale and output concepts in this sector of the industry, it also facilitated substantial quality improvements, which developed even further under the stimulus of increasing demands in this direction from such end users as the automobile industry.

Innovations whose diffusion was dominated by cost considerations include the basic oxygen process, the continuous miner and the mechanical coal loader. In the case of the former, once its potential for operating economies had proved realizable through a major scaling-up of the small facilities originally developed in Europe, diffusion increased sharply. Increasing application of the continuous miner, despite a pronounced decline in the total output of underground coal mines, was stimulated by rapidly rising wage rates. Although the mechanical coal loader was adopted during the 1920s in those few states where strong unionization kept wages high, it was not until a decade later, when wage rates rose in other states, that rapid growth in mechanical loading developed elsewhere [13].

Each of the above illustrations highlights the positive factors which more than offset concomitant considerations tending to favor rejection or delay. But such retardants may at times predominate and therefore brake rates of diffusion even in the face of growing output. For example, the relative slowness with which by-product coking was adopted may be attributed to an interaction of two of the forces discussed above. In the initial stage, the plentiful supply of excellent Pennsylvania coking coal and the availability of organic chemicals from foreign suppliers clearly retarded adoption of the new technology during the early period of its availability. Not until World War I did shortages of both lead to a rapidly growing interest in the by-product process. The slow diffusion of the open hearth in the face of sharply growing output was clearly attributable to the industry's heavy financial and technical commitments only a few years earlier to the Bessemer process as well as to uncertainties about open hearth technology. It may also be of interest to note that the open hearth's ability to absorb considerable proportions of scrap did not turn into a major economic advantage until the expanded output of the industry generated sufficient quantities of home scrap [15, pp. 108 ff.; 21].

Still another form of retardant is illustrated by the slow diffusion of the machine cutting of coal despite booming coal production. A multiplicity of designs on the market and conflicting opinions about their respective performances encouraged delay in changing over to machine cutting until one type of equipment emerged as clearly superior. Finally, delays in the adoption of mechanical coal cleaning may be traced to the disadvantageous output mix and cost structure during its early period of availability. Specifically, as long as lump coal commanded a premium in the market, it made little sense to crush coal to the much smaller size at which cleaning is efficient. Moreover, inasmuch as such cleaning is largely a remedial operation to offset the inability of mechanical loading devices to discriminate between coal and waste materials, the more rapid adoption of mechanical cleaning had to await the emergence of mechanical loading as economically attractive. On the other hand, washing was adopted much more rapidly for coking coal, where crushing improved the quality of the output and reductions in sulphur and ash provided additional benefits.

The need for scale increases in adapting new technologies to mass production requirements has already been mentioned as retarding the adoption of basic oxygen furnaces in large American steel mills.

A similar process is currently under way in respect to the adaptation of continuous casting. Incidentally, even in some sectors of the industry where one finds no 'major innovations', one of the main thrusts of technological development has been in the direction of scale increases, as is especially well illustrated by blast furnaces. Major changes of this kind pose decision issues comparable in many respects to those associated with new technologies. For example, the blast furnace was widely characterized in the mid-1930's as on its way out—and renewed expressions of this expectation are being publicized in 1969, at the same time that successively larger blast furnaces are being built in this country and abroad [21].

VI. TOWARDS A BROADER ANALYTICAL FRAMEWORK

The preceding analysis suggests the desirability of penetrating beneath 'black box' approaches which seek out variables correlated with experiential data on diffusion and then combine these into models purporting to explain past results and to predict future decisions and outcomes. In particular, the diversity of our findings indicates that aiming directly at any universal model at the current crude stage of exploring managerial decisions about major technological innovations may prove less fruitful than searching for the sources of such diversity. Significant dissimilarities might be found among various kinds of innovations, among decision foci representing different constraints or successive stages of commitment, and at different levels of aggregation. If such internal groupings actually proved to be important, further analysis might yield differentiated models for several of the resulting combinations. In addition, the preceding discussion also raises questions concerning the relationship of eventual post-decision profits and other outcomes for innovation-adopters to the determinants of their earlier decisions.

A. Decision-Making Processes

Inasmuch as technological diffusion is rooted in decisions by the managements of individual firms, a brief review of the stages leading up to and following such decisions may help to clarify the processes encompassed within the 'black box'. As shown in Chart III, decision-making channels have continuous inputs representing pressures from product markets, factor markets, technological developments and internal operating as well as organizational problems. Proposals for coping with such pressures—including technological innovations—may be generated by external suppliers of facilities and services as well as by various internal groups. The bearing of such proposals on

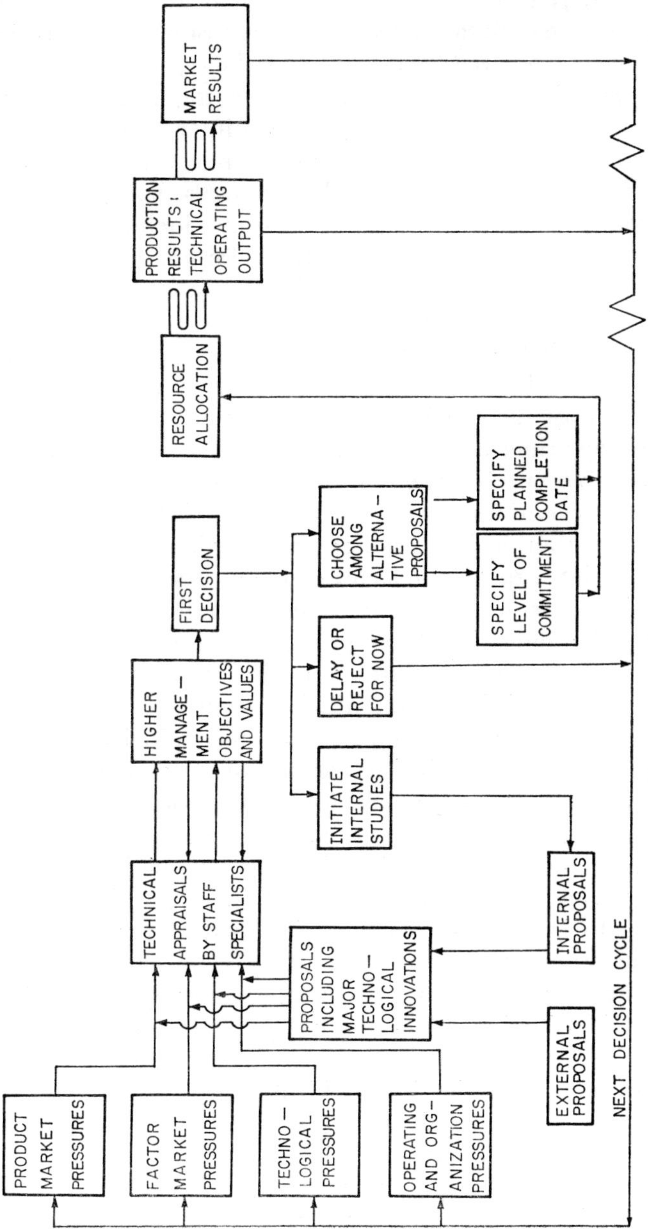

CHART III. Decision process for major technological innovations.

each of the channels of pressure is appraised by staff specialists and assembled into technical recommendations to higher levels of management. Whenever these fall short of yielding inescapable conclusions, because of data inadequacies or substantial uncertainties or implications not covered by prevailing policies, successive exchanges may take place involving responses to higher management's inquiries. Only then is a decision made: to initiate internal studies including research and development projects; or to reject action for the present; or to choose among available proposals, specifying both the level of commitment and the period within which resulting acquisitions or construction should become ready for use. After resources are then allocated, a considerable period may elapse before production results are experienced (including technological findings, product yields and needed operational adjustments), followed by another extended period before an adequate array of market responses is secured. Both of these delayed sets of results constitute additional inputs to the various channels of pressure as well as to the technical assessments prepared as the basis for the next round of decisions.

There are several reasons for introducing this broader framework. It emphasizes that decisions about technological innovations fit into general decision processes instead of being essentially unique, that technological pressures are continuous instead of arising only when technological innovations are proposed, and that technological pressures affect a wide range of decisions in addition to those involving new facilities, often making it very difficult indeed to separate out the differential effects of technological innovations. Secondly, the focus on decision cycles stresses that many major decisions do not take the climactic form of once-for-all choices among alternatives, but rather represent temporary commitments subject to successive extensions or modifications on the basis of intervening results and other information [10, p. 400]. Hence, it may be quite misleading to infer the bases for original decisions from eventual profits and other operating results. This view also serves as a reminder that diffusion rates are affected not only by firms which have hitherto delayed adoption, but also through progressively larger commitments by early adopters experiencing favorable results from exploratory initial applications. Thirdly, this flow chart highlights the problems of reaching beyond available authoritative data and recognized computational procedures to account for top level management decisions [9, pp. 106–8] by suggesting the role of organizational objectives and managerial values both in reshaping technical judgments and in supplementing them to arrive at major decisions [10]. Finally, the chart underlines the likelihood that periods of 1–10 years may elapse before the facilities embodying a major technological innovation are in place and functioning, with further delays to be expected before market responses are adequately plumbed.[4] This raises questions about the significance of findings concerning utilization rates and other conditions at the time when innovations become operative[5]—for wide differences in the periods required to implement decisions involving the adoption of innovations means that conditions at the time when these come on stream need have no consistent relationship to those in effect when the decisions were made, and it is presumably the latter which are of primary analytical concern.

B. The Decision Model

Decision models concerned with the adoption of major technological innovations seem to have succumbed to the temptations both of over-generality and of over-rationality. To say that major innovational decisions are based on profitability expectations adjusted for the estimated probabilities of adverse outcomes may be unobjectionable, and may even be correct in some sense; but it is certainly unenlightening. As an 'explanation' of past decisions, it offers nothing more than a tautology: i.e., if an innovation was adopted, management must have expected it to be sufficiently profitable; and if not, not. And as an empirical 'test' of such expectations, it is hardly more helpful to demonstrate that the innovations which survive and achieve eventually wide diffusion are those whose utilization has been associated with profitability. Serious analysis surely requires digging deeper.

The diversity of diffusion patterns presented earlier suggests that firms appraising newly available major technological innovations usually emerge with widely differing estimates of the desirability of immediate adoption. In seeking to account for such disparate conclusions, it may be useful to examine possible sources of difference in the pre-decision environment, in the characteristics of the innovation and in the bases for making evaluations relative to each criterion as well as for combining the results into a decision.

Perhaps the most important elements of the pre-decision environment are the urgency of the needs leading to a consideration of major

[4] In the case of iron ore pelletizing, preliminary plans were made by Reserve Mining in 1944 for a plant that issued its first output in 1956. But the commercial success of the plant was not certain until full-scale blast furnace tests of pellets were carried out in 1960.

[5] This refers to the finding that innovations are most likely to be introduced when utilization rates are around 75 per cent [17, pp. 109 ff.]. Incidentally, the use of industry utilization rates in this study as a surrogate for those of the individual firms making these innovative applications cannot but generate further doubts about the significance of such findings.

innovations, the nature of these needs, the availability of alternatives to technological innovations for coping with such needs and the existence of any marked preferences by management among such alternatives. Firms may obviously differ widely in the degree of felt urgencies, defined as the period within which management considers it essential that measures for dealing with specified pressures become operative.[6] Those facing the greatest urgencies might then be expected: (a) to act sooner than others with comparable evaluations of the prospective benefits and burdens of available innovations; (b) to favor innovations promising more immediate gains; and (c) to be willing to accept greater risks relative to expected gains.

Differences in the specific needs constituting the pressures to action are also likely to engender dissimilar environments within which alternative innovations are evaluated by individual managements. Even if the list of such pressing needs is limited to a few broad categories—increasing or replacing capacity, increasing the scale of some or all operations, improving product quality, lowering requirements of inputs in short supply, decreasing production costs via reduced inputs relative to output levels, decreasing such costs through lower factor prices and increasing sales—it is clear that the potential contributions of technological as compared to marketing and other innovations are likely to be more dominant in respect to the first five than the last two; and it is also clear that individual innovations would likewise differ substantially in their usefulness in promoting such disparate ends. However, the more general the terms in which corporate urgencies are defined, e.g., as a need to increase profitability, the wider range of alternatives to technological innovations which invite consideration. And inasmuch as firms may have deeply rooted preference orders as among alternative approaches to major problems—reflecting differences in managerial training, experience and past sources of company success—they may well differ both in their readiness to consider technological solutions at all, and in the relative levels of net advantage required of technological as compared with marketing or other preferred innovational alternatives [10].

While the aspects of technological innovations which engender different managerial reactions are not yet clear, they may include the

[6] Such urgencies might include pressure to expand into newly burgeoning markets; or to offset serious losses in, or impending threats to, its competitive position; or a need to ease rapidly developing imbalances in its production flows—such as is being currently experienced by the steel industry as a result of the shift to basic oxygen furnaces, and which is intensifying consideration of continuous casting. It may even be useful to distinguish between 'discretionary' decisions which allow management a choice between action and delay, and those permitting a choice only among alternative proposals, as suggested in Chart III.

source and nature of the innovation as well as the kinds of prospective benefits and risks involved. The first of these concerns whether the innovation has been developed by the firm's own technical staff, or is being offered by an external source on an exclusive basis, or is available from a supplier seeking to promote widespread use. The second might include such matters as whether the technology involved is alien or kindred to the company's current fields of specialization[7] and whether resulting products would flow through existing channels to established customers or would involve breaking new ground in these respects. Managerial responses to available alternatives among technological innovations are also obviously dependent on the distinctive arrays of benefits and burdens offered by each relative to company rankings of their respective urgencies and preferred forms of burdens. Merely defining each prospective innovation's relative contributions to each of the seven broad categories of need suggested above would at least partially explain divergent evaluations by companies seeking to cope with dissimilar patterns of urgencies. For example, even innovations offering lower costs might be of limited interest to firms confronted by urgent demands for higher quality products. At a deeper level of detail, innovations with a limited scale or product range would obviously be rated as less attractive by firms whose needs would consequently remain largely unmet. Moreover, innovations likely to yield marketable benefits only 5–10 years hence are likely to be rated as relatively less desirable among firms facing critical shorter-term pressures.

Among the deterrent factors associated with prospective innovations, it might suffice for current summary purposes to list four potential burdens (displacement of undepreciated assets, need for new investment funds, change-over costs including attendant labor and organizational turmoil, and the possibility of higher unit costs accompanying desired product improvements or other gains) and three potential risks (that the innovation won't function acceptably, that product or cost improvements will fall short of expectations, and that the innovation under consideration is likely to be displaced by more advantageous innovations before recovery of the attendant investment can reasonably be expected). Inasmuch as available innovations are likely to warrant different ratings in respect to each of these deterrents and inasmuch as different firms might attach unequal emphasis to these several criteria, another important source of disparate evaluations of given innovations by prospective adopters has been identified.

[7] For example, companies with products long rooted in mechanical engineering and staffed by such specialists tended to resist the early incursion of electronic approaches to effectuating similar design, manufacturing and production control objectives.

Attention may now be focused on the decision-making model for which the pre-decision factors and the evaluations of the benefits and burdens of alternative innovations which have been discussed serve as inputs. Almost all managerial decision models assume that each criterion affecting decisions is somehow translated into cost and revenue equivalents and that these are then combined to yield profitability estimates as the ultimate determinant of the decisions made. Pervasive as they are, however, these assumptions are not without alternatives worth some consideration.

In respect to the over-riding role of profitability, one of the more extreme dissidents was Keynes, who argued that many major business decisions are taken 'as a result of animal spirits—of a spontaneous urge to action rather than inaction' [14, pp. 161–2]. Others have emphasized the need to keep moving with the stream of change, even though its eventual outcomes are unclear and even though the short range outcomes of individual projects do not seem unduly attractive. Some even argue that innovations are necessary to attract and hold good personnel and to encourage innovative efforts.[8] An intriguing hybrid between 'profit-directed' and 'other-directed' views suggests that major technological decisions tend to be dominated by the judgments of technologists, who tend to *evaluate* the physical improvements of prospective innovations and to *assume* parallel economic benefits via *ceteris paribus* assumptions commonly associated with the work of economists. While the forms of such assessments and their shortcomings have been discussed elsewhere [9, pp. 106 ff.], it should be recognized that such technical judgments tend to be regarded as convincing not only because of their apparent objectivity and precision, but also because too little research has yet been done to indicate the magnitude of the errors which may be involved in assuming parallel economic benefits. Moreover, the fact that most commitments to major innovations unfold progressively over several decision cycles may constitute a significant safeguard in that the dominance of technological judgments concerning gains in physical input–output relationships during early decisions may be gradually offset in later decisions as firmer cost and market data become available.

The logic of rigorous rational models implies a need to identify the major categories of benefits, burdens and risks considered in making a decision, to explain how their respective magnitudes are estimated and how the results are combined to yield a conclusion. If it should

[8] Illustrations of such 'dissident' views include Hershey [11, p. 263], Sutherland [19, pp. 118–35], Carter and Williams [7, p. 56], Nelson [18, p. 124] and Andrews and Brunner [4, pp. 355–6].

turn out that the available factual content of such efforts is often fairly low in respect to newly available innovations and that the estimates used to supplement them are recognized as subject to wide margins of error, the very focus of analysis may have to be shifted, however reluctantly, to more influential albeit less measurable determinants of such major policy decisions [10]. And it is quite possible, of course, that final managerial outcomes are based not on any formally weighted combination of favorable and unfavorable factors, but on the extent of 'concrescence' (to use Max Black's term in accounting for how 'scientific' a given methodology is [6]) among those pointing in a given direction—much like our current practice in interpreting the 'net' implications of 'leading' and 'lagging' business cycle indicators.

One means of attempting to circumvent these difficulties has been to use *ex post* performance data to infer the primary determinants of the original adoption decisions. But this approach raises several problems. The first, which was mentioned earlier, is that eventual results need not have much relationship to the expectations underlying the initial decision, which may have been modified repeatedly during successive stages of extending the original commitment to encompass more, larger and even improved facilities. A second is that estimates of the differential effects of given innovations on profits are frequently subject to serious error, because most innovations serve as parts of larger complexes of facilities whose results cannot be disentangled from one another,[9] because firms which are especially successful with major innovations are likely to have managements which are above average over a wider range of performance and because profits represent the interaction of technological improvements with a variety of adjustments in product and factor markets as well. A third is that the differential benefits of innovations tend to be limited during the early period of their full functioning because of attendant efforts to learn how to operate them effectively [12] and how to adapt to market responses; and they also tend to erode with time under competitive conditions, as has been discussed at some length elsewhere [9]. This raises the questions of when evaluations should be made and, even more interesting, what the benefit patterns may be expected to look like through time. A fourth is that studies of the outcomes associated with eventually successful in-

[9] 'The overwhelming majority of business investment projects are of this segmental component type—replacements, improvements, expansions or some combination thereof. They become a part—usually a small part—of an existing operation. Since it is impossible in most cases to compute their separate revenue generation and operating cost incurments after they are in service, it is even more impossible to predict these magnitudes before the projects are acquired' [20, p. 52].

novations can hardly provide effective models for deciding whether or not to adopt proposed new innovations, when the probabilities of failure may far overshadow those of successes. And finally, the data offered concerning the profit expectations 15–60 years ago, when recently studied innovations were first adopted [17, p. 143, n. 20, 21] represent recollections, inferences, estimates and guesses, most of which seem open to substantial margins of error.

One might well add that in order to account for empirical diffusion patterns, it would seem necessary to explain not only the decisions of 'pioneer' adopters, but also the changing bases for decisions confronting individual firms during later stages of diffusion as well as the characteristics of the changing mix of firms dominating adoptions during such successive stages. In particular, laggard managements would not only be confronted by changing estimates of technological and market uncertainties, but they might also face changes in materials prices, wage rates and even in product prices and product specifications generated by market responses to the spreading innovation [9]. Thus, further adoptions might come to be motivated increasingly by threats to competitive position and even to survival rather than by the attractions of added benefits. As for the changing mix of adopters between early, intermediate and later stages of diffusion, there is little basis as yet for even formulating interesting hypotheses comparing diffusion rates among different classifications of firms inasmuch as the critical distinguishing variables are not yet clear. In the meantime, efforts to compare the responsiveness of large *vs.* small firms may significantly under-estimate differences in the optimal scale and product range of the innovations covered as well as their relative impact on the effectiveness of total operations and on the level of average total unit costs.

C. The Innovation

Finally, closer scrutiny is needed of the concept of 'the innovation' which is presumably the focus of such decision and diffusion models. 'It' frequently appears in a variety of forms with differing combinations of advantages and disadvantages to complicate the managerial decision. Among the innovations studied in this paper, such a multiplicity of designs emerged not only in the coal cutting case cited earlier, but also in respect to open hearth and by-product coke furnaces, continuous rolling methods, coal loading machines and coal washing methods. And similar uncertainties exist currently concerning alternative methods of continuous casting and the direct reduction of iron ore. Nor is choice necessarily limited to the current array of alternatives, inasmuch as the very multiplicity of competing designs at a given time evidences intensive developmental activity which may well yield improved, if not entirely new, alternatives within reasonable time horizons. Moving further along the technological continuum, one may identify 'substantial' or 'major' improvements in existing technologies and facilities. These may well yield sharp gains in productive capacity or in product quality or in production costs without involving the replacement of older facilities —e.g., the use of oxygen lancing in open hearths, the speeding up of rolling mills, etc. Still another sector of the technological continuum is characterized by major changes in the scale of productive facilities, perhaps doubling and re-doubling as in the case of blast furnaces, or increasing 10 or 20 fold as in the case of oil tankers, without requiring new technological 'breakthroughs'.

One implication of this more detailed view bears on the sharpness with which studies of adoptions and of diffusion rates and effects can be focused consistently on a particular 'new' innovation as differentiated from a network encompassing various and changing forms. Analytically even more interesting, however, is the resulting challenge to explore the relationships among these various forms of technological advance.

In discussing the nature of innovations, it may also be useful to note that the frequent distinction between product and process innovations may prove to be less widely applicable than has been supposed. At least in the iron and steel industry, there is hardly a major process innovation which did not have significant effects on product characteristics. Indeed, recognition of this interaction is institutionalized in the requirement of formal approval by various specification-writing agencies of products resulting from new processes.

CASE WESTERN RESERVE UNIVERSITY

REFERENCES

[1] A. C. ADAMS, President of Jones & Laughlin Steel Co., in *American Steel Market*, September 23rd, 1959.

[2] W. ADAMS and J. DIRLAM, 'Steel Imports and Vertical Oligopoly Power', *American Economic Review*, LIV/5, September 1964.

[3] ——, 'Big Steel, Invention and Innovation', *Quarterly Journal of Economics*, LXX/2, May 1966.

[4] P. W. S. ANDREWS and ELIZABETH BRUNNER, *Capital Development in Steel*, (Oxford, 1952).

[5] A. W. BELDEN, 'Metallurgical Coke', *U.S. Bureau of Mines, Technical Paper No.* 50, 1913.

[6] MAX BLACK, 'The Definition of Scientific Method', in W. Stauffer (ed.), *Science and Civilization* (University of Wisconsin Press, 1949).

[7] C. F. CARTER and B. R. WILLIAMS, *Investment in Innovation* (London, 1958).

[7a] G. C. CHOW, 'Technological Change and the Demand for Computers', *American Economic Review*, LVII/5, December 1967, p. 1117.

[8] D. R. DILLEY and D. L. MCBRIDE, 'Oxygen Steelmaking—Fact vs. Folklore', *Iron and Steel Engineer*, October 1967.

[9] B. GOLD, 'Economic Effects of Technological Innovations', *Management Science*, XI/1, September 1964.

[9a] ——, 'Industry Growth Patterns: Theory and Empirical Findings', *Journal of Industrial Economics*, November 1964.

[10] ——, 'The Framework of Decision for Major Technological Innovation', in K. Baier and N. Rescher (ed.), *Values and the Future* (New York, 1969).

[11] R. L. HERSHEY, 'Finance and Productivity in Industrial Research and Development', *Research Management*, July 1966.

[12] W. Z. HIRSCH, 'Firm Progress Ratios', *Econometrica*, April 1956.

[13] W. E. HOTCHKISS *et al*, *Mechanization, Employment, and Output Per Man in Bituminous Coal Mining* (U.S. Work Projects Administration, National Research Project Report No. E–9, 1939).

[14] J. M. KEYNES, *The General Theory of Employment, Interest and Money* (London, 1936).

[15] C. D. KING, *Seventy-five Years of Progress in Iron and Steel* (New York, 1948).

[16] F. LYNN, 'An Investigation of the Rate of Development and Diffusion of Technology in Our Modern Industrial Society', in *Studies prepared for the National Commission on Technology, Automation, and Economic Progress*, Appendix Volume II, Technology and the American Economy (Washington, D.C., 1966).

[17] E. MANSFIELD, *Industrial Research and Technological Innovation* (New York, 1968).

[18] R. R. NELSON, 'Economics of Invention—A Survey of the Literature', *Journal of Business*, April 1959.

[19] A. SUTHERLAND, 'Diffusion of an Innovation in Cotton Spinning', *Journal of Industrial Economics*, March 1959.

[20] G. TERBORGH, *Business Investment Policy* (Washington, D.C., 1958).

[21] 33/*Magazine of Metals Producing*, June 1969.

APPENDIX: *Sources of Statistical Data*

1. Bessemer Process

V. S. Clark, *History of Manufacturing in the United States*, Vol. II (New York, 1929; reprinted 1949), p. 20.

C. D. King, *Seventy-five Years of Progress in Iron and Steel* (New York, 1948), p. 94.

American Iron and Steel Institute (AISI), *Annual Statistical Report* (New York, annual).

2. Continuous Cold Rolling, Sheets
   AISI, *op. cit.*
3. Electrolytic Tinplating
   AISI, *op. cit.*
4. Wide Continuous Hot Strip Mill
   AISI *Annual Statistical Report* (various years).
   D. A. Fisher, *The Epic of Steel* (New York, 1963), p. 145.
5. Continuous Cold Strip Mill
   AISI, *op. cit.*
6. Basic Oxygen Furnace
   AISI, *op. cit.*
7. Pelletizing of Taconite Concentrate
   AISI, *op. cit.* Data used are consumption of pellets compared with consumption of iron ore and agglomerates in iron and steel. For 1956–1958, 'shipments' of pellets were used since 'consumption' was not available.
8. Continuous Coal Mining Machine
   U.S. Bureau of Mines, *Minerals Yearbook* (various years).
9. Washing of Coking Coal
   Frederick H. Wagner, *Coal and Coke*, McGraw-Hill, 1916, p. 102.
   Sheridan and DeCarlo, *Coal Carbonization in the United States*, 1900–62, U.S. Bureau of Mines Information Circular 8251, 1965.
10. Machine Loading of Coal
    National Coal Association, *Bituminous Coal Data*, 1962.
11. By-product Coke Oven
    Sheridan and DeCarlo, *op. cit.*
12. Machine Cutting of Coal
    U.S. Bureau of the Census, *Historical Statistics of the United States, Colonial Times to 1957.*
13. Open Hearth Steel Making
    C. D. King, *op. cit.*, pp. 94, 109.
    AISI, *op. cit.*
14. Strip Mining of Coal
    National Coal Association, *op. cit.*

MEANINGFUL BANK FAILURE: A PROPOSAL

by A. Dale Tussing*

I

The ultimate test of the efficacy of bank supervision, if one speaks to officials of the regulatory agencies at the Federal or state level, is the absence of bank failure. Yet the extensive regulation of banking in the United States was not ostensibly designed to prevent bank failure, but rather to protect the economy and the depositor. Over the years, 'protection of the public interest' and 'prevention of bank failure' have become so linked in the minds of legislators, supervisory personnel, and bankers, that they are used interchangeably.

The purpose of this paper is to argue, first, that the two are not the same but are quite separate issues, and, second, to demonstrate, through a proposed reorganization of the means of bank regulation, that the two are separable in practice.

This writer has argued earlier that bank failure, once an inherently destructive force in the American economy, can be made to be an essentially constructive one.[1] This earlier work has raised two additional questions:

1. What changes in banking structure and regulatory procedure are necessary? Here the reference is not to the ultimate reforms sought: freer entry, more managerial initiative over asset composition, more opportunity for price competition, etc. Instead, the question concerns the changes which would make bank failure tolerable and hence permit movement toward the ultimate reforms.

2. Precisely what is, or should be, meant by 'bank failure?' If a banking structure is going to make constructive use of the competitive pressure of the threat of failure, it must be prepared (lest the threat be a hollow one) to permit some additional banks to fail. What is meant by this involves a consideration of precisely whom to threaten, and with what. Does the bank actually have to close down? Should stockholders suffer? *Only* stockholders? And to what

* An earlier version of this paper was presented under the title 'Bank Failure: A Meaningful Competitive Force?' at the Conference on Bank Structure and Competition, Federal Reserve Bank of Chicago, May 13th, 1968. The author is indebted in a variety of ways to Professors Melvin A. Eggers, Syracuse University; Thomas G. Gies, University of Michigan; Oscar Goodman, Roosevelt University; Irving H. Plotkin, Massachusetts Institute of Technology; and Edward J. Stevens, Syracuse University; and to Dr. Paul M. Horvitz of the Federal Deposit Insurance Corporation and Dr. George G. Kaufman of the Federal Reserve Bank of Chicago.

[1] A. Dale Tussing, 'The Case for Bank Failure', *Journal of Law and Economics*, 10 (1967), pp. 129–47.

extent and in what ways is the public to be protected from the undesirable social consequences of bank failure?

The answers to these two questions are intertwined, and the two issues must be dealt with simultaneously. In what follows, there will first be a discussion of the essential reasons for bank supervision and of its historic association with preventing bank failure. Second, a scheme will be proposed, whereby the essential public interest can be protected even while bank failure is permitted, so that society can reap the advantages both of a safe and sound banking system and a competitive one. Finally, the paper will compare the proposed scheme with the recent and highly controversial Federal Deposit Insurance Corporation action in the case of the failing Public Bank of Detroit.[2]

II

The essential reason for the long-standing policy of avoiding bank failure is the existence of two important linkages. The first is the linkage between the failure of an unsound and/or poorly managed bank and the failure of other banks. This is the problem of bank runs and panics. It would not make economic sense to allow the forces of competition to operate sufficiently freely to endanger any bank if the failure of that bank were to lead to failures of, or even significantly uneconomic behavior by, sound and well-managed banks, even if there were no important effects of bank failures on the payments mechanism, on depositors and borrowers, or through them on third parties.

We have not seen bank runs in the United States for three decades, but that in and of itself does not mean that we need not be concerned with this linkage, since we have achieved this record in an environment of protective regulation. It is still possible to argue that, should a more competitive banking structure be developed, and should a significantly larger number of banks begin to fail each year, public confidence in banks would decline sharply, and failures of some banks would produce difficulties for others. In some recent cases of bank failure, pressures have indeed been strong upon other local banks, especially newer and smaller ones in metropolitan areas.

It is the effects referred to on depositors, borrowers, and third parties, that constitutes the second linkage. The failure of any

[2] This writer first learned the details of the Public Bank case at the Federal Reserve Bank of Chicago Conference on Bank Structure and Performance, where an earlier version of this paper was presented. Because of striking similarities to this paper's proposed scheme, the Public Bank case must be discussed here, with both the similarities and some important differences noted.

business has harmful effects on persons and businesses whose behavior was not responsible for the failure—employees, creditors, even customers. In many cases, these effects are more troublesome and severe for the failure of non-banking businesses than they are for isolated, individual bank failures. Nonetheless, we must accept the social judgment, whether well-founded or not, that this linkage is of over-riding importance. Moreover, when both linkages work in tandem, as they did in the 1930s, then the destructive effects of waves of bank failures on the payments mechanism, on the integrity of the public's assets, and on employment and income can be profound.

It can be argued that the literature and our patterns of regulation, in concentrating on the depositor, and, through him, the payments mechanism, give insufficient attention to the effects of bank failure on borrowers. Even today, the failure of a locally important bank can be immediately disruptive to a business whose planning has been predicated upon the continuance of a credit relationship with a familiar and understanding lender; the uncertainty and delay involved in establishing a new banking relationship with another institution may be needlessly dangerous to the viability of sound firms, especially those which are new and/or small, those with seasonal business, and in general most construction contractors, merchants with large working-capital needs, automobile and appliance dealers originating installment-loan paper, and the like. In the 'thirties, this aspect of the bank failure–third party linkage manifested itself in the forced liquidation of loans by cash-hungry banks, and often in business failures which aggravated the economic collapse.

The existence of these two sets of linkages has led to the elaboration of a vast, complex and detailed system of protective regulation. Given the linkages, there seems no alternative. So long as the two linkages exist, little progress can be made in banking reform.

The only other strategy conceivable is one of breaking the linkages. What this means is that society can tolerate a competitive banking structure, complete with banker initiative over entry, product line, price and exit, and with the possibility of failure, only if failure can be achieved without its spreading to other banks, and without its having significant effect upon third parties.

Both these linkages are considerably weaker than they were in the 1930s, a fact far from adequately reflected in relaxation of Federal and state protectionist measures, but one reflected in the impatience of academic and supervisory economists with the present order. But there is little feeling that they are weak enough to permit competition sufficiently untrammeled that there be a significant increase in the threat of bank failure.[3]

III

The two linkages described, which shall be called the other-bank linkage and the customer linkage (short for 'customer-and-third-party linkage'), are mutually reinforcing. In the absence of the other-bank linkage, the customer linkage becomes considerably less important, and occasionally even trivial compared with the customer linkages of other, nonbank business failures. On the other hand, the most important step in breaking the other-bank linkage is to break the customer linkage, since the former is largely a consequence of self-protective behavior in an atmosphere of economic crisis. Indeed, the most important step we have thus far taken in breaking the customer-linkage, the establishment of deposit insurance, has achieved its most notable effects through breaking other-bank linkages. Some observers give deposit insurance the lion's share of the credit for the disappearance of bank runs and collective failures in the post-World War II era, and it is hard to argue with this view.[4] We shall be content, in this paper, to deal with a means of effecting a complete breaking of the customer linkage, on the theory that this breaks the other-bank linkage as well.

Breaking the customer linkage means the following: A bank can fail as a consequence of a bad location, poor personnel policies, poor internal security, technological and competitive ineptitude, bad asset selection, poor planning, or the like. (The above include so-called 'overbanking' as a cause of failure, in that the bank or banks to fail in an overbanked market will be the one or ones weakest in the above respects.) The equity of stockholders is wiped out, and top management lose their positions. But there is an uninterrupted banking business for depositors and borrowers; there is no forced repayment of loans; nor is there any loss in ability to conduct business predicated on existing lines of credit, real estate loan commitments, and the like. To owners and top management, failure is the end; to everyone else, there is no effect.

[3] It is not only in banking policy that linkage-breaking must be sought. In the labor-relations area, for instance, we need imaginative attention to breaking the linkages between the public interest and what are essentially labor-vs.-ownership endurance struggles. How can we develop an economic equivalent to strikes, one which penalizes both employers and employees as strikes do, but does not disrupt service to innocent third parties, cost sales to suppliers, or reduce employment and output through multiplier effects? There are roughly similar linkage problems in the areas of anti-trust policy, transportation, farm price supports, welfare and income maintenance, and elsewhere.

[4] Milton Friedman and Anna Schwartz, *A Monetary History of the United States, 1867–1960*, 1960, pp. 440.

Note that the requirements include 'an uninterrupted banking business for depositors and borrowers', *not* that the banking office remain open. Certainly one way of maintaining an uninterrupted business would be to keep the bank operating, and that approach might be appropriate where the source of failure had nothing to do with location or the number of competing institutions. But an uninterrupted banking business can also mean the distribution of the bank's assets and liabilities, as a package or in pieces, to other institutions.

This extreme of linkage-breaking may be impossible in practice; this discussion of linkage-breaking defines the problem, not its solution. In practice, some linkage-breaking will not be necessary. We do not have to provide for employees, since we have a system of unemployment compensation which covers them as well as others; and if this system is regarded as inadequate, it should be improved as a matter of employment and income-maintenance policy, not of bank regulation. We do not generally provide protection against business failure for suppliers, landlords, nearby merchants, etc.; and there is no reason to provide this protection in banking unless we choose to do it elsewhere.

We have a system of linkage-breakage which operates in some cases, where supervisory authorities arrange for the absorption of a bank by a stronger competitor, a holding company, or a branch system previously unrepresented in the market. But our use of this device is limited not only by the nature of the state banking law but also by its applicability only to a fraction of the sources of failure. What is needed is a system which can cover the cases left uncovered by this informal system, can do so without gain to stockholders and top management of the affected bank, and which goes much further in its linkage-breaking than deposit insurance, in coverage, promptness, and certainty.

IV

Can a banking system with little or no customer linkage be constructed or approximated? The following scheme is offered with some hesitation, because of a concern that it may be interpreted as the major purpose of this paper. The more important purpose has been to indicate the nature of the problem. The following is offered to demonstrate that such a system is in fact conceivable. For practical application it would need much discussion, articulation, and, probably, modification.

To simplify the discussion, the system will be described in terms of a single, major regulatory body, and a single set of procedures, based on the present Federal Deposit Insurance Corporation, the main linkage-breaking institution presently in existence. The same techniques could be employed, but with more difficulty, within a 'dual' or 'multiple' bank-supervision arrangement.

The FDIC would broaden its conception from that of deposit insurance to 'bank life insurance', i.e., the contingency on which benefit payments would be made would be the death of a bank. As with any other life insurance, benefits would be paid to surviving beneficiaries, not to the deceased. The precise nature of the claims to be paid will be discussed momentarily.

And as with life insurance, premiums would be based on risk of death. This requirement poses a somewhat more formidable problem for bank life insurance than it does for ordinary life insurance, because of our greater actual experience with mortals. That is, too few banks fail today for actuaries to work with. Even so, this problem is not insuperable. Premiums could be assessed in accordance with an objective formula (though some judgment seems inevitable), including the following features: (1) Premiums would be paid, as now, on dollars of deposit liabilities, though not at the same rate for all banks. (2) Premiums per dollar of deposit would be based on the mix of asset types held by the bank, those with a high loss experience requiring higher premium rates than those with lower empirically determined risks. There could even be a form of progression in the rate structure within each asset-type group, to make diversification within banks more attractive. (3) Loans classified by examiners could be subject to penalty premiums; and these penalties could increase rapidly if the same loans are classified in report after report. (4) There would, however, be a credit against the premium for a high ratio of equity capital to risk assets. Thus a bank could afford the luxury of a higher-risk loan portfolio, including more classified loans, without penalty, to the extent that the risks were borne by the shareholders rather than the FDIC. For the insurance premium to become an effective market force, other kinds of examiners' exceptions, such as those dealing with internal controls and security, would also have to be given dollar-premium equivalents.[5]

The insurance premium would become the principal device for asset-choice and bank-performance regulation, and most explicit asset-choice rules would be abolished. Bank examinations would become, in effect, underwriters' examination, whose principal pur-

[5] Cf. Tussing, *op. cit.*, p. 146; Thomas Mayer, 'A Graduated Deposit Insurance Plan', *Review of Economics and Statistics*, 47 (1965), p. 114.

pose would be the setting of premium rates. Bankers' judgments and market processes could be given freer rein; different judgments would lead to different policies among banks. Some would readily accept higher premiums in order to invest in statistically more risky assets, perhaps because they do not believe past loss patterns will be maintained, or perhaps because present yield patterns increase the revenue potential of some assets relative to their premium costs. Other banks will economize on insurance premiums by accepting assets primarily from the less risky end of the spectrum.

The credit against premiums for a high capital ratio is a two-edged sword. Should a bank sustain losses, its capital ratio would decline, and its premiums would rise. It would be forced, through this cost inducement, to restore its equity before paying dividends, thus imposing an immediate cost to stockholders of a sort not now consistently imposed.

Should society decide to accept some of the risk of loss of certain kinds of loans, such as loans to poor people in the ghetto, it could do so through subsidizing the differential insurance premiums associated with such high-risk assets.

Most important, for present purposes, banks would be permitted to play the game of brinksmanship, taking risks that no bank today would be permitted to take—and to pay for them. And they would be permitted to fail.

The proposed procedure for bank failure, much of which can be applied today, without waiting for revisions in procedures for determining insurance premiums or for changes in restrictive laws and regulations, is a more moderate change than it at first appears to be. It moves in the direction that current *de facto* regulatory procedures now tend. In outline, the procedure would be:

1. The bank is declared to be insolvent by the FDIC, by other supervisory authorities, or by the bank's own directors, subject to FDIC approval. This power would go beyond the corporation's present powers, which are limited to denying deposit insurance.

2. Immediately upon this declaration the FDIC, through a modified liquidation division, moves in and takes over the bank and operates it, or perhaps turns it over to another bank or holding company to run on its behalf, as the FDIC's agent, not as its own business. This 'trusteeship' or 'receivership' is temporary only, and is intended only to guarantee an uninterrupted banking business. The public is to be reassured about this takeover through the posting of signs and the mailing of notices with wordings such as:

For your protection, the local National Bank is under United

States government operation. All legitimate business will be continued without interruption. You are, of course, free to transfer your business elsewhere if you choose.

3. All existing business will continue, except that a quick judgment must be made to suspend or block transactions where the top management, directors, and major shareholders are involved, until a decision can be made respecting the legitimacy of such business. The regular examination procedure will already have paved the way for making these exceptions by locating and isolating this business. No new business will be initiated during the trusteeship period, except where the acting management decides that the continuance of a largely unchanged banking relationship is necessary to protect a customer from injury.

4. All stockholders' equity is wiped out. Moreover, should liabilities exceed assets, bondholders' interests would be reduced, *pro rata*, to the extent necessary. Thus the bank would be decapitalized. It would also be decapitated, with all top management and directors dismissed automatically (with exceptions allowed upon appeal).[6]

5. As soon as possible, the bank would be put on the auction block, to be sold to the highest eligible bidder. Bidders would have to agree to supply a minimum amount of capital to the bank, and would have to satisfy Federal and state laws respecting branching, holding companies, the character of the new organizers, and the like. The standards currently employed in passing on charter applications can be readily adapted to this purpose of establishing eligibility to bid. Ideally, the bidders would include, where consistent with law, branch systems or holding companies not previously represented in the locality. One novel feature of the auction procedure, and one requiring some additional comment, is that bids could be negative as well as positive. That is, the possibility would exist that the new organizers would be paid, rather than pay, to take over the suspended bank.

Negative bids would become, one would suspect, the rule rather than the exception, since the new organizers would be taking over insolvent banks, guaranteeing depositors' claims from their own assets, and providing new capital. Payment to the new owners would be the counterpart, in this scheme, of the payment of deposit-insurance claims under today's system of bank protection. It would represent (except for the administrative costs of handling the trusteeship) the only major use of the insurance premiums funds paid by the banks. But there is a possibility that, even with an insolvent

[6] Exceptions could be allowed, for instance, where new and qualified management had recently been brought in in a vain effort to save the bank.

bank, bidders will see sufficient advantage in taking over an on-going business that they will enter positive bids. (This is especially likely to be true under today's limited-entry regime.) Thus there is the possibility that the new scheme may in fact cost less, in FDIC outlays, than the present one.

6. As an alternative to step 5, above, where there is no bid, or at the option of the FDIC where all bids are negative, i.e., where a continued banking operation requires some form of subsidy, the bank could be liquidated. Marketable securities could be disposed of, in such a manner as to avoid disrupting the markets; arrangements could be made, preferably at the initiative of the borrowers themselves, to transfer loan business to other lenders; and depositors would be advised to transfer their accounts to other institutions, transfers financed by the FDIC, to the extent necessary, by drawing on the insurance-premium fund. A major consideration in the FDIC's decision whether to accept negative bids or to liquidate the bank would be which procedure is less expensive, in use of these funds.

The procedure described might be rarely used, because banks—on their own initiative or at the prodding of supervisory authorities—can ordinarily anticipate their own demises, and can arrange for mergers long before failure would otherwise occur.

The overall effect of such a system would be to effect a final divorce between effects on those definitionally responsible for the failure of the bank—shareholders, directors, and top management—and effects on innocent depositors and borrowers. The former stand to lose their investments, their positions, and their prestige; at the risk of these, they are permitted more freedom to innovate, compete, develop new banking arrangements, satisfy demands for new credit arrangements, and accommodate themselves and their banks to demand and technology. The latter are fully protected, and protected by a procedure financed by the banks themselves, where even the financing technique represents a use of the market, rather than administrative discretion, in inducing efficient and economic behavior.

In a sense, the proposed scheme would abolish bank failure altogether, rather than make it tolerable. 'Bank failure' has really meant two things; the closing of a business firm, and the effects of that closing on individual others and the economy generally. In the latter sense, 'bank failure' is abolished; the effect is to divest 'bank failure' in the former sense of any unique social importance.

The most salient change is to remove the present $15,000 limit on deposit insurance, so that deposit insurance becomes unlimited in amount. This represents a change from this writer's earlier proposal that the limit be established at some high level, such as $1,000,000, on the theory that depositors with accounts that large are sophisticated enough to choose banks on the basis of their judgment of the quality of the bank's management and its asset-selection policies; with such a high limit, the threat that a large depositor would transfer his account if the bank followed perilous policies would provide a market force for careful management.[7] With unlimited deposit insurance, and particularly with an uninterrupted banking business—no delays or uncertainties over claims—this market force is removed, and even the largest depositors have no concern over the quality of bank management policies.

Nonetheless, it is wiser to remove the limit altogether, even at the sacrifice of this useful market force. The reason is that a completely free banking policy is not tolerable as long as customer linkages of any kind exist. Large depositors should compare banks according to service, price, and other such characteristics; even they should not have to feel that they will be among those to lose should a bank fail for any reason.

The proposed scheme goes much further than making deposit insurance unlimited. Even with unlimited deposit insurance, there are reasons for both borrowers and, still, depositors to be concerned about injury to them in the case of a bank failure. Borrowers, as noted, have to worry about the continuity of their own business when a credit relationship is broken; depositors must worry about when, and perhaps whether, they will be compensated, and whether they will continue to accrue interest. Unlimited deposit insurance is the most important step in breaking the customer linkage; but in itself it does not assure 'an uninterrupted banking business'.

A scheme such as the one proposed can be adopted immediately; it need not be combined, in a package, with the elimination of protective regulations. The latter can be achieved gradually and experimentally, within the context of a new system without links between the failure of banks and the welfare of others. Even in the absence of changes in protective regulation, such a scheme could permit more 'risk-taking' by regulatory authorities in such decisions as chartering new banks; and it could provide them with a technique for dealing with the problems raised by the failure of banks under the present order.

V

Between the mid-1950s and late 1966, the Federal Deposit Insur-

[7] Tussing, *op. cit.*, pp. 146–7.

ance Corporation followed a policy of liquidating rather than attempting to sustain failing banks; and throughout the FDIC's history there has been no consistent policy of attempting to maintain 'an uninterrupted banking business'. Perhaps because of criticism of this policy, but more likely because of the size of the bank involved, the FDIC followed a different and in some respects quite novel policy when, in the fall of 1966, it and state banking supervisors were faced with the incipient failure of the Public Bank of Detroit, a state bank with over $100 million in deposits.[8] In the Detroit case, the FDIC employed some rarely used and one never-before-used techniques, which in combination share some characteristics of the proposed bank-failure approach discussed above.

The FDIC is empowered by law to act as receiver for failed banks. It is also empowered to make loans to or deposit funds with ailing banks, or to take over their assets, if the bank is essential to the community, or if by so doing it will reduce the risk or avert a threatened risk to the FDIC. In Detroit, the FDIC used these powers together in a wholly new way.

On October 12th, 1966, the Michigan Banking Commissioner filed a petition with the County Circuit Court Judge asking that the FDIC be appointed receiver for Public Bank. The judge's order was signed at 1 a.m. The FDIC then immediately sold its newly acquired bank to another Detroit institution, the Bank of the Commonwealth, a $600 million bank, and the eleven offices opened the next morning as branches of the acquiring institution. Signs had been erected overnight on all offices showing the new owners' names, and business was carried on as usual throughout the old Public Bank system, not only with respect to the honoring of checks but with respect to all transactions of any kind. There was 'an uninterrupted banking business'.

The Bank of the Commonwealth did not enter a 'negative bid', but the technique actually employed was very similar. Commonwealth paid $550,000 for the eleven Public offices, plus an amount equal to 2 per cent of demand deposits and ½ per cent of all other deposits to FDIC as receiver. The securities portfolio was sold at market rather than face value; other assets, including several millions in home-modernization loans already charged off, were sold at face value (nil for charged-off loans), less unearned interest and discounts. Most important, the FDIC provided $10 million in

[8] As of year's end, 1965, the Public Bank's deposits were $117.1 million, though they were less at the time of the bank's demise. At the time of its failure, the Public Bank was the largest bank to have failed in the United States since the 1920s. The events leading up to and the reasons for the failure of the bank are not relevant here, and will not be discussed. See, however, the *American Banker*, October 14, 1966.

standby protection against further losses on the bank's assets; that is, within the $10 million limit, Commonwealth was guaranteed the value of all Public Bank assets—the securities portfolio at market, and other assets at book, with the guaranty fund to make up any difference. On the other hand, any receipts on previously charged-off loans were to be added to the price paid by Commonwealth to the FDIC.

The settlement has many characteristics in common with the arrangement proposed above. The customer linkage was broken, as an uninterrupted banking business was maintained. Because of this, the other-bank linkage was also broken. In fact, in Detroit over-the-counter markets for bank securities, all Detroit banks showed gains in bid prices the next day, even though the failure of Public Bank was front-page-headline news.[9] Public Bank stockholder equity was completely wiped out; there was nothing left for distribution to them when accounts were settled eighteen months after the merger.

Most important, the Detroit case shows that the FDIC has much of the statutory authority it needs to break these linkages in all cases.

Since the FDIC's approach to the Public Bank failure had the effect of breaking both linkages, it would appear to satisfy the objectives of the proposal made in this paper. Actually, however, there are important differences; and on closer examination, the FDIC's approach has grave weaknesses.

One difference which is immediately apparent is that there was no open, public bidding process by which Public Bank was sold; instead, there were private negotiations. All major Detroit banks were, however, given a chance to make proposals. The application of this approach could mean that the FDIC might not minimize its own costs, and it could also raise the possibility of charges of favoritism and/or graft, though neither of these appears to have been involved in the Detroit case. More seriously, it almost certainly limits this kind of approach to branch-banking states.

The *Detroit News*' banner headline the first morning of the merger read, 'PUBLIC BANK FOLDS: DEPOSITS SAFE'. The same headlines could have appeared had the FDIC, rather than Commonwealth, operated the bank, while the Corporation awaited bids for the closed institution. The bank need not close, even temporarily, for a bidding settlement; thus its value as an ongoing institution need not decline. The difference in the Detroit case is perhaps trivial; but the Detroit

[9] *Ibid.* The City of Detroit provides an unusually strong test of customer and other-bank linkages, because of the city's unusually bad record of bank failures. The standard history of the banking collapse of 1933, including the national 'holiday' declared by President Roosevelt, is that it began with the failure of the Union Guardian Trust Company of Detroit. Only two Detroit Banks survived the depression, one of them Commonwealth.

approach, as noted, is not applicable in all cases. There must be a technique applicable in all cases for the approach to have the effect desired—an uninterrupted banking business, and the breaking of customer and other-bank linkages, so that a more freely competitive banking environment may be hazarded. The Detroit approach is inapplicable in two kinds of cases: where banks fail in unit-banking states; and when banks fail where liquidation, rather than merger, is appropriate, i.e., where it is desired that, for the customer, an uninterrupted banking business be maintained, but where it is not desired that the banking offices be perpetuated.

The most serious weakness of the approach in the Public Bank case is, however, that it is a unique instance, not a policy. It provides the FDIC and supervisory agencies in general with a new and probably better technique for dealing with failing banks; but that in itself is a trivial advantage, outside the FDIC itself. It does not provide the certain linkage-breaking that itself is necessary before supervisory authorities can accept greater risks of bank failure. There is nothing in the Detroit case *per se* that would encourage chartering authorities to grant more charters, move legislative bodies to remove restrictions on price competition, or lead legislatures or examiners to provide banks with more freedom in asset selection.

Thus the chief significance of the Detroit case lies not in what was actually done, but rather in its demonstration of what could be done. It indicates that both linkages can be broken through maintaining an uninterrupted banking business; that this can be done while maintaining the usual penalties of business failure for stockholders and top management; and that, consequently, a banking system can be devised under which a virtually complete divorce can be made between the legitimate public interest and the question of bank failure. What remains is to articulate a scheme which is applicable in all instances, so that we can get on with the job of relaxation of the manifold restrictions on competition in banking.

SYRACUSE UNIVERSITY

PRODUCTIVITY, LABOR DEMAND AND COST IN A CONTINUOUS PRODUCTION FACILITY*

by L. S. Zudak

In Hicksian theory, the short-run demand for labor and marginal cost of a single output firm are derived from the marginal physical product curve. Marginal productivity analysis will be proved inapplicable to a steel mill department and the marginal cost and demand for labor will be derived from a local union contract, the standard crew agreement.

The term 'firm' in traditional theory was clearly not meant to apply to a multi-process, multi-product steel plant. Its basic production facilities include fifty iron and steel furnaces and 500 coke ovens which must be operated continuously during the planning period. Semi-continuous, partially adaptable, processes include fifteen rolling mills and processing lines for transforming steel ingots into hundreds of different types of structural beams, plate, cold rolled and galvanized sheets and tin plate. The steel plants' raw material inputs include six million tons of iron ore, three million tons of scrap and two-thirds as much water as the city of Chicago. Overhead capital may include 100 miles of railroad tracks and 900 cars. This description should be sufficient to establish that output is the joint product of many separate production units or departments. The total and marginal products do not exist because, as Eiteman[1] showed, a marginal change in the output of the firm is the sum of coordinated and often non-proportional changes in the output of the departments which are the fundamental cost and production units, like the theoretical 'firm'.

Departments are given current output goals every ten days which they must meet in order to synchronize their output with other departments. Overall plans are established for three months. Some firms issue labor constraints on the number of workers permitted at each level of output but state that these are seldom binding. The department is supposed to minimize cost. If it succeeds in reducing it below its historical level, management and even the workers may receive a bonus for doing so. The minimization of cost and technical

* I would like to thank my thesis supervisor Professor E. Ames, Professors Blomqvist, Saraydar and Melvin, and the U.S. Manpower Administration, Grant No. 91-16-68-35. This analysis was part of a Ph.D. dissertation done at Purdue University on the Chicago-Gary steel complex under Professor Ames, Ullman and Brown. The faculty and facilities of Indiana University, Gary, were also of great help.

[1] Eiteman's basic point, ignored by his critics, will be proved later on. See also Lester Richard, 'Shortcomings of Marginal Analysis for Wage Employment Problems', *American Economic Review*, 1946.

fixity of labor requirements is institutionalized in each department's standard crew agreement.

Besides being multiprocess, many steel firms and their departments are also multiproduct which also makes the single product Hicksian model inapplicable. The only departments in which single product outputs are produced are the continuous, chemical type department. Since large steel firms often divide the continuous processes[2] and non-continuous into separate plants, the demand and marginal cost of the open hearth would be characteristic of these functions in continuous plants. The use of the open hearth as our example will also eliminate the need to consider problems of market structure, product price and kinked demand curves, because the output is intended for internal consumption. Therefore the unit value of output will be assumed to be given, as in fact it is.[3]

In short-run applications with fixed capital, standard price theory asserts that the profit maximizing point is where $MPP_L \cdot P_0 = MW$, where $MPP_L = \mathrm{d}O/\mathrm{d}L$. The fixity of capital in steel, from five years for a non-continuous process to twenty years for a continuous,[4] imposes restrictions on output, O, and labor, L, and therefore wages, W, which were assumed away in the theoretical model. In the analysis that follows it will be proved that a total productivity function which is continuous, convex and differentiable cannot be derived from open hearth production data for single product output because: (1) output is not continuously variable, it must jump by at least the technical minimum of the production process, here the capacity of a furnace; (2) the organization of capital requires specific types of skilled labor, a crew, which are specialized to the user and in general cannot be obtained outside the firm; (3) the crew cannot be assumed as the homogeneous labor input nor can linear programming be used because the number of each type of worker does not vary proportionally with output; (4) finally, if labor is not a single input then neither is its return, the wage.*

The first point will be discussed alone in section one, with labor assumed homogeneous in order to establish that the characteristics of either labor or output are sufficient to invalidate traditional theory. This homogeneity assumption would be justified in tradi-

[2] U.S. Steel has Gary works, 20,000 men, for processing from raw ore to open hearths to slabbing, and primarily semi- and non-continuous processes in two separate plants 'Sheet and Tin', 7000 men and 'American Bridge'.

[3] We cannot base our (pricing) commercial planning on sporadic fluctuations in demand, p. 45, *Steel and Inflation*, United States Steel Corporation, 71 Broadway, New York, N. Y.

[4] For a more thorough discussion and empirical evidence see page 52 *op. cit.*, p. 2.

* I would like to thank the Editors, and Mr. John E. King for their suggestions from which the discussion above especially benefited.

tional theory because steel mills only hire unskilled workers in the external labor markets. Since traditional theory ignores internal markets, an observer applying that theory to a change in output accompanied only by a change in the hiring of unskilled production workers would be forced to conclude that these homogeneous inputs caused the change. In section two the homogeneity assumption will be relaxed and the three remaining points will be discussed. The derivation of the traditional demand function in terms of wages implicitly assumes that labor units will respond to wages, and that at some positive wage enough units will be supplied. Since skilled labor is not hired externally, wages are fixed by contract and the skilled labor requirements must be filled, it is necessary to explain the supply of labor to internal markets. A definition and measure of micro-underemployment and a brief summary of the sequence will establish that management can expand the supply of labor in each market by lowering the continuous service requirement, training, and promoting workers from lower markets. Since the only market which cannot be supplied internally is the lowest, the unskilled, only unskilled workers are hired in the external market. Steel mill wages are high enough to assure a waiting list for unskilled vacancies.[5] A numerical example of the marginal change in labor and wages of the actual crew will be compared with that derived from the theoretical model to establish its inapplicability. Finally, it will be established that the discontinuities in the demand for labor which make the crew expansions non-homogeneous, also make it impossible to derive the demand for labor from Leontief type linear programming. Having established the inapplicability of marginal productivity theory or linear programming and redefined labor and wages, the demand for labor and then the marginal cost will be derived from the standard crew agreement.

THE DERIVATION OF THE TOTAL PHYSICAL PRODUCT

A brief discussion of technological restrictions in the open hearth and the derivation of the demand for labor at each level of output when labor is assumed homogeneous will establish the initial conditions necessary to derive the total product function. Open hearths are similar to oil cracking plants, generators and battleships. They cannot in general be started and stopped at random because the cost is too high. Failure to cool or heat the furnaces very gradually (over a period of several weeks) causes severe damage to their linings. Even

[5] In periods of abnormal demand, it may be necessary to accept less qualified workers with respect to education, usually high school, or age, etc.

after being correctly cooled, several days are required to rebrick certain parts of the system damaged by cooling. During a production period,[6] furnaces are either run at capacity or not used at all. There are seven furnaces in the department. The firm operates the furnaces in order of their relative efficiency. The three-furnaces level would utilize the three most efficient furnaces, etc. However, any statement of the level of output of any furnace is a probability statement. The level of output actually obtained is a function of atmospheric conditions, temperatures, etc. The maximum output of any furnace with an oxygen lance is 300 tons per eight hours. It will be assumed for simplicity that the actual output of each furnace is 300 tons. Whatever the level of output, the department is operated at that level 24 hours a day, three shifts, and seven days per week. There are seven levels of output technically possible during a production period but the cost of auxiliary equipment makes three furnaces the minimum feasible level of output economically. Seven furnaces is full capacity. Thus the number of furnaces listed at the top of each column in the standard crew table[7] (Table I) means the total number of furnaces operating full time per week, 18,900 tons at the three-furnace level, 300 tons $\times$ 3 furnaces $\times$ 3 shifts $\times$ 7 days.

Table I illustrates explicitly the demand for labor in the open hearth as a function of the level of operations, three furnaces to seven, with current technology and capacity as agreed to by local contract.[8] Beginning with the highest of the three bottom rows in the Table, the first row states the total number of workers required per shift at each level of operations, the second row states the total number of workers required if workers work four days per week, the third row states the number required if they work five days per week. The total number of workers required per shift to operate three furnaces can be found by simply adding the number of workers required in each job, 1 through 26, in the three-furnace column. The result is $29\frac{1}{3}$ which can also be obtained by adding the subtotals, $5+9+9+6\frac{1}{3}$. The total number of jobs per shift must then be multiplied by three shifts per day and seven days per week in order to obtain the total number of jobs per week, 616 jobs at three-furnaces level. If each worker only works four shifts per week, 616 must be

[6] Open hearths are started only if the production plan allows them to produce at least 500 heats, 175 days.

[7] Zudak, p. 257, see three-furnaces column in Table 1, *A Theoretical Analysis of the Supply and Demand for Labor in the Steel Industry*, Vol. II, 184070, Clearing House for Federal Scientific and Technical Information, Springfield, Virginia, 1969.

[8] Local standard crew agreements tend to stand longer than the contract. This is because they are only permitted to change when the company makes a change in technology sufficiently substantial to justify any change in the crew. How substantial the change is, is determined by an outside arbitrator.

TABLE I

PRODUCTION SHIFT CREWS

	Furnaces				
	7	*6*	*5*	*4*	*3*
MATERIALS					
1. Ladle operator	1	1	1	1	1
2. Conductor	1	1	1	1	1
3. Switchman	1	1	1	1	1
4. Stocker leader	1	1	1	1	1
5. Stocker	2	2	2	1	0
6. Ladle operator helper	2	2	2	1	1
	8	8	7	6	5
FLOOR					
7. 1st helper	7	6	5	4	3
8. 2nd helper	7	6	5	4	3
9. 3rd helper	7	6	5	4	3
	21	18	15	12	9
PIT					
10. 1st steel pourer	1	1	1	1	1
11. 2nd steel pourer	1	1	1	0	0
12. 3rd steel pourer	1	1	1	1	1
13. Steel pourer helper	2	2	2	2	1
14. 4th steel pourer	3	2	2	1	1
15. Conductor	3	3	2	1	1
16. Switchman	3	3	2	1	1
17. Pit hooker	3	3	2	2	2
18. Mould yard hooker	2	2	1	1	1
	19	18	14	10	9
CRANES					
19. Ladle	3	3	2	2	1
20. Charging	3	3	2	2	1
21. Combination	0	0	0	0	0
22. Hot metal	2	2	2	1	1
23. Scrap	2	2	2	2	1
24. Stripper	1	1	1	1	1
25. Mould yard	2	2	1	1	1
26. Raw material	$\frac{2}{3}$	$\frac{2}{3}$	$\frac{2}{3}$	$\frac{2}{3}$	$\frac{1}{3}$
	$13\frac{2}{3}$	$13\frac{2}{3}$	$10\frac{2}{3}$	$9\frac{2}{3}$	$6\frac{1}{3}$
TOTAL JOBS*	$61\frac{2}{3}$	$57\frac{2}{3}$	$46\frac{2}{3}$	$37\frac{2}{3}$	$29\frac{1}{3}$
No. men at 4 days/week	—	—	245	$197\frac{3}{4}$	154
No. men at 5 days/week	259	$242\frac{1}{5}$			

* Assuming 7 days per week.

divided by 4 to obtain the total number of workers which must be employed, 154. If instead the men worked five days per week, the total number of jobs per week obtained in the six-furnace column by summing, $57\frac{2}{3}$, would be multiplied by 21 shifts and divided by five job-shifts to obtain $242\frac{1}{5}$. Since each entry in the Table states the minimum number of each type of worker required at a level of output, the demand for first helpers, (7), can be computed by multiplying 6 by 21 shifts and dividing by 5, $25\frac{1}{5}$ for the six-furnace level of output. Workers work only four days a week instead of five at low levels of output protecting the firm's stock of skilled labor by retaining it at a reduced weekly wage to protect their investment in training which is specialized to the user. The work is not reduced below four days per week because those workers most affected by the reduction can earn more by staying home and receiving social security and supplementary unemployment benefits.[9]

The theoretical penchant for treating the firm as a black box, observing only inputs and outputs in the outside market, can lead to a totally incorrect analysis of a real problem. This approach undoubtedly leads to similar mistakes in studying industries other than steel.

In the discussion that follows, just as in traditional theory, the analysis will be made in ignorance of internal labor markets. The intent is to establish inapplicability of marginal theory and its assumptions in deriving the demand for labor. The firm will thus be treated as a black box. It will be assumed that the change in output is a function of the increase in unskilled workers employed. If the firm is currently operating three furnaces per week, 18,900 tons, 154 workers are demanded to work four days per week. If the firm increases its operations to four furnaces per week, 25,200 tons, the demand increases to $197\frac{3}{4}$. An observer applying traditional theory to the external market would observe that this increase in output had been accompanied by the department's hiring of $43\frac{3}{4}$ workers for four days each. Since the workers hired are all unskilled, it could be assumed that they were homogeneous labor units. An increase in total physical productivity of 6300 tons per week has taken place. The increase from four furnaces to five shows up in the external labor market as a hiring of $47\frac{1}{4}$ unskilled laborers, etc. Since all newly hired inputs can be assumed homogeneous, the application of traditional theory should lead to the derivation of the total physical productivity curve designated TPP. However it is obvious that the above process does not permit infinitely small changes in output. Therefore the total product is not a continuous function and the marginal product, the first derivative, does not exist. Hicksian theory including realistic modifications[10] are inapplicable.[11] It will nevertheless be helpful to plot the actual graphs.

From the normal procedures:

$$APP = \frac{TPP}{\text{No. of workers}} \text{ is the average physical product}$$

[9] About $80 per week, tax free, in the state of Indiana.

[10] Cartter, Allan M., pp. 49–51. *Theory of Wages and Employment*, R. D. Irwin, Homewood, Illinois, 1959.

[11] Hicks, J. R., pp. 78–82. *Value and Capital*. The Clarendon Press, Great Britain, 1961.

$\Delta PP = \Delta TPP$ the increase in output ascribable to all additional workers.

The number of workers required for each level of output is stated both in terms of crews working four days a week and crews working five days a week. The difference will be eliminated by multiplying the number of men in the row marked four days times 4 and those in the last row times 5, i.e.,

TABLE II

OPEN HEARTH PRODUCTIVITY TABLE

TPP	*No. of workers employed*	*Man days*	*ΔPP*
18,900	154	616	
25,200	197	791	36.5
31,500	245	980	33.3
37.900	242	1,211	27.2
44.100	259	1,295	70.7

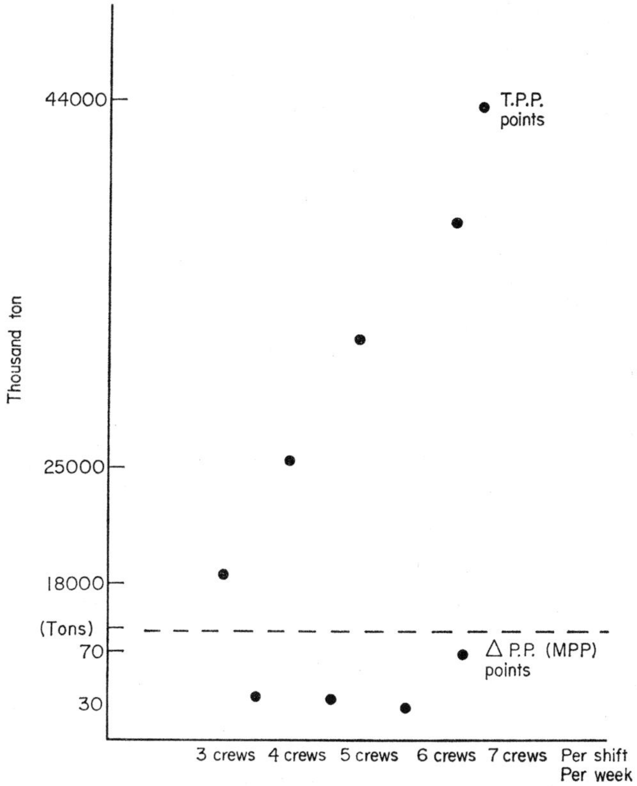

FIGURE 1. Open hearth productivity graph.

From Table II the Total Physical Productivity and Marginal Physical Productivity diagrams are plotted on Fig. 1. Even if continuous curves could be drawn for the total physical product and marginal physical product, they would still be confusing because the ΔPP is increasing at capacity, not diminishing. Thus, it is possible that the Hicksian cost line originating at some positive point K on the ton axis in Fig. 1 could be tangent at more than one point to the productivity curve.[12] Thus the discontinuous output characteristics of the organization of capital alone are sufficient to render marginal theory inapplicable even if labor is assumed homogeneous.

Labor, the Wage and Underemployment

In order to prove that the capital stock alone precluded the application of marginal productivity theory, it has been assumed that the theory was correct in assuming that the change in output was caused by hiring unskilled, homogeneous, workers in the external market. In this section, a discussion of the internal labor markets will establish that the changes in output discussed in the preceding section were not caused by the hiring of unskilled workers as assumed in the Hicksian model but by changes in the intensity of utilization of the existing stock of skilled labor. A definition of micro-underemployment and the sequence will explain the firm's ability to expand the supply of skilled labor in internal markets while hiring only unskilled labor externally. Having redefined the labor variable, a numerical example of the actual change in labor, ΔL, and wages, ΔW, accompanying a change in output in the open hearth will be compared with the results predicted by the traditional model. It will be proved that discontinuities in the demand for labor make it impossible to derive that demand or the marginal cost from linear programming.

Output rose from 18,900 tons a week to 25,000 in Fig. 1 not primarily because of the input of the $43\frac{3}{4}$ unskilled workers listed on the horizontal axis but because of the increase in skilled workers in several jobs caused by the more effective utilization of the 154 men already on the job. The addition of $43\frac{3}{4}$ laborers (or even 197 laborers if the critical labor force had been zero) would not by itself have produced a single extra ton of steel. They do not know how to operate the machinery. Any engineer or personnel man in the steel industry will agree with this statement. On the other hand, the existing labor force of 154 men can produce 18,900 tons a week by working four

[12] Hicks, J. R., pp. 78–82. *Value and Capital*. The Clarendon Press, Great Britain, 1961.

days per week. Promoting workers currently in the labor force and letting them work five days instead of four would permit the opening of another furnace which Table I states would increase output to 25,200 tons (or even beyond it) without any additional labor inputs. Beyond some point, of course, this 154-man crew would be incapable of increasing output any further. But there would have been no increase in output even from the addition of the required skilled workers unless they had been added in the correct proportions. This is why the standard crew agreement is required. Workers with skills must be supplied, but in correct proportions.

It might seem crews could be defined as the fundamental labor unit but looking at Table I again it is obvious that only the floor sequence 7, 8, 9 increased in fixed proportions. Considered alone it shows strictly constant costs. In actual fact, as Eiteman showed, the 300 ton increase from the three-furnace level to four requires different increases in manpower and a different distribution of these workers among different jobs than the change between the four- and five-furnace levels. This means that the fifth crew is not a simple duplication of the fourth crew. On the horizontal axis of the traditional productivity curve, labor, the units are assumed to be alike. In the above example they are not, and neither are crews.

The firm is able to expand its supply of labor out of a previously under-utilized stock of skilled labor because two types of involuntary underemployment are present:

1. Underworked employees who are not contributing as much to production as they are willing to contribute at the current hourly wage. The fact that output could be expanded without increasing the number of workers demanded in certain jobs—ladle operators—implies that the worker is not fully employed in his present job at lower levels of output. He may not even be fully employed at capacity.
2. Promotable workers who have the specialized skills and training required for higher jobs but work below their maximum wage and skill level at lower levels of output.

In order for promotable workers to be available for promotion it is necessary that they remain with the firm, be allocatable by some variable beside wages which are fixed and that the correct workers be promoted since qualified workers must fill critical jobs such as pourer, first helper, etc. In the steel mill the problem of training, allocating and retaining skilled labor is solved by the promotional sequence which is also common in other industries. Related jobs in the standard crew are hierarchically organized on the basis of skill and wages.[13] Each step in the sequence trains workers for the next step. The supply to a job is increased by promoting the worker on the job below with the most continuous service in the sequence. Demotion to the next job down is given to the worker with the least continuous service. Only after offering the job to every worker in the sequence can it be offered to other workers in the plant. If they refuse, it is offered to workers outside the plant. Only the lowest level job in each sequence can be filled by hiring outside the sequence. This eliminates competition from outside the sequence for semi-skilled and skilled jobs. This is not too serious a handicap because the specialized nature of many of these jobs precludes filling them by outside hire.

One example is the helper sequence. The first helper, second helper, and third helper's job form a sequence. The worker enters the sequence as a third helper and when he becomes the worker with the most continuous service and training time, he is promoted to second helper, etc.[14] All jobs covered by the standard crew are organized into such sequences. When an expansion in demand occurs, it creates a demand for additional skilled workers, first helpers, etc. This demand is filled by promoting the senior semi-skilled workers, second helpers, etc., to the skilled openings in their respective sequences. The promoted worker is compensated for working at a higher level job by being paid the higher wage. Demoted workers[15] remain in the sequence because the cost of changing sequences is too high.

The discussion of the firm's internal markets and underemployment has established that the 43¾ workers hired when output expanded to four furnaces were not primarily responsible for the increase. They were replacements for the unskilled, semi-skilled, or skilled workers previously in the pool who were capable of higher jobs and were promoted. These 45 workers were promoted to replace other workers who were promoted to fill the new jobs created in all levels by the expansion. Thus there are two separate causes for the increased need for workers in each occupational labor market in the department. Demand increases to provide the increase in manpower necessary to open another furnace. Supply decreases as a result of workers being promoted to fill demand increases in higher jobs.

In traditional theory there is one wage paid to a single variable

[13] For a more complete discussion of the sequence see pp. 66–71, Zudak, Volume I, *op. cit.*, p. 5.

[14] Only a few critical jobs such as the first helper are not strictly filled by continuous service, a test is also required. For empirical evidence of continuous service criterion, see pp. 92–194, *op. cit.*, p. 13.

[15] Pp. 89–91, *op. cit.*, p. 13.

output, labor. Here there are many types of labor, each with a different wage. Because labor cannot be expressed in terms of a common unit, *à la* Marx or Marshall, each job in each sequence is given a classification by industrial engineers. Jobs in each classification receive the same wage. Every job in the standard crew falls into one of the thirty-five classes.[16]

It is obvious that treating the firm as a black box, analyzing only the external markets, can lead to a complete misconstruction. It will nevertheless be helpful to quantify the mistake with a numerical example. This will facilitate the derivation of the demand and marginal cost by an unambiguous example of the marginal wage and the labor variable in the steel industry. Any column in Table I can,

TABLE III

THE MARGINAL WAGE OF A CREW INCREASE

ΔL		ΔW
5	New ladle operators	× \$4.02 = \$20.10 × 32 = \$643.20
+5	1st helpers	× \$3.50 = \$17.50 × 32 = \$560.00
+5	2nd helpers	× \$3.332 = \$16.660 × 32 = \$533.12
+5	3rd helpers	× \$2.720 = \$13.600 × 32 = \$435.20
+5	2nd pourers	× \$3.332 = \$16.66 × 32 = \$533.12
+5	Steel pourer helper	× \$3.332 = \$16.66 × 32 = \$533.12
+5	4th steel pourer	× \$2.720 = \$13.60 × 32 = \$435.20
+5	Conductor	× \$2.60 = \$13.00 × 32 = \$416.00
+5	Hot metal cranemen	× \$3.00 = \$15.00 × 32 = \$480.00
45		ΔTC = \$4568.96

to a point, be considered a type of input–output table. Each row states a skilled worker constraint on that level of output. If the theoretical approach were correct, the firm's labor marginal wage cost for increasing output by one furnace per week should have been $\Delta Q \times \$2.385$[17] or $43\frac{3}{4} \times 2.385$ times four days times eight hours per day. Referring again to Table I, it is obvious that the firm's wage bill increased by an increase in manpower in several different occupations and different sequences at various wage rates. Taking the base rate in each occupation, the actual increase in the firm's wage bill can be approximated. For each job in which the number of workers increased with output, an entry is listed Table III. The entry is computed by multiplying ΔL in each job market by 21 turns and dividing by four days per week, $5\frac{1}{5}$. Dropping the $\frac{1}{5}$ for simplicity yields the total change in labor required to increase output for three furnaces to four.

[16] P. 116, Volume I, 184069, *op. cit.*, p. 13.
[17] Contract wage for unskilled labor job class 2, *op. cit.*, p. 13.

The real increase in wage cost is $4,568.96 which is much greater than the $3,271.76 predicted by the traditional approach. The reason for the discrepancy is that the increase in output was not achieved by the 43¾[18] homogeneous new workers but by the promotion of the additional workers required in each job in each sequence in the department in order to raise output from three furnaces to four. Therefore, the actual change in labor in Table III is not a number but a vector. Similarly the wage is not a number but a vector. Therefore the increase in cost associated with the hiring of unskilled labor in the external market implied by the theoretical approach is substantially smaller than the real figure. Thus, traditional theory is inapplicable because it ignores the phenomena of internal markets for labor and the interrelationships between these markets.

The organization of the internal markets also precludes the use of linear programming to minimize cost and derive labor demand *à la* Leontief because of the non-proportionality of crew expansions which implies previously existing unemployment. Leontief intended his model as a model of an entire economy over time in which all goods except labor are currently reproducible.[19] Nevertheless, production models with Leontief's characteristics have been used by other writers as the production functions of firms, implying a short-run application, and are typically solved by linear programming to maximize profit or minimize cost.

In the Leontief system[20] labor is assumed to be homogeneous, the coefficients of production are fixed, and the amount used of any good will be minimized if it has a positive price. Each type of labor in the standard crew could be labelled x_0 to x_n. In the Leontief model, coefficients of production, x_0 to x_n, change proportionately with changes in output. Looking at the standard agreement, it is obvious that this condition is not met. Doubling output does not double the number of workers in each job, therefore ordinary linear programming is inapplicable. The change in these coefficients is partly caused

[18] Notice that the Table understated the increase in semiskilled and skilled workers promoted, 20 turns rather than 21, and there will still be more workers promoted than unskilled workers hired. Nevertheless, the Table shows that more workers were promoted from the labor pool, 45, than were added, 43¾. This unequal expansion means that the ratio of workers in sequences contributing to output has increased relative to the non-productive workers and pool workers. The productivity of the crew should rise, which provides one reason that the average productivity of labor rises as output increases. If increases in output are also accompanied by decreases in the pool, the net ΔTC woufd be computed by taking ΔTC above subtracting the decrease in unskilled workers, 1½ times the wage rate. A decrease in unskilled workers' wages would increase net ΔTC!

[19] pp. 130–183. Dorfman, Samuelson and Solow, *Linear Programming and Economic Analysis*, McGraw-Hill, New York, N.Y. 1958. For short-run applications see Kemeny, Schleifer, Snell and Thompson, *Finite Mathematics*, Prentice-Hall, Englewood Cliffs, N.J. 1965.

[20] See Table 7–9 on p. 296, Samuelson, *op. cit.*, p. 15.

by the fact that the steel mill violates Leontief's assumption that only the minimum amount of any input with a price will be employed to produce a given output. In the steel industry, workers who have a positive price are often not fully employed because of the non-divisibility of a real worker and more important the non-divisibility of his skill.

Derivation of Demand and Marginal Cost from Standard Crew

The standard crew agreement assumes that capital, technology and the organization of production are fixed. Since wages are also fixed by contract, it can be shown that the demand for labor and marginal cost are solely functions of the level of output.

The demand for each type of labor for each crew size is fixed by contract. Once the firm chooses a level of output and thereby the crew size, the quantity of each type of labor in each sequence

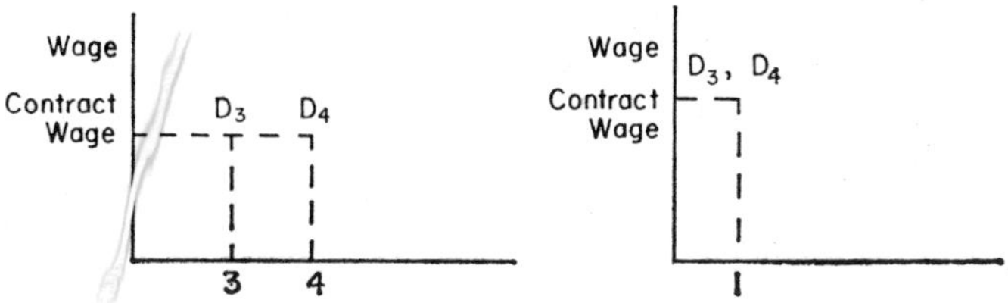

FIGURE 2. Demand functions for direct and indirect crew.

demanded is fixed by contract. A shift in the demand for labor in one of these markets causes a shift in supply, not in horizontally competing markets but in markets in the same sequence, above or below the market in question. Thus in Table I, a level of output of three furnaces per week requires three first helpers, etc. An increase in output from three to four furnaces shifts the demand for first helpers to the right by one first helper but does not affect the demand for first pourer at all, etc.

Given that the wage is fixed by contract and that the company knows what it is, the demand in each labor market is a point for each level of output as shown in the two representative markets in Fig. 2, where D_i = demand when i furnaces are operating.

The demand can be read off the standard crew sheet, Table I, for any level of output. For a change in output such as from three furnaces to four, ΔD can be defined as the four-furnace column minus the three-furnace column for each job on the standard crew sheet.

Let jobs be designated by j
where $1 \leqslant j \leqslant 26$.

Let the number of furnaces operating be g, then the change in

$$\Delta D = \sum_{j=1}^{26}(D_{g,j} - D_{g-1,j})$$

or

$$\Delta D = \sum_{j=1}^{26}\Delta D_j$$

Thus the demand is a composite, simultaneous demand for many different specialities. Unless all the jobs are filled none of the jobs can produce an output. If these jobs were filled in horizontal markets as postulated by traditional theory, the firm would spend more time looking for workers with these skills[22] than producing steel. Every department would generate such lists, the quantitative problem could be astronomical. The minimization of this search-cost and time provides a reason besides training cost minimization for labor hoarding in the sequence. Even more difficult is the qualitative problem of producing dozens of workers with specialized skills simultaneously. There is no separate demand curve for pourers unless restrictions such as the sequence can be derived which automatically and simultaneously fill the other posts. In terms of traditional analysis this shopping list is the demand for labor.

Validity of the declining wage hypothesis. In looking at Fig. 2 a hypothetical question arises. What if wage rates in the economy fell? Might not the firm automatically increase output from three furnaces to four, thus tracing out a negatively sloped series of demand points approximating the traditional negatively sloped demand curve? The answer is not obvious. A fall in wage rate theoretically makes it profitable to hire a marginal worker, or group of workers.[23] In the traditional model, it is assumed that the demand for steel is elastic and that income effects are negligible. A decrease in wages lowers the marginal cost, decreasing price and increasing the quantity demanded. But a fall in wages in the external market does not make it possible for the steel firm to accept a lower marginal revenue product because unskilled workers were not hired or paid on the basis of their immediate contribution to revenue product. It was shown in the numerical example that the wage of unskilled workers does not enter into the marginal wage and thus the marginal cost. It is

[22] Unlike workers in the next job in the sequence, management has no way of testing to make certain they have these skills. Imagine trying to produce steel while testing hundreds of workers on various jobs.

[23] See footnote 18. Lester felt that firms would not decrease output in response to wage increase because a firm is normally operated at less than capacity, and a reduction in output would increase cost still further. This is substantiated in this study by the open hearth marginal cost derived above.

productivity of the semi-skilled and skilled workers relative to their wages that determines the level of output.

The firm could expose the internal markets to the external by the direct training of duplicate crews.[24] Additional unskilled workers could be hired and exposed to full time training to prepare them for semi-skilled and skilled jobs. This training, the investment in these workers, would be much greater than for those trained by vertical mobility. The higher cost would be due to the fact that these workers would have to be kept on the payroll strictly as trainees; in some cases for several years. Also, the production process would have to be interrupted to give these duplicate crews time to acquire practical experience. In order to justify this investment, the fall in wages would have to be very large and long-term. If wages rose to their original level during this process, the firm would have to raise the wages of its duplicate crews or lose them. In either case the firm loses its investment. Of course, the union contract promotion clause makes the above suggestion for increasing the supply in the internal market totally impractical.

Besides the problem of determining the nature of the traditional marginal physical product of ΔPP and failure of changes in external markets to be automatically transmitted into the internal markets, there is one further cause for indeterminacy. If a reduction in wages is to succeed in increasing output, the decrease in wages, cost and price usually assumed must be sufficient to increase the quantity demanded by 6300 tons, not infinitesimally or there will be no increase in output. These three complications would cause the model to be indeterminate if wages were variable.

It is possible that a severe depression would cause sufficient pressure to force the decline in wages needed to break the system. The fact that steel wages remained virtually unchanged for the first three years of the depression in the early 1930s in the United States[25], even without a union, suggests the level of severity required to break the system. For an exploration of why an oligopolist may find it advantageous to maintain factor prices in a depression, see Sylos Labini.[26]

[24] It might be argued (as suggested by John King), that this is 'a bargaining problem and that the employer can transmit external wage pressures because employees are earning more than its outside opportunity wage.' But Becker disagrees because the result would be to increase both current and future turnover. Marshall also states that '[a worker's] departure would injure the employer by several times the value of his salary but Marshall does not make the causal link between internal wages and turnover and argues a bargaining solution', p. 22, Becker and Gary, *Investment in Human Capital,* National Bureau of Economic Research, New York, 1964.

[25] Wages were not reduced in steel during the first three years, the entire effect of reduced demand fell on employment.

[26] Sylos Labini, *Oligopoly and Technical Progress,* Harvard Economic Studies, Harvard University Press, Harvard University, Cambridge, Mass., 1960.

The Marginal Cost

In traditional theory the Marginal Revenue Product Curve serves another function besides defining the demand for labor. It is also the inverse of the marginal cost curve, assuming that labor is the only variable input. If the marginal revenue product cannot be derived, can the marginal cost be derived? Although the non-homogeneity of the labor input precludes the derivation of the marginal product, the specialized jobs within each crew size can be expressed in homogeneous units (money) when the crew demand is viewed as a cost.

It will be recalled that all labor *in the department in question is subdivided into jobs* on the basis of the standard crew agreement. Management knows the number of workers required at that job for that level of output by reading it off the standard crew agreement. This number will be: $q_{ij}(o)$, where o is the level of output, one to seven furnaces, for the *i*th job in the *j*th sequence.

For planning purposes the firm knows how long any level of output is to be maintained, T_{ij} for the time during which the *i*th job in the *j*th sequence must be filled and w_{ij} for the wage at which it must be filled.

$$\therefore \qquad TVC(o) = \sum_i \sum_j q^{(0)}{}_{ij} T_{ij} W_{ij}$$

$$\Delta TVC = \Delta C = \sum_i \sum_j (q^{(2)}{}_{ij} - q^{(1)}{}_{ij}) \; T_{ij} \; W_{ij}$$

Thus a series of points for finite changes in cost can be plotted assuming a single output.

In order to simplify the cost calculations, assume that the furnace crew only includes the ladle operator, his helper and the first, second, and third helpers. This gives a simplified crew which is nevertheless reflective of the real crew. Part of the simplified crew, the ladle operator, does not vary at all with output just as in the real crew. Another part of the simplified crew varies with output, the ladle helper, and part of the crew varies proportionately with output, the floor crew.

From Table I and the wage rates a series of total variable cost, *TVC*, and ΔC, instead of *MC*, can be plotted (see Fig. 3).

Where $$\Delta C = \frac{TVC(1) - TVC(0)}{\Delta Q}$$

Since the change in quantity is always the same here, 6300 tons = one furnace per week, the division need not be carried out.

The delta cost curve derived from the standard crew agreement does not fulfill the requirements of marginal analysis. It is impossible to employ the rule that below the profit maximization point $MR > MC$ and above that point $MR < MC$ even for discrete changes in the total cost. If there is discontinuity in the slope of the total cost (a sharp break or termination) as in Fig. 3, 'this implies a (finite or infinite) discontinuity in the marginal curve and hence indeterminacy of the marginal magnitude'.[27]

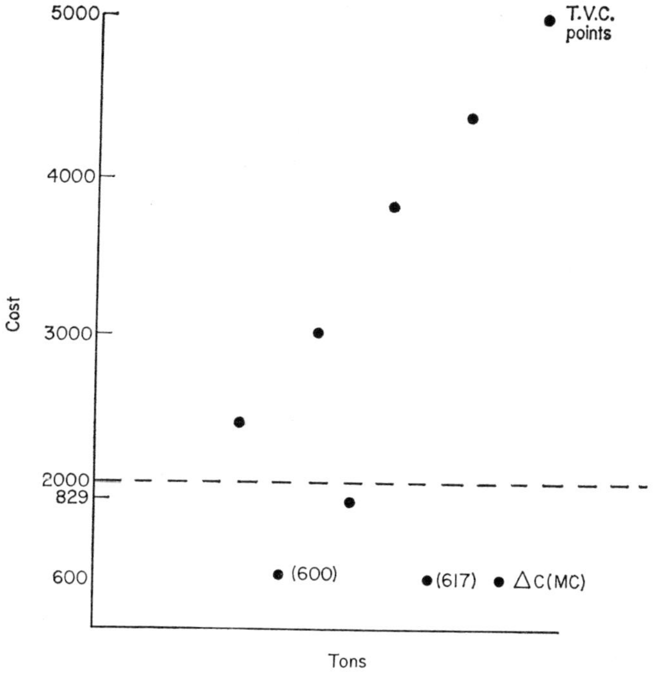

FIGURE 3. Open hearth cost graph.

The delta cost does not satisfy the requirements of marginal theory because plants are not continuously adaptable with respect to labor inputs either with respect to quantity or to the skills of workers employed. This unadaptability is reflected in the demand for labor generated by the standard crew agreement. Given existing capital, technology and the organization of production, the firm is limited to a few feasible outputs, the demand for labor is a vector at each level of output which varies discontinuously between outputs, and wages are a multi-dimension parameter, not a single variable. These conditions generate a marginal cost which does not have the properties of

[27] P. 616, Bishop, 'Cost Discontinuities, Declining Costs and Marginal Analysis', and Haines, *American Economic Review*, Volume XXXVIII, September 1948.

the textbook marginal cost. It is not a continuous function but a set of discrete points. Although the marginal cost is not a 'curve', Reynolds predicted that 'A partially divisible plant would show a saw-toothed curve.'[28] The saw tooth occurs in the simplified crew because the portion of the crew which does not vary proportionately with output, the ladle operator helper, increases only once between four and five furnaces. The actual standard crew might be expected to have more than one tooth since the non-proportional part of that crew, the number of workers and their jobs, changes with every output step. Moreover, there is added irregularity in the cost curve because of differences in wages paid to each worker. If it is assumed that the firm can inventory, then the relevant points on delta cost are a set of minimum points lying in the lower horizontal plane.[29] It seems apparent that for perfect competitors and kinked demand oligopolists, 'One cannot really say that output and employment are determined by the intersection of [a set of discrete delta cost points in a horizontal plane] and the [discontinuous] marginal revenue.'[30]

The shape of the marginal cost function raises two fundamental questions: cost minimization in relation to the 'teeth' and the adjustment of output to orders given the small number of feasible outputs. Reynolds suggested that it was 'quite unlikely that a plant would operate for any length of time at some higher point on one of the "teeth"; operations would be carried on at one of the minimum points, and deviations between output and sales would be taken care of by inventory adjustments.'[31] But the steel mill product is not inventoried because each customer's order specifies a particular grade, chemistry and size. 'Since there are thousands of products with different specifications, the steel mill product is only produced after the customer's order is on hand.'[32] The main variable available to the firm is time. If, for example, it is obtaining more than enough orders to operate three furnaces but not enough for four, it operates three furnaces and begins to backlog its orders. In clause 7 in the conditions of sale from a typical mill order, it is noted that almost infinite delay in filling an order is permitted. With only five feasible outputs, it seems unlikely the firm would reject those which represented higher teeth. Especially since customers already contend that unless one bought steel from more than one firm, one could go broke waiting for delivery. The firm does not backlog orders because of its

[28] Pp. 296–298, L. G. Reynolds, 'Short Run Theory of Wages', *The American Economic Review*, Vol. XXXVIII, June 1948.
[29] *Ibid.*
[30] *Ibid.*
[31] *Ibid.*
[32] P. 44, *Steel and Inflation*, *op. cit.* footnote 3.

unliquidated monopoly gains but because of the small number of feasible output points, i.e., technology. The firm will backlog orders until it has enough to add an additional furnace for a long enough period to justify its start-up cost.

CONCLUSIONS

1. The technological peculiarities of the production process discussed should not be permitted to mask the impact of the fact that labor is a vector whose coefficients do not expand proportionately with output on definitions of productivity.

   A. The productivity of any given type of worker—roller, heater, welder, etc., is indeterminate. Traditionally theory has ignored this indeterminacy because of an inadequate definition of output. Whether a welder is welding in a mill, ship, or on construction, the output is not the weld but tons of steel, ships or houses.

   B. The only marginal product possible is a joint one. Output is produced by a given combination of skilled, semi-skilled and unskilled workers. Changes in output are produced by changes in the total crew. Crews cannot be used as interchangeable labor units on the horizontal axis because the crews are not simple multiples since the ratios of various types of labor vary from one crew size to another.

2. Since labor is a vector so is the wage. The marginal wage has the same non-proportionality properties as the labor vector and is not necessarily decreased by a fall in wages in the unskilled labor market.

3. The standard crew agreement provides a basis for deriving both the marginal cost and demand for labor. Given the fixity of wages, technology, and organization implied by the standard crew, labor demand and marginal cost can be derived as functions of output alone.

   A. The marginal product cannot be derived by classical techniques or cost minimization using linear programming. The demand for labor is fixed at each level of output by the standard crew. With fixed wages, the demand is a point at each level of output in each job market. Each point is constrained by the requirement that all demands must be simultaneously met. The sequence makes it possible to meet all demand simultaneously by promotion, vertical mobility.

   B. The total cost and marginal cost are a series of discrete points for each level of output when output was homogeneous, the output of a single commodity. The marginal and total cost are not the continuous convex functions of traditional theory nor even a continuous linear function. Instead, as Reynolds predicted, it is a set of discrete points. In a firm with these types of continuous parallel processes, equilibrium, wages, prices and quantities are indeterminate contrary to the results predicted by Carter and others. Within an integrated steel mill composed of stages beyond the open hearth, the discontinuous marginal cost nevertheless imposes severe restrictions, a series of feasible output points, on the whole firm, since inventorying is not permitted. Steel firms claim to be job shops and do not generally produce for stock.

4. The foregoing discussion implies a micro-model which is compatible with the existence of underutilized labor. Keynes pointed out that the weakest link in productivity theory was a marginal productivity theory of wages which precluded involuntary unemployment. Keynesian macro-unemployment has been analyzed with little discussion of a micro-theory which would generate macro-involuntary unemployment. Two types of underemployment can be defined and measured in the model above.

A. The firm can increase output because two types of involuntary unemployment are present: (1) promotable workers working below their maximum skill level; (2) underworked employees, whose numbers do not expand with output. The sequence ensures that required workers are trained, retained, and supplied.

B. It is possible to state underemployment explicitly, to list the workers—and skills being underutilized. The loss in output can be imputed from their wage losses. It can be more accurately calculated by comparing the output of current crews with the output of potential crews which could be formed by full utilization of skills of the steel mill labor force, currently laid off workers and the requisite number of unskilled unemployed workers. Summing this loss of output over all industries is by definition underemployment for the economy.

THE UNIVERSITY OF WESTERN ONTARIO, LONDON, CANADA

THE ACCURACY OF SHORT-TERM BUSINESS FORECASTING: AN ANALYSIS OF A FIRM'S SALES BUDGETING*

by E. A. Lowe and R. W. Shaw

INTRODUCTION

The ability of firms to predict the movement of their future sales and other short-term variables is of interest to economists both for macro- and micro-economic planning reasons. If firms, in the aggregate, fail to provide fairly accurate predictions of the level, or at least the direction, of change, in these variables, then anticipations surveys, providing series for predicting the behaviour of the economy either directly or by suggesting causal relationships,[1] are likely to be misleading. At the micro level, if individual firms are unable to predict satisfactorily their own sales, and other variables, then doubt is cast on theoretical formulations of firm and market behaviour which tend to ignore, or play down, uncertainty.

A number of sales and employment surveys have been completed in the United States[2] and elsewhere[3] so that a body of evidence has accumulated on the short-term predictive accuracy of such aggregated data and some tentative analyses have been made. However, little attention has been devoted to measuring the accuracy of individual company forecasts.

Two questions are important: how accurately do firms anticipate

* The authors are particularly indebted to Mr. K. W. Bamforth (Dept. of Management Studies, University of Leeds) for participating in the fieldwork in the earlier stages of the research project, and to Mr. C. Bamford and Mrs. Margaret Williams for extensive statistical assistance. Thanks are also due to Dr. C. M. Cannon and Mr. A. G. Witts for their comments on earlier drafts of this paper.

[1] See, for example, F. Modigliani and K. J. Cohen, 'The Significance and Uses of Ex Ante Data', in *Expectations, Uncertainty and Business Behaviour,* edited by Mary J. Bowman (Social Science Research Council, New York, 1958).

[2] See, for example, R. Ferber, 'The Railroad Shippers' Forecasts and the Illinois Employers' Labor Force Anticipations: A Study in Comparative Expectations', in *The Quality and Significance of Anticipations Data: A Conference* (National Bureau of Economic Research, 1960); F. Modigliani and O. H. Sauerlender, 'Economic Expectations and Plans of Firms in Relation to Short-term Forecasting', in *Short-Term Economic Forecasting* (National Bureau of Economic Research, 1955); F. Modigliani and H. M. Weingartner: 'Forecasting Uses of Anticipatory Data on Investment and Sales', *Quarterly Journal of Economics,* February 1958; B. P. Pashigian: 'The Accuracy of the Commerce–S.E.C. Sales Anticipations', *Review of Economics and Statistics,* Vol. XLVI, No. 4, November 1964; M. C. Lovell, 'Sales Anticipations, Planned Inventory Investment and Realization', in *Determinants of Investment Behaviour,* edited by R. Ferber (N.B.E.R., 1967). Also see Comment to it by R. Eisner.

[3] See, for example, D. Hartle, 'Predictions Derived from the Employment Forecast Survey', *Canadian Journal of Economics and Political Science,* Vol. XXIV, No. 3, August 1958; H. Theil, *Economic Forecasts and Policy* (1961, North-Holland Publishing Company, Amsterdam), Parts 4, 5 and 9.

the level and direction of change of a variable?; are the aggregated results the consequence of the cancelling out of large individual firm errors or does the predictive accuracy cluster closely around the mean error? Concerning the prediction of sales and employment levels, for instance, it appears that firms, in aggregate, make fairly good estimates though when compared with some naive techniques, such as reporting expectations for the next period to be equal to actual sales, etc., for the current period, this ability is less remarkable. Whether firms show strong ability to forecast the direction of change is a more contentious issue[4] but there does seem to be substantial agreement that changes are underestimated.[5] *When sales, etc., are rising there is a tendency to underestimate and when falling there is a tendency to overestimate the level. Also it seems clear that whatever the accuracy of aggregated predictions individual firms show markedly differing ability in this respect.*[6] The general tenor is that even for relatively short-term forecasts the accuracy attained by businesses is very variable and, even in the aggregate, somewhat disappointing.[7] Attempts to explain these inaccuracies have generally stressed uncertainty about *external economic factors* (growth of market, competitors' reactions, the rate of inflation, etc.) and the consequential decisions of forecasters *as individuals*. These explanations neglect the systematic influences of the economic information flows *within* a firm's forecasting process. In order to throw light on this aspect, studies at the individual firm level seem called for[8] as a further step in providing for the integration of all these influences within the framework of an economic decision process.

In this paper a partial explanation is offered of forecasting errors, within one firm, using statistical analysis of forecasts and actual sales and relating these to evidence obtained in budget meetings and interviews. In conclusion, we discuss the consequences of our findings for some of the important aspects of the economic analysis of the firm's activities. The firm is a medium-sized retail business with

[4] F. Modigliani and H. M. Weingartner, *op. cit.*, claimed a 100 per cent success record for one series of sales forecasts but Pashigian, *op. cit.*, has suggested that the test used was a weak one and a more rigorous one reduced the success rate to only 60 per cent.

[5] See Theil, *op. cit.*, and Modigliani and Sauerlender, *op. cit.*

[6] R. Ferber found, in a study of forecasts of manpower requirements, *Employers' Forecasts of Manpower Requirements: A Case Study*, Bureau of Economic and Business Research (University of Illinois Bulletin, 1958), that the coefficients of variation were generally around 100 per cent and hence average errors were unlikely to be representative of the accuracy of individual forecasts. Also see D. Hartle in a Comment on R. Ferber and R. A. Levine, 'Capital Expenditure Forecasts by Individual Firms', both in *The Quality and Economic Significance of Anticipations Data: A Conference, op. cit.*

[7] See A. M. Okun, 'The Predictive Value of Surveys of Business Intentions', *American Economic Review, Papers and Proceedings* of the 74th Annual Meeting of the American Economic Association, 1961.

[8] See D. Hartle in a Comment on R. Ferber's paper in *The Quality and Economic Significance of Anticipations Data, op. cit.*

about 350 branches, many of which are small. Separate forecasts were made annually for each shop, building up into composite area and company forecasts for the succeeding year. In the two budget years studied over 650 individual forecasts made by nine people are analysed on the basis of our observation of budget meetings, the examination of company sales and budgeting documents and interviews with senior managers involved in budgeting.

THE FORMAL FORECASTING PROCESS

The Managing Director and General Manager gave instructions to the Senior Marketing Officer (S.M.O.) to produce a sales forecast for the year ahead. He, in turn, requested the nine Area Managers (A.M.s) to produce a shop-by-shop sales forecast prior to a meeting with himself to agree area forecasts. The basic instructions issued by the S.M.O. were:

1. Appraise every shop in terms of its [previous year's] performance.
2. Unless you are aware of local circumstances which indicate differently, assume that, where there is a growth trend, it will continue at or near the [previous year's] rate.
3. In shops where sales are falling do not fail to take into account the likely effect of management attention.
4. Assume a Company Sales Promotion Programme similar in style [to the previous year].
5. Do *not* allow for price changes. If these occur they will be allowed for in the final Budget calculation.
6. The figure required is the single figure total for the year for each branch.

Hence the forecast for each shop consisted of an evaluation of current trend, and its projection, and an adjustment for factors likely to affect the trend.

While the basic instructions seem reasonably clear their implementation presented difficulties: there was a general feeling in the Company that the industry sales trend had changed; an attempt to modify the seasonal pattern of sales was continuing; and many shops in the Company were experiencing increased competition and local redevelopment.[9] A conventional time series analysis to extract seasonal, cyclical and trend factors was neither attempted formally

[9] The S.M.O. reported after the 1966/67 forecast that one-third of the Company's shops were directly affected by changing local competitive conditions and one-quarter by town redevelopment.

nor did our observations suggest that managers would have placed much confidence in it in these changing conditions. Hence we observed that the assessment of sales trend was a rough and ready approximation: up or down, faster or slower or about the same.

The effect of factors likely to cause a change in trend was similarly treated with caution: managers were ready to accept a classification of the factors into competitive change, general and local environmental changes, state of shop (space; condition of shop front, decorations and equipment) and a (small) miscellaneous group (e.g. staffing problems) but they resisted a request by the S.M.O. to include a quantitative analysis of expected total change broken down according to these factors.

The organizational technique adopted, 'the sales manager composite' was designed, as part of a budget control system, to utilize the local knowledge of A.M.s and increase their involvement in the Company,[10] whilst providing for the scrutiny of each forecast by a senior head office manager (S.M.O.).

ANALYSIS OF FORECASTS

In this section the analysis seeks to ask what pattern of inaccuracy occurs, and why, in this particular firm.

1. *Analysis of Forecasting Errors*

This sub-section is concerned with the investigation of what pattern of inaccuracy exists.

In both the years studied the Company changed its prices despite the original forecasts being based explicitly on the assumption of no price change.[11] In 1965/66 the change occurred after only $\frac{2}{13}$ of the year and in the absence of specific forecasts for this short period a detailed analysis of forecasting errors was abandoned. The 1966/67 price changes were made after $\frac{7}{13}$ of the year and over eight months after the forecasts were made. Despite our doubts about allocating the A.M.s annual forecasts over a shorter period the analysis of errors up to the price change was carried out in order to enable comparisons with previous studies and because the acid test of

[10] Variations on the sales force composite method of forecasting are widely used in industry. See, for example, R. S. Schultz, 'Sales Forecasting', in *How Business Economists Forecast* edited by W. F. Butler and R. A. Kavesh (Prentice-Hall, Inc.), 1966; *Forecasting Sales*, National Industrial Conference Board, Business Policy Study No. 106, 1964. See also D. J. Liston, 'Sales Forecasting: An Evaluation of Some Practical Results', *Applied Statistics*, Vol. IV, No. 3, November 1955, for some discussion of the practical merits of this approach.

[11] See the S.M.O.'s budgeting instructions on page 277. The firm amended its total sales revenue forecast to allow for an intended price change according to a rule which implied an inelastic demand curve.

TABLE I

ANALYSIS OF 1966/67 FORECASTING ERRORS[1]

Areas: 1965/66 *Actual Sales Growth Rank*[2]	GROWING SHOPS[3]			DECLINING SHOPS[3]		
	Forecast Mean Error Rate (%)	*Forecast Median Error Rate* (%)	*Forecasts Overestimating Sales* (%)	*Forecast Mean Error Rate* (%)	*Forecast Median Error Rate* (%)	*Forecasts Overestimating Sales* (%)
Growing 1	+3.6	+4.7	68.4	+4.0	+2.7	50.0
2	+1.7	−0.1	47.6	−3.2	−5.0	28.6
3	+2.2	+1.7	53.3	+9.4	+5.0	66.7
4	+1.7	+0.6	52.4	−0.8	0.0	44.4
5	−1.7	−3.9	23.5	−2.8	−3.3	30.0
Declining 6	+6.5	+3.9	60.0	+12.9	+13.8	89.5
7	+3.8	+3.0	62.5	+11.6	+8.0	95.2
8	+2.9	+3.1	72.7	+2.8	+1.4	69.6
9	+2.7	+1.9	60.0	+7.2	+6.0	64.7
Growing areas	+1.6	0.0	50.0	+1.3	−0.9	43.9
Declining areas	+4.3	+3.1	63.8	+8.4	+7.1	80.0
Company	+2.5	+1.2	54.2	+6.0	+6.0	67.8

Notes

[1] Forecast Error $= \dfrac{\text{Forecast}-\text{Actual Sales}}{\text{Actual Sales}}$. Area Manager forecasts for the first seven periods up to the price change are estimated using the Company's official budget split of 56.2 per cent of annual sales to accrue in those periods. (See text, Analysis of Forecasting Errors.) All percentages have been taken to the nearest first decimal place.

[2] Sales growth rates are adjusted to exclude shops opening and closing during the year and are based on the agreed estimation of sales made after $\frac{10}{13}$ of 1965/66 at the time of the 1966/67 forecast.

[3] Growing shops include all shops showing any sales increase compared with the preceding year. Declining shops include all shops showing any decline compared with the preceding year. An alternative criterion of 'clearly' growing and declining shops, being those with growth or decline of $\geqslant 3$ per cent, was also used and the results are qualitatively unaffected. For example, the mean error rates for growing areas, growing and declining shops respectively are +1.6 and +1.1, and for declining areas +5.0 and +9.6 respectively.

forecasts is their ability to predict. The Company management also found it useful to split annual forecasts.[12]

We define forecast error as the difference between the forecast and actual sales expressed as a percentage of actual sales. The A.M.'s forecasts for each shop up to the price change are estimated by taking their annual forecasts and adjusting them by the Company's official sales budget split for 1965/66. This procedure, while crude, seems justified by the fact that the proportions of annual Company sales accruing in the first seven periods of 1964/65 and 1965/66 were both within 1 per cent of the budget estimate and by a simple correlation of period sales with period sales budgets which revealed a fairly close correspondence of sales and budgets.[13]

Summary results of the analysis are presented in Table I. The classification of areas and shops according to whether sales were greater or less than in the previous year follows Company practice. A tendency to overestimate sales in declining shops is revealed consistently for declining areas though not for growing areas.[14] A similar though less marked differentiation, with A.M.s of declining areas again overestimating, arises in the case of growing shops. A chi-squared analysis was carried out to test whether these tendencies are statistically significant. In the case of the declining areas the percentages of forecasts overestimating sales differs significantly from the expected 50 per cent[15] for both growing and declining shops and at the 10 per cent and 0.5 per cent levels respectively. In the case of the heterogeneous error pattern of growing areas the collective percentages of forecasts overestimating sales do not differ significantly from the expected 50 per cent for either growing or declining shops. A possible cause of the heavy overestimation of sales in declining shops in declining areas (not apparent in growing areas)

[12] The Company used four-weekly periods for budget control reports.

[13] For the four-weekly periods of 1965/66, $r = 0.7509$ and $r^2 = 56.39$ per cent but by excluding the first period which was generally acknowledged in the industry to have been subject to exceptional conditions, $r = 0.9170$ and $r^2 = 84.09$ per cent. At a lower level of aggregation no area had a sales percentage accruing in the seven periods of more than 2.5 per cent away from the budget percentage used. There seems to be no relation between an area's rate of sales growth and the sale percentage experienced.

[14] Area 5 was the only one to record forecasts underestimating sales in both growing and declining categories. Our analysis (see Table II) distinguishes this A.M. as the only one who *directly* stated that he sought to obtain as low a budget as possible.

[15] In this analysis we assume that in the absence of bias 50 per cent of forecasts would overestimate and 50 per cent underestimate sales. It is further assumed that this would be true of two hypothetical populations of growing and declining shops. The differentiation of the two categories is necessary because of the clearly separate treatment of each within the Company's control system: A.M.s were given asymmetrical budgeting instructions and on their own admission forecasted them differently. Growing and declining areas were commonly referred to as such and reward schemes differentiated them. The independence of each shop forecast is inferred in the analysis. A.M.s did in fact forecast each shop separately and according to them, as well as our observations of budget meeting proceedings, the area forecast was the result of a mere aggregation.

TABLE II

FACTORS INFLUENCING AREA MANAGERS' FORECASTS IN 1965/66; EVIDENCE FROM QUESTIONNAIRES AND INTERVIEWS[1]

AREA MANAGERS[2]	TREND AND COMPETITIVE FACTORS			ORGANIZATIONAL FACTORS			
	Current Trend, Recent Months	*Trend over Recent Years*	*Information Likely to Cause Change in Trend*[3]	*Recent Company Sales Growth Standards*[4]	*Profit Target*[5]	*Reward System*[6]	*A.M. Forecast Standards*[7]
1	× ×	×	—[9]	—	—	—	—
3	—[8]	—	× ×	× ×	—	—	—
4	× ×	× ×	× ×	—	—	—	—
5	× ×	—	× ×	× ×	×	× ×	—
6	× ×	× ×	× ×	×	—	—	—
7	× ×	—	× ×	×	× ×	×	×
8	× ×	—	× ×	×	×	×	× ×
9	× ×	×	× ×	—	× ×	—	—

Notes

[1] Questionnaires were sent out and interviews held after the 1965/66 forecasting meeting. The evidence consists of either a direct statement that the factor was considered which is signified by '× ×', or an inference from the discussion which was supported by statements made in the forecasting meetings which is signified by '×'.

[2] Area Managers are listed according to their areas' 1965/66 growth rate as in Table 1. One area has been excluded from the 1965/66 analysis as the A.M. concerned had just received notice of dismissal and consequently took little part in the forecasting process.

[3] An assessment of the effects on sales trend of such things as changes in competitive pressure, shop and site improvement or deterioration, changes in management and general locality situations.

[4] Budgeted sales growth rates for areas and shops in recent years.

[5] Concern that some minimum level of sales would be necessary for either some shop or company profit to be achieved.

[6] The influence of the Company's system of determining salaries, bonuses, promotions and general attitudes to individual managers. There is evidence that managers other than those for whom there is questionnaire and interview evidence took this factor into account.

[7] An individual standard set by an A.M. for himself.

[8] It is clear from observation of the budgeting meeting that this A.M. did in fact base his forecasts partly on current trend despite the lack of a statement to that effect.

[9] The A.M. concerned explicitly excluded from consideration any factor other than the projection of sales trend at least for the 1965/66 forecast.

is the use of the budget split to estimate the A.M.s' forecasts up to the price change. While this cannot be excluded, a 'sensitivity' test reveals that even if the critical error rate is moved from zero to plus 5 per cent the proportion of shops with forecasts overestimating sales is still significantly different from the expected 50 per cent at the 5 per cent level.[16]

Although the results are tentative they are similar to those obtained in several surveys of forecasting errors.[17] Aggregation of forecasts results in the cancellation of opposing errors so that in total the forecast is quite accurate (Company mean+4.0 per cent, standard deviation 11.0 per cent). The tendency to overestimate sales is concentrated on the declining shops (about two-thirds of the declining shops in the Company in 1965/66 were in the four declining areas, and nearly three-quarters of the other area, G3, which shows a strong tendency to overestimate, is added to these). On the other hand there seems to be no general tendency to underestimate sales in growing situations.[18]

2. *A Comparison of Forecasts with Recent Experience*

In this sub-section we seek to answer why the particular pattern of inaccuracy observed arose.

In Table II a summary is given of the analysis of questionnaire and interview notes concerning the factors influencing A.M. forecasts. It appears from these (as well as our observations of budget meetings) that the budgeting instructions were followed in so far as this concerned appraising each shop in terms of its recent performance followed by projection and allowance for changing circumstances. It is also apparent that A.M.s' forecasts were influenced by a variety of intra-organizational factors such as past Company sales growth standards and in particular by the injunction to take into account the likely effect of management attention in declining shops. The considerable strength of these organizational factors may be inferred from the subsequent statistical analysis.

This analysis consists of a number of comparisons of shop forecast growth rate distributions with those experienced over a period of four years up to and overlapping the forecast period. The results of

[16] In the case of growing shops in declining areas, raising the critical expected error rate to plus one causes the overestimation percentage to become insignificant at the 10 per cent level.

[17] See, for example, R. Ferber: 'The Railroad Shippers' Forecasts and the Illinois Employers' Labor Force Anticipations: A Study in Comparative Expectations', and D. Hartle's Comment, *op. cit.*, and H. Theil, *op. cit.*

[18] R. Ferber has called the tendency to overestimate a variable in declining situations and a weaker tendency to underestimate in growing situations the 'permanent optimism hypothesis'.

TABLE III

COMPARISON OF RECENT ACTUAL AND FORECASTED SHOP SALES GROWTH RATE DISTRIBUTIONS

	NUMBER OF AREAS[1]						
	1965/66 Forecasts			*1966/67 Forecasts*			
Actual Sales	*1962/63*	*1963/64*	*1964/65*	*1962/63*	*1963/64*	*1964/65*	*1965/66*[2]
Actual variance greater than forecast variance	7	7	8	8	8	8	9
Levels of significance:[3]							
1%	7	7	6	7	6	6	8
5%	—	—	—	—	—	2	—
10%	—	—	1	1	2	—	—
> 10%	—	—	1	—	—	—	1
Actual variance less than forecast variance	1	1	—	—	—	—	—
Levels of significance: > 10%	1	1	—	—	—	—	—

Notes

[1] One area has been excluded from the 1965/66 analysis (see note 2, Table II). The area is included in the 1966/67 analysis for the one comparison for which sales figures are available.

[2] The 1965/66 actual sales used in calculating that year's growth rate and the 1966/67 forecast growth rate are estimates for the full year made after $\frac{10}{13}$ of the year.

[3] The F-ratio test with one tail was used.

the first comparison, concerning the variances of the distributions, are presented in Table III. In a total of 57 comparisons the recent actual variance of the *area shop* growth rate distribution exceeded the forecast variance 55 times. Of these, in 47 cases the difference was significant at the 1 per cent level[19] and only two were not significant at the 10 per cent level. In the two cases in which the forecast exceeded the recent actual variance the difference was not significant at the 10 per cent level.

A similar comparison of the variances of *aggregate area* recent actual and forecasted annual sales growth rates reveals that the recent actual variances always exceeded the forecasted variances and that three of the seven cases are significantly different at the 5 per cent level (including the years immediately preceding the two forecasts) and a further two at the 10 per cent level.

The above results suggest that A.M.s collapsed the distribution of growth rates when making their sales forecasts in a manner difficult to justify by their recent actual sales experience. Indeed the comparison of the shop forecast and actual growth rate variance for 1965/66 shows that the forecast variances were unrealistically low: of the eight areas, the actual exceeded the forecasted variance at the 1 per cent level of significance in six cases and at the 5 per cent level in the other two.[20]

The failure of the sales forecasters to draw on recent experience in the matter of the variances of growth rate distributions suggests that strong organizational pressures intervened. The nature of these may be examined further through an analysis of area growth rates coupled with the proportions of shops expected to decline. In Table IV recent experience and forecasts are again considered. It is noticeable, as one would expect, that there is a tendency for the proportion of shops in an area that are declining to fall as the area sales growth rate increases.[21] This relationship was also predicted in the forecasts but in this case the percentage of declining shops seems to be well below that normally experienced for similar growth rates. Indeed for any given area sales growth rate the lowest percentage of declining shops recently experienced is almost always above the highest percentage of declining shops forecasted (see note 6 to Table IV).

[19] The F-ratio test with one tail is used as we hypothesize that organizational factors will lead to a collapsing of the forecasted growth rate distributions.

[20] This result should not be stressed too strongly as the *ceteris paribus* assumption on price was broken and this may have affected the results. However, as we are concerned here with the distribution as a whole and not error rates and particular growth rates, this qualification may not be serious. The research was concluded before the end of the 1966/67 budget year so the parallel comparison for that year was not made.

[21] It appears that the relationship is not quite linear. There seems to be a 'floor' below which the proportion of declining shops does not fall (at least within the observed spectrum of growth rates).

TABLE IV

THE RELATIONSHIP BETWEEN RECENT[1] ACTUAL AND FORECASTED AREA SALES GROWTH RATES[2] AND THE ASSOCIATED PERCENTAGES OF DECLINING SHOPS[3]

	Area Sales Growth Rates[4]															
	−7	−6	−5	−4	−3	−2	−1	0[5]	+1	+2	+3	+4	+5	+6	+7	+8
Recent experience																
Number of cases	1	—	3	1	1	5	—	2	5	4	5	2	1	1	1	1
Mean % of declining shops	68.6	—	71.5	56.1	68.9	59.3	—	50.2	44.4	36.1	31.8	23.7	23.5	32.3	29.4	25.0
Lowest % of declining shops	68.6	—	65.5	56.1	68.9	52.8	—	43.7	29.4[6]	28.6	24.1	18.4	23.5	32.3	29.4	25.0
A.M. forecasts																
Number of cases	—	—	—	—	—	—	1	2	3	3	3	4	1	—	—	—
Mean % of declining shops	—	—	—	—	—	—	40.0	34.6	19.0	19.7	12.5	6.2	13.5	—	—	—
Highest % of declining shops	—	—	—	—	—	—	40.0	34.8	24.3	23.9	16.7	12.0	13.5	—	—	—

Notes

[1] The period considered is the four years prior to and overlapping with the forecasting period.

[2] Area sales growth rates are based on cash value of sales. Shops newly opened or closing during the year are excluded. The 1965/66 growth rates are those projected after $\frac{10}{13}$ of the year had elapsed and constitute the 'recent experience' underlying the 1966/67 forecasts.

[3] Declining shops percentage includes all shops with sales less than the previous year, except those closing during the year, as a percentage of all shops excluding new and closing shops.

[4] Calculated to the nearest whole figure.

[5] The four cases are all positive.

[6] Using the growth rate intervals +0.1 to 1.0 and +1.1 to 2.0 the observation lowest actual percentage 29.4% moves into the same interval as the highest forecast percentage, 34.8%. In no other case would the order of lowest actual percentage and highest forecast percentage be reversed.

It seems clear from this evidence that whatever the likely area sales growth rate, A.M.s were chronically unwilling to forecast shops to decline.[22]

3. *Conclusions from Foregoing Analysis*

The evidence presented strongly suggests that avoidance of forecasts of sales declines and the collapsing of the expected sales growth rate distributions cannot be explained easily in terms of sales experience and expectations. Furthermore it may be inferred from the magnitude of the discrepancies between experience and forecasts, the pattern of error rates and the pressures acknowledged by A.M.s that organizational factors were an extremely important influence on forecasting behaviour.

The organizational factor which seems to have affected forecasting behaviour in this case was a control system apparently designed to differentiate performance into either acceptable or unacceptable categories.[23] Uncertainty about both the future generally and the present parameters of market functions in an oligopolistic situation resulted in the use of rather crude criteria for assessing performance. The use of acceptability criteria as part of the control system generated behaviour patterns such that managers responded to the external environment in a manner heavily conditioned by the internal situation.[24]

Sources of Acceptable Levels of Performance

A problem with organizational procedures which use acceptable levels as guidelines is to find their derivation. In this section, for reasons of space, we give only an outline of our interpretation of interview and budget meeting evidence on this subject.

Four sources of acceptable performance levels in particular seem to be apparent: recent profit performance of the Company; top management aspiration levels about growth; recent budget standards used in the Company; and recent performance of other

[22] In 14 of the 17 area growth forecasts the percentage of shops expected to decline was less than 25 per cent whereas in only 5 of the 22 recorded cases of growing areas was the actual percentage of declining shops 25 per cent or lower.

[23] Details of this particular control system are examined in a previous paper: see E. A. Lowe and R. W. Shaw, 'An Analysis of Managerial Biasing: Evidence from a Company's Budgeting Process', *Journal of Management Studies*, Vol. 5, No. 3, October 1968.

[24] R. J. Monsen and A. Downs, 'A Theory of Large Managerial Firms', *Journal of Political Economy*, Vol. LXXIII, No. 3, June 1965, for instance, suggest that managers at all levels tend to pass upwards only information favourable to themselves and that for similar reasons they tend to carry out only some of their orders. See also H. Leibenstein, 'Allocative Efficiency Vs. "X-Efficiency"', *American Economic Review*, Vol. LVI, No. 3, 1966, especially p. 407.

companies in the industry.[25] Our research experience in this case makes it clear that the dual role of forecasts as predictors (and hence planning information) and also as control devices is a central feature in understanding the derivation of the sales forecasts.

The starting point of the budgeting process, of which the sales forecasts were a part, was an estimate of 'expected' profit[26] made by the Board of Directors. This appears to have emerged as an aspiration level from a consideration of the likely current year's profit, past years' profits and desire for growth.[27] There is little doubt that the aspired profit was operative in that it influenced the budgeting process at all levels of management[28] (see Table II). In addition recent cost and sales experiences of shops, areas and head office departments were projected forward as standards of performance: for sales, becoming an injunction to do at least as well as last year (compare recent area sales growth rates with forecasted growth rates in Table IV).

Recent budget standards were also projected forward. One A.M. apparently even regarded a 5 per cent sales growth norm, taken from previous budgeting exercises, as the basis of his forecasts. In recent years a head-office-determined budgeted sales growth rate had been allocated more or less pro-rata to each shop with almost all being expected to grow. Furthermore current sales forecasting instructions made it clear that to forecast sales to decline would reflect on the manager's competence.[29] These combined to reinforce A.M.s' belief that anything less than last year's sales would be unacceptable.[30]

In addition the Company obtained information about the performance of other firms at all levels from the Managing Director to individual shop competitor checks by managers. Although the evidence is sketchy it appears that this information served not only as an input for competitive strategy decisions but also as a control device in setting up minimum performance standards.

[25] Similar kinds of sources are discussed by J. G. March and H. Simon, *Organisations* (Wiley, 1958); R. M. Cyert and J. G. March, *A Behavioral Theory of the Firm* (Prentice-Hall, 1963); C. P. Bonini, *Simulation of Information and Decision Systems in the Firm* (Prentice-Hall, 1963).

[26] 'Expected profit' is used advisedly to imply a mixture of planned, anticipated and aspired profit.

[27] The Managing Director summarized this: 'the Board gave some indication bearing in mind past years' profits' and 'wanted realistic but growth'.

[28] One A.M. after having forecast a small area growth rate acknowledged that 'objectively' none was present.

[29] For instance, see the Company's Budgeting Instruction 3 on page 277 above.

[30] Several Managers talked of A.M.s' justifying themselves by *forecasting* improvement. It seems likely that the Company's standards were reinforced by becoming a measure of professional competence partly accepted by A.M.s themselves.

Economic Consequences of Acceptable Forecasts

In an earlier paper,[31] we analyzed the complete sales forecasting process from an organizational viewpoint, concluding that Head Office amendments were of minor importance and that generally counter-biasing behaviour by higher management is unlikely to be successful. Although this question remains open we proceed here (as if the initial forecasts were used directly for decision-making purposes) to discuss briefly the important economic consequences.

1. *The scale of expenditures on resources*

First, the sales forecasts, although only short-term, were part of a comprehensive budget in which the Company management estimated the scale of capital investment it could afford based on a 'residual funds' approach to capital budgeting.[32] Secondly, the budgeted profit was tested against the aspired profit level and, in so far as the former was inadequate, reductions, some of a strategic type, were made in departmental budgets (e.g. training and sales promotion expenditures).

In these two ways the acceptability criterion had long-run economic consequences for the Company.

2. *The allocation of these resources*

The individual forecasts exercise an important role in the allocation decisions within the Company. The reluctance of A.M.s to write a shop's sales significantly up or down when they believed this could or would happen resulted in the setting of unrealistic budgets. Several managers recognized that this is likely to lead to a failure to realize potential because of the great effort spent on redeeming poor situations at the expense of 'hounding success'. Thus managerial and other resources tended to be diverted to areas and parts of areas where the marginal net revenue was lower than elsewhere. The opportunity cost to the firm of this inefficient allocation of resources is difficult to analyse formally, in a simple manner, but the opportunity loss depends upon the length of time over which the misallocation persists, as well as on the quality of information and decisions of its competitors. The loss may be the difference between the present value of the missed opportunity and that of the best alternative opportunity remaining when resources are finally shifted. In a dynamic situation the loss might be represented by a series of such differences arising from the firm being generally one step behind some of its competitors.

[31] E. A. Lowe and R. W. Shaw, *op. cit.*

[32] Funds available for investment were calculated as follows: (Expected Profit + Depreciation Provision) − (Taxation Due + Expected Dividend).

3. *The Quality of these Resources*

A major consequence of the use of 'acceptable' levels of performance concerns the quality of managerial, and other, resources employed. The tendency to classify performance as 'acceptable' rather than more appropriately as 'superior' or 'inferior' may result in the employment of less efficient sets of managers. Since managers are the co-ordinating factor then it is likely that both the quality and efficiency in use of the firm's other factors of production are also adversely affected.[33] In this firm the allocative function of the external price system and the application of factor substitution at the margin, seems to have been distorted by the workings of the internal control system.

MANCHESTER BUSINESS SCHOOL and
SCHOOL OF ECONOMIC STUDIES, LEEDS UNIVERSITY.

[33] As Leibenstein has pointed out, this kind of misallocation cannot be handled by micro-economic theory in its present state (*op. cit.*, p. 397).

THE BOARD OF TRADE CAPITAL-INVESTMENT-FORECASTS: THE PREDICTION OF GROSS-FIXED-CAPITAL-FORMATION IN U.K. MANUFACTURING INDUSTRY AND BUSINESS EXPECTATIONS*

by C. M. Cannon

I. INTRODUCTION

The Board of Trade publishes a figure of percent-change in the capital-investment of U.K. industry which is expected by businesses. This figure is obtained from sample surveys of businesses' investment-forecasts. These business forecasts are expectations of future capital-expenditure decisions. Hence both these expectations and the actual capital-expenditure decisions themselves depend upon business evaluations of prospects for capital-investment. These investment-forecasts are *forecasts*, they are not one of many causes of capital-investment. A forecast can take into account any possibility which may affect actual outcome. Therefore investment-forecasts can be used alone, as direct predictors of capital-investment. Nevetheless the accuracy of their predictions must be open to influence by risk and uncertainty. This is so because investment-forecasts must use less dependable information than do investment-decisions, since for forecasts a longer period of time exists between evaluation of the prospects of investment and final outcome of investment.

In this paper I report on my investigation of the results of the surveys of the annual investment-expectations of U.K. manufacturing industry which are published by the Board of Trade (B.O.T.). First, I construct a time-series of these investment-expectations, and I criticize the method by which Ball and Drake have compiled a series from the same source. Second, I consider the '*forecast-errors*' which arise from the use of this and three other series as direct predictors of the actual annual gross-fixed-capital-formation of U.K. manufacturing industry at unadjusted and at 'fixed' prices. Third, I consider the accuracy with which the direction of change in investment is forecast by this series. Fourth, I consider whether my series is a biased predictor of actual investment. Fifth, I construct a quarterly expectations-series from my annual series, which it might be worthwhile for the B.O.T. to produce, and I use it in a simple model of

* I thank my colleague Z. K. Kmietowicz for his comments and I thank C. G. Bamforth, Computing Officer in the School of Economic Studies, University of Leeds, who undertook the calculations.

plan-adjustment. Sixth, I use all this evidence in tests of decision theories.

II. THE PUBLISHED INFORMATION ON PERCENT-CHANGE IN INVESTMENT-EXPECTATIONS

In this Section II, I explain just what is published by the B.O.T. on investment-expectations. Since 1955, the B.O.T. has used a large sample of companies in manufacturing as a source of evidence on expected and actual fixed-capital-expenditure. Three surveys are made of future expenditure in each year: one is made in the early summer of the forecast year; another is made in the late autumn of the forecast-year; and the third is made in the late autumn of the actual expenditure year itself. This information is then used, in the light of knowledge of its coverage, to obtain estimates of the future expenditure of manufacturing industry as a whole.[1] Next, each successive forecast is compared by the B.O.T. with the *forecast* of current expenditure which was compiled at a comparable date during the previous year, and a percent-change *in expectations* is published.[2] So this published percent-change *does not* represent a comparison of expected future expenditure with current expenditure. Since 1966 enquiries have been more specific, for volume changes.[3]

I make use of information on manufacturing industry only, because the coverage of distributive and service trades was thin before a general enquiry was made in 1960.[4] Also one can reasonably expect budgetary discipline to be less in distributive and service trades than in manufacturing.

III. AN ABSOLUTE INVESTMENT-EXPECTATIONS TIME-SERIES

Ball and Drake have constructed an annual aggregate investment-expectations series from the survey-material which is collected by the B.O.T. in the late autumn of the forecast-year. In order to calculate their forecast they apply the published percent-change in expecta-

[1] *Board of Trade Journal*, February 4th 1956. 'Changes in Fixed Capital Expenditure 1954–6 Shown by the New Board of Trade Enquiry'. 'Changes in capital-expenditure in the U.K. have been calculated by grossing-up the expenditure of responding companies to obtain estimates of the expenditure by companies in the population from which the sample was selected, and comparing this with a similar estimate of the expenditure of the same companies in the previous period. [We] obtain changes for manufacturing industry as a whole by weighting the change of separate industry groups by the estimates of total capital-expenditure obtained from the Census of Production', pp. 207–8.

[2] T. Paterson and A. Sorrell, 'The Board of Trade's Sample Enquiry into Capital Expenditure Introduction', *Transactions of the Manchester Statistical Society*, March 21st 1958, pp. 35–6. *Board of Trade Journal*, February 21st, 1958, p. 406.

[3] *Board of Trade Journal*, January 27th, 1967, p. 204.

[4] *Board of Trade Journal*, April 28th 1961, p. 998; August 4th, 1961, pp. 251 and 297.

tions to the figure of actual investment in the forecast-year.[5] But this is incorrect. The percent-change should be applied instead to *expectation* of investment for the forecast-year, and *not* to actual investment in the forecast-year. By applying percent-change to actual investment Ball and Drake disguise much systematic difference between expectations and actual expenditures because thereby they incorporate the assumption that for each forecast-year investment-forecast is equal to actual investment. Hence the usefulness of their series is limited, and for some purposes use of their series is misleading: for example their assumption makes a circularity of their test of the hypothesis that expectations are an unbiased predictor of actual investment.[6]

It is possible to trace a time-series of annual expectations which does not depend upon this assumption, entailed by Ball and Drake's method. I have built up such a time-series upon the relation, which has been published by the Board of Trade, between actual investment in manufacturing in 1954 and 'estimated investment in manufacturing in 1955'. I use this relation to calculate expected investment in manufacturing in 1955, then I combine this with percent-change in expectations for 1956, in order to provide an absolute base for my time-series which approximates to absolute expectation for 1956—I cannot use 'estimated investment for 1955' as my base because the forecast period was so short, only up to three months. Then I apply the published percent-change in expectations for 1957 to this base of absolute expectation for 1956, and by continuing this exercise I obtain a time-series of annual absolute investment-expectations. But this new time-series does rest upon the assumption that 'forecasted investment for 1955', which was calculated by businesses with knowledge of actual investment during the first six months of that year, did equal 'estimated investment for 1955', which was calculated by the B.O.T. with knowledge of actual investment during the first nine months of that year. I have to make this assumption because expectations for 1956 are expressed as a percent-change on forecasted investment for 1955, while forecasted investment for 1955 is unobtainable. However my base of calculated investment-expectation for 1956 is extremely close in total to actual business investment in manufacturing in 1956, at unadjusted prices, which increases one's confidence in it. There are good reasons for believing that actual investment in 1956 is the best base for my time-series.[7]

It is necessary to enter into a full discussion of the compilation of

[5] R. J. Ball and P. S. Drake, 'Investment Intentions and the Prediction of Private Gross-Fixed-Capital-Formation', *Economica*, August 1964, p. 232.

[6] Ball and Drake, *op. cit.*, pp. 238, 243.

[7] Read Footnote 19.

my base of absolute expectations for 1956 and of the results for the earlier years of my time-series because a regular publication procedure was not followed by the B.O.T. until 1958.[8]

Gross-fixed-capital-formation in U.K. manufacturing in 1955 which was *estimated* in winter 1955 by the B.O.T. was 18 per cent more than actual *business* capital-expenditure in 1954. But only *establishment* capital-expenditure in 1954, obtained from the Census of Production, has been published. However, this establishment expenditure can be converted to a business basis by multiplying it by the ratio of actual business capital-expenditure to actual establishment capital-expenditure in 1956, 1.05. Expectations for 1956 were expressed by businesses in autumn 1955 as 17 per cent more than their *forecast* stated in summer 1955 for 1955.[9] As I have stated in my penultimate paragraph I assume that this relationship between the forecast for 1956 and the forecast for 1955 holds too for the relation between the forecast for 1956 and the B.O.T.'s estimate of investment in 1955. Then calculated absolute investment-expectation for 1956 at unadjusted prices, with a forecast period of up to fourteen months, is: £591m × 1.05 × 1.18 × 1.17 = £852.89m—see Table I. A second business forecast for 1956 was made in late spring 1956: 21 per cent more than expectation for 1955.[10] Subsequently the expectation for 1957 in late autumn 1956 was expressed as a percent of this second figure: 1 per cent more than spring 1956 expectation for 1956.[11] Therefore, calculated absolute investment-expectation for 1957 at unadjusted prices, with a forecast period of up to fourteen months is £852.89m × 121/117 × 1.01 = £890.86m—see Table I. From 1958 onwards the B.O.T. based its percent-change upon the forecast made at a comparable date in the previous year. Thus the autumn 1957 expectations for 1958 were 2 per cent above those of the previous year for 1957.[12] So absolute expectation for 1958 at unadjusted prices, and with a forecast period of up to fourteen months, is £890.86m × 1.02 = £908.68m—see Table I.

Throughout my series I use the revised forecasts which are collected in the autumn of the forecast-year, because the initial forecasts made in the summer of the forecast-year seem likely to be less dependable, and this series is not complete. The published percent-change for 1967 was in volume-terms specifically.

I identify my expectations-series as the '*absolute-series*'. In Section III of this paper I investigate the 'forecast-errors' of this series and

[8] *Board of Trade Journal*, February 21st, 1958.
[9] *Board of Trade Journal*, February 4th, 1956.
[10] *Board of Trade Journal*, August 4th, 1956, pp. 262–3.
[11] *Board of Trade Journal*, December 29th, 1956, p. 1365.
[12] *Board of Trade Journal*, February 21st, 1958.

TABLE I

PREDICTED AND ACTUAL CAPITAL-EXPENDITURE IN U.K. MANUFACTURING INDUSTRY: UNADJUSTED PRICES, £m.

	Actual expenditure	*Absolute expectations*	*Percent expectations*	*Naive Model I* (*No change in expectations from expenditure in forecast-year*)	*Naive Model II* (*Expected change = last year's change in expenditure.*)
1956	854	853	843	719	823
1957	947	891	892	854	988
1958	922	909	966	947	1040
1959	867	818	829	922	896
1960	1021	932	989	867	813
1961	1239	1212	1327	1021	1175
1962	1168	1200	1227	1239	1458
1963	1044	1032	1005	1168	1097
1964	1216	1114	1127	1044	919
1965	1401	1226	1337	1216	1388
1966	1495	1250	1429	1401	1587
1967	1425	1128	1349	1495	1589

FORECAST ERRORS: Actual expenditure *minus* expectations/actual expenditure.

	Absolute expectations	Percent expectations	Naive Model I	Naive Model II
Average absolute error (%) (This neglects sign of error.)	7.62	4.74	10.33	10.23
Absolute error variance (%)	53.85	2.42	22.50	66.78
Mean error (%)	7.16	1.92	5.82	0.89
Mean error variance (%)	60.64	21.19	95.34	170.64

TABLE II

PREDICTED AND ACTUAL CAPITAL-EXPENDITURE IN U.K. MANUFACTURING INDUSTRY: ADJUSTED TO 1958 PRICES, £m.

	Actual expenditure	*Absolute expectations*	*Percent expectations*	*Naive model I*	*Naive model II*
1956	925	980	969	828	910
1957	978	965	966	925	1110
1958	922	938	998	978	1031
1959	871	818	829	922	865
1960	1016	936	993	871	820
1961	1195	1206	1321	1016	1162
1962	1098	1157	1183	1195	1374
1963	964	970	944	1098	1001
1964	1092	1029	1041	964	830
1965	1203	1101	1201	1092	1219
1966	1233	1073	1227	1203	1314
1967	1172	966	1110	1233	1263

FORECAST ERRORS: Actual expenditure *minus* expectations/actual expenditure.

	Absolute expectations	Percent expectations	Naive model I	Naive model II
Average absolute error (%) (This neglects sign of error.)	6.24	4.35	9.04	9.87
Absolute error variance (%)	23.89	9.82	15.58	72.08
Mean error (%)	3.78	−0.86	2.39	0.59
Mean error variance (%)	48.54	28.00	91.59	169.15

Source: *Annual Abstract of Statistics.*

the 'forecast-errors' of a series which is compiled by Ball and Drake's method, which I term the '*percent-series*'—see Tables I and II.

III. THE 'FORECAST-ERRORS' OF THE PREDICTORS

In this Section III, I investigate the 'forecast-errors' of expectations-series when they are used as predictors of the gross-fixed-capital-formation of U.K. manufacturing industry. I define 'forecast-error' as actual expenditure minus expected expenditure, expressed as a percent of actual expenditure. Four predictors are presented in Tables I and II: an absolute-series; a percent-series; and two other series, from 'Naive Models I and II'. 'Naive Model I' assumes that there is no change in expectations from the actual expenditure of the forecast-year. 'Naive Model II' assumes that the expected-change from last year's actual expenditure will be equal to last year's change in actual expenditure, in absolute terms.

I make two sets of forecasts for each of these series. One set is valued at unadjusted prices: this supposes that forecasters have made systematic allowance for price inflation. The other set is revalued at constant 1958 prices (see Table II); this supposes that forecasters make no allowance for probable price-change, so that they make their statements in prices current for the *forecast-year*. This revaluation requires that expectations be revalued to 1958 prices from the prices of the forecast-year—thus adjusted expectations for 1959 are equal to unadjusted expectations for 1959 in all series except Naive Model II.

I investigate these forecast-errors in three exercises. First, I test the hypothesis that expectations neglect the probability of future price-change; for this test I assume that expectations *should* tend to equal actual expenditure. So I test whether the mean-error and average-absolute-error of forecast-errors at unadjusted prices are greater than the mean-error and average-absolute-error at adjusted prices, first from the *absolute-series* and then from the *percent-series*. From the *absolute-series* the mean-error at unadjusted prices is greater than that at adjusted prices (i.e. 7.16 per cent as against 3.78 per cent), but only at 85 per cent confidence. Also from the *absolute-series* the variance of the average-absolute-error at unadjusted prices is greater than that at adjusted prices, at 90 per cent confidence. Therefore from my *absolute-series* alone there is evidence which is consistent with the hypothesis that business expectations neglect the probability of future price-change.

In a second exercise I test two hypotheses. The first is that expectations are in substantial error, and the second is that expectations are biased in direction of error. In order to examine these I test whether the average-absolute-error is greater than zero, and whether the mean-error is greater or less than zero, first from the *absolute-series* and then from the *percent-series*. I find that the average-absolute-error from all series is greater than zero. Also, from the *absolute-series* the mean-error with both unadjusted and adjusted prices is greater than zero at 90 per cent confidence. Therefore from both series there is evidence which is consistent with the hypothesis that business expectations are in substantial error. While from my *absolute-series* alone there is evidence which is consistent with the hypothesis that expectations are biased *downward* in direction of error.

In a third exercise I test the hypothesis that business expectations do provide a *closer* prediction than Naive Models I and II. For this I test whether the average-absolute-error from the naive models is greater than the average-absolute-error from my *absolute-series*. Average-absolute-error has the advantage that it reflects the magnitude of error irrespective of direction of error, so it does not automatically penalize biased series. I find that the average-absolute-error from both naive models with prices adjusted is greater than that from my *absolute-series*—i.e. 9.04 per cent and 9.87 per cent as against 6.24 per cent. Therefore there is evidence from my *absolute-series* when adjustment for price-change is made, which is consistent with the hypothesis that business expectations do provide a closer prediction than the two naive models.

In summary, my evidence is consistent with the following statements. Business investment-expectations do neglect the probability of future price-change. Business investment-expectations are in substantial error and are biased downwards even after neglect of price-change has been eliminated. Business investment-expectations do provide closer predictions than two naive models if expectations are adjusted for neglect of future price-change.

IV. FORECASTS OF THE DIRECTION OF CHANGE IN INVESTMENT

One requirement made of a good predictor is an ability to foretell direction of change, because knowledge of turning-points is crucial for policy—I define 'forecast of direction of change' as direction of *change in forecast* so that a biased predictor is not penalized automatically. From Tables I and II it is obvious that the *absolute-series* performs equally as well in this respect as the *percent-series* and that both are good. Indeed the *absolute-series* provides a mistaken forecast of direction of change for only 1958 at unadjusted prices, while at adjusted prices it provides a mistaken forecast of direction of change for only 1966. The *percent-series* provides a mistaken forecast for only

1958 at both unadjusted and adjusted prices. The naive models are very poor predictors of direction of change in investment.

V. ANNUAL ABSOLUTE-EXPECTATIONS AND ANNUAL INVESTMENT

In this Section V, I re-examine the hypothesis that investment-expectations are unbiased predictors of actual investment, by testing the composite hypothesis that the slope of the regression of actual annual-gross-fixed-capital-formation in manufacturing, I_t, on my *absolute-expectations-series*, I_t^*, is more or less than unity and the intercept is more or less than zero.

In the relation with prices unadjusted (1) the residuals are autocorrelated.

$$\hat{I}_t = -\underset{(192.12)}{207.90} + \underset{(0.18)}{1.28}\, I_t^* \qquad (1)$$

$$d = 0.61 \quad \overline{R^2} = 0.83$$

But by taking transformed variables, autocorrelation can be reduced substantially, and an improved relationship in terms of the original variables can be determined (2).[13]

$$\hat{I}_t = \underset{(225.4)}{365.8} + \underset{(0.16)}{0.90}\, I_t^* \qquad (2)$$

$$d = 1.02 \quad \overline{R^2} = 0.78$$

This suggests that the expectations-series at unadjusted prices is a biased predictor of investment, because the intercept of the relation is greater than zero at 90 per cent confidence.

In the regression relationship when prices are adjusted (3) again the residuals from the original data are autocorrelated. But this is eliminated by transformation in (4).

$$\hat{I}_t = \underset{(245.58)}{154.61} + \underset{(0.24)}{0.89}\, I_t^* \qquad (3)$$

$$d = 0.41 \quad \overline{R^2} = 0.58$$

$$\hat{I}_t = \underset{(205.9)}{532.0} + \underset{(0.13)}{0.76}\, I_t^* \qquad (4)$$

$$d = 1.53 \quad \overline{R^2} = 0.80$$

The slope of this regression relation is less than unity at 95 per cent confidence; the intercept is more than zero at 98.5 per cent confi-

[13] J. Johnston, *Econometric Methods*, 1963, pp. 192–9.

dence. This is consistent with the existence of bias when prices are adjusted.

Thus there is evidence of bias in investment-expectations. Further the values and standard errors which have been calculated for slopes and intercepts in both of these sets of regression relationships indicate that business expectations have been biased downward over observed levels of expenditure.[14] Nevertheless the *absolute-series* is a useful predictor, for it explains up to 80 per cent of the variance of actual investment.

VI. ANNUAL ABSOLUTE-EXPECTATIONS AND QUARTERLY INVESTMENT

In this Section VI, my purpose is to investigate the potential of a quarterly investment-expectations-series. In order to pursue this end I establish the proportion of the variance of quarterly investment which can be explained by my annual *absolute-series* when this is converted into a quarterly form. Unfortunately such a conversion is difficult. So I use a step-like series which assumes expectations to be the same in each quarter. This rudimentary conversion is likely to be that method which is least sympathetic to the worth of the expectations-series as a predictor.

I use this series in a model which explains actual quarterly manufacturing investment, I_t, by seasonal effects, Q_{it}, and by quarterly expectations, I_t^*. The Q_{it} are set with value one in the appropriate quarter and zero otherwise. The sample-period extends from 1956/I to 1967/III by quarters. All variables are seasonally unadjusted. The gross relationship between I_t and I_t^* is presented in (5) and (6) below. In (5) prices are unadjusted, autocorrelation is significant and 83 per cent of the variance is explained. In (6) prices are adjusted, autocorrelation is significant and 60 per cent of the variance is explained.

Next I include a plan adjustment variable, $Y_t - Y_{t-1}$, in the model in an attempt to improve the level of explanation. As this measure of the change in sales after the statement of expectations I use the difference between G.D.P. at factor cost in the quarter of the investment outcome and G.D.P. in the same quarter of the forecast-year. In (7) prices are unadjusted, autocorrelation is significant and 83 per cent of the variance is explained. In (8) prices are adjusted, autocorrelation is significant and 63 per cent of the variance is explained.

These levels of explanation and these standard errors point to the

[14] I.e. from (2) the intercept is significantly greater than zero, while the slope is not significantly greater or less than one; from (4) the intercept is greater than 160 and no more at 95 per cent confidence, while the slope is less than only 0.995 and no less at 95 per cent confidence.

importance of the constructed quarterly expectation variable I_t^* in the explanation of quarterly investment. They suggest that the plan-adjustment variable is not important.

$$\hat{I}_t = -48.69 - \underset{(10.69)}{44.95}Q_{1t} - \underset{(10.69)}{32.72}Q_{2t} - \underset{(10.69)}{23.59}Q_{3t} + \underset{(0.10)}{1.36}I_t^* \quad (5)$$

$$d = 0.58 \quad \overline{R^2} = 0.83$$

$$\hat{I}_t = 41.52 - \underset{(10.09)}{34.08}Q_{1t} - \underset{(10.09)}{24.92}Q_{2t} - \underset{(10.09)}{19.32}Q_{3t} + \underset{(0.14)}{0.95}I_t^* \quad (6)$$

$$d = 0.41 \quad \overline{R^2} = 0.59$$

$$\hat{I}_t = -47.99 - \underset{(10.75)}{40.93}Q_{1t} - \underset{(10.74)}{29.43}Q_{2t} - \underset{(10.74)}{19.91}Q_{3t} + \underset{(0.11)}{1.30}I_t^* + \underset{(0.03)}{0.03}(Y_t - Y_{t-1})$$

$$d = 0.67 \quad \overline{R^2} = 0.83 \quad (7)$$

$$\hat{I}_t = 43.95 - \underset{(10.00)}{32.45}Q_{1t} - \underset{(10.00)}{23.05}Q_{2t} - \underset{(10.00)}{17.30}Q_{3t} + \underset{(0.13)}{0.93}I_t^* + \underset{(0.02)}{0.025}(Y_t - Y_{t-1}) \quad (8)$$

$$d = 0.50 \quad \overline{R^2} = 0.63$$

VII. TESTS OF DECISION THEORIES

One interesting use of investment-expectations is in a test of the hypothesis of 'rational expectations', that is in a test of the effect of risk and uncertainty upon expectations. Muth has expressed this hypothesis in the following form: the subjective-probability distribution of future possible outcomes tends to be distributed about the objective-probability of outcomes. This hypothesis presents a testable inference for investment-expectations: expected expenditure is an unbiased predictor of actual expenditure. Investment-expectations can be used for this test because they are a forecast of actual expenditure; thus expectations and actual expenditure can represent an evaluation of the same prospects, except that the expectations are constructed earlier with less-dependable information.[15] Nevertheless this interpretation of rational expectations does have limitations, for it provides maximization only under linear conditions, that is when the expected-value at the forecast-date of total perceived opportunity is in fixed proportion to total forecast, and when the expected-

[15] J. F. Muth, 'Rational Expectations and the Theory of Price Movements', *Econometrica*, 1961. Okun, 'Predictive Ability of Intentions Surveys', *American Economic Review*, 1964. Pashigan, 'Commerce—S.E.C. Sales Anticipations', *Review of Economics and Statistics*, 1964.

value at the expenditure-date of total perceived opportunity is in the same fixed proportion to total expenditure. Only when this condition is met can the rational business also maximize by forming a relationship between investment-expectations and actual expenditure which leaves disturbances normally distributed; because only then will disturbances in expected-values also be normally distributed.

While not conclusive my evidence suggests that, useful although investment-expectations are, they are biased and biased somewhat downwards. This bias does indicate a response by businessmen to risk and uncertainty which is inconsistent with the hypothesis of rational expectations. This bias is inconsistent too with the corresponding hypothesis that risk and uncertainty has no effect upon the level of any discount-rate which is used or required in evaluation of capital-investments. Further, downward bias does suggest a response by businessmen to risk and uncertainty which is consistent with theories which incorporate aversion to risk and uncertainty into business evaluation of proposed capital-expenditures.[16]

I can speculate on the magnitude of this aversion to risk and uncertainty in recent capital-expenditure decisions. For this again I must assume that the expected value at the forecast-date of perceived opportunity is in fixed proportion to forecast total, and I must assume that the expected-value at the expenditure date of perceived opportunity is in the same fixed proportion to expenditure total—i.e. that expenditure from perceived opportunity changes with change in discount-rate as does expected-value of perceived opportunity. Given these assumptions I can interpret the proportion which each forecast of expenditure is of *estimated* actual expenditure, as an estimate of the proportion which expected-value at the forecast-date of perceived opportunity is of expected-value at the expenditure-date of perceived opportunity. Then my final step is to calculate the discount-rate p.a. which over a period of seven months on average (my average forecast-period) will account for each of these estimates of the proportion which expected-value at forecast-date is of expected value at the expenditure-date.[17]

$$\hat{I}_{n+1} = \alpha + \beta I^*_{n+1} + p[I_n - (\alpha + \beta I_n^*)] \qquad (9)$$

My best linear estimate of actual expenditure, conditional on observed sample values, is given by (9) with regression coefficients and errors from (2) and (4). These parameters utilize my knowledge of auto-regressive structure, the form of the predictor takes due account of the estimated disturbance in the previous period; this disturbance-

[16] S. A. Ozga, *Expectations in Economic Theory*, 1965, Part 3.

[17] A. B. Curtis and J. H. Cooper, *Mathematics of Accounting*, 1961, Table IV, 'Present Value of 1 at Compound Interest', p. 461.

term was an integral part of the exercise in which the parameters were estimated.[18] I calculate from my unadjusted-series that on average over the sample period, a discount-rate of at least 11 per cent p.a. will eliminate the difference between expected and estimated actual expenditure. While I calculate from my adjusted-series that on average over the sample period, a discount-rate of at least 12 per cent p.a. will eliminate this difference.

Hence I estimate that *either* the average premium for risk and uncertainty which has been added recently to required 'cost-of-capital' in investment appraisal in U.K. manufacturing industry has been at least 11–12 per cent p.a.; *or* that the recent usual effect of risk and uncertainty upon the subjective-probabilities of expected-values has been such as to reduce expected-value and so expenditure to that level which would have been chosen *if* risk and uncertainty were represented instead by a 11–12 per cent p.a. premium added to cost-of-capital. This estimate of the premium is almost twice the yield from equity investments and is an indication of the importance of risk and uncertainty. It suggests a usual recent requirement in investment appraisal for a discounted-cash-flow yield of at least 18–19 per cent p.a. net of tax, with orthodox cost-of-capital at 7 per cent.

VIII. CONCLUDING REMARKS

This investigation has confirmed the usefulness of the information published by the B.O.T. on the capital-investment-expectations of U.K. manufacturing industry. This information can assist in the prediction of gross-fixed-capital-formation, and in the prediction of turning-points in the cyclical movement of capital-formation. Further, it appears to disclose some important characteristics of business expectations. Therefore one can recommend that the B.O.T. should improve the survey-information and construct a quarterly-series, as available for the U.S.A. Nevertheless, a cheap and substantial improvement in the available evidence would be publication of the absolute total of expected investment, rather than the percent-change, and of the absolute total for each individual industry, constructed as I suggest, on the base of *actual* investment for, say, 1956.[19]

[18] Johnston, *op. cit.*, p. 197. $p = 0.85$ when prices were adjusted; $p = 0.91$ when prices were unadjusted.

[19] Absolute business forecasts of fixed-capital-expenditure in U.K. manufacturing can exaggerate for three reasons. Firstly, businesses can return forecasts for their overseas as well as their U.K. investment. Secondly, businesses will frequently derive these forecasts from *cash budgets*. These estimates of future cash requirements will be the sum of fixed *and working* capital investment, as well as including precautionary balances. Thirdly, spending can be reduced more easily than increased.

My series avoids these problems. It provides a somewhat better explanation of actual investment than does that of D. Smythe and G. Briscoe, 'Investment Plans', *Economica*, August 1969, Table 4, p. 290.

Such information is necessary for fully satisfactory use even of annual figures and it is essential for the next step in research on this subject, which is investigation of the determination of business investment-expectations.

SCHOOL OF ECONOMIC STUDIES,
THE UNIVERSITY OF LEEDS

PUBLICATIONS RECEIVED

Card Network Planning, by J. A. Larkin, Scottish Academic Press, 1970.

Communist International Economics, by P. J. D. Wiles, Basil Blackwell, 1968, 84s.

A Dictionary of Computers, by Anthony Chandor with John Graham and Robin Williamson, Penguin Reference Books, February 1970, 10s.

Distributive Trades Statistics, a guide to official sources, by the Distributive Trades EDC, H.M.S.O., 1970, 13s.

Economics of the Construction Industry, Studies in Business Economics No. 111, by Peter J. Cassimatis, The National Conference Board, $2.50 or $12.50.

Economics, Industrial Training and Management, Pergamon Press, 1969.

The Effective Use of Capital, by A. M. Alfred, Industrial Educational and Research Foundation, April 1970, 8s.

Electronic Computers, by S. H. Hollingdale and G. C. Tootill, Pelican Books, Ltd., 10s.

Exchange-Rate Systems, Interest Rates, and Capital Flows, Essays in International Finance, No. 78, January 1970, Thomas D. Willett, Samuel I. Katz, William H. Branson, International Finance Section, University of Princeton.

Federal Funds for Research, Development, and Other Scientific Activities, Fiscal Years 1968, 1969 and 1970, Volume XVIII, National Science Foundation.

Federal Support of Research and Development at Universities and Colleges and Selected Nonprofit Institutions, Fiscal Year 1968, A Report to the President and Congress, National Science Foundation, March 1970.

Financial Statements, A Crusade for Current Values, Howard Ross, Sir Isaac Pitman and Sons Ltd., April 1970, 60s.

Financing of Industry and Trade, by D. J. Darby, Sir Isaac Pitman and Sons Ltd., February 1970, 16s. (Paperback), 30s. (Hardback).

Forms of Wage and Salary Payment for High Productivity, International Management Seminar, Versailles, 26–29 September 1967, Basil Blackwell & Mott, Ltd.

Fundamentals of Business Analysis, by Howard B. Baltz, Richard B. Baltz, Prentice-Hall, Inc., 1970, 90s.

A Guide to the Study of Management, by Thomas Kempner, A.T.M. Occasional Papers, Basil Blackwell, Oxford, 1969, 25s.

Industrial Relations and Communications, by William Walsh, A.C.I.S., Gee & Co. (Publishers) Ltd., March 1970, 35s.

Intercompany Transactions in the Multinational Firm, by James Green and Michael G. Duerr, The Conference Board, Managing International Business, No. 6.

Job Vacancies in the Firm and the Labor Market, Studies in Business Economics, No. 109. A Research Report from the Conference Board, by John G. Myers, $2.00 (students and teachers), $10.00 to others.

The Management of Research and Development, by George F. Thomason, B. T. Batsford Ltd., April 1970, 65s.

Manpower Problems and Policies: Full Emoloyment and Opportunity for All, John A. Delehanty, International Textbook Co. Ltd., February 1970, 50s.

Marketing Research, Edited by Joseph Seibert and Gordon Wills, Penguin Modern Management Readings, April 1970.

The Neurotic Trillionaire, A Survey of Mr. Nixon's America, by Norman Macrae, Harcourt, Brace & World, Inc., 1970.

The Penguin Dictionary of Commerce, by Michael Greener, Penguin Books Ltd., 1970, 10s.

Planning in East Europe, Michael Kaser and J. Zielinski, Background Books published by The Bodley Head, 1969, 21s.

Politica Commerciale Nelle Imprese Industriali, Maurizio Theodoro, Vita E. Pensiero, 1968.

Programming for Optimal Decisions, edited by P. G. Moore and S. D. Hodges, Penguin Modern Management Readings, April 1970.

The Reform of Sterling, Essays in International Finance, No. 77, December 1969, by Benjamin J. Cohen, International Finance Section of the Dept. of Economics of Princeton University.

Reshaping Government in Metropolitan Areas, by the Research Policy Committee of the Committee of Economic Development, February 1970, $1.00.

The Role of Fleet Leasing in Motor Vehicle Fleet Plans of Business Firms, by Clyde William Phelps, Studies in Commercial Financing No. 4, Commercial Credit Company, Baltimore, 1969.

Some Theoretical Problems Relating to the Euro-Dollar Market, Helmut W. Mayer, International Finance Section, February 1970.

Specification and Uses of Econometric Models, by T. Merritt Brown, MacMillan & Co. Ltd., 1970, 90s.

Sterling and the City, by Benjamin J. Cohen, Reprints in International Finance, March 1970.

Three Lectures of Economic Development, Beirut Arab University, by Mohamed Z. Shafei, Beirut 1970.

The Value-Added Tax, The U.K. Position and the European Experience by T. M. Rybczynski with a Foreword by Sir Robert Shone, Basil Blackwell, Oxford, 1969, 15s.

THE JOURNAL OF INDUSTRIAL ECONOMICS

VOLUME XVIII

1969–70

BASIL BLACKWELL

OXFORD

Printed in Great Britain by
Alden & Mowbray Ltd
at the Alden Press, Oxford

CONTENTS

VOLUME XVIII

Number 1, November 1969

PAGE

Business Pricing Policies and Inflation—Some Evidence from E.E.C. Countries, by LOUIS PHLIPS 1

Operational Marketing Research, by A. MERCER 15

Some Effects of Policy on Productivity in Soviet and American Crude Petroleum Extraction, by EARL R. BRUBAKER 33

Cost Functions for the Water Industry, by J. L. FORD and J. J. WARFORD 53

The Water Supply System up to A.D. 2001, by DOUGLAS WOOD 64

Symposium on Advertising and Concentration:

An Empirical Investigation of Advertising and Concentration: Comment, by ROBERT B. EKELUND, Jr. and CHARLES MAURICE 76

Testing Hypotheses in Industrial Economics: a Reply, by H. M. MANN, J. A. HENNING and J. W. MEEHAN, Jr. 81

Another Look at Advertising and Concentration, by L. G. TELSER 85

Statistical Testing in Industrial Economics: a Reply on Measurement Error and Sampling Procedure, by H. M. MANN, J. A. HENNING and J. W. MEEHAM, Jr. 95

Number 2, April 1970

Project Evaluation of Multinational Plants in Africa, by R. ROBSON 105

The Concentration of Patent Ownership in Corporations, by DONALD STEVENSON WATSON and MARY A. HOLMAN 112

Short-Run Cost Functions of a Multi-Product Firm, by RONALD S. KOOT and DAVID A. WALKER 118

On the Sales Revenue Maximization Hypothesis, by C. J. HAWKINS 129

Effective Competition in the Television Rentals Industry: a Note, by J. F. PICKERING 141

A Note on Advertising and Uncertainty, by IRA HOROWITZ 151

A Survey into the R & D Evaluation and Control Procedures Currently Used in Industry, by J. M. ALLEN 161

Number 3, July 1970

Competition in the Sausage Market, by DENNIS LEES and JOHN MORLEY 185

The Determination of Selling Prices, by R. C. SKINNER 201

Diffusion of Major Technological Innovations in U.S. Iron and Steel Manufacturing, by BELA GOLD, WILLIAM S. PEIRCE and GERHARD ROSEGGER 218

Meaningful Bank Failure: A Proposal, by A. DALE TUSSING 243

Productivity, Labor Demand and Cost in a Continuous Production Facility, by L. S. ZUDAK 256

The Accuracy of Short-term Business Forecasting: An Analysis of a Firm's Sales Budgeting, by E. A. LOWE and R. W. SHAW 276

The Board of Trade Capital-Investment-Forecasts: The Prediction of Gross-Fixed-Capital-Formation in U.K. Manufacturing Industry and Business Expectations, by C. M. CANNON 291